The Fort at Prospect Bluff

The British Post on the Apalachicola & the Battle of Negro Fort

Dale Cox

2020

ISBN-13: 978-0578634623
ISBN-10: 0578634623

Old Kitchen Media
4523 Oak Grove Road
Bascom, Florida 32423

www.oldkitchen.org

He hath sent me to heal the brokenhearted, to preach deliverance
to the captives, and recovering of sight to the blind,
to set at liberty them that are bruised.
Luke 4:18

This book is respectfully dedicated to Andrea Repp and Rhonda Kimbrough.

Contents

INTRODUCTION

THE DESTRUCTION OF THE NEGRO FORT at Prospect Bluff on the Apalachicola River was one of the most horrific and noteworthy events in American history. The fort was on Spanish soil, but U.S. Army, U.S. Navy, and Lower Creek forces attacked it in a siege that lasted from July 20 to July 27, 1816. The battle ended when a heated cannonball from Gunboat No. 154 ricocheted from a pine tree and ignited a gunpowder magazine. The explosion shook the ground for miles in all directions. Nearly 300 men, women, and children lost their lives from the deadliest cannon shot in American history.

The U.S. Forest Service preserves the site today as part of the Apalachicola National Forest. Trenches, moats, and the remnants of earthworks testify to the size of a settlement and magnitude of the tragedy. Prospect Bluff was the largest community in Florida during the final months of the War of 1812. The size diminished in the next year, but it was still the largest free black colony in North America when American forces destroyed it.

The narrative that follows is the result of years of research. The story it tells is one of desperation, hope, and tragedy. It is the story that determined the outcome of the history and future of Florida.

Many different people and institutions made this book possible. The list is too long to remember, let alone include, but special acknowledgments are due to the following:

Rhonda Kimbrough and Andrea Repp of the U.S. Forest Service have been my constant exploring buddies and sounding boards in nearly five years of visits to the site. Their love for its story is unparalleled. The work they have done to preserve and learn more about the fort and the people who lived there deserves the thanks of multiple nations. All the other friends I have made in my interactions with the forest service have been kind, friendly, and professional.

Historians Bill Steele, Matthew Shack, Brian Rucker, Joe Knetsch, John McNish Weiss, Christopher Kimball, John and Mary Lou Missall, Joyce Southard, Samantha Arroyo, and Sue Tindel all contributed information and expressions of support for this project. I appreciate them all.

Special thanks likewise are due to Dean DeBolt and Timothy Bulger of the University Archives and West Florida History Center, John C. Pace Library, University of West Florida; James G. Cusick of the P.K. Yonge Library of Florida History, Special & Area Studies Collections, George A. Smathers Library, University of Florida; Claudia Campbell of the Friends of Fort Mims, and Rev. Ken Beard of Collins Chapel Baptist Church, who helped with translations of William Hambly's letters.

I am indebted to the staffs of the National Archives, Library of Congress, National Archives of Great Britain, British Museum, the Archivo Nacional de la Republica de Cuba, the National Archives of Trinidad and Tobago, State Archives of Florida, Georgia Archives, the Alabama Department of Archives and History, and many other repositories and institutions, large and small.

My special thanks must go to Rachael Conrad, who had traveled everywhere with me as I worked on this book. Without her help, encouragement, and support, the book would have overwhelmed me, and I would never have finished it.

I also appreciate the help and support of my friends Farris Powell and Patti McMullen Powell, Angie Powell, Todd and Paige Powell, Ben W. Ferguson, Robert Daffin, Lorrin "Bernie" Howell, John Dolan, J.J. Dolan, Ed William, Timothy Richardson, George Floyd, Chelsey Venrick, Ralph and Pam Medley, Billy Bailey, and many others.

As always, I am thankful for my grown sons, William and Alan Cox, my mother, Pearl Cox, and of course, my friend and buddy Dodger D. Dogg.

THE FORT AT PROSPECT BLUFF

The British Post on the Apalachicola
& the Battle of Negro Fort

1

CRISIS ON THE FRONTIER

THE UNITED STATES FIRST DETERMINED TO CONVERT the proud and powerful Muscogee (Creek) people to the ways of the whites during the days of George Washington. The "Father of our country" himself sent Col. Benjamin Hawkins to live among the Creeks and introduce to them a "Plan of Civilization." Unspoken was an expectation among whites of authority that the introduction of the plow and chattel slavery would end the culture of the hunt among the Native Americans. The Muscogee would no longer need their vast hunting lands, opening millions of acres for white settlement.

Many great chiefs led the *talwas* or towns of the Creek Confederacy during its centuries of existence, but Hawkins came to see himself as the wisest and most benevolent of all. He changed the lifestyles of many Creek families by introducing plows, European-style farming, and hundreds of African slaves to their fields. As the warriors became more dependent on the agent for seed, tools, and supplies, he was able to exert greater and greater control over their laws and political affairs. It was at Hawkins' instance that the Creeks established a National Council to direct the affairs of the nation. A speaker presided over this panel, but any pretenses he might have to real power were disabused by the colonel when he broke Peter McQueen (*Talmus Hadjo*) from the position and replaced him with the Big Warrior.

McQueen was a powerful and well-connected war chief from the Tallassee towns of the Upper Creeks. The son of a Muscogee woman and a long-lived Scottish trader, he was affluent and popular. He objected to

1

the growing control of the whites over the affairs of his nation, and Hawkins used his influence to remove him. From that day forward, he viewed Benjamin Hawkins as his mortal enemy.

McQueen was not alone in expressing his disdain for the United States and their agent. His influence was strong among the Tallassee and Atasi (Autossee), many of whom had family connections among the Hillabee, Alabama, and Coushatta. An opposition party slowly formed to the American agent's hand-picked leadership on the Creek Council. Still too weak to act by 1811, they waited and hoped for some event that might unite more of the nation behind them.

As McQueen and his followers waited, white pressure on the Muscogee increased. The expanding frontiers of the United States swept west to the Mississippi River and beyond, threatening the territorial integrity that Alexander McGillivray fought to provide his people. McGillivray's war forced George Washington to sign the Treaty of New York with the Creeks in 1790. It established the territorial limits of their nation but gave the United States permission to open a horse path through the Muscogee country. The treaty also prohibited whites from building bridges along the route or making their road passable for wagons. The Creeks also maintained control of the ferries along the path.

The Upper Creeks were never thrilled about the new "Federal Road." They watched as increasing numbers of white settlers passed through their country, heading to the Mississippi Territory established by the United States in 1798. Migration along the road was a trickle at first, but Benjamin Hawkins dreamed of opening the floodgates.

The Creek National Council of 1811 is remembered primarily for a speech given by the Shawnee leader Tecumseh. He visited the Muscogee as the head of a delegation sent by his brother Tenskwatawa, the Shawnee Prophet. Tecumseh was not yet famous in his own right, but the Prophet was the leader of a major religious and political movement sweeping the region from the Great Lakes to the Ohio. He hoped to expand his influence into the Southeast by sending Tecumseh and the others on a mission to the Choctaw, Muscogee, and Cherokee. Legend to the contrary, there is no evidence that Tecumseh also planned to visit the Seminole.

Benjamin Hawkins was at the National Council and knew of Tecumseh's presence, but considered it to be of little consequence. His primary interest that year was in pushing through a proposal to widen the Federal Road that ran east-west through the Creek country while also securing permission for the building of a second path that would connect Tennessee to the Mississippi Territory. Despite wariness voiced by council members, the agent succeeded:

> A gentleman who left Tuckabatcha the 25th ult. informs us, that the chiefs of the Cherokees, Choctaws, Chickasaws, and Creek Indians, and the agents of the United States, which met at this place on the 17th, had been three days debating on the subject of cutting a road through the Indian country, and the Indians fully refused to give their consent. Colonel Hawkins, at length, told them, he did not come there to ask their permission to open a road, but merely to inform them that it was now cutting. Colonel Hawkins did not apprehend any attempt would be made to stop the progress of the workmen employed on the road, as the best informed chiefs of the nations were in favour of it personally, but thought it impolitic to give their public assent.[1]

The agreement gave the United States authority to widen the horse path into a wagon road. It also stripped many prominent Creek businessmen of their profits by replacing the ferries they operated with wooden bridges. The people of the nation did not immediately learn of the agreement, which invalidated a key part of the Treaty of New York, but anger rose as the news spread.

Tecumseh does not appear to have been aware of the road negotiations. Had he learned of them, his mission to the Creeks might have been much more successful. He delayed giving his speech until Hawkins and other whites had left Tuckabatchee, but finally spoke in the final hours

---

[1] Report dated Carthage, Tennessee, November 16, 1811, published in *The Pennsylvania Gazette*, December 18, 1811.

of the council. Despite modern writings to the contrary, most of the key Muscogee leaders were not impressed:

> ...One of the most respectable chiefs of the Upper Creeks reported that the Shawnee deputation spent a whole day in the public square at Tookaubatchee, talked much of conversations with GOD on Indian affairs; that after the day was spent, the reporter & some other chiefs consulted with each other, as to the meaning of what they heard, so as to detail it to col. Hawkins. But their opinion was, the leader was a mad man or a great liar, in fact both, and as they could not understand him, they would take no notice of his foolish talks.[2]

The frontiersman Sam Dale and others claimed in later years that they heard Tecumseh's speech, giving vivid descriptions of the Shawnee's exhortations to war. Their versions, however, do not match those given by Native Americans in the days and weeks following the Council. Hawkins later emphasized that visitor used guarded language in his comments to the Creeks:

> Tecumseh, in the square of Tuckaubatchee, delivered their talk. They told the Creeks not to do any injury to the Americans; to be in peace and friendship with them; not even to steal a bell from any one of any color. Let the white men on this continent manage their affairs their own way. Let the red people manage their affairs their own way, and this, too, in the name of the British. What was the actual meaning of this British talk? Your whole nation can answer this question. Kill the old chiefs, friends to peace; kill the cattle, the hogs, and fowls; do not work, destroy the wheels and looms, throw away your ploughs, and every thing used by the Americans. Sing "the song of the Indians of the northern lakes, and dance their dance."

---

[2] Timothy Barnard to Messrs. Grantland, May 14, 1812, *The Georgia Journal*, May 27, 1812.

> Shake your war clubs, shake yourselves; you will frighten
> the Americans, their arms will drop from their hands, the
> ground will become a bog, and mire them, and you may
> knock them on the head with your war clubs. I will be
> with you with my Shawanese, as soon as our friends the
> British are ready for us. Life up the war club with your
> right hand, be strong, and I will come and shew you how
> to use it.[3]

So popular is the legend of Tecumseh delivering a fiery oration that exhorted the Creeks to war that some writers have excised parts of this quote to make it appear more supportive of traditional versions. There are claims that after delivering his peaceful speech, Tecumseh returned to the council and gave a second version. There is no evidence to support such statements.

In truth, it was not Tecumseh's words that outraged the Upper Creeks in the weeks after the National Council, but the spread of news that Hawkins had obtained permission to build a wagon road through their territory. A force of some 300 fighters turned out to stop a U.S. Army survey crew that began marking the expanded right-of-way almost as soon as the council ended:

> We are indebted to the politeness of several travelers,
> who have just arrived here from the Mississippi, for the
> following account of the detention of a detachment of
> troops under the command of liut. Lucket of the United
> States' army, who was sent on command from fort
> Stoddart for the purpose of surveying or marking out a
> road from Tensas, (M.T.) thro' the Creek nation to the
> frontiers of Tennessee. They had proceeded some
> distance on their route, when they were arrested near

---

[3] Col. Benjamin Hawkins to the Big Warrior, Little Prince, and other Chiefs, June 16, 1814, *American State Papers: Indian Affairs*, Volume I: 845.

Manna'cs (a half breed) by a party of 300 or more Indians.[4]

The Upper Creeks disarmed the soldiers and escorted to Fort Stoddert on the Alabama River. They crossed on a ferry run by Samuel Mims, who soon figured prominently in the accelerating course of events. The "Manna'c" mentioned in the account was Samuel Moniac, a mixed-race or *metis* businessman who ran a tavern, store, and ferry on the Federal Road in present-day Montgomery County, Alabama. His son David later became the first Native American to graduate from the U.S. Military Academy at West Point.

Anger over the widening of the road increased in 1812. Murders and the harassment of travelers surged in the Upper Creek country and concerns grew among the Lower Creeks as well. This faction of the nation lived along the Chattahoochee and Flint Rivers, and some chiefs began complaining to Col. Hawkins about white settlements and intrusions on Muscogee lands east of the Flint. Hawkins, though, was caught up in his duties as "advisor" to the Creek Council and the implementation of the "Plan of Civilization" and failed to recognize the signs of growing unrest. He blamed the accelerating problems on a few malcontents. The road was widened, the previously banned bridges were built, and the agent soon advertised for contractors to build large ferry flats on the Flint River near the Creek Agency and the Chattahoochee at Coweta.

Three incidents took place in 1812 that had an enormous influence on coming events. The first involved a man named Josiah Francis who ran a small trading post on the Federal Road near present-day Montgomery, Alabama. The son of a white deerskin trader and a Creek mother, he was a friend of the deposed speaker Peter McQueen. His marriage to Hannah Moniac, a niece of Alexander McGillivray and the sister of Samuel Moniac, gave him powerful connections. One of her sisters was married to another important *metis* named William Weatherford.

Francis lived on the road and watched with alarm as traffic surged along the newly widened highway. This rush of white travelers passing

---

[4] Letter to the Editor, undated but apparently written in mid-October 1811, *Georgia Journal*, October 24, 1811.

through with their household goods packed in their wagons and carts led Francis to reflect on the message that Tecumseh delivered to the Creek National Council the previous year. The Shawnee had urged the Muscogee to join the alliance formed by his brother, the Prophet, or face inundation by the westward movement of the U.S. frontier. Tecumseh had left a missionary from his brother named Sikaboo or Seekaboo among the Creeks, and at some point, Josiah Francis sought him out to learn more about Tenskwatawa's religion and teachings., Benjamin Hawkins failed to notice at all when Francis suddenly set fire to his home and store on the Federal Road and disappeared to live among his Alabama relatives. He founded a town that he called Ecanachaca or "Holy Ground" and announced that he was the recipient of visions and visits from the Master of Breath. Josiah Francis declared himself a prophet and welcomed all to come and hear his message of hope for the Muscogee.

A second influential incident took place in the Spring of 1812 when a party of Creeks led by the Little Warrior of Wewocau returned from a winter-long pilgrimage to hear the teachings of the Shawnee Prophet. Filled with religious fervor, they were somewhere in southern Indiana when they heard that war had broken out between the Native Americans and the whites. Little Warrior quickly led his men across the Ohio River and fell on settlements near the mouth of the Duck River in Tennessee. Several whites died, and one woman, Martha Crawley, was carried as a prisoner back to Creek country.

The warriors passed through the Chickasaw towns after their raid, proudly showing off the hats they had obtained and announcing their deeds to all that would listen. The information received by Little Warrior, however, was wrong. There was not yet war between the United States and Great Britain. White militia flooded the Tennessee frontier in pursuit but failed to come up with the Muscogee. In Nashville, a lawyer and politician named Andrew Jackson called on the governor for permission to raise an army and punish the Creek Nation for the bloodshed.

Cooler heads prevailed for the moment, and the invasion from Tennessee did not take place. Col. Hawkins, however, exerted his influence, and the Creek Council ordered a Coweta war chief named William McIntosh to form an execution squad and hunt down Little

Warrior and the members of his party. Individually or in groups, the perpetrators of the Duck River attack were hunted down and killed. All fought with unexpected fury, refusing to surrender and taunting their executioners to the bitter end. Little Warrior himself, it was said, announced with pride that he had eaten the flesh of white people.

Martha Crowley, meanwhile, escaped captivity and was rescued by Tandy Walker, a government blacksmith assigned to the Choctaws. He delivered her in safety to George S. Gaines, the Choctaw agent and a brother of a young military officer named Edmund Pendleton Gaines. The latter man achieved national fame as a lieutenant when he arrested former Vice President Aaron Burr for treason in 1807.

The third incident influencing future events was perhaps the most important in leading to the British intervention on Florida's Apalachicola River, and yet it has gone completely unrecognized by historians for more than two centuries.

Thomas Perryman was a powerful chief who lived on the Chattahoochee River in what is now Seminole County, Georgia. He was the father-in-law of the late adventurer, pirate, and self-proclaimed "Director-General" of the Muscogee, William Augustus Bowles. Perryman and his son William—who lived across the river in today's Jackson County, Florida—fought in the American Revolution on the British. Thomas received the largely honorific title of "colonel" and William as a "captain" for their roles in leading Creek warriors against the American Patriots in Georgia.

The chief and his sons were accustomed to trading in Georgia, although William also owned both a schooner and large pirogue and occasionally made maritime voyages as far as the Bahamas to secure trade goods. Two of the sons, one of them possibly William himself, were on a routine trading visit to Hartford, Georgia, when things went wrong:

> Mr. Barnard informs me he has communicated to you
> an outrage committed by some people of Hartford on two
> sons of Perrymans. I wish it would be examined into that
> justice may be done. I am informed some scout parties of
> course said to be from Jones [County], have been out

above me and reported their orders were to kill every Indian they saw who had not something white about their heads. I do not know who could have given such an order.[5]

The brutal attack infuriated the entire Perryman family, which was quite large and boasted great influence among the Eufaula, Okitiyakani, and Wekiwa towns of the Lower Creeks and the Tocktoethla and Tellmochesses towns of the Apalachicola River Seminoles.

In response to the Georgia attack on his son, Thomas Perryman began efforts to open talks with the British. He wanted guns and ammunition so his people could defend themselves against the coming American attacks. William took at least one more trip to the Bahamas, where he purchased what supplies he could and spoke with authorities about the need of his warriors for modern weapons and ammunition. The requests came in the earliest days of the War of 1812 and disappeared in the British bureaucracy.

The angry chief refused to give up, and his efforts eventually paid off. War was coming to the frontier, and Benjamin Hawkins was too caught up in politics and intrigues to notice it.

---

[5] Col. Benjamin Hawkins to Gov. David B. Mitchell of Georgia, September 6, 1813, Georgia Department of Archives and History.

2

DISASTER AND EXODUS

THE EXECUTION OF LITTLE WARRIOR'S PARTY was the spark that brought war to the Creek Nation. War clubs were a traditional sign of conflict among the Muscogee and soon appeared at Econachaca, where the followers of the Prophet Francis made clubs made from white oak runners. These "sticks" looked a bit like an inverted letter "L." The club or large end was left rough and unshaped, making the sticks fearsome weapons. Warriors sharpened the outer side of the angle of the "L" into a blunt wooden blade. They smoothed the rest of the club for use as a long handle. Once shaped, the sticks were painted red except for the club end itself. This part, the warriors planned to redden with the blood of their enemies. The completed weapon was called a "red stick" or "red club," and the name quickly came to describe the Prophet and his followers as well.

Outraged by the violent deaths of their friends, Red Stick warriors soon struck back against members of the execution squad. Much like the Scot-Irish settlers of the Southern backcountry, the Muscogee followed an eye for an eye philosophy. The killing of a family member called for justice, which under traditional Creek law meant the death of the killer or one of his family members. As Red Sticks struck back against individual members of the McIntosh squad, they spread the word of the involvement of Benjamin Hawkins in ordering the deaths of their friends. Simmering resentment exploded, and armed warriors flooded to Econachaca and the red stick standard of the Prophet Francis. Town after town raised the red stick, and civil war erupted in the Creek Nation.

Recognizing an opportunity to strike back against Hawkins and the Big Warrior for their removal of him as speaker, Peter McQueen brought the powerful Tallassee warriors into the fight. Joining with their allies from Atasi, they attacked Tuckabatchee in mid-June 1813. The large town on the Tallapoosa River was the seat of the Big Warrior and the Creek National Council. Its warriors fortified as best they could and fought for their lives for weeks against the growing Red Stick army.[6]

The Big Warrior pleaded for help from the whites in Georgia, but the stunned Hawkins could send only a few rifles and a small supply of powder. The agent urged the warriors of Coweta, Cussetuh, and other Lower Creek towns to go to the rescue of the Tuckabatchees. McQueen and the Atasi King likewise called for support, and a massive siege developed for control of the Creek capital.[7]

Benjamin Hawkins had promised the Big Warrior the power of the United States if a situation ever required it. The situation now faced the Muscogee leader, but the expected support did not appear. The United States had declared war on Great Britain, and the War of 1812 was raging with full fury. U.S. troops were also either in or on the border of Spanish Florida, supporting a group of men who called themselves "Patriots" and were attempting to seize the colony and hand it over to the United States. Spanish soldiers, volunteers, and Seminole warriors from the Alachua bands were driving them back with slow but steady success.

Unable to send soldiers as he had promised, Hawkins pleaded with the chiefs of Coweta and Cussetuh to go to the rescue of the Tuckabatchees. William McIntosh led the warriors on this mission, and they successfully extracted the Big Warrior and his followers from the besieged town. The capital of the Creek Confederacy fell to the Prophet Josiah Francis.[8]

---

[6] Brig. Gen. James Wilkinson to Hon. Harry Toulmin, June 25, 1813, John Francis Hamtramck Claiborne, *Mississippi, as a Province, Territory, and State*, (Volume I), Jackson, MS, Power & Barksdale, 1880: 321-322.

[7] Col. Benjamin Hawkins to Secretary of War James Armstrong, July 6, 1813, *American State Papers: Military Affairs*, Volume I: 848; Col. Benjamin Hawkins to Gov. David B. Mitchell of Georgia, July 7, 1813, Georgia Department of Archives and History.

[8] James Durozeaux, a trader at Coweta, to Mr. McIntosh, July 14, 1813, Telamon Cuyler Collection, University of Georgia.

Francis, McQueen, Atasi, possibly William Weatherford, and others now planned to annihilate their enemies once and for all. They would strike at Coweta on the Chattahoochee River—where the "white faction" and Big Warrior were forting in—and then drive east to the Flint to destroy the Creek Agency and kill or drive away Hawkins himself. Like their opponents, however, they were short on ammunition. McQueen volunteered to lead a supply party to Pensacola in hopes of obtaining powder, lead, and other supplies from the Spanish. His party was returning with the needed ammunition when it was attacked by a force of volunteers from the Mississippi Territory north of present-day Brewton, Alabama, on July 27, 1813.[9]

The Battle of Burnt Corn Creek was a disaster for the frontiersman. They caught McQueen by surprise and seized his packhorses, but the seasoned war chief reorganized his men in a ticket of tall river cane and led a furious counterattack. Disorganized and caught in the process of looting the Red Stick supplies, the Mississippi volunteers fled for their lives as war cries and gunfire erupted from the cane. McQueen's warriors pursued, driving volunteer soldiers from the field and recapturing many of their supplies. Capt. Sam Dale's company continued to fight, waging an unplanned rearguard action to help the panicked men from the other companies to escape.[10]

Word of the fight at Burnt Corn Creek spread quickly through the Creek Nation and Florida borderlands. Family members of warriors slain in the battle demanded vengeance, and the Red Stick plan to move immediately on Coweta fell apart. Submitting to the demands of the outraged families, the Prophet Francis agreed to strike back against the settlers. The Red Sticks knew that many of those engaged in the Burnt Corn attack were now forted in at the home of Samuel Mims near Boatyard Lake in the Tensaw community. Francis and Paddy Walsh led their army south in August 1813. The strike force included warriors from thirteen Upper Creek towns and numbered anywhere from just over 400 to more

---

[9] Col. Benjamin Hawkins to Secretary of War John Armstrong, July 20, 1813, C.L. Grant, ed., *Letters, Journals, and Writings of Benjamin Hawkins: 1802-1816*, Beehive Press, Savannah, Georgia, 1980: 648.
[10] Hon. Harry Toulman, Letter of July 29-30, 1813, Washington, DC *Universal Gazette*, September 9, 1813.

than 1,000. Several white traders, long resident in the nation, accompanied the expedition prepared to help should they be asked for advice or to treat the wounded.[11]

The Battle for Fort Mims was a pivotal event in North American history. Red Stick warriors stormed the crude stockade as its inhabitants gathered for lunch, attacking from all four sides at once. The fight lasted for hours as men, women, and children sold their lives dearly, but Fort Mims fell before the end of the day. More than 250 of its occupants died.[12]

News of the Red Stick victory at Fort Mims spread like lightning through the towns of the Creek Nation. Thomas Perryman knew of the battle within days. He was still angry over the assault on his sons at Hartford, Georgia, but also recognized that the destruction of the fort would likely bring the full power of the United States down on the Muscogee people. He gathered a group of chiefs—his son William among them—and set out for Pensacola to request arms and ammunition from the Spanish. To their surprise, however, they arrived in the city to find a British warship riding at anchor in the bay.

The vessel was HMS *Herald*, an 18-gun *Cormorant* class sloop of war sent by Governor Charles Cameron of the Bahamas to gather intelligence on the condition of the American Indians in the Southeast. British records indicate that Clement Milward was the captain of *Herald* in September 1813, but Lt. Edward Handfield was the senior officer on board when the Perryman party arrived. He met with the chiefs and agreed to carry a letter from them to Gov. Cameron:

> We hope you will eade and assist us as your alis and
> friends Sir you know that our four fathers owned the Lan
> Where we now live But and Ever since our father the King
> of Grate Briton Left us the Americans had Ben Robing us

---

[11] Josiah Francis, the Old King, Old Interpreter, and Mougceweihche to Gov. Mateo Gonzales Manrique, August 1813, Papeles de Cuba, Forbes Papers, University of West Florida.

[12] *Ibid.*; Brig. Gen. Ferdinand L. Claiborne, Mississippi Territory Militia, to Brig. Gen. Thomas Flournoy, U.S. Army, commanding 7th Military District, September 3, 1813, *Daily National Intelligencer*, October 9, 1813.

of our Rights and now the americans has maid war against our nations and we aply for armes and amenisun to defend our silves from so Greid a Enemy and as you Know that this nations all ways was frinds to the English we hope you will send us Seplys by Henry Durgen as soon as possible and we hope that you will send sum of our old frind the British troops to eade and assist us a ganst our Enemeys.[13]

The letter was signed by Col. Thomas Perryman, Capt. William Perryman, Alexander "Sandy" Durant, and an enigmatic individual whose Creek name was spelled "Noah Hoeo" by the writer. "Noah" probably represents an attempt to spell the title "Eneah." "Hoeo" is more difficult to identify but may be "Hadjo," "Mico," or "Emathla." It is tempting to identify the individual as Eneah Emathla or Neamathla, a chief long recognized for his resistance to U.S. expansion in 1813-1836, but without additional documentation, it is impossible to do so.

Alexander "Sandy" Durant, who also signed the letter, was a member of a prominent Creek family who had settled on the Apalachicola River. He was a nephew of Alexander McGillivray and the brother-in-law of Peter McQueen. Durant penned a personal appeal to Cameron that he enclosed with the group letter. He pointed out his family's long history of service to Great Britain, his relationship to McGillivray, and his white education, telling the governor that, "I love my Country and my people" – a reference to the Creek Nation and Muscogee people. He requested a military commission from Cameron and urged him to send on arms and ammunition as the Spanish governor in Pensacola was unable to supply the needs of the Creeks.[14]

At least three of the chiefs could speak English to at least some degree, and Durant had at least a rudimentary education, but they chose to communicate with Handfield through an interpreter named Henry Durgen.

---

[13] Col. Thomas Perryman, Capt. William Perryman, Alexander Durant, and Noah Hoeo to Gov. Charles Cameron, September 11, 1813, Cochrane Papers, Public Records Office, Colonial Office, 23/60.

[14] Alexander "Sandy" Durant to Gov. Charles Cameron, September 11, 1813, National Archives of Great Britain, Colonial Office, 23/60.

The lieutenant agreed to carry Durgen to New Providence for them and promised to deliver their appeal to Gov. Cameron.

The information provided Durgen matched intelligence received by Cameron from two British spies remain unidentified. They may have been deerskin traders who lived in the Red Stick towns or Pensacola residents with excellent ties to members of the movement. Whatever the case, they presented the situation of the Red Sticks in vivid terms to the British governor. The movement could succeed if Francis and his warriors received arms, and coordinated their operations with the British war effort, reported one of the spies. Without such support, however, he warned that "it is evident that they must be crushed." The writer, who penned his report before hearing news of Fort Mims, expressed fear that the Red Sticks would damage their chances with a premature strike against the Americans.[15]

The second spy offered specific recommendations for British intervention on the Gulf Coast. Using a Spanish port such as Pensacola to supply the Creeks with arms would violate Spain's neutrality, he warned, suggesting instead that the establishment of a supply depot and a military presence on the Apalachicola River. The informant went on to recommend that Great Britain supply the Red Sticks with 50,000 pounds of powder, 100,000 musket balls, 1000 trade guns, provisions, and other supplies.[16]

Gov. Cameron recommended to Earl Bathurst in London that Great Britain intervene in the Creek War. His communique, which left the Bahamas on November 30, 1813, took time to cross the Atlantic. Bathurst and his advisors used more time as they discussed the implications and possibilities of opening a new front in the War of 1812. And finally, more time was consumed as the reply made its way back across the Atlantic to the Bahamas. In the Creek Nation, meanwhile, the fight went on.

Three U.S. armies closed in on the Red Sticks as they sought to consolidate their control over the nation. Brig. Gen. Ferdinand L. Claiborne led a force of volunteers, militia, and the 3rd U.S. Infantry from the Mississippi Territory into the Creek country by way of the Alabama

---

[15] Intelligence report enclosed in Gov. Charles Cameron to Earl Bathurst, November 30, 1813, National Archives of Great Britain, Colonial Office, 23/60.
[16]

River. Maj. Gen. John Floyd pushed west from Georgia to Coweta on the Chattahoochee River, the recently widened Federal Road easing the movement of his troops, supply wagons, and cannon. Maj. Gen. Andrew Jackson, who advocated such an invasion nearly two years before, commanded an army of Tennessee volunteers who marched south to Huntsville and the Tennessee River. The armies moved independently but were to converge on the sacred Hickory Ground of the Creeks at the confluence of the Coosa and Tallapoosa Rivers.

Jackson's army struck first. Crossing the Tennessee River, he sent mounted forces to destroy the Black Warrior's town on the river of the same name. No real fighting resulted, but the troops burned abandoned Red Stick villages. The main army crossed the mountains to the Coosa River and built Fort Strother at the Ten Islands near present-day Ohatchee, Alabama. Brig. Gen. John Coffee—one of Jackson's favorite subordinates—attacked Tallushatchee on November 3, 1813. The battle was bloody and brutal. Tennessee troops surrounded the town and killed more than 186 men, women, and children while losing only five killed and 41 wounded of their number. Frontiersman Davy Crockett, who fought at Tallushatchee, wrote that "We shot 'em down like dogs." Andrew Jackson reported that "Fort Mims has been avenged." To this day, no one knows if the warriors of the town really were Red Sticks.[17]

Other battles followed. Jackson destroyed a definite Red Stick force at the Battle of Talladega on November 9, 1813. Brig. Gen. William Cocke, unaware of a truce granted them by Jackson after Talladega, attacked the unresisting warriors of the Hillabee towns on November 18, 1813. Sixty-four inhabitants died, 29 were wounded, and another 237 taken prisoner in a massacre that turned the survivors into bitter enemies of the United States. The Georgia army struck two weeks later, burning hundreds of homes and killing 200 Red Sticks at the Battle of Atasi (Autossee) on November 21, 1813. The Mississippi force entered the fray by attacking Econachaca (Holy Ground) on December 24, 1813. Soldiers destroyed the town of the Prophet Francis, and William Weatherford entered the realm of legend with a famed leap into the Alabama River.

---

[17] Brig. Gen. John Coffee to Maj. Gen. Andrew Jackson, November 3, 1813, Jackson Papers, Library of Congress; David Crockett, *The Autobiography of David Crockett of Tennessee.*

None of the 1813 campaigns, however, succeeded in reaching the Hickory Ground or the rumored new Red Stick stronghold at a place called Tohopeka in a 'horseshoe bend" of the Tallapoosa River.

John Durant, a warrior fighting in the Red Stick forces, wrote to his brother Alexander on the Apalachicola that winter, assuring him of the safety of his mother and sister:

> Dear Sandy I imbrace this oppertunity of informing you that we are all well what is yet alive your mothere is liveing yet and your Sister betsy is very desiours to go and live still with you if she nowed how to get there it is trubsome time here now in this part of world but all we lack is powder and led we have had two powerful armes in our country this winter but they had to run back faster then they cam the Creek has been counted cowards the turne out to be brave soldere they meet enemes and put them to flight the spanards do not seem incline to supply us they and the inglish is one and the inglish has rote on to them to supply us but we see no supply we cant tell the reason no more at present but remain your Brother John Durant[18]

In a postscript on the back of his letter, Durant asked his brother to send him six pounds of powder and lead if possible. As his letter demonstrates, the Red Sticks entered the year 1814 reeling but still full of fight. They were in desperate need of arms and ammunition, but slow communications meant that the British government in London was beginning to consider Thomas Perryman's request for military assistance. The armies arrayed against them had supply problems of their own but were growing in strength.

The Tennessee force resumed the offensive first. Short on supplies and with the enlistment terms of many of his men expiring, Jackson launched a dash deep into the heart of Creek country. The troops left Fort Strother on January 17, 1814, and reached Euckfaw Creek near the Horseshoe Bend

---

[18] John Durant to Alexander "Sandy" Durant, ca. December 1813, Alabama Department of Archives and History.

of the Tallapoosa River five days later. The general planned to storm a fortification that the Red Sticks were building at the bend but found himself under attack instead. Menawa, Peter McQueen, the Prophet Francis, and others led warriors out of the new town of Tohopeka and attacked the soldiers on the heights overlooking the Emuckfaw. Jackson's men drove him back, and he sent Brig. Gen. John Coffee forward with a mounted force to examine the Horseshoe Bend fortification. Coffee was surprised by the strength of the defenses and fell back on the main force, telling Jackson that they would need more men. Unable to advance and facing constant sniping from the Red Sticks, Jackson ordered a retreat. His men started back to Fort Strother and were crossing Enotichopco Creek near the Hillabee towns when the Red Sticks attacked again. The rear guard of the army collapsed, and only the personal courage of Jackson and his officers and brave fighting by a small group of soldiers prevented the destruction of his entire force.

The Battles of Emuckfaw and Enotichopco Creek were followed on January 29th by an encounter that almost destroyed Maj. Gen. John Floyd's Georgia army. The general left Fort Mitchell on the Chattahoochee River in mid-January and advanced 40-miles to the west. The army built Fort Hull and Fort Bainbridge as supply depots, and new sections of the road opened, but a massive force of Red Sticks was waiting. Led by Paddy Walsh and William Weatherford, as many as 1,800 warriors gathered to fight the Georgians. Despite Jackson's claim that he had drawn off Native American forces in Floyd's favor, there is evidence that Peter McQueen, the Prophet Francis, and many of their warriors joined the army under Walsh and Weatherford in time for the fight.

Walsh, who, despite later legends about Weatherford, had led the primary Red Stick army since the attack on Fort Mims, devised a plan for a night attack. He wanted to approach Floyd's army, then camped near Calabee Creek in today's Macon County, under cover of darkness and then charge directly into the center of the white encampment and kill as many of the senior officers as possible. The loss of leadership would disorganize the citizen-soldiers and open the door for total victory. William Weatherford disagreed with this plan and argued instead for a defensive battle along the line of Calabee Creek. Many of the warriors had been present for a similar Weatherford-led defensive battle at Holy Ground and were wary of his suggestion. The principal chiefs present sided with Walsh, and Weatherford left the ground with several hundred followers.

His force still numbering roughly 1,200 men, Paddy Walsh went forward with his attack on the Georgia army. The warriors crept into position around the encampment—which Floyd called Camp Defiance— and at 5:30 a.m. slipped past the white sentries and attacked from three directions. Calabee Creek was a hard-fought and close battle. The warriors bloodied Floyd's army, and Walsh's plan of reaching the officers' tents at the center of Camp Defiance almost succeeded. The army's artillery saved the day, fighting hand to hand while reloading and blasting the Red Sticks with successive rounds of canister at point-blank range. Gen. Floyd ordered a bayonet attack at dawn, and Walsh pulled his warriors from the field.

Like Emuckfaw, the Battle of Calabee Creek was a tactical victory for the whites but a strategic one for the Red Sticks. Floyd's army suffered 200 casualties, and he ordered an immediate withdrawal to the Chattahoochee River. There is no way of knowing whether the Creeks might have achieved total victory had Weatherford and his followers remained on the field and taken part in the battle.

The Red Sticks suffered heavy casualties at Emuckfaw, Enotichopco Creek, and Calabee Creek, losing a reported 104 men killed and an unknown number of wounded. Their expenditure of ammunition was heavy, and the already meager supply on hand dwindled dramatically. Many would fight their next battle armed only with their namesake war clubs, tomahawks, and bows and arrows. Chiefs and warriors engaged in the fighting and their allies in the Perryman towns near the Gulf Coast waited anxiously for a response to September 1813 plea for military support from Great Britain.

The British were coming, but not fast enough. Admiral John Warren commanded the King's forces in American waters and sent two sloops of war to cruise off the Florida coast. Unfortunately for the Red Sticks, neither carried a supply of arms and ammunition for them. Great Britain was fighting its war with Napoleon, and until that fighting ended, there was little the country could do to support its allies in the Creek Nation. Admiral Warren informed London that he was unable to send additional ships or troops to the Gulf of Mexico without risking the safety of his operations on the Atlantic Coast. The situation did not change until Napoleon abdicated and went into exile on the Mediterranean island of Elba on April 6, 1814. Unfortunately for the Red Sticks, Napoleon's temporary departure came ten days too late.[19]

Three American armies had moved against the Red Sticks in the fall and winter of 1813-1814, but only one still held its ground. Maj. Gen. Andrew Jackson forced his starving men to live off acorns and even threatened to shoot would-be deserters personally, but somehow kept enough of an army together to hold his ground on the Coosa River. The desperate gamble paid off in March 1815 as thousands of reinforcements and a somewhat adequate supply of provisions reached Fort Strother. The U.S troops moved down the river to its confluence with Cedar Creek in modern Talladega County and built Fort Williams. Handmade wooden boats brought provisions, ammunition, and other supplies down from Fort Strother, and by mid-March, Jackson was ready for a second attempt at the Red Stick force entrenched at Horseshoe Bend.

The Red Sticks called their stronghold *Cholocco Litabixbee*, a Muscogee term that translates roughly to "horse's flat foot." The name came from the horseshoe shape formed by the Tallapoosa River as it flows around the site. A war or refugee town stood at the interior foot of the bend, built following the destruction of nearby *New Yaucau*—named after the Treaty of New York—and other communities by white troops. The new town was named *Tohopeka,* and as many as 1,000 Red Stick warriors lived there in as many as 300 log cabins or huts. The people came from towns that included *Oakfuskee, Oakahaga*; *New Yaucau, Hillabee, Fish Ponds*, and *Eufaula*. Following the curve of a rising elevation, they built a massive wall of log and earth across the neck of the bend.[20]

Jackson left Fort Williams with an army of 3,300 men on March 23, 1814, reaching the old Emuckfaw battlefield three days later after opening more than 50-miles of a new road. He ordered Brig. Gen. John Coffee to

---

[19] Admiral John Warren to John Croker, March 9, 1813, National Archives of Great Britain, Foreign Office 5/96.
[20] Maj. Gen. Andrew Jackson to Maj. Gen. Thomas Pinckney, March 28, 1814, S.G. Heiskell, *Andrew Jackson and Early Tennessee History*, Volume I, Nashville, 1920: 501-502.

cross the Tallapoosa with 600 Cherokee and white faction Creek allies and 700 Tennessee mounted volunteers. Coffee moved into position on high ground overlooking Horseshoe Bend and spread his soldiers out along the riverbank to prevent any attempt by the Red Sticks to escape by water. The rest of the army—numbering 2,000 men—moved into position north of the Red Stick "barricade" or fortification. Two cannons were pushed forward to a knoll overlooking the Creek line. It bears the name "Gun Hill" to this day.[21]

The barricade proved too strong for Jackson's artillery, and it was not until some of the allied warriors in Coffee's command swam across the river and brought back canoes that the tide of the battle changed. The Cherokees used the canoes to cross over and set the Tohopeka town on fire. Plumes of smoke rose over the battlefield as the warriors lining the barricade could hear the cries of their wives and children coming from behind them. The cause became apparent as the Cherokees pushed forward and started shooting at the Red Sticks from their rear. This rear attack forced Menawa, who commanded the Red Stick army, to divide his force and created a moment of opportunity for Jackson, who ordered his infantry to storm the fortification.[22]

The Thirty-ninth U.S. Infantry led the attack, its commander Maj. Lemuel P. Montgomery falling from mortal wounds as he led his men over the wall. Ensign Sam Houston was also wounded at this stage of the battle but continued to fight.

Along with regiments of citizen-soldiers from East and West Tennessee, the regulars swarmed over the wall and the day devolved into hand to hand fighting and massacre. Jackson reported that his men counted 554 bodies of Red Stick warriors and thought that another 200-300 were killed in the river by Coffee's men. The hope of the Red Stick movement died as the Tallapoosa River ran red with blood.[23]

Jackson and Coffee believed that no more than a handful of Red Sticks escaped the slaughter at Horseshoe Bend, but the number was probably much higher. Menawa, wounded many times and disfigured for life,

---

[21] *Ibid.*

[22] *Ibid.*

[23] *Ibid.*

remained beneath a pile of dead bodies well into the night before slipping down into the river and floating away. A Hillabee warrior named Tulwa Tustunuggee was wounded nine times but escaped with assistance from his brother and other survivors. He was the grandfather of future Muscogee (Creek) principal chief George W. Grayson and had been known early in life as Johnie Benson, the name given him by his white mother.[24]

How many warriors escaped from Horseshoe Bend is a matter for speculation, but the number could easily be 100 or more. It did not take long for the first of them to reach the Hickory Ground at the confluence of the Coosa and Tallapoosa Rivers. This was the traditional sacred ground of the Muscogee, the place where the Creeks kept their sacred plates, and the cultural center of their nation. The other primary Red Stick army—led by Peter McQueen, Josiah Francis, Holms, Homathle Mico, Tallassee Mico, William Weatherford, and others—was building fortifications there but all construction stopped as news of the disaster at Horseshoe Bend rippled through the town. Warriors and chiefs alike were shocked as bloody and wounded survivors came in to confirm that Jackson had destroyed Menawa's powerful army. Morale collapsed, and most of the leaders present decided to pull their people out and flee for safety to Spanish Florida. Jackson soon arrived at the Hickory Ground, expecting one last major battle but found it abandoned and the Red Sticks gone.

The retreat to Florida was a human catastrophe. The Red Sticks withdrew south to the headwaters of the Choctawhatchee, Pea, and Conecuh Rivers through rain, cold, mud, and floodwaters. The healthiest pushed ahead to beg food from Gov. Mateo Gonzales Manrique in Pensacola. They reported that thousands were starving and dying in the swamps in a desperate attempt to reach the international border:

> The hostile Indians are retreating from us in various
> directions mostly towards Conecuh, a few miles above
> our line of limits. The terrible chastisement inflicted by

---

[24] Chief George W. Grayson, *A Creek Warrior for the Confederacy: The Autobiography of Chief G.W. Grayson*, University of Oklahoma Press, Norman, Oklahoma, 1988: 22-25.

the Army of militia, regulars, Cherokees and Creeks under General Jackson, at New yaucau, on the hostile Indians, has alarmed the whole party. Believing blood enough has been spilled to atone for past transgressions, general Pinckney on the 23d communicated through me to the enemy the terms upon which piece will be granted them. "The United States will retain as much of the conquered territory as may appear to the government to be a just indemnity for the expenses of the war, and as a retribution for the injuries sustained by its citizens and the friendly Creek Indians.[25]

Maj. Gen. Thomas Pinckney of the regular U.S. Army arrived on the scene after Jackson's victory at Horseshoe Bend. His terms called for the Red Stick warriors to disarm and return home with their families. All of the prophets and "instigators" of the conflict, however, were to be surrendered to the whites and executed. The general either did not know or ignored the fact that the actual instigators of the war were the Mississippi volunteers who attacked Peter McQueen's supply party at Burnt Corn Creek on July 27, 1813. William Weatherford and some chiefs and warriors came in, but thousands of others—starving, cold, and desperate—preferred death to surrender:

> The Chiefs directed Mr. Cornells to inform me they did not believe the Hostile Indians were ready for peace altho' a part of them had suffered so severely in battle against our armies. They were still haughty, brave and moved by fanaticism. Those of the towns on Tallapoosa, below Tookaubatche, and Alabama had suffered the least although they were the most culpable; and it was probable they would mistake our object and offering terms of peace to them. The friendly Indians had no confidence in our promises they might make until a great part of them were destroyed. "The friendly Indians as soon and they had put

---

[25] Col. Benjamin Hawkins to Gov. William Hawkins of North Carolina (his nephew), April 26, 1814, published in *The Georgia Journal*, June 8, 1814.

their families down to planting their fields would be ready
to join and cooperate with our armies in such manner as
you may direct, and believed with but little aid would be
able to destroy their enemy and their fanaticism." I replied
Blood enough had been spilled and if the terms offered
were not accepted the war of course would continue. They
must by such means as were in their power apprise the
enemy of them; and that every one of the warriors must
aid which of course would soon enable us to determine
the course to be pursued.[26]

Benjamin Hawkins tried to use white faction chiefs to negotiate with
the Red Sticks but failed. He had no influence with the war faction before
the war, and his standing had not improved with them since. He made
matters worse for both him and the Muscogee through his failure to
recognize that the coming conflict in the nation had cost him respect in the
eyes of his own country as well. Many of the military and political
authorities on the Southern frontier spoke dismissively of him in the
months and year after the Battle of Horseshoe Bend.

As Hawkins tried to achieve a peaceful end to the war, military
operations continued. Jackson built a new fort adjacent to the site of the
old French post of Fort Toulouse on the peninsula formed by the
confluence of the Tallapoosa and Coosa Rivers. The post was named in
his honor and became the center for mopping operations targeting Red
Stick parties still in the field. An officer writing to friends in Charleston,
South Carolina, reported a flurry of continuing activity:

...Scouting parties of from 2 to 700 men are daily sent
out to discover any of the enemy that may be lurking
behind, and to burn their towns. Prisoners are frequently
bro't in, both by the whites and friendly Indians. All the
males that are captured by the latter are immediately
butchered by them. – The Indian war may now be said to

---

[26] Col. Benjamin Hawkins to Maj. Gen. Thomas Pinckney, April 25, 1814, C.L.
Grant, ed., *Letters, Journals, and Writings of Benjamin Hawkins*, Volume II,
Beehive Press, Savannah, Georgia, 1980: 679-680.

be at an end. Several of the chiefs of the hostile party have delivered themselves up, with many of their followers, and more are daily coming in. The lives of these are spared, and they are dismissed to cultivate their grounds in peace. Offers of peace have been made them, and a party has been sent after those who have fled, to acquaint them with it. The lives of all are to be spared, except those of the prophets, who are to be delivered up and executed. It is thought that these proposals will be gladly accepted. They perceive that these men have deceived and ruined them, and they will gladly sacrifice them as a peace-offering for their own lives.[27]

The writer of the above, who penned his letter in mid-April, briefly made a note of another rumor:

It is not possible that the Spaniards would afford these wretches a shelter, as they must be well assured that they would be involved with their destruction. The only foundation on which, in my opinion, a journey to Pensacola can be made is, that the British have landed there and of course will endeavor to give succour to all who may fly to them; a report of this kind as reached our camp, which, in the minds of some, may procure us a sight of Pensacola.[28]

The rumor of a British landing at Pensacola was false, but the Spanish were already doing what they could to feed the desperate Red Stick families entering their territory. Supplies in Pensacola were not plentiful, but the governor, garrison, and many of the citizens shared what they had with the starving men, women, and children who appealed to them for

---

[27] Unidentified officer at Camp Jackson to a friend in Charleston, South Carolina, April 17, 1814, published in the *New Jersey Journal*, May 31, 1814.
[28] *Ibid.*

help. There was not enough food, and although the people of Pensacola saved many lives, a number of them went hungry as well.

Andrew Jackson reported on April 18 that surviving prisoners from Fort Mims were coming into his camps, even as his troops continued their pursuit of the retreating Red Sticks. He did not mention rumors of a British landing at Pensacola:

> …Many of the negroes who were taken at fort Mimms, have been delivered up, and one white woman, (Polly Jones) with her two children. They will be properly taken care of. The Tallapoosce king has been arrested, and is here in confinement. – The Tostabatchee king of the Hickory Ground tribe has delivered himself up. – Weatherford has been with me, and I did not confine him. He will be with me again in a few days. Peter M'Quin has been taken, but escaped. He must be taken again. Hillishagee, their great prophet, has also absconded; but he will be found – They were the instigators of the war, and such is their situation.[29]

The man that Jackson referred to as "Hillishagee, their great prophet" was Josiah Francis. His Muscogee name was one commonly given to prophets or conjurors among the Creeks and was generally spelled "Hillis Hadjo" by 19th-century writers. It translates roughly to "maker of mad medicine," an indication that Francis was a powerful conjuror and his medicine or magic was strong. He and McQueen were then in the swamps of the Conecuh and Escambia Rivers, making their way to Pensacola to seek food and emergency supplies for their followers.

The general's mention that William Weatherford had been with him but not imprisoned like other captured war leaders is interesting. The former Red Stick came into Jackson's camp and surrendered in a legendary scene that was described as simple but moving by eyewitnesses but took on much embellishment in the retelling. Jackson spared his life, and Weatherford showed gratitude by guiding North Carolina militia

---

[29] Maj. Gen. Andrew Jackson to Gov. Willie Blount of Tennessee, April 18, 1814, *Alexandria Herald*, May 25, 1814.

detachments in raids against his former Red Stick friends. Mounted units from the Mississippi Territory joined in these raids, as did parties of allied Creek and Choctaw warriors. Fleeing refugees were captured, killed, or driven from their temporary camps with the loss of what few possessions they had left.[30]

Conditions became so bad that many of the Red Sticks concluded that they must either sue for peace or watch their families starve in the swamps of the Conecuh, Escambia, Yellow, and Choctawhatchee Rivers. They approached William Boyles, an American then living north of Pensacola in Spanish territory, and asked him to carry a message to the commanding officer at Fort Pierce near the charred ruins of Fort Mims:

> After general Jackson's battle at the Horse Shoe, the remains of the warlike Indians in that neighborhood being much pressed for want of provisions, almost famished with hunger, flocked towards Pensacola, and finding there little or no prospects of getting supplies formed a determination, in this emergency to sue for peace. They accordingly selected a Mr. Biles [*i.e., Boyles*], who was well known among the whites, as an embassador to make propositions. He came up to Pierce's fort, where Colonel Russell was, being the commanding officer of the whole force at that time, and state to him the wishes of the Indians – he was informed that they could have peace and the conditions, and he (Biles) returned. – Shortly after he came up a second time to Col. Milton, who had taken the command, with similar propositions. The Col. Selected Major Carson, who immediately proceeded to Pensacola, where the chiefs and warriors had been convened for the purpose. He stated to them in council the disposition of our government to be at peace. They entered into an

---

[30] For details of Weatherford's role in leading attacks on the fleeing Red Sticks, see the accounts of North Carolina officers from April-June 1814.

HURRICANE MICHAEL RECOVERY

✝AWFUMC
In partnership with UMCOR

Repair, Rebuild, Restore Together

Our team of case managers, volunteer coordinators, and construction coordinators is committed to helping people recover from Hurricane Michael through Repairing, Rebuilding, and Restoring. We are working with long-term recovery groups from Panama City to Marianna to Port Saint Joe, and thousands of volunteers from across the country.

Our Promise

Assisting individuals and families through the recovery process without bias by utilizing thousands of volunteers to repair and rebuild resilient communities affected by Hurricane Michael.

 Supported by the People of the United Methodist Church

Express need. Volunteer. Donate.
www.hurricanemichaelrecovery.org | 850.740.3966

engagement to come up to this place in twelve days, and assured him that the terms would be complied with.[31]

The expected surrender never took place. Just as it appeared that thousands of Red Stick warriors might come in—and surrender Francis and McQueen as well—news reached Pensacola that British ships had arrived at Apalachicola Bay.

---

[31] Letter from a gentleman at Alabama Heights (Fort Claiborne) to the editor of the *Nashville Clarion*, July 6, 1814, published in the Bedford, Pennsylvania, *True American*, August 3, 1814.

3

RED COATS ON THE APALACHICOLA

THE U.S. PLAN TO REUNITE THE MUSCOGEE in a new territory isolated from the support of Spain and Great Britain ended dramatically on May 10, 1814. The royal and topgallant sails of HMS *Orpheus* slowly rose above the horizon off St. George Island at the mouth of Florida's Apalachicola River. Six months had passed since Thomas Perryman and other Native American leaders watched their plea for help leave Pensacola aboard HMS *Herald*. The long-awaited British response had arrived.

The five-year-old *Orpheus* was a 145-foot *Apollo*-class frigate rated for 36 guns and a crew of 264 men. A fifth-rate warship designed for speed and maneuverability in scouting missions or on independent cruises, she was about half the size of the famed American frigate USS *Constitution* ("Old Ironsides"). The ship and her crew had demonstrated their capabilities just 20 days before by running down and capturing the sloop of war USS *Frolic*—soon to become HMS *Florida*—off the coast of Cuba. Accompanied by her smaller consort, the 99-foot and 12-gun schooner HMS *Shelburne*, the *Orpheus* carried 2,000 muskets, accouterments, and a corresponding amount of powder and ball for distribution to the Creek and Seminole Indians. Also, onboard was a detachment of Royal Marines under the command of a former deerskin trader, slave smuggler, and adventurer named George Woodbine. He was now a commissioned second lieutenant with the brevet rank of captain. His mission was to distribute the arms and ammunition aboard the ships and to initiate the training of Great Britain's new Native American allies.[32]

The arrival of the two British vessels off Apalachicola Bay culminated in a series of administrative and military movements that began on March 27, 1814—ironically the same day that Andrew Jackson defeated the Red Sticks of Tohopeka at the Battle of Horseshoe Bend. With Napoleon temporarily in the bottle after the surrender of Paris to coalition forces, Great Britain viewed the War of 1812 with the United States in a new light. Earl Bathurst notified Gov. Cameron in the Bahamas that the Royal Navy was authorized to reinforce and supply the Red Sticks in their war against the United States. Bathurst and Cameron, of course, were unaware of Jackson's victory on the Tallapoosa. Vice-Admiral Sir Alexander Cochrane, an aggressive and seasoned naval officer, was named the commander-in-chief of British military operations in North America in April 1814. He quickly picked a favorite officer to spearhead Great Britain's intervention on the Gulf Coast.[33]

Vice-Admiral Sir Alexander Cochrane, an aggressive and seasoned naval officer, was named the commander-in-chief of British military operations in North America. He immediately picked a favorite officer to spearhead a movement on the Gulf Coast. Brevet Maj. Edward Nicolls of the Royal Marines was called "Fighting Nicolls" by those who knew him. He fought in as many as 107 battles during his lifetime:

> He was born at Coleraine [Ireland], in 1779, and was educated at the grammar-school of that town and at the Royal Park Academy, Greenwich. He entered the Royal Marines at the age of sixteen, and was attached to the corps up to the period of his retirement. He became Colonel in 1837, and Lieutenant-General in 1854. In 1803 he distinguished himself by capturing a French armed cutter off St. Domingo with the aid of only thirteen volunteers, and on this occasion was severely wounded.

---

[32] Capt. Hugh Pigot to 2nd Lt. George Woodbine, May 5, 1814, Cochrane Papers; Capt. Hugh Pigot to Brevet Capt. George Woodbine, May 10, 1814, Cochrane Papers.
[33] Earl Bathurst to Gov. Charles Cameron, March 27, 1814.

He was at the passage of the Dardanelles, in 1807, and in several minor affairs, including the capture of an armed Italian gun-boat near Corfu, and at the reduction of Anholt, in the Cattegat.[34]

When he received his first commission in the Royal Marines at age 16, Nicolls already had five years of military experience having school at age 11 to join the Royal Navy. His qualities as an officer were obvious, but there was another facet to the 34-year-old major that likely appealed to Cochrane for this specific mission. He was a devout Ulster Protestant and an outspoken Abolitionist.

The admiral saw something in the reports of the two British spies and the request for arms and ammunition from Chief Perryman's delegation that others before him had not. The intelligence and plea for help offered Cochrane the chance to open a new and profitable front in the War of 1812. The target? New Orleans and—with a bit of luck—the entire Mississippi Valley. While the admiral led his main fleet and army against the Chesapeake, Baltimore, and Washington, D.C., Nicolls would sail for the Gulf of Mexico with a detachment of Royal Marines and a supply of arms and ammunition. Entering Florida via the Apalachicola River as recommended by one of the British spies, he would build a fort and supply depot. The Red Stick Creeks and Seminoles could come there to receive not just arms and ammunition, but formal military training as well. Cochrane intended to supply his Native American allies not with trade guns as recommended by the spies in 1813 but with 2,000 Brown Bess muskets complete with slings, bayonets, cartridge boxes, and every other necessity. The Royal Marines were crack light infantry, and the admiral planned to turn his allies into the same by providing them with regular military training that would enable them to stand on the battlefield against U.S. regulars.[35]

The second phase of the plan entrusted to Nicolls was of equal importance. He was to organize a new Royal Colonial Marines regiment

---

[34] *The Illustrated London News*, February 18, 1865.
[35] Rear Admiral Sir Alexander Cochran to Gov. Charles Cameron, July 4, 1814, National Archives of Great Britain, Colonial Office, 23/61.

by enlisting Maroons or escaped slaves from the United States into the service of King George. Slavery was illegal in Great Britain by 1814, and British law was very specific about the status of escaped slaves. Any Maroon who made it to British territory was free, and since the ships of the Royal Navy were sovereign "soil," slaves reaching them also were set free. The Royal Marines regarded their shore installations as "ships on land," and any slave who came aboard one likewise was emancipated. British law also specified that only free men could serve in the country's armed forces, so any escaped slave from the United States could likewise gain his freedom by enlisting in the military. Maj. Nicolls was to set free as many American slaves as possible and bring them into the war effort against their former masters.[36]

Although he never put such into words, it is clear from Cochrane's orders that he anticipated the occupation of Spanish military posts in Florida by Nicolls' command. This would be a serious violation of Spain's neutrality in the war, but the British admiral harbored no doubts that the Americans coveted Florida and would use the least pretext for occupying it. He had plenty of support for this belief. The U.S. Army and Navy invaded East Florida in 1812 to support a group of self-styled "Patriots" who claimed to be staging a revolt against Spain. Most of them were actually from the United States, and the Madison Administration disavowed the invasion when confronted by Spanish diplomats. The East Florida controversy failed to stop an even more serious violation of Spain's sovereignty in West Florida in 1813 when Brig. Gen. James Winchester led an amphibious operation against Mobile. U.S. forces seized not just the city but the entire Mobile Bay region as far east as the Perdido River. Spanish Gov. Mateo Gonzales Manrique protested from his headquarters in Pensacola but lacked the military power to reclaim his nation's lost territory.

Admiral Cochrane planned to move first against the Chesapeake Bay region and anticipated that Nicolls' activities along the Gulf Coast would be a powerful diversion in his favor. Apalachicola Bay was separated from the nearest U.S. military posts by hundreds of miles of swamp and forest.

---

[36] *Ibid.*

Red Sticks and their Seminole allies still controlled much of the region despite Jackson's victory in the Creek War. American authorities would have a difficult time trying to obtain accurate intelligence about British activities on the Gulf Coast and would hesitate to send additional troops to the East Coast. This would improve the chances of success for the British operations against Washington, D.C., and Baltimore, Maryland.

The grand prize of the entire campaign, however, was New Orleans. The Crescent City controlled the international commerce of the Mississippi, Arkansas, Missouri, Ohio, Cumberland, and Tennessee River valleys. It was a vast region with unlimited resources, and the levees of the city were piled high with cotton, rice, lumber, and other products of the American frontier. The wealth to be gained from a successful operation against the city was enormous, and the admiral was determined to have the largest share.

A move against New Orleans also served important strategic interests. With the city under his control, Cochrane could push naval and land forces up the Mississippi River and seize thousands of square miles of territory for Great Britain. If the war ended with an agreement for each side to retain the land it possessed, the British would occupy a swatch from the Gulf of Mexico to Canada while hemming in the Americans. The future of the entire continent was at stake.

The city, however, was surrounded by swamps, lakes, bayous, and watery prairies. Just reaching it from the mouth of the Mississippi required an upriver sail of 104-miles. American forts and warships guarded the channel, and even the current would fight hard against an attacking British fleet. Nor was it any easier to reach New Orleans from other directions. The region west of the Mississippi was one of vast wetlands controlled by the pirate crews of Jean Lafitte and his brother Pierre. Largely of French descent, they had no love for the British. The city's eastern approaches required a lengthy sail through lakes and inlets such as the Rigolets. Like the Mississippi, these were fortified to some degree and patrolled by American gunboats.

As he considered these difficulties—likely with input from officers who had first-hand experience visiting the city—the admiral concluded that the best way to attack was from the north. By taking Mobile, his forces could use its large bay as the base of an overland campaign against Baton

Rouge on the Mississippi River. British guns mounted on the lever would halt supplies and reinforcements from traveling downriver to New Orleans. Without food and defenders, the city would surrender.

To accelerate its fall, Cochrane decided to approach the Lafitte brothers. If they chose to assist in his operations, British troops would be able to move through the labyrinthian bayous and channels and emerge on the west bank opposite the city. He decided to offer them legal pardons for all their "offenses" against shipping in the Gulf and Caribbean, plus commissions in the Royal Navy. If the bribe worked, the pirate ships and crews would come under his control.

As these operations were underway, Nicolls, with his army of Native Americans and Maroons, would strike against the frontiers of Georgia, Tennessee, and the Mississippi Territory. This would pin down U.S. forces in the region and prevent them from rushing to the assistance of New Orleans. A third army, meanwhile, would come ashore at Cumberland Island on the Georgia coast and push north up the Atlantic seaboard to Savannah.

The key to this ambitious plan was the immediate occupation of Apalachicola Bay by British forces. The lead ships of this effort were the *Orpheus* and *Shelburne*, which arrived off St. George Island on May 10, 1814. The success of the operation was entrusted to Capt. Hugh Pigot of the Royal Navy. With his ships safely anchored offshore, he ordered Capt. George Woodbine to land on the white sand beaches. The British invasion of the Gulf Coast was underway:

> *You are hereby directed to proceed up the river Appalachicola and endeavour by every means in your power to procure an interview with the Chiefs of the Creek Nation. You will inform them that the Orpheus Frigate has arrived on the coast with two thousand muskets, ammunition, &c. &c. for them, and...and should cavalry be able to act inform me what arms and furniture they stand in need of.*
>
> *You will take under your command Sergt. Smith & Corporal Denny (who have volunteered their services) giving them such orders from time to time as you may find*

necessary for the good of His Majesty's Service in instructing the Creek Nation in the use of arms and acting against the United States of America and by adopting every measure to forward their interest, to the furtherances of which, it is my desire you act with full power as British Agent to the Creek Nation, for which this is your authority until the pleasure of the Commander in Chief is known.[37]

Woodbine started upriver in a launch from the *Orpheus* and quickly reached the John Forbes and Company trading post at Prospect Bluff. The Spanish called this location the *Loma de Buena Vista* or "Hill of Good View," a name that became "Prospect Bluff" in English. It is a low elevation on the east side of the Apalachicola 20-miles above its mouth. The captain interviewed storekeeper Edmund Doyle, who introduced him to William Hambly, a sometimes employee of the company who lived upstream at Spanish Bluff. Another low elevation compared to some others on the river, this bluff is on the west side of the Apalachicola at what is now Blountstown, Florida. It probably took its name from either Hambly or his father, as both were of Hispanic descent.

A literate man, William Hambly could speak not only English and Spanish but the mutually unintelligible languages of the Muscogee and Hitchiti branches of the Creek Nation as well. The powerful Miccosukee of North Florida spoke the latter dialect while most of the Red Sticks used the former. He was married to a Creek woman and lived with his family on a farm that he humorously called "Poverty Hall." Newly settled nearby was a Tuckabatchee chief named John Blunt or "Lafarka." Whites of his day often used the latter name, but its origin is somewhat mysterious as there is no "r" sound in the Muscogee dialects. Blunt led his surviving ten warriors and their families down the Chattahoochee River after suffering heavy losses of cattle and property in the Creek War. The available documentation is silent as to whether he was a Red Stick or a supporter of the Big Warrior. Blunt's removal to Spanish Florida instead of returning to his home on the Tallapoosa River at war's end, however, suggests that

---

[37] Capt. Hugh Pigot to Capt. George Woodbine, May 10, 1814, Cochrane Papers.

he may have been a Red Stick. He was on good terms with both Red Sticks and the British in the months that followed.

Woodbine continued upstream from Spanish Bluff, eventually making it as far as Eufaula Talofa in what is now Barbour County, Alabama. He drew a detailed map of the journey, showing the locations of villages, refugee camps, natural landmarks, and more. Not far above Hambly's place, he showed a "Negro settlement" on the west bank of the river near today's John Redd Landing. Little is known about this community, but it may have been the home of a band of Maroons led by Vacapachassie, a man called the "Mulatto King" by Americans.[38]

The British did not include the men of this village in their initial enumeration of warriors available for their cause, but the community disappeared during the War of 1812, and its inhabitants undoubtedly moved down to Prospect Bluff. They may have been left off the list of Native American warriors because Woodbine considered them recruits for the regiment of Colonial Marines authorized by Admiral Cochrane. The other towns identified, and the number of warriors reported for each is as follows:

Iola (Blunt's town)	10 warriors
Tamathli and Ocheesee	150 warriors
Tocktoethla (Perryman's town)	100 warriors
Okitiyakani	250 warriors
Saockulo (Sawokli)	50 warriors
Fowltown (Tutalosi Talofa)	300 warriors
Yuchi (Red Stick refugees)	20 warriors
Tallasee (Red Stick refugees)	30 warriors
Canholva	15 warriors
Emussee	50 warriors
Chehaw towns	400 warriors
Ekanachatte (Red Ground)	20 warriors
Chiscatalofa	60 warriors
Kiva Rawon and Cedar Creeks	100 warriors
Miccosukee	700 warriors
Tallahassee Talofa	200 warriors

---

[38] Woodbine Map, May-June 1814, National Archives of Great Britain.

Red Sticks near Pensacola   800 warriors

TOTAL   3,255 men

The list prepared by Woodbine does not include Eufaula Talofa, Etohussewakke, and other towns in the area of today's Lake Eufaula, although some of those warriors clearly expressed support for the British. The principal chief of Eufaula Talofa, for example, reported that some of his young men went down to receive arms and ammunition from the magazines at Prospect Bluff.

The Eufaulas warned the British that it was unsafe for them to continue upriver as they would be entering the area influenced by the powerful Cowetas. Woodbine expressed regret that he did not have a cannon on the launch as he felt he could have attacked Fort Mitchell, the southernmost U.S. post on the Chattahoochee River:

> ...I hope Sir Thomas Trowbridge will shortly arrive as you suppose, and bring field pieces with him. Had I had a gun in the launch, I would have attacked Fort Mitchell, about 280 miles up the river both by water and land in less than 3 weeks. There is only one gun mounted on it and a garrison of 200 men, however, I don't despair having it, and one or two more forts ere long.[39]

Woodbine made it up to Eufaula and back down to the Gulf in ten days, meeting many chiefs and warriors and gathering considerable intelligence about conditions on the frontier. He saw a region generally untouched by the Creek War, although he did encounter some refugee Tallassee and Yuchi, as well as the Fowltown warriors who had been defeated at the Battle of Uchee and forced to retreat down to the confluence of the Chattahoochee and Flint Rivers. He encountered no opposition and was able to invite a large number of Creeks and Seminoles to come down and receive arms.

---

[39] Capt. George Woodbine to Capt. Hugh Pigot, May 31, 1814, Cochrane Papers.

The first delegation to respond to the captain's invitation arrived at Apalachicola Bay on May 20, 1814. Thomas Perryman and Cappachimico were among them and approved the British request to land troops and supplies on St. Vincent Island. Capt. Pigot entertained them aboard the *Orpheus* and gave orders for a landing the next morning:

> It being for the good of His Majesty's Service, I feel it my duty to accept the voluntary offer of your services to instruct the Creek Nations in the use of small arms & assist them against our common enemy the Americans.
>
> For which, it is my positive directions you put yourselves under the command of Brevet Captain Woodbine of the Royal Marines, and follow such orders as he may give from time to time for the performance of this service.[40]

Sgt. Samuel Smith and Corp. James Denny of the Royal Marines led a detachment to the island. A log house was built there as a repository for supplies from the ships, which were too deep of draft to cross the bar into Apalachicola Bay. Small boats started carrying muskets, kegs of powder, and other items to shore, and soldiers built three more log houses to provide shelter for the men on St. Vincent. Warriors were armed as they reached the island, and Smith and Denny began training them with military-style load and fire drills.

Woodbine and Pigot recognized almost immediately that St. Vincent Island was remote and difficult to reach for Native Americans coming down to receive the promised arms. They decided to move their main operation upriver 20-miles to Prospect Bluff while continuing to use the island as a temporary storehouse for arms and ammunition. Capt. Woodbine established new headquarters on the bluff just south of the Forbes and Company store on May 25, 1814. Things now began to happen very fast. An immediate council gathered and Woodbine offered his services as agent and commandant:

---

[40] Capt. Hugh Pigot to Sgt. Samuel Smith and Corp. James Denny, May 21, 1814, Cochrane Papers.

...The Proclamation of the Commander in Chief, I intend to forward in a day or two to Georgia, Tennessee & New Orleans by trusty Indians, who have been appointed at a general meeting of the chiefs, for such purposes, and I have no doubt of several hundred American slaves joining our standard the moment it is raised, which shall be done when the arms are all up, and an encampment formed on the Forks of the River. At this same meeting the chiefs have unanimously decided that all power to conduct operations shall be taken out of their hands and lodged solely in mine, as chief of all, as also the appointment of all officers, and that no interference of a single individual shall be allowed. This command I have accepted on condition, that they will make prisoners (and give them up to me for the purpose of working on any public works I may order) that they put to death no one but those resisting with arms in their hands, which is agreed to, and all chiefs individually have pledged themselves, that their tribes will comply.[41]

The proclamation referenced was a call from Admiral Cochrane to the American citizens of the region, calling on them to offer their loyalty to Great Britain in exchange for guarantees that their persons, families, property, and possessions would be protected. John Yellowhair, a young chief from Tamathli, was sent overland to inform the Red Stick groups around Pensacola of the British arrival. Thomas Perryman and Cappachimico were named "Generals" by Woodbine, who promised to share all intelligence and reports with them and to seek their approval on all operations.[42]

Woodbine addressed the assembled warriors at Prospect Bluff on May 25, telling them more about his mission and calling upon them to show mercy to their enemies:

---

[41] Capt. George Woodbine to Capt. Hugh Pigot, May 25, 1814 (actually edited and sent on May 28, 1814), Cochrane Papers.
[42] *Ibid.*

Your father King George sends me among you, to bring arms and ammunition to defend yourselves. Your father got only one letter from you, and I now give you the Answer – Hear – Your father told me to tell you that he had never forgot good children the Creeks, but that many Nations of Enemies had tried for some years past to destroy your Father, but the Great Spirit had stood his friend and had made him so strong that he had beat them all. Your father told me to tell you that he was sorry to hear that those wicked people the Americans, were robbing his children the Creeks of their lands and were driving them, their women & children into the woods like Tigers. Your Father wishes you to talk the straight talk with his Captain about all your business.

Your Father wishes to know what things you want to make you all happy. If you tell me, I will write to his Admiral and Great Warrior, who will send them. Your Father told me to tell you, that he wants to protect all the Indians and to make them into one family that they may unite and drive the Children of the Bad Spirit (the Americans) out of the lands and hunting ground. Your father told me to tell you that he wants some Americans, men women & children, and if you will take them all prisoners, instead of killing them, he will send you good presents every year and plenty of Powder & Ball to hunt with.

You must bring them all to me his Captain, and I will write to the Admiral and great Warrior, who will then write to the King your father, all good talks about you.[43]

The assembled chiefs agreed to the British request that they spare the lives of any prisoners taken. Thomas Perryman and Cappachimico signed their consent in a written document prepared by Woodbine:

---

[43] Capt. George Woodbine, Talk of May 25, enclosed in Woodbine to Pigot, May 25, 1814 (edited and sent on May 28, 1814), Cochrane Papers.

> In the name of all the chiefs of the Creek Nations, now assembled in arms against the Americans, we promise to spare the lives of all prisoners taken, wither man, woman or child, and to give them to Captain Woodbine of the Royal Marines who has informed us that they should be a gratefull present to our Father King George.
>
> For all the Chiefs, we sign by their desire,
>
> Thomas Perryman, King of the Seminoles
>
> Cappachamico, King of the Mickasukis
>
> Witness to Signatures
>
> Wm. Hambly[44]

Woodbine did not know it, but American spies were already present. The chief and trader John Stedham, who lived on the Chattahoochee River, had sent several of his employees down to the Forbes and Company store to secure supplies. They arrived on his "boat" (probably a keelboat) to learn with surprise that the British had arrived:

> ...When Mr. Steddam's boat arrived at the store, he found a good many of the British officers and soldiers at the store. The British officers wanted to borrow the boat of Steddam's men to go to Deer Island. The men refused for some time, and would not land the boat. After a great deal persuasion they agreed to land it and went with the British officers to Deer Island and when they arrived there they found two vessels, one a fifty gun ship, the other a small vessel, and saw the whole British force that had landed there. They supposed to be about one thousand upon said Island. The British had landed on shore guns and ammunition. The Indians had four houses built for them. One house was filled with ammunition. The British had all left there before Steddam's men left the Island. About

---

[44]Promise of the Chiefs given at Prospect Bluff, May 28, 1814, Cochrane Papers.

50 of the British troops were left. The remainder said they would all return again in about twenty days.[45]

The "Deer Island" referenced in the report from Big Warrior, Little Prince, and John Stedham to Col. Hawkins is often identified by historians as St. George Island but was St. Vincent. It appears that Stedham's boat reached Prospect Bluff just as Woodbine was moving his headquarters to that point from the island. Stedham's employees reported that the warriors of Tutalosi Talofa (Fowltown) and Oketeyacanne had received arms and powder from the British. Both towns requested 200 kegs, but Woodbine explained that he was unable to provide that quantity.[46]

The boatmen also described the talk given by the British to warriors from different towns as they arrived at the bluff:

> You Red people, our Children,
>
> We thought you were all done over; and the Heads of our Nation sent us here to see you. We were told you, our Children, were very poor. When we arrived we found it was true, and we make a present to you of this ammunition, not to do any mischief with it, we give it to you for your hunting and support your families. You are not to do any mischief to no person. Whatever you do, do not lift up your hands against the American people. If you do, your nation will be ruined and destroyed.
>
> We understand your nation was fighting one another, which was a bad policy among you. You must quit that if you do not stop it, you will lose the whole of your country. Our Heads gave us a talk which brought us here. We were sent here to Talk to the Cussetau and Cowetaw, these two fires, and also Cherokees, Chickasaw & Choctaw to the whole of the Four Nations, there is none left out. We was sent to come a shore here. A part of our troops is to land

---

[45] Big Warrior, Little Prince, and John Steddam to Col. Benjamin Hawkins, June 13, 1814, Hargrett Rare Book and Manuscript Library, The University of Georgia Libraries, Telamon Cuyler Collection.
[46] *Ibid.*

near Savannah and Amelia Island, and others are to land below Mobile, which last place will not be for some time. The white people are fighting their own battles, and we are in hopes to have peace with the American people sometime this year. We want the Red people to have no hand in it, in our warfare. We don't want the red people to assist the white people in any of the white peoples' affairs. We do not give you arms and ammunition for that purpose."[47]

A strange accident took place in the Native American camps at Prospect Bluff on the evening of Tuesday, May 31, 1814. A party of warriors from Oketeyacanne received four kegs filled with cartridges and went off a short distance to camp for the night. What happened next was strangely prophetic:

> ...A great squall of thunder & lightning come up, and the lightning struck one of their kegs, burnt a good many of their people very badly, one they expect will die, and one of the kegs blew up. They returned again to the English and told them their misfortune. They give them another keg in the room.[48]

Woodbine also described the incident. According to his version, one warrior suffered wounds—undoubtedly the one reported by Stedham's boatmen as being expected to die—when lightning struck a tree "near the magazine" and blew up a keg of powder. The captain's mention of a magazine and the boatmen's description of a "room" where the Oketeyacanne warriors received a replacement keg indicate that the British had done some quick construction on Prospect Bluff as early as the last week of May 1814. Whether any temporary fortification work was taking place at that time is not known.

---

[47] *Ibid.*
[48] *Ibid.*

The response to the Royal Navy's arrival was electrifying. As soon as they heard that supplies were available at Prospect Bluff, hundreds of Red Stick families began moving in that direction. The British did not know of Jackson's victory at Horseshoe Bend or the desperate flight of the surviving Red Sticks into Florida until the ships arrived at Apalachicola Bay. Woodbine came expecting to provide arms and training to Creek warriors engaged in combat with the United States. Instead, he stumbled into a full-blown humanitarian crisis. Thousands of starving men, women, and children were at refugee camps in the swamps of the Choctawhatchee, Yellow, Shoal, Escambia, and Conecuh Rivers. Others were on the lower Chattahoochee River near the Perryman towns.

Woodbine's recognition of the situation is clear in a letter he wrote to Lt. David Hope of HMS *Shelburne* on May 31, 1814:

> I am sadly afraid I shall be badly off for provisions up the country till the crops (which will be in six weeks at least) ripen. If I had two hundred barrels of flour to take up the river with me, I would carry destruction among the Yankees, before three weeks. If you come across any vessel with provisions, I think you could most materially benefit the service by bringing him directly in. From some letters I intercepted yesterday from the American agent for purchasing cattle, the small body of troops they have in this nation are almost in a state of starvation, and the Indians with them are quite discontented on that account, so much so that I am offered their services by the Chiefs privately if I will victual them which I am at present unable to do. Some of the Choctaws the most numerous tribe the Americans have are now with me. They tell me that the moment it is known in their nation that the British intend to aid them with arms and ammunition, they will all come over to us. The Americans some time ago sent them home owing to their being unable to victual them.[49]

---

[49] Capt. George Woodbine to Lt. David Hope, May 31, 1814, Cochrane Papers.

The Choctaws mentioned by Woodbine were overly optimistic about the prospects of their nation joining the British. They were part of a small group that converted to the religion of the Prophet Francis early in the Creek War and against all the odds had survived the various battles with the American armies. They were now on the Apalachicola, and their journey was far from over.

John Yellowhair volunteered his services as a runner to carry news of the British arrival to the refugees in the swamps of Northwest Florida. He set out in the last week of May, slowly working his way west to Pensacola and searching the wilderness for signs of Red Sticks. One by one, he located the refugee camps and delivered Woodbine's invitation for them to come to the Apalachicola. By May 31 more than 1,000 were at Prospect Bluff, and nearly that many more were on their way:

> I have been entirely unable to distribute a musquet or ammunition for these three days last, owing to the Belts and Cartridge Boxes not being sent up. Do for God's sake load the canoes with them, as I have more than 1200 men waiting here & 7 or 8 hundred coming tomorrow or next day; hurry the canoes away, and if the boats can take more than the accoutrements break open the boxes and put the muskets loose in them, not forgetting to tye each bayonet to the musket or the Indians will mix them and create confusion.[50]

The captain also pleaded for additional troops and a section of field artillery, but Pigot was unable to provide them. Rumors became rampant as the Red Sticks flooded into the Prospect Bluff camp. The most intriguing one to Woodbine was a report that British forces were attacking Mobile:

> There is a report of Mobille being attacked by the British. If I was certain it was true, I would purchase cattle on credit & march with a thousand or fifteen hundred men there directly, to co-operate and could leave that number

---

[50] Capt. George Woodbine to Capt. Hugh Pigot, May 31, 1814.

behind to meet the Americans up the country. Negroes are flocking in from the States & I make no doubt that I shall have occasion for a considerable supply more of musquets &c. &c. &c., particularly when the Upper Town Indians join of which I have not the slightest doubt.[51]

The report was false, but the entire borderlands were a rumor mill run wild. Benjamin Hawkins first learned of the British arrival via a rumor passed along by several express riders making their way from the Alabama River across to the Chattahoochee and Flint. On May 25, the same day that Woodbine moved his operations to Pensacola, Zachariah McGirth arrived at the Creek Agency on the Flint reporting "an arrival from Havanna with munitions of war for the "Red Clubs," and orders to supply them with provisions."[52]

Two weeks passed before the American agent learned that the vessels arriving from Havana were British and that a landing had taken place at the mouth of the Apalachicola:

We have reports of supplies of munitions of war, an order for the supply of provisions to the Red Clubs being arrived at Pensacola; we have also a report that some British have arrived, and are making settlements near the mouth of Apalachicola; the truth or falsehood of both reports I expect soon to receive. The road of communication has been traveled in perfect safety between our posts, and we have not had a man killed on it during our war.[53]

As rumors and bits of real intelligence made its way to the Creek Agency and U.S. forces on the Alabama River, John Yellowhair completed his mission to the Red Sticks camped along the Spanish border.

---

[51] *Ibid.*
[52] Col. Benjamin Hawkins to the Government, May 25, 1814, *Connecticut Spectator*, June 22, 1814.
[53] Col. Benjamin Hawkins to John Armstrong, Secretary of War, June 7, 1814, Grant, *Letters Journals and Writings of Benjamin Hawkins*, 1980: 682-683.

He reached Pensacola on June 9 and met with Josiah Francis and Peter McQueen. They immediately dashed off a letter to the British pleading their case and begging for help:

> Our Case is really miserable and lamentable, driven from House and Home without Food and Clothes to cover our Bodies by disasters and an Enemy, who has sworn our ruin, and hovering about Pensacola and its Vicinity, where We can get no Assistance, as the Spanish Government tells Us that it is scarsely able to support its Own Troops.[54]

HMS *Orpheus* and HMS *Shelburne* sailed back to Nassau for more supplies as Yellowhair was making his way across Northwest Florida. On arrival there, Capt. Pigot found Capt. Nicholas Lockyer of the brig-sloop HMS *Sophie* ready to sail for the Apalachicola. He directed Lockyer to load his vessel and her consort, HMS *Childers*, with arms, ammunition, and other supplies. Lockyer also assumed command of the *Shelburne* and the three vessels set sail for Florida. After calling at Apalachicola Bay and delivering all weapons requested by Capt. Woodbine, they were to proceed west along the coast to Pensacola. Pigot anticipated the desperate condition of the Red Sticks around the Spanish capital and instructed Lockyer to do everything possible to assist them. He cautioned Lockyer, however, to "give no offence to the Spanish Government in execution of the orders." The second shipment of British supplies set sail for the Gulf of Mexico.[55]

American authorities, meanwhile, slowly learned more about the new threat to the Southern frontier. Two U.S.-allied Lower Creek chiefs—the Wolf Warrior and Fullausau Hadjo—reported on June 7 that a courier sent by Col. Hawkins to communicate with William Hambly had paid with his life:

---

[54] Joshua [Josiah] Francis, Yahollasaptko, Hopoyhisihlyholla to British Commander at St. George's Island, June 9, 1814, Cochrane Papers.
[55] Capt. Hugh Pigot to Capt. Nicholas Lockyer, June 11, 1814, Cochrane Papers.

The English has taken possession of Pensacola and given a large quantity of arms and ammunition to the Simmonolies. They keep it a secret from me I have seen by accident and talked with a man right from there. It is not for war they say but it looks very suspicious in my eye. The Indians from below say an express from Colo. Hawkins to Hambly was put in care of Sandy Durant and an Indian to conduct him safe, that Durant killed him and robed him.[56]

Sandy Durant was one of the signers of the original request for British help sent by the Perryman delegation from Pensacola in September 1813. His violent move showed a determination to prevent Hawkins from learning specifics about the situation on the Apalachicola. Other spies, however, succeeded in getting more information to the agent:

...Fullaussau Haujo saw a young man of his town who had been to Deer Island in the mouth of Apalatchecola where he saw two British ships. An officer sent to invite the Indian to come there, a number arrived mostly Seminoles and Hostile Indians. The officer said "I am a British officer sent to see whether the Indians were distroyed or not, in their war with the United States, if not, to afford them help. I have some supplies and I give to each town four large casks of powder and some short muskets with slings and other things. I have 1000 men in each of the ships." During his being there, they issued daily to the Red people assembled two beef cattle and some dried salt meat from the ships.[57]

---

[56] Col. Benjamin Hawkins, "Report of supplies to the Indians by the British and Spaniards at Pensacola and mouth of Chattahochie," June 14, 1814, Telamon Cuyler Collection, Hargrett Rare Book and Manuscript Library, The University of Georgia Libraries.

[57] *Ibid.*

Fullausau Hadjo was the principal chief of Eufaula, the northernmost town reached by Woodbine in May. He never mentioned this fact to Hawkins or his assistants, but did provide some detail on the British plan of operations as learned by the warrior from his town. The Red Sticks had halted at Yellow River and planned to concentrate their forces on the Choctawhatchee until they received word as to what they should do. The British planned to occupy Mobile, Perdido Bay, the Yellow and Choctawhatchee Rivers, "an island near St. Marys, an island near Savannah and that town and an island near Charleston at the same time." They were to continue recruiting their strength until the second shipment of supplies reached the Apalachicola, at which time they would strike all along the Gulf Coast and Georgia seaboard.[58]

Wolf Warrior and Fullausau Hadjo also relayed concluded their report with an ominous warning from the Prophet Francis and another Red Stick chief:

> The prophet observed to the Semenolies in presence of the reporters "we have brought our difficulties on ourselves without advise from any one. The old chiefs need not expect we will be given up. We have lost our country and retreated to the sea side where we will fight until we are all destroyed, we are collected and find a few more than 1000 warriors left; and mean to form our settlement on Choctau hatche."
>
> Tustunnuggee Haujo who fled with the fowltown and Oketeyoanne people below the confluence of the Flint & Chattahooches sent a message to the Big Warrior & Little Prince "I have now friends and arms, you compelled me to fly and if you attempt to track me up I shall spill your blood."[59]

Col. Hawkins reacted such intelligence with a message to the Big Warrior, Little Prince, and the chiefs on the Creek Council, telling them to

---

[58] *Ibid.*
[59] *Ibid.*

be ready for action. He linked the interests of the Creeks to those of the United States:

> As your corn is now planted, we must begin to look about us. If the enemy are not conquered, we must go after them again, and follow them up, until we conquer them. It matters not who comes to help them, British or Spaniards; the United States will help us, and we shall be an over match for them. We fight on our own ground, and they are foreigners, who, if they come, it will be to deprive us of our rights. The British have tried us before, when we were not half so powerful as we are now, within our recollection, and found us strong enough to defend our rights.[60]

The agent was speaking of the Creeks when he said, "We fight on our own ground" but drifted to speaking of the United States when he noted that "the British have tried us before." He forgot, at least temporarily, that many of the Muscogee had sided with Great Britain in the American Revolution.

---

[60] Col. Benjamin Hawkins to the Big Warrior, Little Prince, and other chiefs, June 16, 1814, *American State Papers: Indian Affairs*, Volume I: 845.

4

RED STICK REVIVAL

CAPT. NICHOLAS LOCKYER REACHED THE WATERS off St. George and St. Vincent Islands after a three-week sail from Nassau. Although none of his ships approached the size of HMS *Orpheus*, all three brought cargoes of arms, ammunition, blankets, corn powder, and other material. Dropping anchor off the entrance to East Pass, he sent small boats up the river to Prospect Bluff where Capt. Woodbine and his detachment eagerly awaited the arrival of more supplies. Work went forward on the British depot in June and July, but details are few. Several buildings are known to have been built, among them a more substantial magazine. The Royal Marines undoubtedly built houses for their shelter, and Woodbine likely had a cabin thrown up for himself as well. Storage buildings of some sort for muskets and accouterments were also necessary.

The shore party reached the bluff on July 16, 1814. Other boats continued to land weapons and supplies on St. Vincent Island during its absence. Woodbine sent a letter down to Lockyer informing him that it would take some time for canoes to arrive from the upriver towns to help move the material from the island to Prospect Bluff. He also reported the capture of an American purchasing agent who was trying to buy beef in the Lower Creek country:

> I send a Packet of Papers herewith found on Wilson & in
> his trunk, which with himself I will be obliged by your
> delivering up to the Commander in Chief. He came down
> from an American Fort, with a letter to the two principal

53

chiefs of the lower Creeks, to tamper with them and to secure myself and party (according to their report) to be delivered up to the Americans. At any rate, among his papers will be found a letter wherein he acknowledges himself U.S. Contractor for fresh beef, and also his contract with the regular contractor for the U.S. troops. This circumstance with his lurking about this part of the country, and occasionally going up to the American forts, in such times, is highly improper. I have therefore thought it right to send him out of this part of the world – and leave him at the disposal of the Commander in Chief.[61]

Capt. Woodbine asked Lockyer to allow him the use of HMS *Cockchafer*—named after a European beetle—which he hoped would take him to Pensacola for 48-hours and then back to the Apalachicola. The little schooner was something of a celebrity in the Royal Navy, having captured much larger U.S. ships in armed combat. She had not yet arrived off Apalachicola Bay but was expected soon. By going to the Spanish capital, Woodbine expected to gain intelligence that would prove valuable to Admiral Cochrane:

> I could most fully satisfy him on every point respecting which he craves information, and which Capt. Pigot particularly desired to convey to the Commander in Chief. I know the Commander in Chief is very anxious to gain information on his various queries, and your compliance with my request would enable me to ascertain many circumstances very favorable to my present undertaking, indeed without which, I shall act on a very great uncertainty, and most probably fail. Should you capture a small vessel with provisions of which I am entirely out, I will thank you to send her to me. The want

---

[61] Capt. George Woodbine to Capt. Nicholas Lockyer, July 17, 1814, Cochrane Papers.

of the latter prevented me acting offensively against the Americans six weeks ago.[62]

Lockyer approved the use of *Cockchafer* should she arrive before he left the vicinity. He moved his ships around Cape San Blas and into St. Joseph Bay in search of a safer harbor. The bay had sufficient water for the ships to enter, and they were able to sail up to a point near its eastern end. A "haulover" there allowed supplies to be portaged across the narrow neck of St. Joseph Peninsula to small boats waiting on the other side in Apalachicola Bay. This route proved much faster and safer than trying to move weapons and supplies through the open Gulf to St. Vincent Island. The *Cockchafer* reached St. Joseph Bay on July 24, having already made one quick run to Pensacola. Lockyer notified Woodbine that if he would come down, the vessel was at his disposal.[63]

The naval captain's brief letter did not provide much more important news regarding the *Cockchafer*. Onboard when she entered St. Joseph Bay were the Prophet Josiah Francis and Peter McQueen, by then the most wanted men on the southern frontier. They were furious that their former ally, William Weatherford, was leading U.S. troops in raids across the Spanish border against Red Stick camps north of Pensacola. One of the British spies in Pensacola gave details on the attacks in an unsigned report:

> At your request I have put to paper, what appears to me to be the most probable situation of affairs in this neighbourhood. For some days past it had been pretty well understood that six hundred Americans were posted at the head of the River Scambia about 25 miles from this place, that the Americans and Indians were very near this place, supposed by some to take possession, by others, that this was not intended, but committing depredations and murdering &c. &c.[64]

---

[62] *Ibid.*

[63] Capt. Nicholas Lockyer to Capt. George Woodbine, July 19, 1814 & July 21, 1814, Cochrane Papers.

[64] Unsigned report dated Pensacola, July 19, 1814, and addressed to Lt. Perc. Jackson, HMS Cockchafer, Cochrane Papers.

Col. Joseph Carson of the Mississippi Territory was the leader of the first attack. He headed the First Mississippi Regiment during the main fighting of the Creek War and took part in the Battle of Holy Ground. He now headed a company of mounted volunteers. The colonel and his men crossed the line into Spanish Florida, striking into present-day Escambia and Santa Rosa Counties:

> ...This morning I find the facts to be these – A party of American horsemen about 40 (no Choctaws) headed by Colonel carson, and joined by Wm. Weatherford an Indian chief, are pursuing the Creek Indians and are killing them wherever they meet them. They were yesterday at Mr. Marshalls about 16 miles off the other side of this Bay, and killed 7 or 8 Indians there. They then went to Mr. Miller's Plantation, but did no damage there. They have also attacked a new Indian settlement called Coneta, and killed all the Indians they could lay hands on, have taken what women & children could be found, and the report among the Americans in this place is that Genl. Jackson is at the head of 9500 men, and are proceeding to Apalachicola. My own belief is, that half this number of men are not as yet collected into one body in this neighbourhood, nor do I think that the Americans will dare to attack this place, at the same time there is no accounting for the acts of madmen I observe. Marshall's Plantation is in Spanish Territory. Wm. Weartherford was lately fighting alongside of McQueen, and has given himself up to the Americans.[65]

Unaware of the *Cockchafer's* arrival with McQueen and Francis, Capt. Woodbine was making plans for a sudden strike against Fort Hawkins on the Georgia frontier. Sgt. Samuel Smith and Corp. James Denny were up the river drilling warriors—probably at Perryman's town—when they received intelligence that the fort was weak and vulnerable. The enterprise

---

[65] *Ibid.*

was made even more intriguing by the presence in the stockade of Col. Benjamin Hawkins and his family, whose capture would be a major coup for the British. Woodbine promoted Smith to acting lieutenant for "your good conduct" and decided to attack.[66]

In orders issued on July 21, he indicated that Smith proposed the plan of attack:

> The enterprize you have solicited my permission to undertake, I have from your representation of the practicability thereof consented to your attempted. But recollect to temper that laudable ambition you have to distinguish yourself in some dashing affair with prudence, and use every endeavour to obtain correct information of the strength of the object of attack. Should you succeed, I know I need scarcely inform you that "Humanity is the first quality in a truly brave man." The Indians will spare as few as possible but impress it on the minds of the party that accompany you that prisoners are my object, and that I set y face against putting any one not resisting to death or scalping them, and that according to the humanity they shew, so will you report their conduct to me and procure them rewards accordingly. Should any females (of which I understand the Colonels family are likely to be part) fall into your hand, you too well know the duty of an Englishman and a soldier to require my saying a word to you on the line of conduct to pursue.[67]

The American forts along the Federal Road were uncharacteristically weak in June and early July 1814, when the Smith gathered his intelligence. Fort Hawkins was a well-designed regular post that even defended by a small garrison would have been much more difficult to take than one of the temporary stockades thrown up during the advance of the Georgia army. The British had been working for over six weeks to arm

---

[66] Capt. George Woodbine to Sgt. Samuel Smith, July 20, 1814, Cochrane Papers.
[67] Capt. George Woodbine to Lt. Samuel Smith, July 21, 1814, Cochrane Papers.

and train Red Stick, Seminole, and Miccosukee warriors, and with enough men and proper leadership, a successful strike was possible.

The situation changed quickly on the next day when a boat arrived with Capt. Lockyer's announcement that the *Cockchafer* was in St. Joseph Bay and ready to carry Woodbine to Pensacola. He immediately rescinded his orders to Smith and replaced them with new instructions according to a previous attack plan the two had discussed:

> You will instead of proceeding on the intended enterprize immediately place yourself at the head of at least three hundred picked men, and march with all possible speed to Pensacola and there join me for an attack on the place we mentioned.
>
> Secrecy and dispatch is requisite. Take Col. Perryman, Ben Perryman, Fulsahlanny and the Burgesses with you – and all volunteers let them be able men. Tallafaggys cattle will follow you (Daniel comes up to you, as quick as possible. George Perryman I am obliged to take with me as the business requires the best interpreter. Now is your time to make a dash! I will give you every chance. Keep your journal.[68]

Woodbine tried to ensure operational security by not identifying the new target in writing, but it was Mobile. The American occupation of the city was a thorn in the sides of both the Red Sticks and Spain. The Prophet Francis offered to recapture or destroy it for the Spanish shortly after the fall of Fort Mims, but Gov. Mateo Gonzales Manrique declined. Now the British were ready to make a move regardless. Lt. Smith's taking of Col. Thomas Perryman on the expedition gave it legitimacy among the Native Americans of the borderlands. Ben, Daniel, and George Perryman—also mentioned in the orders—were among the old chief's sons while the Burgesses were sons and grandsons of the late frontier trader James Burges. Both families had supported Great Britain during the American Revolution.

---

[68] Capt. George Woodbine to Lt. Samuel Smith, July 22, 1814, Cochrane Papers.

Sending a running upriver to alert Smith to the change of plans, Capt. Woodbine dropped down the Apalachicola River to the bay, and by July 25 was aboard HMS *Sofie* off Cape San Blas. Before going aboard *Cockchafer* in St. Joseph Bay, he prepared a report of his recent activities to be delivered to Admiral Cochrane by Capt. Lockyer. He blamed his failure to attack the enemy on the horrible food shortage that existed throughout the region:

> ...You will, Sir, I trust find that no exertion have been omitted to perform the orders left by Capt. Pigot, but the very distressed situation of this country for provisions has alone prevented me attacking the Americans, not only in Georgia, but also in various parts, particularly Mobille, which I do not hesitate to say, I would have destroyed even with the Indians that had joined me, could I have fed them. I have been unable to gain over the Upper Creek Indians that were acting with the Americans and in a few weeks I trust I shall have to report to your Excellency some movements tending to the annoyance of the United States in this quarter. My situation here, without an assistant I may almost say to manage a race of men that require I assure you every endeavour to please, will I trust exonerate me for having allowed more than two months since my arrival to pass without doing something that might distress our Enemies. But I must reiterate the same complaint to your Excellency that I did to Capt. Pigot that the very distressed state of the Creek Nation, was thrown into by the Americans having created a civil war among them, with the scarcity of provisions, prevented me acting offensively.[69]

Woodbine went on to report that he had promoted both Sgt. Smith and Corp. Denny to acting lieutenants of Royal Marines. Because non-commissioned officers did not wear epaulets, he found the promotions

---

[69] Capt. George Woodbine to Rear Admiral Sir Alexander Cochrane, July 15, 1814, Cochrane Papers.

necessary to allow the men to adopt uniforms that their Native American trainees would respect. The captain urged the admiral to approve the new ranks. He then reported that the British had considered a change of base from Prospect Bluff to St. Andrew Bay:

> ...I applied to Captain Lockyer on his arrival here to land the supplies he had brought at St. Andrews Bay, and to throw up a small fort, as from the situation it would be more central than Prospect Bluff and enable me to draw on my supplies with more facility. He used every endeavour to accomplish it, but regret to say, he failed but he can explain the reasons better than myself.[70]

The project failed because St. Andrew Bay proved no more accessible for the British warships than Apalachicola Bay. Its entrance was shallow, and the draft of the vessels too great. Lockyer fell back on St. Joseph Bay, using the haul-over previously described to move arms and supplies across to small boats in Apalachicola Bay. The second shipment went to Prospect Bluff in the launches and other boats of the ships instead of by Native American canoe. Woodbine requested that future deliveries be made in the same way:

> ...[S]hould any other men of war, be ordered on this station and you should honor me by continuing me in my present situation, and the store should be at Prospect Bluff, I hope you will order all supplies to be transported by their boats to the Depot, as on arrival of any vessel I am compelled to send for canoes nearly two hundred miles up the river, wait for their coming down, and then going down to Vincent Island and returning.
> They are compelled when loaded to cross the Bay of St. Georges, to enter the river and should any squall take them, run a great risk of sinking as was the case with one canoe two days ago, with sixty stand of arms and accoutrements complete. The four Indians in her were

---

[70] *Ibid.*

fortunately saved, but the arms &c. it being in deep water, in the center of the Bay were lost.[71]

The captain explained to Cochrane that multiple sources—Lockyer, Lt. Jackson of the *Cockchafer*, and John Yellowhair—indicated that the Red Sticks near Pensacola were in desperate straits "from immediate starvation of them, and their families." They also had immediate need of arms and ammunition, both for self-defense and for military operations:

> In consequence I have judged it necessary to proceed immediately to Pensacola, from whence I shall have the honor of further continuing to your Excellency my report of proceedings in this quarter. I shall most strictly comply with Capt. Pigot's instructions, as also with Capt. Lockyer's directions, respecting avoiding giving the slightest offence to the Spanish Government but I do not think I should at all do my duty as Indian Agent without I personally attempted to rescue these unfortunate and loyal subjects of his Majesty.
>
> Intend if Act. Lieut. Smith joins me in good time to attempt with his body (and the Indians in and about Pensacola) the capture or destruction of Mobille as also the burning of a frigate nearly ready to launch and only drawing 8 foot water and a new man of war brig, lately off the stocks.[72]

Woodbine boarded the *Cockchafer* at St. Joseph Bay and sailed west along the Northwest Florida coast, reaching Pensacola on July 28. The 5-gun schooner was able to sail up to the city itself, while Capt. Lockyer anchored in the bay with the larger vessel HMS *Sophie*. HMS *Shelburne* was ordered to the Bahamas with Woodbine's reports and a request for additional stocks of arms, ammunition, and food, while HMS *Childers* went to cruise for American vessels off the coast of Cuba. Capt. Woodbine first stepped ashore near the foot of Palafox Street at a site now covered

---

[71] *Ibid.*
[72] *Ibid.*

by fill. The shoreline was extended into the bay in later times to allow expansion room for downtown Pensacola and its wharves to extend into deeper water. He immediately walked up through the deep sand to the home of Gov. Mateo Gonzales Manrique:

> ...[O]n his arrival there he was received by the Spanish Governor on the greatest terms of friendship and solicited by the Governor for his assistance in protecting the town of Pensacola from the supposed meditated attack of the Americans. The Cockchafer rejoined me off Mobille with a letter from Captain Woodbine soliciting me to proceed to Pensacola to land 120 stand of arms I had on board which I complied with, on my arrival there I found about 1000 Indians near 700 of which are warriors of the Lower Creek Nation, and from every information there is reason to suppose a much greater number will soon arrive there. I have thought it expedient to dispatch the Cockchafer for your information and having completed my provisions at Pensacola I shall continue to Cruize calling occasionally at that place to render any assistance the Indians or Captain Woodbine may stand in need of.[73]

Woodbine reported that "with the Governor's sanction," he distributed six cases of muskets and eight kegs of powder to the Red Sticks at Pensacola. He learned from the chiefs and warriors in the city that reports of Andrew Jackson concentrating his army on the Escambia River north of the city were false. He had returned to Fort Jackson at the Hickory Ground, but intelligence indicated that U.S. troops were massing at Mobile and Baton Rouge for an attack on Spanish Florida:

> They are withdrawing all their marauding parties, and have dismantled several Forts. They will strain every nerve to get hold of this Town, ere reinforcements can arrive. I am preparing every possible mode of defense.

---

[73] Capt. Nicholas Lockyer to Admiral Sir Andrew Cochrane, August 12, 1814, Cochrane Papers.

> With the Indians I am levelling a high hill, formerly a Fort
> (was constructed on it,) that commands the principal Fort
> (St. Michael) of this town, and am repairing it also, it
> being much out of order. The Governor has requested me
> to take possession of it, and defend the Town, which I will
> do with a body of white men, mulattoes & blacks that I
> am raising here, and encamp the Indians round it.[74]

The hill that Woodbine described "levelling" was the site of the Prince of Wales Redoubt, a small fort built by the British during the American Revolution. The redoubt was 300 yards north Fort George, which the Spanish renamed Fort San Miguel or St. Michael. It guarded the heights that overlooked Fort George to protect against an enemy force occupying them and placing cannon to fire down into the main fort. A third fort, the Queen's Redoubt, occupied another hilltop 300 yards north of the Prince of Wales. These three forts were the focus of the Battle of Pensacola, one of the largest and yet least known actions of the Revolutionary War.

Gen. Bernardo de Galvez's allied army of Spanish, Irish, French, and a few American soldiers attacked Pensacola on March 9, 1781, igniting a two-month siege for control of the British occupied city. The battle continued until a Spanish cannon shot exploded the magazine of the Queen's Redoubt on May 8. Spanish grenadiers and soldiers from the Havana militia stormed the hilltop and seized the ruins of the fort. They brought up cannon during the night and by the next morning were ready to rain fire down on the Prince of Wales Redoubt and Fort George. The British raised the white flag, and Pensacola surrendered.

Spain rebuilt the Queen's Redoubt in the years after the American Revolution, renaming it Fort San Bernardo. The Prince of Wales Redoubt, which the Spanish called Fort Sombrero for its unique "hat-shape" design," slowly eroded. Woodbine destroyed most of its remnants during his 1814 leveling operation.

The British captain still believed that the bulk of the Choctaw Nation would join his cause in fighting the Americans. There is no indication that the leadership of the nation ever considered such a proposition, but this is

---

[74] Capt. George Woodbine to Admiral Sir Alexander Cochrane, August 9, 1814, Cochrane Papers.

likely what the small group of Choctaws from Prospect Bluff told Woodbine:

> ...The Governor proposes retreating to Fort Barrancas, which commands the entrance of the Harbour, and to leave the protection of the Town to me. He has desired me to do as I please either in destroying or erecting Forts. The whole Country is ripe for a change and longing anxiously to rid themselves of the Americans. Even a smaller British force than I mention to your Excellency, would make us Masters of this Country. I hope to have the Choctaws on the rear of Genl. Jackson's army shortly, but at present it is impossible to convey arms and ammunition to them till we capture Mobille which I must give up the idea of attempting for a while. Nothing but that prevents them striking the blow and drawing off the attention of the Americans from this place.[75]

The Red Sticks began to emerge from the swamps of the Escambia, Conecuh, Yellow, and Choctawhatchee Rivers as soon as they learned of the British arrival in Pensacola. Woodbine was shocked by their appearance. Most were mere skin and bones, their clothing nothing but rags:

> ...The Indians that were driven into the Woods are now flocking in daily, the picture of wretchedness and misery displayed by these poor people beggars description, many with not a rag to cover them. I trust you will approve my having purchased some osnaburgs to clothe them. Those that I first saw are however beginning to look better, and I hope shortly to bring them all round so that they may do some credit to your protection. Ere my arrival they were dying in numbers daily, but a little assistance will not materially alter their appearance.[76]

---

[75] *Ibid.*
[76] *Ibid.*

The number of Red Sticks now in Pensacola or the adjacent swamps reached more than 2,000, perhaps 800 of whom were warriors. Woodbine sent three private vessels weighted with ballast to attempt purchases of corn and other provisions from Mobile and New Orleans. At the same time, he requested that the Spanish governor place an embargo on all shipments of provisions from Pensacola to other ports. He reported to Admiral Cochrane that he was unable for the time being to arm the Red Sticks who were coming in because he did not have transportation to bring arms and ammunition from Prospect Bluff. He planned to purchase a small schooner for that purpose but feared its loss to pirate or American vessels since it would go unarmed.[77]

It did not take long for news of the British occupation of Pensacola to reach the nearby American frontier. The Pierce brothers, who ran a sawmill near Fort Mims in the Tensaw settlement, wrote to U.S. District Judge Harry Toulmin on August 5, 1814:

> We have this moment received the following information from a Mr. John Morris, who has just arrived from the neighborhood of Pensacola, he left there three days ago. He states that about ten days ago, some British officers called the Indians together, about a mile or two out of town, and gave them a talk; (no Americans, and but a few Spaniards were permitted to hear it) the Indians say that the British directs them not to kill women and children. They say that a number of the British were expected at Pensacola every day, and when they arrived, they should be supplied with arms, ammunition, and provisions. Two British vessels were said to have arrived the day before he, (Morris) came away. They are daily mustering, parading, and exercising the Indians, which seems to be very disgusting to them – they appear to be in confusion, and are not well pleased with the general proceedings of the British towards them, and many of

---

[77] *Ibid.*

them are determined not to fight for them – a few of them are gone to Escambia, for the purpose of interceding with their families and friends, to come and give themselves up to the Americans – It is expected they will be here in a few days if they proceed; the number of Indians in and about Pensacola, we believe to be about 350, and more are daily expected from Appalachicola.[78]

The information was essentially correct, although Woodbine's reports indicate that the actual number of Red Stick warriors present might have been much higher. Lt. Smith and Col. Perryman probably had not arrived with their warriors by the time the American spy, John Morris, left the city. He was fluent in the Muscogee language, having lived for several years in the Creek Nation, and reported that the British were aware of the weakness of the American posts along the frontier. The spy eavesdropped on Red Stick conversations and found it was one of their topics of discussion. He also carefully observed the military situation of Pensacola:

He further states that the town is guarded principally by Indians, under the command of British officers – there are now three in town; all the British troops at Appalachicola were daily expected, and soon after their arrival a part of the British and Indians were expected to come up this way, another part were expected to go on to the Cogeta. They direct the Indians to kill every American who attempts to go into Pensacola. They are also instructed, on the arrival of the British, to confine every American in and about Pensacola, if they refuse to fight for them. The Spanish troops are all moved to the Barrancas.[79]

The Pierce brothers expressed concern that the newly armed Red Sticks would soon strike against the frontier. "If there is not more troops

---

[78] W. and J. Pierce to Hon. Harry S. Toulmin, August 5, 1814, *Western Monitor*, September 9, 1814.
[79] *Ibid.*

sent here soon," they wrote, "we fear ere long, we shall share the same fate of the people who fell in Mims' fort."[80]

The Mississippi Territory was not the only part of the South with a threatened frontier. One day after the Pierce brothers penned their letter at Tensaw, a party of Red Sticks struck on the Georgia frontier below Hartford:

> It is with great pain I have to communicate to your Excellency, that we had a very serious alarm from the Indians yesterday evening at three o'clock, in the field of Mr. John Rabun, which is between seven and eight miles below Hartford and immediately on the river – The said Rabun being in his field, three Indians arose out of the corn, and one of them fired on him and wounded him severely in the back – He immediately took to flight – The pursued him with the most horrid yells, and as he crossed the fence both the others fired on him and wounded him slightly in the shoulder. They continued to pursue him near his house, where he got his gun and would have fired on them but for the interference of his wife, who clung around him and prevented him.[81]

The Red Sticks struck next at two nearby farms, taking a horse and household items. Lt. Col. Allen Tooke of the 35th Georgia Militia sent a detachment in pursuit of the warriors, but they eluded capture. A lieutenant's guard went out to occupy three small forts along the local frontier and watch for signs of other raiding parties.[82]

The new trouble found Maj. Gen. Jackson, Col. Hawkins, and the principal chiefs remaining in the Creek Nation assembled at Fort Jackson near modern Wetumpka, Alabama. Two chiefs arrived on August 6 to

---

[80] *Ibid.*
[81] Lt. Col. Allen Tooke, 35th Georgia Militia, to Gov. William Rabun of Georgia, August 6, 1814, *Georgia Journal*, August 10, 1814.
[82] *Ibid.*

report that they had been down to the mouth of the Apalachicola and conversed with a British officer:

> I have been down to John Forbes & Co. store and saw and conversed with a British officer (Hambly, interpreter). I told the officer I was sent by the Chiefs to see him. He said "he was glad of it. He had seen but one, Capitchuchee Micco (King of the Seminoles) who appeared to be of any account, he was a correct man. The Chief of his government had sent him to see the situation of the Creeks, it had been a long time since the British had left them, but he had retained his friendship for them. He, the Capt., had three vessels. They were not large. He had some arms and ammunition for the Chiefs and some clothing, but on the sea 1,500 men sailing along. He had been searching for a port for his vessels but had not yet found one and would have been lost in his search if he had not had his compass. The water was shoal and his vessels could not get near the land which he wished.[83]

The report is a little unclear about the identity of the officer who met with the two chiefs, but it was Capt. Woodbine. Lt. William Hambly interpreted for them. The captain told them that he had orders to encourage peace along the frontier and had no hostile intentions for the United States. These words indicate that he suspected the two—Fallaupau Hadjo and Noocoosa Hadjo—were spies for Benjamin Hawkins. He told them that he believed he and Hawkins would get along well and promised that he would write them when he returned from Pensacola, for which place he was about to leave. This information places the date of their visit to around July 20.[84]

Their report to Jackson was appended at 3 p.m. by Col. Hawkins with a note that one of his sub-agents, Alexander Cornells, had heard them deliver a second less-peaceful message to the other chiefs present:

---

[83] Fallaupau Haujo and Noocoosa Haujo to Maj. Gen. Andrew Jackson, August 6, 1814, Jackson Papers, Library of Congress.

[84] *Ibid.*

Mr. Cornells reported in confidence "the two reporters and their companions had communicated to the Chiefs the foregoing was for the ear of Col. Hawkins. The officer directed him to say to the Chiefs which they would act on as they like, that the British and other powers had conquered France and seven powers were now united against America. A little before the white frosts you will hear of smoke all around the United States in the sea ports and the burning of powder. The war is just beginning, there will be several armies landing in different places. His King George said the seven powers would be able to conquer America and the British would be masters of it. They need not expect to be deceived, the wood fulfill their promise and never leave this land again."[85]

The clumsy attempt to deliver one talk to the Creek chiefs and another to Jackson did not settle well with the general. He railed against the British on the next day in a talk that Hawkins interpreted for the chiefs:

…Upon being appointed to the command in this quarter and having received orders to settle the war with the hostile Creeks, he came here. Whilst he is engaged in this business he finds that Oketeyoconne Tuttallossee, the Seminoles and other Indians near the fork of Flint and Chattahochee are running to the British for arms and ammunition for muskets with Bayonets and cartridge boxes to kill squirrels, crows and turkeys. And yesterday what was his surprised to hear in his own tent but to Chiefs sent after information to come with two talks, one for the ear of Col. Hawkins, and one for the Chiefs. He has a runner from Pensacola. The British is there with some Creeks with redcoats, caps and sidearms and he has the second talk in his pocket. While he is geathered your poor people and feeding thousands to save their lives, the

---

[85] *Ibid.*

lower towns are running after the British for arms to fight against us. In a little time we should have mischief in this quarter, the paths are already smooth with the hatchets of mischief running to and from the British making and circulating lies.[86]

Jackson went on to tell the chiefs that he had marked a new southern boundary for the Creek Nation to prevent communication between the Muscogee and the British. Those who loved the British, he said, "may go to them." The general even offered "provisions and ammunition for the path." Anyone caught trying to cross the line after the expiration of his offer, Old Hickory warned, "shall be put to death."[87]

The sudden resurgence of the Red Sticks as a fighting force came as Jackson was laying out his demands for the cession of more than 21 million acres of Creek land to the United States. The parties signed the Treaty of Fort Jackson on August 9, 1814. It was technically an agreement to end the Creek War of 1813-1814 but most of the principal Red Stick leaders—the Prophet Francis, Peter McQueen, the Alabama King, the Tallassee King, Homathlemico, Holms, Neamathla, and others—did not sign the document and refused to recognize it. It stripped the Creek Nation of a vast amount of territory, reducing the lands of Muscogee to a mere fraction of their former holdings. The treaty forced the Creeks to pick sides. Some drifted south to join the British and Red Sticks along the Florida border. The rest settled into the remaining lands allowed them by the general they had fought and bled for at Horseshoe Bend.

---

[86] Col. Benjamin Hawkins to Maj. Gen. Andrew Jackson, August 6, 1814, Jackson Papers, Library of Congress.
[87] *Ibid.*

5

NICOLLS AT PROSPECT BLUFF

TWO MORE BRITISH WARSHIPS LEFT NASSAU ON AUGUST 5, 1814. They carried more weapons for the growing auxiliary force in Florida. The largest of the two vessels was HMS *Hermes*, the namesake of a class of 20-gun ships. Full-rigged with a complement of 135-men, she had once been commanded by the brother of novelist Jane Austen. The ship was now under Capt. the Hon. William Percy, but aboard was someone perhaps as famous in Great Britain as Miss Austen. Brevet Lt. Col. Edward Nicolls, "Fighting Nicolls" of the Royal Marines, was on his way to assume command of land operations in Florida.[88]

It took *Hermes* and HMS *Carron* just eight days to reach the mouth of the Apalachicola River. Capt. Percy accompanied Nicolls up to Prospect Bluff in the days that followed:

> We arrived at the entrance of the Appalachicola River on the 13th day of the same month where having landed the Marines under the command of Brevet Lieutenant Colonel Nicolls on Vincent's Island I proceeded with him to Prospect Bluff where we learned that Brevet Captain Woodbine had proceeded to Pensacola in His Majesty's Sloop Sophie for the purpose of assisting and communicating with a party of friendly Indians driven by

---

[88] Capt. W.H. Percy to Adm. Sir. Alexander Cochrane, September 1814, Cochrane Papers.

the Americans into Spanish Territory near that place. On my return from the Bluff I found a vessel had arrived from Pensacola hired by Captain Woodbine to bring the arms and the ammunition from the depot at the Bluff to Pensacola having leave to that effect from the Governor.[89]

Just getting to the bluff proved to be something of an adventure for the two seasoned British officers. The Apalachicola Estuary is one of the richest biospheres in the world. The freshwater that comes down the river spreads out through numerous channels to enter a bay noted as an incredible fishery. Hundreds of different species live there in a vast area that extends 50 miles inland from the barrier islands. Navigation can be tricky in its channels and rivers even today, and there is a reason that adventurers and outlaws once used the estuary as a hideout for their smuggling and piracy operations. As Nicolls and Percy soon learned, it was easy for even an experienced guide to lose his way:

> We arrived here this morning, and lost no time in disembarking the men on Vincent Island, but did not land the stores. I ordered the men to build strong Hutts, and continue to do so until I returned. Captain Percy and myself went off the same day for the bluff, but owing to the stupidity of a guide given to us by Captain Umpherville we were lead astray for two days and obliged to return for a supply of provisions.[90]

The frustrated officers tried again on about August 16 and were more successful in negotiating the twists and turns. Nicolls reported that they reached the bluff but found that "Captain Woodbine had gone to Pensacola, that the Sergeant and Corporal were up in the nation drilling the men." He does not seem to have learned that Woodbine had ordered Sgt. Smith and Corp. Denny—to whom he had given temporary promotions to lieutenant—to organize their partially-trained warriors and

---

[89] *Ibid.*

[90] Lt. Col. Edward Nicolls to Adm. Sir Alexander Cochrane, August 12, 1814-ca. December 1814, Cochrane Papers.

lead them overland to Pensacola as well. The Irish officer quickly assessed the situation, though, and realized the magnitude of the provision crises:

> …[I]n consequence of their coming in such numbers upon Perryman and Capachamico, they had created a famine, and were actually eating the corn before it was ripe. About 50 Warriors and 30 women and children came to the Bluff for arms, such objects I never saw the like of, absolute skin and bone, but cheerfull and resolved to do their utmost against the common enemy. An old man told me, when I asked him how far it was to where the enemy were, and if he knew the way to lead me to them, he said it was seven days Journey to them, (about 300 miles) that he could not miss the way, for it was marked by the graves of his five children.[91]

The Red Stick warriors who came in told the lieutenant colonel through Lt. Hambly that shortages of weapons and ammunition had caused their defeat. Without bayonets of their own, they were unable to stand against the bayonet charges directed at them by Jackson's troops. The same older warrior who described the journey as marked by the graves of his children expressed great joy at receiving a Brown Bess musket and bayonet. "He always thought something was wanting, for that while the enemy was loading, and he was loading, much time was lost," Nicolls wrote, "that now he had a bayonet he would rush on the American, when he was sure of victory."[92]

The two officers spent only 8-hours at Prospect Bluff before climbing back into their launch or longboat for the return trip downriver. Nicolls wrote that he intended to go down and bring up his Royal Marines, arms, and supplies. He planned to "fortify the place, as strong as circumstances would permit." Since the shortage of provisions was so acute, he would send out his men into the various villages and refugee camps to train the warriors instead of concentrating the whole greater force at the new fort. When he and Capt. Percy reached the bay, however, they found that a

---

[91] *Ibid.*
[92] *Ibid.*

private schooner sent by Capt. Woodbine to retrieve arms and ammunition had arrived:

> ...[O]n our return, we had the pleasure of getting a letter from Captain Woodbine at Pensacola, informing us of the Governors request to land there for the defence of the place, and that he had sent two Schooners to bring everything from the bluff, particularly 600 stand of arms, but as I saw, and was informed, that partys of 30 and 40 men, were coming in daily for arms to the bluff, from a great distance, I deemed it proper not to take away the 600 stand, as they might think we were not sincere in our promises, and return disappointed. I was the more positive in doing this, as I had the 1000 stand with me, which would more than supply all the Warriors at Pensacola.[93]

The news that Gov. Mateo Gonzales Manrique had requested the presence of British troops in Pensacola was especially welcome as Admiral Cochrane had anticipated using the city as a base from the earliest days of his command. Col. Nicolls attempted to expedite his move to Pensacola by ordering his marines to embark on the two schooners sent from Pensacola. They were in the process of doing so when disaster struck:

> ...[U]nfortunately the largest schooner [ran] on shore, bulged and filled on the bars, we lost no lives but had a great many things spoiled, among the rest, the medicine chest. I have ordered a protest to be made out, and an estimate of the loss sustained by the Spaniard, who owned and commanded her, which will be sent for your consideration, and I trust you will be so good as to order a fair remuneration for him, as no one but himself would venture in our service.[94]

---

[93] *Ibid.*
[94] *Ibid.*

Warriors from Fowltown led the first attack against the Georgia frontier, striking near Hartford, Georgia. They crossed the Flint River just above the mouth of Kinchafoonee Creek and headed for the white settlements on the Oconee and Ocmulgee Rivers. Timothy Barnard tried to warn the settlers of the danger:

> ...The man that saw them, he says he said every thing he could to stop them but to no purpose. They crossed the river and pushed on. Yesterday [August 4, 18114] was the fourth day since they crossed Flint river therefore I fear before this they have committed some murder or stole of some horses, perhaps both. The Aumauculle Chiefs has appointed seven men to way lay the river and if they return back the same way and bring horses, to take them from the robbers and have them sent to Hartford.[98]

The warriors struck even as Barnard was writing his warning. Lt. Col. Allen Tooke of the 35th Georgia Militia reported that three homes faced attack on the morning of August 5, 1814:

> It is with great pain I have to communicate to your Excellency, that we had a very serious alarm from the Indians yesterday evening at three o'clock, in the field of Mr. John Rabun, which is between seven and eight miles below Hartford and immediately on the river – The said Rabun being in his field, three Indians arose out of the corn, and one of them fired on him and wounded him severely in the back – He immediately took to flight – The pursued him with the most horrid yells, and as he crossed the fence both the others fired on him and wounded him slightly in the shoulder. They continued to pursue him near his house, where he got his gun and would have fired on them but for the interference of his wife, who clung around him and prevented him.[99]

No other injuries took place, but warriors carried off one horse and anything else of value that they could move. One of their red war clubs or

---

[98] Timothy Barnard to Mr. Mumford, August 5, 1814.
[99] Lt. Col. Allen Tooke to Gov. Peter Early, August 6, 1814, printed in the *Georgia Journal*, August 10, 1814.

"Red Sticks" was left at the scene of the Rabun attack. Lt. Col. Tooke called out detachments from his regiment to chase the Creeks, but they had no success.

The raid marked the beginning of a fall and winter of predatory warfare on the Georgia frontier. Other groups joined the Fowltown warriors in the attacks. Warriors from the new Oketeyacanne and Yuchi camps west of the Chattahoochee River participated in some, as did men from other towns. Col. Hawkins responded by ordering William McIntosh, the war chief of Coweta, to march south with a large force and capture the arms and ammunition stockpiled on the Apalachicola and Chattahoochee Rivers. Rumor spread that McIntosh was on his way to attack the British. Hawkins soon confirmed that a force of 196 warriors left Coweta on September 23, 1814. Another 100-200 warriors joined the column as it headed for Prospect Bluff.[100]

The strike force paused first at Eufaula Talofa, a Muscogee town on the west side of the Chattahoochee immediately north of today's Eufaula, Alabama. The chief, who now held the rank of major in the U.S. auxiliary forces, was given interesting news by the leaders of the town:

> …On his arrival at Eufaulau he was informed the British officers with the runaway and stolen negro's had left the Seminolie Country for Pensacola. He continued his march notwithstanding to Perrymans square where all the Seminolie Chiefs were [gathered]. – They seemed surprised at his appearance in arms among them, assured him of their pacific disposition and wish to remain in peace and quietness with everybody. They said the negro's in their country who had not gone to Pensacola had run into the Swamps to hide themselves. He might return home, all runaway negros which are in their country shall be hunted up and sent to their owners.[101]

---

[100] Col. Benjamin Hawkins to John Armstrong, Secretary of War, October 5, 1814, *American State Papers – Indian Affairs*, Volume I, page 861; *Georgia Journal*, September 7, 1814.

[101] Col. Benjamin Hawkins to Gov. Peter Early, October 12, 1814, Telamon Cuyler Collection, Hargrett Rare Book and Manuscript Library, The University of Georgia Libraries, Box 76, Boulder 25, Document 10.

The Fowltown chiefs and warriors lived directly across the river from McIntosh's stopping point at Thomas Perryman's town. They could not have been happy with the presence of the major and his Creek soldiers in their community or with his decision to leave behind two chiefs as observers. They waited for him and his observers to leave before convening a second meeting:

> The Seminoles have had a gathering at Perryman's for mischief. They are making their war-food. They have received orders from the British to make ready, and to strike on this side without delay when the British are ready to strike on the other. They were to be ready by this full moon. A large party was soon after this full moon to march off some where for mischief, supposed the frontiers of Georgia below Fort-Hawkins and probably near Hartford. One of the informants says he heard several of them say they had been ill-treated near Hartford, and the day was not far off when they would be revenged.[102]

The spy's report that several participants complained of being "ill-treated near Hartford" was likely a reference to the assault committed on Perryman's sons in 1813. Hawkins learned of the second meeting from several informants and immediately ordered assistant agent Christian Limbaugh to raise as many allied warriors as possible. This force was to occupy the empty forts along the Georgia frontier until more white soldiers could arrive. The speed of events was accelerating, and the British were riding the wave.

Col. Nicolls recognized the opportunity created by the weak American defenses of the frontier, but the starving condition of the Red Sticks slowed his ability to react. Knowing that Cochrane planned operations against New Orleans, he outlined plans for the forts on the Apalachicola River that would allow him to assist:

> ...My intention now is to throw up strong works at the Bluff. I have written for cannon and stores, to Governor Cameron. I shall continue to raise as many men as I can, in order to be ready for whatever expedition you may

---

[102] Col. Benjamin Hawkins to Gov. Peter Early, October 30, 1814, published in the *Georgia Journal*, November 2, 1814.

order. From present appearances I think it probable, by the time you want them, I can have 4500 Indians ready to embark, on any service in the Gulf, and plenty to guard or even attack from their own neighbourhood. They entreat me to build two forts, one at the bluff, and the other at the point of land formed by the Flint and Chatahatchee rivers. This is I think a reasonable request, as they say if you take us away you ought to have a protection for our wives and children. The red sticks have behaved (with a very few exceptions) entirely to my satisfaction.[103]

The colonel told Admiral Cochrane that he hoped to negotiate a peace between the Red Sticks and the Big Warrior. If successful, this would allow the formation of a new alliance and allow him to "enter Georgia with a strong hand." He knew that the admiral was coming, just not when.[104]

The main British focus by September 1814, however, was on Pensacola. The Spanish city, as expected, proved to be an excellent base for operations against U.S. forces around Mobile Bay. Nicolls and Woodbine focused on drilling their new allies in light infantry tactics, and multiple American spies reported seeing Francis and McQueen in uniform. The flow of accurate information from the city soon became a concern for Col. Nicolls:

…The generality of the Spaniards here, are very disloyal to their Government. They were fully prepared, and had made up their minds to receive General Jackson with open arms, and actually made a sale, and distribution of the Crown lands, expecting the Americans every day. This is confined to the rich part of the community. The lower orders are pretty well, but I do not calculate any assistance from them. Our presence certainly saved the place, as untill the day after our arrival, the American Cavalry were within twelve miles of the place, but on my sending out a detachment of Indians, they soon went off. Ever since I

---

[103] Lt. Col. Edward Nicolls to Admiral Alexander Cochrane, August 12, 1814 – November 1814, Cochrane Papers. This section of the report appears to have been written on November 13, 1814.
[104] *Ibid.*

have kept a post there, which has not been molested. I lost no time in sending out spies, and soon learned that the enemy had plenty intelligence from this place.[105]

The spies sent out by Nicolls intercepted a letter from Forbes and Company partner John Innerarity to his brother James in Mobile. James was the First President of Commissions or mayor of the city and in regular communication with U.S. military officers. The letter urged him to halt all shipments of food to Pensacola to starve the British out. The colonel was surprised by this intelligence, as John Innerarity had expressed support for Great Britain. "I hope soon to destroy this nest of iniquity," he wrote of Mobile.[106]

As the British focused on providing arms, supplies, and training to their allies, U.S. authorities reacted with growing alarm. It was difficult to know where and when the redcoats might strike, but one Kentucky newspaper editor figured it out:

The Creeks who are between the Mobile and Pensacola and on the Escambia who are said to amount to 1500 warriors, continually carrying off the cattle of the people on the Tombigbee, but (probably respecting, the injunction of the British) have not lately committed any murders. The circumstance of the British having landed MARINES seems to point out New Orleans as the final object; and if they can organize a sufficient number of Indians and negroes will probably attempt to penetrate by land in the settlements on the Mississippi river above the city. Their whole scheme whatever it be might be, rendered abortive by a vigorous attack on the Indians collected below the line, and on the British force collected at the Appalachicola. Col. Benton was to start the 6th or 7th inst. with the 39th regiment and some citizens to give battle to the Indians on the Escambia and Coneche, but it is feared they will not be found unless he follows them to Pensacola. Gen. Flournoy has removed the 7th regiment from the pass of Christiana, to the north side of lake

---

[105] *Ibid.*
[106] *Ibid.*

Pontchartrain that they may be ready for the defence of Orleans when attacked. The second regiment is at Mobile, and it is expected the works at the Point (the mouth of Mobile bay) now evacuated will presently be occupied by the Spaniards or British. The third regiment was ascending the Alabama for Fort Jackson. No part of our army seems to be going towards the enemy but the regiment raised in Tennessee.[107]

There is little doubt that the occupation of Pensacola by the British took the U.S. military by surprise. Militia forces in the Creek Nation were standing down and going home due to the end of major fighting. Even Maj. Gen. Jackson was looking forward to time home at the Hermitage near Nashville, Tennessee. The occupation of the Spanish capital changed everything:

> We continue to receive daily rumors of hostile appearances at Apalachicola and Pensacola. The British armed vessels off that coast have maneuvered dexterous slowly by landing and assembling their crews to deceive the Indians in that neighbourhood. They have unquestionably furnished a considerable supply of the munitions of war and some clothing and are training the Indians and some negros for purposes hostile to us. The Indian training is to fire a swivel, sound the war whoop, fire three or four rounds of small arms, send the war whoop to every village who repeated and are ready to march with the shortest notice. Four have recently been to the frontiers of Georgia and done mischief. The British officers have applied to the stock holders in that quarter to supply beef to the Indians and they will pay for it. They have informed me they are apprehensive they shall not be paid.[108]

Col. Hawkins forwarded a steady flow of intelligence-filled letters to Gens. Pinckney and Jackson, urging them to deal with the situation before

---

[107] *Western Citizen* (Paris, Tennessee), August 13, 1814.
[108] Col. Benjamin Hawkins to Secretary of War John Armstrong, August 16, 1814, Grant, 1980: 694.

the British intervention grew too strong. He might have misjudged the danger posed to his efforts by the Red Stick movement in 1812-1813, but as a veteran of the Revolution, he saw red when it came to Great Britain.

So did an American businessman who arrived in Savannah during late August. He was in Havana, Cuba when the *Hermes* and *Carron* stopped on around the first of the month, so Capt. Percy and Lt. Col. Nicolls could meet with the captain-general:

> The colonel commanding dined at a public table – he spoke freely of great cruelties committed by the troops under General Jackson during his expedition against the Indians; and seemed exasperated against the Americans. – He urged that the country belonged to the Indians – they were the first settlers, and it was his intention to restore it to them. His first stand would be at Colerain in Georgia, and from thence to Savannah. The colonel reported that he expected a reinforcement of 4000 men – that he had on board the two ships 3000 uniforms, epaulets, swords, &c. for officers whom he intended to commission. A gentleman who was on board the Hermes read one of the proclamations signed by colonel Woodbine inviting all classes and descriptions of people to the British standard for protection and freedom.[109]

Nicolls, of course, was already in Florida by the time the businessman reached Savannah with his intelligence. The merchant was still able to provide U.S. authorities with their first clear picture of what the British were doing. He correctly reported that several British ships were making voyages back and forth to Florida carrying arms, ammunition, and other supplies. The amount of material delivered to the Native Americans, he warned, was "large."[110]

Col. Hawkins soon turned to the use of silver as a means of obtaining good intelligence. He provided Christian Limbaugh with a supply of coin for use in buying information from allied Creeks who had been down to the Apalachicola and for paying others to make the trip. Hawkins reported on August 30—the first anniversary of the Red Stick capture of Fort

---

[109] Report dated Savannah on August 25, 1814, published in the *Georgia Journal* on September 7, 1814.
[110] *Ibid.*

Mims—that warriors armed at Prospect Bluff were ranging far up the Chattahoochee and Flint Rivers. They were taking cattle, horses, and other supplies and—much more importantly in the mind of the American agent—were liberating slaves and taking them to freedom in Spanish Florida. He wrote to the Big Warrior and Little Prince:

> ...This Second Bowles with his negro stealing must be put a stop to. You are the masters of the land to the seacoast and must see that such doings are stoped. Send Major McIntosh with your young warriors to receive all the ammunition and arms landed in your country, let them take it peaceably if they can, or forceably if necessary. I do not wish to see you shed the blood of each other, but attack and take or destroy all the white and black people you find and arms. Take such white people as you see encouraging the black to mischief, and bring them prisoners to me, if they refuse to surrender to you, fire on them and compell them. The captain as he calls himself has begun by stealing Stedham's negros, and James Perryman's, and next to steal the Beef cattle you have at Fort Mitchell. You all know these cattle are sent there by order of the President to feed the Red people in distress, and this man wants to steal them from you to feed your enemies. Take him and all white people with him by force and send him & them to me. Treat him and them kindly when prisoners with you. The negros you take who have no white masters will be your property and those who have white masters shall pay you 50 dollars a head. The Red people who will not listen to the terms of peace offered by Gen'l Pinckney are our enemies, those who have been doing mischief in Georgia must be shot. Mr. Limbaugh will furnish you provisions and such things as you want.[111]

Intelligence from Pensacola that reached the United States via New Orleans in late August made clear that a sudden demand from Andrew

---

[111] Col. Benjamin Hawkins to Tustunnuggee Hopoi (Little Prince), Speaker for the Lower Creeks, and Tustunnuggee Thlocco (Big Warrior), Speaker for the Upper Creeks, August 30, 1814, Jackson Papers, Library of Congress.

Jackson was responsible for Gov. Mateo Gonzales Manrique inviting the British to occupy the city:

> On the 19th [July] arrived here, Col. Jno. Gordon with dispatches from Gen. Jackson, demanding in rather peremptory terms, two Indian chiefs M'Queen and Francis the prophet, saying that if he was refused, that he should be under the disagreeable necessity of coming here after them. This has much enraged the governor & his officers; & the governor, they say, has refused the general and put him at defiance. As it respects the chiefs, preparations of defence are making – orders have been issued at the Barrancas to sink any American armed vessel that should attempt to pass it. A copy of the order I was to have sent to Capt. Jones commanding in Mobile bay, certified by the governor and the letter signed by Don Benegras de Calderow, the representative of the province.[112]

As such reports slowly trickled into the United States, the British attempted to form another alliance that could quickly alter the balance of power on the Gulf of Mexico. HMS *Sophie* sailed from Pensacola with a message for Jean Lafitte, the leader of the Barataria pirates:

> I have arrived in the Floridas for the purpose of annoying the only enemy Great Britain has in the world, as France and England are now friends. I call on you with your brave followers to enter the service of Great Britain, in which you shall have the rank of Captain; lands will be given you in proportion to your respective ranks, on a peace taking place; and I invite you on the following terms – your property shall be guaranteed to you, and your person protected.
>
> In return for which I ask you to cease all hostilities against Spain or the Allies of Great Britain. Your ships and vessels to be placed under the orders of the

---

[112] Gentleman in Pensacola to a friend in New Orleans, July 25, 1814, published in the *Richmond Enquirer*, September 17, 1814.

commanding officer on this station, until the Commander-in-Chief's pleasure is known; but I guarantee their fair value to you at all events.

I herewith inclose you a copy of my proclamation to the inhabitants of Louisiana, which will, I trust, point out to you the honourable intentions of my Government. You will be a useful assistant to me in forwarding them; therefore, if you determine, lose no time. The bearer of this, Captain Williams, will satisfy you on any other points you may be anxious to learn, as well as Captain Lockyer of the *Sophie*, who carries him to you. We have a powerful reinforcement on its way here, and I hope to cut out some other work for the Americans than oppressing the inhabitants of Louisiana. Be expeditious in your resolves, and rely upon the veracity of your very humble servant.[113]

The move was certain to provoke the outrage of U.S. authorities. The British were reaching out to Red Stick Creeks, Maroons, and now pirates. Had Lafitte accepted the offer, his men, ships, and knowledge of the bayous and waterways of Louisiana would have proved critical in the coming campaign to take New Orleans. The idea of allying with the hated English, however, was too much for a French pirate. He sent Nicolls' letter to Gov. William C.C. Claiborne with a message offering his services to the United States in defense of Louisiana. Lafitte's decision was a key factor in assuring American victory in the Battle of New Orleans.

While the British consolidated their positions at Prospect Bluff and Mobile, U.S. forces did the same on Mobile Bay. The primary defense of Mobile was Fort Charlotte, the antiquated French Fort Conde, and there was little hope that it could hold off a determined attack. The fight for control of the city would instead take place at the entrance to the bay, where regulars from the 2nd Infantry were finishing a semi-circular fort of log and sand that they called Fort Bowyer. The little battery stood on the western end of Mobile Point at the site of today's Fort Morgan. This position allowed its cannon to control the channel leading into Mobile Bay

---

[113] Lt. Col. Edward Nicolls to Monsieur La Fete, or the Commandant at Barataria, August 31, 1814, *The Times of London*, November 22, 1814.

from the Gulf of Mexico. The channel was so far from the eastern tip of Dauphin Island that the Americans made no efforts to build a second battery there, although hospital camps for sick soldiers did spring up on the island.

Fort Bowyer was not impressive to the eye. Low and built of temporary materials, there were serious questions as to whether it could withstand a sustained bombardment from British warships. Like Fort Moultrie at Charleston Harbor during the American Revolution, the little fort on Mobile Point soon became a symbol of American courage in the War of 1812.

Photographs
Section One

The Prophet Josiah Francis, a powerful hillis hadjo, let the Red Stick movement in the Creek Nation. He painted this self-portrait while visiting Great Britain in 1814-1816.
British Museum

Sam and Ben Perryman were descendants of the Seminole chief Thomas Perryman. Ben (right) was a courier during the War of 1812. Library of Congress

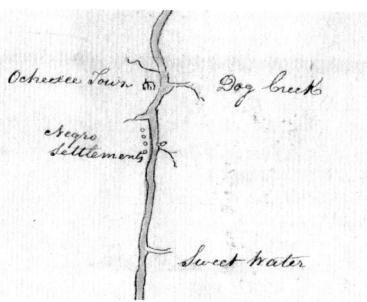

The "negro settlements" near Ocheesee Bluff on the Apalachicola River are shown on the 1813 Woodbine Map. National Archives of Great Britain

A private of the Royal Marines from the War of 1812 era is shown here in a 19th-century lithograph. Nicolls, Woodbine, and their Royal Marines wore similar uniforms.

St. Vicent Island with nearby St. George Island forms Apalachicola Bay. The British troops first came ashore here in 1813 to build storehouses and start a training camp.

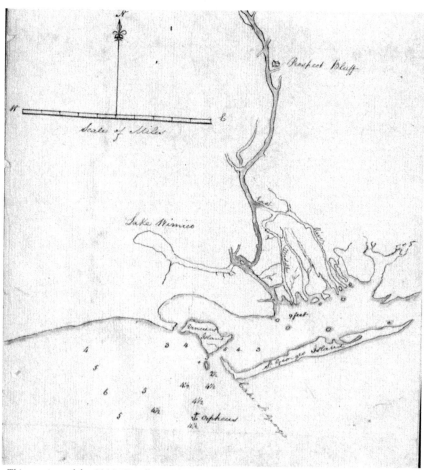

This section of the 1813 Woodbine Map illustrates Apalachicola Bay and the immediate vicinity. From north) to south, notice the locations of Prospect Bluff, St. Vincent and St. George Islands, and the anchorage of HMS Orpheus. National Archives of Great Britain.

The "Loma de Buenaviista" or Prospect Bluff and the surrounding waterways and trails are shown on an 1814 map drawn by Capt. Vicente Sebastian Pintado. Library of Congress

1Prospect Bluff rises less than 15-feet above the surface of the Apalachicola River, but commands miles of the channel. This photograph, taken from the crest of the bluff at the British Post site, illustrates how heavy cannon here could be so effective.

HMS Hermes, seen here crushing a French privateer, was a key vessel in the flotilla that arrived off Northwest Florida in 1814. National Maritime Museum, Greenwich, London

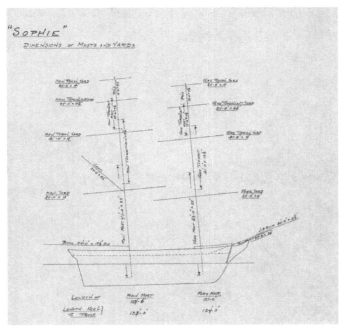

2HMS Sophie carried Capt. Woodbine from the Apalachicola to Pensacola in 1814.
National Maritime Museum, Greenwich, London

6

FORT BOWYER AND PENSACOLA

TWO OF THE MOST SIGNIFICANT BATTLES OF THE WAR OF 1812 took place away from the major fronts of that conflict. The encounters are examined at some length here because of their enormous impact on the history of the Fort at Prospect Bluff.

The British intervention in Spanish Florida reached a point by September that its commanders were ready to take the offensive. Their target was Mobile, a city that could prove key in Admiral Cochrane's plans to take New Orleans and the Mississippi valley. The battalion of Colonial Marines being formed by Nicolls and Woodbine at Pensacola and Prospect Bluff by enlisting escaped slaves was taking shape. So too was the Native American force, which was showing progress in its light infantry training. Scouts sent to examine the Eastern Shore of Mobile Bay reported that there were few U.S. troops in the area and that Fort Bowyer was incomplete and weak. Capt. W.H. Percy was anxious to strike a blow and fully open the war on the Gulf Coast and requested that Col. Nicolls provide some of his Native Americans to seal off the neck of Mobile Point and prevent the escape of the garrison at Fort Bowyer. Always aggressive, Nicolls made clear that he would be going in person.[114]

The arrival of HMS *Childers*, an 18-gun brig, at Pensacola on September 6, 1814, gave Percy the firepower he needed to make his

---

[114] Capt. W.H. Percy to Adm. Sir Alexander Cochrane, September 9, 1814, Cochrane Papers.

attempt. The last intelligence reports to arrive indicated that American troops would soon begin work to strength Fort Bowyer. The Royal Navy officers agreed that it would be foolish to delay their attack further:

> It being necessary to have possession of the town of Mobile to hold communication with the very numerous tribe of the Choctaw (who are supposed to be friendly towards us) I have determined if found practicable to attack with the squadron Fort Bowyer on Mobille Point, it appearing from every information I have been able to obtain that it is a low wood battery of little strength mounting at the most fourteen guns of small caliber en barbette, though others state the number at six, the men are exposed as low as the knee and there is depth of water sufficient for the squadron to within pistol shot of their guns. The capture or destruction of it will enable us effectually to stop the trade of Louisiana and to attack Mobille. I have heard that General Jackson has ordered it to be refortified after having lately dismounted the guns and sent them up to the fort near the town of Mobile.[115]

The captain conferred with Lt. Col. Nicolls, who offered to bring 40 men from the Royal Marines, 20 men and one howitzer from the Royal Marine Artillery, and 130 Red Stick auxiliaries on the expedition. This force would attack Fort Bowyer from the rear and keep its garrison in place while the British warships moved up the channel between Mobile Point and Dauphin Island to engage the battery from the front. The troops embarked aboard HMS *Hermes* on September 11, 1814, and she sailed west past Perdido Bay in company with HMS *Sophie* and HMS *Carron*. The three ships mounted a combined total of fifty-four 32-pounder carronades, two 9-pounders, and four 6-pounders. Compared to these sixty guns, Fort Bowyer mounted 12 to 14 cannons, most of them of light weight.

The land forces went ashore on September 12 to begin closing in on the fort from behind. Nicolls later reported that the warriors advanced in

---

[115] *Ibid.*

conjunction with the westward movement of the ships. A part of his force, headed by Lt. Castle of the Royal Marines, moved overland from Pensacola to occupy Bon Secour and guard against any American movement to rescue Fort Bowyer. The colonel planned to move with his troops to direct the fire on the fort's land face but was stricken with a severe case of dysentery. He remained aboard the *Hermes*, reluctantly entrusting the land operation to Capt. Robert Henry of the Royal Marine Artillery.[116]

The British ships met HMS *Childers* off present-day Gulf Shores. She was returning from her unsuccessful mission to enlist the services of Jean Lafitte and the Baratarian pirates. Her arrival added sixteen 32-pound carronades and two 6-pounders to the firepower of the squadron. The total armament now included 78 guns.

The Royal Navy began its attack on Fort Bowyer on the afternoon of September 12, 1814, forming a line and crossing the bar at the mouth of Mobile Bay. The wind immediately turned on the British:

> …[H]aving a light breeze from the West I made the signal for the Squadron to weigh and at 3:10 passed the bar in the following line of Battle: *Hermes, Sophie, Carron & Childers*. At 4:16 the Fort commenced firing which was not returned until 4:30 when being within pistol shot of it I opened my broadside and anchored by the head & stern at 4:40 the *Sophie* having gained her station did the same, at this time the wind having died away and a strong ebbtide having made notwithstanding their exertions Captains [Robert C.] Spencer and [John Brand] Umfreville finding their ships losing ground, and that they could not possibly be brought into their appointed stations, anchored, but too far off to be of any great assistance to the *Hermes* and *Sophie* against who the great body of the fire was directed.[117]

---

[116] Lt. Col. Edward Nicolls to Adm. Sir Alexander Cochrane, August-November 1814, Cochrane Papers.
[117] Capt. W.H. Percy to Adm. Sir Alexander Cochrane, September 16, 1815, Cochrane Papers.

With half of his firepower taken out of the fight and *Hermes* and *Sophie* fighting alone against the unexpectedly defiant American fort, Capt. Percy gave his best fight. Wracked with the pain of his dysentery attack, "Fighting Nicolls" left his bunk and crawled up to the main deck of the *Hermes*:

> …On the evening of the attack, I was enabled to crawl on deck, and saw the squadron, led by the Hermes in the most handsome style. The fort fired on the ships, with round and grape before they could return it, but when the broadside of the Hermes did bear, she caused them to slacken their fire almost completely. At this moment I thought (notwithstanding the complete manner in which the enemy was covered) that we should have an easy victory, but some misfortune happened to the cables, and the tide…running like a sluice, that the ship ended on to the Battery, her bow on the shore, in this state she lay exposed to a severe raking fire.[118]

The battle was not going any better for the land force led by Capt. Henry. The Royal Marine Artillery and Creek auxiliaries advanced on the fort twice:

> [I]n pursuance of your orders, we advanced with the Howitzer and took up a secure position within about eight hundred yards of the fort and commenced firing before discovered by the enemy, whom we soon ascertained to be too strong for us, in consequence I ordered a retreat and determined on taking a position sufficiently near to enable us at a moment's notice to cooperate with the shipping on this occasion. I am sorry to say we had a man killed by an Eighteen pound shot from the enemy.[119]

---

[118] Nicolls to Cochrane, August-November 1814.
[119] Capt. Robert Henry to Lt. Col. Edward Nicolls, September 20, 1814, Cochrane Papers.

Henry's first attack took place before the British warships crossed the bar and stood in for the fort. Finding the rear defenses and armament stronger than expected, he withdrew about two miles before realizing that the ships were forming for battle. Determined to help if possible, he moved his little force back to within range of Fort Bowyer:

> [W]e moved along the beach with the gun, and halted at the distance of about seven hundred yards from the works, the *Hermes*, and *Sophia*, being at this time in action, we commenced firing shells till having expended all, several of which fell well amongst the enemy, we moved the howitzer to the nearest possible position, in order to fire our case shots with effect, until three rounds only remained, which I thought proper to remove, and leaving the gun we took the whole of the detachment together with the Indians, and advanced towards the point, to assist with the sailors at this time coming on shore with scaling ladders &c.[120]

Col. William Lawrence of the 2nd Infantry Regiment commanded inside Fort Bowyer. He reported that so many of the cannon shots from the British ships flew over the fort and landed in its rear. This overshooting provided such a defense against Capt. Henry's attack that some of the soldiers were withdrawn from n the fort's back wall. Within a pistol shot from the front of the fort, HMS *Hermes* looked high against the western sky:

> The leading ship, supposed to be the Commodore, mounting twenty-two thirty-two pound carronades, having anchored nearest our battery, was so much disabled, her cable being cut by our shot, that she drifted on shore, within 600 yards of the battery, and the other vessels having got out of our reach, we kept such a tremendous fire upon her, that she was set on fire and

---

[120] *Ibid.*

abandoned by the few of the crew who survived. At ten, P.M. we had the pleasure of witnessing the explosion of the magazine. The loss of lives on board must have been immense, as we are certain no boats left her except three, which had previously gone to her assistance, and one of these I believe was sunk: in fact, one of her boats was burned along side of her.[121]

Col. Nicolls described the disaster that befell HMS *Hermes* in his post-battle report to Admiral Cochrane:

> ...[A] scene of carnage took place which I have seldom seen enacted, but as it was we should have been in worse off, but for the animated fire of the *Sophie*, whose gallant commander had placed her in a most judicious position close to us and the enemy. I had the misfortune to be wounded by a grape shot, in the right eye and temple, which has deprived me of its sight, and obliged me to go below for a few minutes to get it dressed. When I came up again, I got slightly wounded in the leg, and knocked down by a Splinter which struck me on the back of my head. I remained until Captain Percy sent me with the rest of the wounded on board the other ships. And he being the last one off the *Hermes*, set fire to and blew the ship up.[122]

Capt. Percy reported that the loss of *Hermes* came after American fire dismounted many of his cannons, and many of the ship's crew had been killed or wounded. He attempted to cut his anchor cables and let the outgoing tide carry the ship away from the fort and out of the battle, but she ran aground with her stern pointed directly at Fort Bowyer. The gunners on the ramparts of the fort increased their fire, and the *Hermes* had no way of replying. His situation critical; the captain signaled for the

---

[121] Col. William Lawrence to Maj. Gen. Andrew Jackson, September 15, 1814, published in the *Farmers Cabinet*, October 26, 1814.
[122] Nicolls to Cochrane, August-November 1814, Cochrane Papers.

captains of the other ships to join him for a conference. They agreed that it was impossible to continue the battle with any chance of success and Percy ordered the evacuation of HMS *Hermes* by her crew:

> The ship being entirely disabled and there being no possibility to move her from the position in which she lay exposed, I thought it unjustifiable to expose the men remaining to the shower of grape and langrage incessantly poured in, and Captain Lockyer and Spencer, who saw the state of the ship, at the same time giving it as their decided opinion that she could not by any means be got off, I determined to destroy her and ordered Captain Lockyer to return to the Sophie and send the boats remaining in the squadron to remove the wounded and the rest of the crew, and to weigh at the same time. I made the signal for the Squadron to prepare to do so, the crew being removed and seeing the rest of the Squadron under way at 7:20 assisted by W.A. Matthews 2nd Lieut, M. Maringy 1st Lieutenant having been ordered away to take charge of the people I performed the painful duty of setting fire to His Majesty's Ship.[123]

Capt. Percy went aboard HMS *Sophie* and ordered the surviving ships to withdraw from the battle. The First Battle of Fort Bowyer was over, and the little fort had survived. The outcome was a disaster for the British, who reported 32 men killed and 40 wounded. Among the latter was Lt. Col. Nicolls, who carried scars from the battle for the rest of his life. The fort's small garrison reported four killed and five wounded.

Maj. Gen. Andrew Jackson was in Mobile when the attack on Fort Bowyer took place. There was little he could do to help once the sound of distant cannon fire started echoing over the bay. The news of Lawrence's victory, however, elicited high praise from Jackson:

---

[123] Percy to Cochrane, September 16, 1814, Cochrane Papers.

The result of this engagement has stamped a character on the war in this quarter highly favorable to the American arms; it is an event from which may be drawn the most favorable augury.

An achievement so glorious in itself, and so important in its consequences, should be appreciated by the government; and those concerned are entitled to, and will doubtless, receive the most gratifying evidence of the approbation of their countrymen.

In the words of Major Laurence "where all behaved well, it is unnecessary to discriminate." – But all being meritorious, I beg leave to annex the names of the officers who were engaged and present; and hope they will, individually, be deemed worthy of distinction.[124]

An interesting footnote to the battle is the report of Capt. Robert Henry, Royal Marine Artillery, which describes the baptism of fire for the newly trained Native American auxiliaries. Henry's account indicates that the Red Sticks and Seminoles—some of whom had joined the British at Prospect Bluff—fought well in the face of heavy U.S. artillery fire. After the howitzer fired the last of its ammunition, Henry moved his men in close per a prearranged plan to storm the fort:

> …Here we remained close under cover, and within six hundred yards of the works, until seeing the Hermes deserted, we returned to the Howitzer set the whole detachment to the [task] and retreated about four miles, where from the extreme fatigue the men had suffered, we were obliged to halt for the night, not expecting any communication with the shipping before morning. However about half an hour after one o'clock, a boat from the Childers with a reasonable supply of provisions and a message from the Commodore, to say he could do nothing

---

[124] Maj. Gen. Andrew Jackson to the Secretary of War, September 17, 1814, *New York Gazette*, October 18, 1814.

more for us, that I had the schooner to do as I pleased with, and that he recommended our retreating to Pensacola.[125]

One of the Colonial Marines died when a cannon shot from one of the fort's 18-pounders took off his head. His body was either buried or abandoned in the drifting sand of Mobile Point, where it may remain to this day. William Ellis, the U.S. Inspector of Revenue for Mobile, was at Bon Secour when the British troops under Lt. Castle seized the community. He wrote in his journal that he could distinctly hear the sounds of cannon fire as the battle raged:

> The express returns this evening with the news that the marines, 75, and Indians, 130, under the command of Capt. Henry, had landed at the point, and had fired four bombs into the fort – that the Colonel's servant had his head carried off by a cannon ball, and an Indian had his belt cut in two by a grape shot; that the Colonel was on board the ship *Armise* [*i.e., Hermes*]; that the vessels were within a league of the fort – Very heavy firing this day. About an hour after night, we heard a great explosion – suppose it to be the fort blown up.[126]

The explosion, of course, was the demolition of HMS *Hermes*. The distance from Mobile Point to Bon Secour by modern road is 30-miles, and it was as difficult to cross on foot in 1814 as it is today. It took two days for the land force to reach Bon Secour where Lt. Castle's Marines waited:

> A party of Indians arrived (24) from the point at 11 A.M. Told us the ships were beat off, and one blown up – that the balance of the Indians and marines were coming on, which proved to be the case. In about two hours they arrived, halted, killed several beeves, opened two

---

[125] Henry to Nicolls, September 20, 1814, Cochrane Papers.
[126] William Ellis, Journal, published in the *National Daily Intelligencer*, January 2, 1815.

hogsheads of tobacco, and several barrels of flour, refreshed themselves, and went on about six miles, put out spies, and encamped. The Indians refused to obey their chief (Woodbine) and would not stand sentry.[127]

The British took William Ellis, "old man Alexander of Fish River," and others as prisoners. They also liberated all of the slaves in the area of their operations, and many of the newly freed men enlisted in the Colonial Marines. Ellis reported that he and the other prisoners were treated well while in captivity at Pensacola, sharing Capt. Woodbine's quarters with him. Casualties in the land troops were light, considering their exposure to sustained artillery fire on two occasions.

The Stars and Stripes flew defiantly over Fort Bowyer as the British ships sailed away. A cannon shot cut the flagstaff in two during one part of the battle, but the garrison raised the flag from the rampart on a cannon sponge. The British, they noted, did not slow their firing even after the flag temporarily came down. Col. Lawrence inspected the works the next morning and was stunned by what he found:

> Upon an examination of our battery this morning, we find upwards of 300 shot and shot holes on the inside of the North and East curtins, and N.E. bastion of all calibres, from musket ball to 32 pound shot. In the N.W. bastion three guns dismounted; one of which, a four pounder, was broken off near the trunions by a 32 pound shot and another much battered. I regret to say that both the 24 pounders are cracked in such a manner as to render them unfit for service.[128]

The British knew that their failure to take Fort Bowyer opened them to the immediate possibility of a retaliatory strike by American troops. The Spanish governor requested that they send a force of 200 Marines and warriors to guard the Perdido River crossings, offering 50 of his men as

---

[127] *Ibid.*

[128] Col. William Lawrence to Maj. Gen. Andrew Jackson, September 15-16, 1814, *Farmer's Cabinet*, October 26, 1814.

support. The troops moved and found that some U.S. scouting parties had already crossed the river and that a larger force was coming. The Americans, though, held back from making an immediate attack.[129]

The failure of Percy's expedition to take Fort Bowyer and Mobile had a telling effect on the reception Nicolls and Woodbine had enjoyed in Pensacola. Gov. Mateo Gonzales Manrique became much more reserved in his dealings with the British, fearing that an American army would soon be on his doorsteps. The town's merchants and others followed suit and Nicolls was soon hard-pressed to pay his growing battalion:

> ...The increase of our force has rendered absolutely necessary to get some money to pay the men, in this populous Town we are at great Expense. I got Captain Woodbine to borrow some money for Captain Allen to pay us, but I am sorry to say, at 25 percent discount. He will send his returns to the 2nd Battalion, by which you will see his expenditure. As we could not get any one to cash a bill on Mr. Adamson, we were obliged to draw on the pay master of marines in London, who is advised by Captain Allen, a copy of whose letter I herewith enclose. I am given to understand, that if one of our cruisers went to Vera Cruise, we could get money there at five, or at a much less expence than here, and by going into the market with money, Captain Woodbine says, (as you will see by his letter to me dated the 3rd of October herewith enclosed) that we shall save considerably. Untill I have your further orders, we must therefore draw on the paymaster in London. Two of our men who deserted to the enemy, said before they went that they would soon be off, as they could get no pay.[130]

Getting food for his troops, Native American allies, and starving non-combatants also became more difficult. Innerarity and other merchants

---

[129] William Ellis Journal.
[130] Nicolls to Cochrane, August-November 1814, Cochrane Papers.

profiteered off the situation, charging extremely high prices even as Red Stick women and children died in the swamps. Recognizing that the defeat had caused a sea change in the potential of British operations from Pensacola, Lt. Col. Nicolls turned his focus more and more to the encampment at Prospect Bluff:

> I have chartered a schooner for 200 dollars to go round to Appalachicola with provisions, stores &c. for those at the bluff. I have also sent Lieutenants Mitchell and Sergiant with half the Artillery, and the Howitzer there. I have directed him to cut wood of all descriptions for building a fort, which will cost nothing but the tools and the labour, also hinges and plank for building boats &c. I am about to go round to the bluff in a few days by land to see those things set about.[131]

Royal Marines and their Native American allies had previously built a magazine and other structures at Prospect Bluff, but this note by Nicolls was the first mention of his plan to build a permanent fort there. His report was written almost like a journal narrative, covering events from August through November 1814, so it is impossible to determine on what date he wrote about his plans. Its placement near the end of the long document suggests that the passage was added sometime in October. It marked the official beginning of British plans for building the post that Americans later called the "Negro Fort."[132]

Nicolls also revealed a plan to make his Colonial Marines truly amphibious:

> ...If you would be so good as to send us three or four small schooners, drawing from four to six feet, it would be a material saving to Government, and if a few active young men were in them, with six sailors in each, we could man them with black men, and soon stop all communication between New Orleans and Mobille.

---

[131] *Ibid.*
[132] *Ibid.*

> Should you be pleased to send these schooners, I hope you will give Mr. Bryerly the command of them; it is impossible for the ships to sail [on] the inland navigation, without such draft. If you send me a few (two or three) good Carpenters, with assistance of the Black men, I can build as fine gun boats at the bluff, as can be seen and we never can reduce New Orleans without them.[133]

New Orleans was clearly in the back of the colonel's mind, but he also faced a much bigger and more immediate problem. Andrew Jackson was preparing to move on Pensacola.

Nicolls reported to Admiral Cochrane that reliable intelligence indicated the Americans were coming. Since his forces were not sufficient to hold them back, he planned to withdraw as they arrived and fall back to Prospect Bluff:

> ...General Jackson is still there [*i.e.,* Mobile), he has about 3000 regulars and about a thousand mounted militia, Choctaws &c. A deserter who came in a few days ago, states that he is going to attack this place, and that 5000 men are coming down to his aid. He is either about to do that, or he is very much afraid himself if he brings such a force as that. I shall retreat to Appalachacola until I can get reinforcements or your further orders. Indeed Sir, it would be very desireable if you could spare them, to send a Battalion of marines. The men I got from the 3rd are the worst I ever saw, not ten of them are fit to drill others, and the noncommissioned officers equally bad. We shall want a great deal more ammunition.[134]

Jackson was most definitely coming. He marched north from Mobile to Fort Stoddert and crossed the Alabama and Tensaw Rivers at Mims' Ferry. Fort Pierce stood near the blackened ruins of old Fort Mims, and

---

[133] *Ibid.*
[134] *Ibid.*

his army camped across a wide expanse between it and the destroyed fort. The famed Tennessee frontiersman Davy Crockett (who preferred to be called David) was present in one of the Tennessee regiments, and took time to visit the tragic scene.

Lt. Col. Nicolls knew that Jackson was on the move almost as soon as his army stepped off definitely by the time the Americans made camp at Tensaw:

> …Also this day a mulato has arrived from Mobille, he states that General Jackson has left that place, that he saw him go off, and send cannon up the river on batteaus to a place called fort Piers, where he is to meet reinforcements to the amount of 10,000 men and attack this place, we are all of opinion that we must retreat from half that force. I am this day getting every thing on board, that I do not immediately want. The fort is so rotten, that as fast as we build one part up, another tumbles down. The firing of the guns causes it to bulge out. There is no water under the distance of 100 yards from it, nor cover for more than 100 men, and it would take 300 at least to garrison it. The people here are not to be depended on. They will neither fortify Barrancas, at the harbour's mouth or let me do it. My present resolution therefore is to meet the enemy in the woods, do what I can to him there, taking care of a good retreat across the harbor to Santa Rosa, where I intend sending all the women and children, make a requisition of all the boats to carry us across, and as much provisions as I can muster. From that Island I can retreat to the bluff or remain as circumstances dictate. I shall have a very disagreeable job with the Spaniards, but as far as I can, the Americans shall have as little as possible from Pensacola. We are to have a counsil of war tomorrow, the result of which I shall give you.[135]

---

[135] Nicolls to Cochrane, August-November 1814, Cochrane Papers.

The timing of events indicates that the colonel wrote this section of his report around October 31, 1814. The council of war mentioned by Nicolls never took place, the governor claiming a press of business. The British officers met under the leadership of Commodore Sir James Gordon, who arrived on Halloween aboard HMS *Seahorse*. He knew something about American determination, having just taken part in the bombardment of Fort McHenry in Baltimore, Maryland. That action gave the United States its national anthem. Gordon quickly learned that the Spanish had lost interest in the British occupation of their city:

> Though Captain Percy and Lieut. Colonel Nichols had done every thing in the power of British Officers, to stimulate the Governor to do something for the defence of the Forts and Town, I felt it my duty in conjunction with the Lieut. Colonel to make another offer of our means, and in consequence delivered to him personally a letter (a copy of which I enclose) but he declined giving any answer to it without first consulting with his officers, and proposed that a Council of War should be held the next morning wishing that the Captains of the Squadron should attend; but as no time could be lost I persuaded him to hold it that evening.
>
> I am sorry to say the Governor and his Officers were determined we should not strengthen Fort Barrancas at the entrance of the harbor, nor would they do so, although the ship's company of the Hermes, had some time before made ready Facines for that purpose. They had no objections to our remaining in the Town to assist in the defence of it or in Fort St. Maguel, but should consider it a breach of neutrality, if the Lieut. Colonel should march to attack the advance of the American Army.[136]

The British originally landed at Pensacola on the urgent pleading of Gov. Mateo Gonzales Manrique, who feared an attack by Jackson's U.S.

---

[136] Comm. Sir James Gordon to Adm. Sir Alexander Cochrane, November 18, 1814, Cochrane Papers.

army. The expected action never materialized, and after the British used Pensacola as a base for the attempt to take Fort Bowyer, he realized that he could be held accountable for a breach of Spain's neutrality. The United States had earlier done the same with raids across the border against the retreating Red Sticks, but those were minor in the governor's eyes when compared to the bombardment of the fort at Mobile Point.

Frustrated with the governor's unwillingness to act, the British began to evacuate Pensacola. Every available boat was pressed into service to carry the Red Stick and Maroon women and children across Pensacola Bay to safety. The warriors went next with instructions to move across Northwest Florida to Prospect Bluff. The British gave them limited provisions and ammunition for the march. Things now began to happen quickly. The American army neared Pensacola on November 5, cutting off and killing four Colonial Marines stationed northwest of town as a picket or sentry force. Nicolls was stunned on the next day to learn that the governor had gone out to meet the U.S. troops without first warning his British allies:

> ...[T]o my utter astonishment I found the Governor had gone out of town, and held a Conference with an American officer, without telling me a word of the matter. I had a message sent to me, from a Spanish Captain warning me of treachery, and indeed it was only owing to the good look out kept by Lieut. & adjutant Chapman, that we were saved the disgrace of being driven into our boats. We drove the enemy's picquets, and advance, from St. Bernardo with the free mulattos, and black Spanish Troops, in order to give time to our sick to embark, and by that means we also gave time to the militia to turn out, and our people to embark unmolested, but we lost some of our horses, from not having craft to embark them in, and owing to the blowing fresh, they could not tow them off.[137]

---

[137] Nicolls to Cochrane, August-November 1814, Cochrane Papers.

Night fell before Jackson could launch his main attack, but the men of each side knew that the battle for Pensacola was coming on the next morning. The American army had approached the city from the Northwest, and the British and Spanish expected the main assault to come from that direction. The militia formed in the streets facing west and a handful of Spanish troops joined them with a couple of field guns. The British warships were turned and anchored to fire on the U.S. soldiers as they advanced. Jackson expected this alignment, however, and instead marched his main army along a hidden route around the north side of town and formed it off to the east. Enough troops were left to the north and west to maintain the ruse of an assault from that direction.

As Commodore Gordon was overseeing the withdrawal of most of the Royal and Colonial Marines by boat on the evening of November 6, Gov. Manrique appeared on the city wharf and appealed to him for help:

> The Governor now came to demand our assistance, wanting the Ships Companies to be landed, and the Indians to be brought back. I told him I could have nothing to do with him, that most of the 1000 Warriors were already on their march for Appalachicola and that the Enemy had already got possession of a post he should have defended; that from his conduct, I was certain he had betrayed his trust, and as it was my duty to provide for the safety of the Troops and the Ships under my orders, I should destroy the Barrancas and the Fort on Santa Rosa, embarking the Spanish Troops who chose to come off whenever I saw the Enemy in possession of the Town. By my direction the Fort on Santa Rosa was destroyed that evening.[138]

The American army marched into view from the east on the morning of November 7, 1814. The Spanish militia and troops reversed front and tried to resist, but it was too late:

---

[138] Gordon to Cochrane, November 18, 1814, Cochrane Papers.

On the 7th the Enemy with five guns and 3000 men commanded by General Jackson entered and took possession of Pensacola with little or no resistance. The Boats of the Squadron annoyed the Enemy so much in their movements from the Town to their Encampment that they were obliged to bring three guns against them.

I directed Captain Lockyer of the Sophie to run down to the Barrancas with the Shelburne, to prepare to spike the guns and destroy the large magazines of powder and stores when the signal was made for that purpose. The Fort of St. Maguel fired a few shot, but I believe was given up on the night of the 7th as they had neither provisions nor water for one day. On the morning of the 8th Lieut. Colonel Nichols landed and sent off the Rear Guards of the Indians, and observing the Enemy march off about 2000 men with three guns toward the Barrancas I weighed, directing Captain Lockyer to put his orders into execution, which was done by the time I arrived there, and two hundred Spanish Troops with the Commandant of the Barrancas embarked. Captain Lockyer reports having rolled into the Water and blown up 300 double barrels of gun powder, a large magazine of every sort of ordnance stores, two stores of provisions for 500 men for one month, spiked the guns, destroyed the carriages in the lower Fort, blew up the Block House and burnt the gun carriages in the upper Fort.[139]

Maj. Gen. Jackson was especially frustrated with the destruction done to the fort and battery at the Barrancas. He had demanded their surrender two days before and then blamed the Spanish for allowing British artillerymen to fire on a truce party that he sent forward to Fort San Miguel. His account of the Battle of Pensacola was not that different from those of the British:

---

[139] *Ibid.*

...I passed in rear of the Fort undiscovered to the East of Town, when I approached within a mile I was in full view, my pride was never more heightened, than viewing the uniform firmness of my Troops, and with what undaunted courage they advanced, with a strong fort ready to assail them on the right, seven British armed vessels on the left, strong Blockhouses, and batteries of cannon in the Front, but they still advanced with unshaken firmness, entered the Town, when a battery of two cannon was opened upon the centre column composed of the regulars with ball & grape and with a shower of musquetry from the houses and gardens, the battery was immediately stormed by Capt. [William] Lavall & company & carried, and the musquetry was soon silenced by the steady & well directed fire of the regulars.[140]

The governor rushed forward with a white flag at this point and approached Col. Thomas Williamson and Col. John Smith, who were leading the dismounted Tennessee Volunteers. He surrendered both the city and Fort San Miguel, but the Spanish soldiers in the fort refused to come out. A flurry of negotiations and accusations followed, but the garrison finally lowered its flag some sixteen hours later at midnight. U.S. losses in the battle were seven killed and 11 wounded. Spain lost around 15 men killed and wounded.[141]

Jackson planned to storm the fort at the Barrancas early the next morning but awakened instead to the thunderous sound of explosions from that direction. The British demolition parties did their work so well that U.S. troops could not occupy the post with any hope of successfully defending it:

...I dispatched a detachment of two hundred men to explore it, who returned in the night with the information that it was blown up, all the combustible parts burnt—the

---

[140] Maj. Gen. Andrew Jackson to Gov. Willie Blount of Tennessee, November 14, 1814, National Archives, Record Group 59.
[141] *Ibid.*

cannon spiked & dismounted except two—This being the case I determined to withdraw my troops, but before I did I had the pleasure to see the British depart.[142]

Jackson made much in his report to Gov. Willie Blunt of the good conduct of his men and especially the Choctaw warriors in his army. They treated the citizens of Pensacola with civility, he said, and showed themselves to be "more civilized than the British." Perhaps, but the Americans were distinctly less civilized in their dealings with slaves and Maroons not under the immediate protection of Spanish citizens. These were rounded up by the army. Citizens of Pensacola later filed claims with the U.S. government seeking reimbursement for losses suffered during Jackson's occupation of the city. Some of them listed slaves among their losses, reporting that soldiers murdered them.

---

[142] *Ibid.*

7

RETURN TO THE APALACHICOLA

THE BRITISH WERE WELL ON THEIR WAY TO APALACHICOLA
BAY by the time Jackson evacuated Pensacola on November 9, 1814.
Nicolls intended to reform his command at Prospect Bluff and prepare for
action either against New Orleans or on the Georgia frontier. Warriors
from Fowltown were planning to strike against American settlements even
as the situation at Pensacola was nearing its moment of truth. The Flint
River trader Timothy Barnard learned from his Yuchi son on November
2, however, that the raiders pulled back:

> My son Timpuge [i.e., Timpoochee] arrived here
> yesterday from his route to Chehaw and old Kenard told
> my son that he had an express come to him that the war
> Indians were on their march which alarmed him a good
> deal which caused him to have an express sent to you.
> Kenerd relates that the day after this happ. Five of the
> Aumauculle Chiefs that had been down at the mouth of
> the rivers where Perriman lives arrived at their town and
> informed Kenerd that the war party had stopped coming
> on in consequence of which Kenerd requested of my son
> to proceed on up to your house and give you the
> information.[143]

---

[143] Timothy Barnard to Col. Benjamin Hawkins, November 3, 1814 (apparently
written on November 2, 1814), Hargrett Rare Book and Manuscript Libraries, The

The chief of Aumuccalee—or Muckalee, one of the Chehaw towns in what is now Lee County, Georgia—sent word via Timpoochee Barnard that he and his warriors would not join the Red Sticks. He requested that the younger Barnard tell Col. Hawkins that they would join with white troops in fighting the British. They would need help, he said, because he did not know how his people could survive on their own if forced to evacuate from their long-established town. Timothy Barnard praised the Aumuccalee chief Hitchufalawa with convincing the Fowltown warriors and their allies to turn back:

> It may give our frontier inhabitants time to be better prepared. It seems the British officer that was up at Perimans at the time urging the Red Stick on was much offended at the red people not proceeding on the route. He and Perriman pushed on down to the stores at the mouth of the river. Should not have wrote you so much as my son was going up by request of the chiefs to tell you all the news but expected you might be gone in to Fort Hawkins. Am still in so low a state am scarcely able to sit up to write or to walk about. My son can tell you about your runaway black. He says when he got down to Aumaucule that there was but very few red people in the town. The Wolf Warrior at the time was laying very sick. The first and only news he could hear of them was that they were seen ten miles off from the east side of the river twenty miles below Obaunes.[144]

Col. Hawkins wrote to Gov. Peter Early from Fort Hawkins on the morning of November 3, urging a preemptive strike down the Chattahoochee River against the British and their allies below its forks with the Flint:

> I shall make Cowetau my head quarters and act from thence as circumstances may require. I shall order all the Uchees to embody under Capt. Barnard and station them

University of Georgia Libraries, Telamon Cuyler Collection, Box 01, Folder 11, Document 16.
[144] *Ibid.*

20 miles below Fort Lawrence. I shall give a like order to the Chiefs of Aumuccullee to remain 30 miles lower still to reconnoiter the movement of the enemy. From Cowetau I can defend the posts, which it is desirable they should attack in preference of your frontiers. If the militia officers in the agency will cooperate under my command with a little aid from you we will soon make the enemy retrace his steps with loss. I shall want 100 mounted infantry. It is bad policy and will never do to act defensively against Indians on a frontier as extensive as yours. On the appearance of hostility they must be traced up to their towns and crushed. The reason is favorable and what provision they have made is ready for us. As they have manifested hostility and made a movement towards us. If the Chiefs of Aumuccullee should prevail on them to desist it will be but temporary as the British force will be ready to act with them. We had better begin and act with effect against them.[145]

Hawkins knew that citizens were deluging the governor with calls for militia protection, so he promised to make his campaign with as little support as possible. He believed that with 500 mounted Georgians and the allied Creek forces then available, he could "crush those people."[146]

The agent and the governor exchanged multiple messages over the next 48-hours, discussing the logistics of the campaign. Hawkins was about to leave for Cusseta when news arrived from "Carr's Ned (a free black man who speaks the Creek tongue well, and is deemed a man of truth)." Ned reported that a large force of enemy warriors had captured him near Hartford but let him go after he swore that he was on his way to join the British on the Apalachicola.[147]

Ned's report spurred Governor Early to action. He immediately ordered Col. Allen Tooke of Pulaski County to use every means at his disposal to repel, pursue, and destroy the party. He also told Capt. Thomas'

---

[145] Col. Benjamin Hawkins to Gov. Peter Early, November 3, 1814, Hargrett Rare Book and Manuscript Library, The University of Georgia Libraries, Telamon Cuyler Collection, Box 76, Folder 25, Document 12.
[146] *Ibid.*
[147] Col. Benjamin Hawkins to Gov. Peter Early, November 5, 1814, published in the *Georgia Journal*, November 9, 1814.

troop of horse to cooperate, and directed Col. Wimberly of Twiggs County to call out rifle and cavalry companies. The governor suspended orders that had been given to the first-class militia of Pulaski County and the frontier districts of Twiggs to march to the support of U.S. troops in Mobile.[148]

Maj. Cook reported from Fort Hawkins on November 7 that he had asked Col. Jones of Jones County to order out part of his militia regiment without delay. He reported that Col. Hawkins had left the post for the Creek Agency on the Flint and planned to march as quickly as possible with the Native American force that was assembling per his orders. The agent promised to "endeavor to get the enemy's rear" so long as Georgia militia units moved to his support. Gov. Early endorsed Cook's move to call our Jones' regiment and also ordered out additional troops from Twiggs County under Col. Wimberly.[149]

The British returned to the Apalachicola and Prospect Bluff as the flurry of activity played out on the Georgia frontier. Hawkins missed a rare opportunity to achieve a major victory by not immediately launching his planned downriver campaign. Supply shortages and uncertainty over the movement of a supporting force of white troops plagued his efforts, even as the Red Sticks crossed the entire Florida Panhandle while dealing with the same issues.

Nicolls reached the bluff a few days after the British ships sailed from Pensacola and met with Thomas Perryman and other chiefs who gathered there for a council with him:

> ...My intention now is to throw up strong works at the Bluff. I have written for cannon and stores, to Governor Cameron. I shall continue to raise as many men as I can, in order to be ready for whatever expedition you may order. From present appearances I think it probable, by the time you want them, I can have 4500 Indians ready to embark, on any service in the Gulf, and plenty to guard or even attack from their own neighbourhood. They entreat me to build two forts, one at the bluff, and the other at the point of land formed by the Flint and Chatahatchee rivers.

---

[148] *Georgia Journal*, November 9, 1814.
[149] *Ibid.*

> This is I think a reasonable request, as they say if you take us away you ought to have a protection for our wives and children. The red sticks have behaved (with a very few exceptions) entirely to my satisfaction.[150]

British efforts to provide military training to the Red Sticks, Miccosukees and Seminoles were paying off. The tactics they were learning would pay major dividends for them in the coming Seminole Wars if not in the closing days of the War of 1812.

The plan to form a battalion of Colonial Marines was also coming to fruition. Nicolls and Woodbine enlisted more than 100 Maroons while in Pensacola, most of them claimed by residents. The British accomplished this by treating Fort San Miguel as sovereign soil once their flag flew over it. Any slave could find freedom simply by walking through the gates of the old Spanish fort. By the time he returned to Prospect Bluff in the second week of November, Nicolls had nearly three companies formed for his battalion:

> ...I found the place in very good order, and the 3rd Company of the Battalion 85 strong. Several of Colonel Hawkins' negroes are among them. They say that the first gun we fire in Georgia, a thousand...black men will join us. 202 are (they add) on their way. They are the finest men I ever saw...I also expect in the course of the month 200 more from the Semanoles Country. They are runaways from the states of a long standing and have lived under the protection of the Semanole King, whose leave I mean to ask for, before I accept of their services, as they pay him a small tribute in grain. Thirteen of them have came away of themselves, and are with me.[151]

The "Semanole King" mentioned by the colonel was not Thomas Perryman, who also identified himself as the king or principal chief of the Seminoles. This king was Boleck ("Bowlegs"), the leader of the Alachua Seminoles. He and his people were driven from their homes along Paynes Prairie by the same Tennessee troops that soon formed the nucleus of the

---

[150] Lt. Col. Edward Nicolls to Adm. Sir Alexander Cochrane, August-November 1814, Cochrane Papers.
[151] *Ibid.*

39th Infantry Regiment. The chief's brother, King Payne, was killed in the fighting in East Florida, and the Americans burned towns and fields in retaliation for the Seminoles fighting on the side of Spain during the so-called Patriot War. This conflict began when a group of men—most of them from the United States—declared a revolution in East Florida, seized Amelia Island, and tried to take St. Augustine. The Spanish held out behind the walls of the city until reinforcements arrived from Cuba. Together with the Seminoles, they systematically drove back the Patriots and reconquered lost territory. Unable to take St. Augustine, the Tennesseans struck the Seminole country instead.

Boleck became the principal chief of the Alachua after the death of King Payne. Leading his people away from their devastated country, he crossed the Suwanee River and built a new settlement at present-day Old Town. Many Maroons, who lived in their town while at Paynes Prairie, moved with the Seminoles and established a nearby village of their own. These men were seasoned fighters and ideal recruits for the British. They were also very motivated to fight against the United States after the destruction of their homes and farms.

Lt. Col. Nicolls moved back and forth from the bay to Prospect Bluff, overseeing the delivery of his troops and supplies. He reported from the former place that he had ordered the construction of the long-contemplated fort:

> I have sent to call all the Chiefs to the Bluff, and Lieutenant Christie of the Royal Artillery I have left there drawing the lines of the Fort. I shall have about 1400 men...and might have more, but for want of Corn or Flour. I have beef plenty. And as I told you about the building of this Fort, it will cost nothing but labour and tools. I am constructing it so as to always admit of immediate defense...The Americans have considerable provision depots along the borders, and if I can possibly take or destroy them I will. The Cherokees have sent for arms. There was none...at the time, but now I can give them as many as they want.[152]

---

[152] *Ibid.*

The Cherokee never came for the requested muskets, but Lt. Christie went forward immediately with carrying out his orders to lay out the new British defenses. The available records are unclear as to whether the British Post was designed by Christie or by Nicolls. Whoever the architect, it was an impressive feat of engineering.

The swampy soil of Prospect Bluff created real issues during the rainy season. The highest point of the bluff is only about 12 feet above sea level, and when the Apalachicola River is at flood stage, virtually the entire surface of the landmark becomes saturated with water. To counter this, the British dug a unique system of ditches and moats. Sluice gates in this allowed water to flow out during times of heavy rain, keeping the main part of the fort dry, or in to fill the ditches and moats should there be danger of an immediate attack. The system is partially still functional after the passage of more than two centuries.

Many writers have described the bluff as "high" or "an eminence," but it is very low. The Apalachicola River laps almost to its surface during major floods. Swamps almost surround Prospect Bluff. Brickyard Creek flows along its northern edge while Fort Gadsden Creek blocks access from the south. Both creeks are swampy and filled with the usual assortment of snakes, alligators, and other natural defenses. Swampy branches feeding into the two creeks delineate the eastern edge of the bluff while the Apalachicola River runs along its western side. The entire formation is about one-mile long and perhaps three-fourths of a mile wide. The fort stood near bluff's southern end, where the face projects slightly closer to the river than at other points. This projection creates a point from which cannons could fire both up and downstream.

The British built a redan or triangle-shaped fortification on the slight projection. Made of earth packed between two walls of horizontal logs, it was open in the rear or at the base of the triangle. The heaviest guns available were mounted here and could control the river for more than one mile both upstream and down. Back away from the river at about the center of the projected fortress, Lt. Christie marked out the lines for an impressive citadel. Octagonal in design, this work featured exterior walls of horizontal logs raised to a height of 12-feet. Workers used axes to mortise the corners or angles like those of a log cabin. Each of the exterior walls measured approximately 50-feet in length. Inside this wall, a second wall was constructed in the same shape but using logs that were 30-feet long. It ran around the inside of the citadel at 18-feet from the outer wall and was of the same construction. A deep moat circled the outside of this structure, the earth from which was packed between the two log walls to create a solid rampart 18-feet thick and 12-feet high. A sally port or gate pierced one of the eastern walls of the citadel, leading from a drawbridge over the moat into its center.

From the central citadel, light stockade walls angled northwest and southwest to the river, creating an "A" shaped fortification with the citadel in the apex of the "A" and the redan or water battery at its base. Eyewitness accounts indicate that barracks, storehouses, and other structures were added to the fort, while the primary magazine and armory were inside the octagonal citadel. The British built at least two other magazines, but their locations remain unknown today. One was likely at or near the water battery. Several writers have either misinterpreted the cursive writing in original reports or repeated the mistakes of other modern writers in claiming that the fort had "stone houses." There were no stone houses at Prospect Blu. The reference is to "storehouses," not "stone houses."

Work on the fort continued through the winter of 1814-1815 and into the following spring. The British eventually traced a large rectangular line around the primary defenses and prepared an outer work that enclosed more than 11-acres. Demi-bastions were located on the ends of this rectangle nearest the river, while full bastions were located at the eastern end away from the river. The bastions were of stronger design, with taller earthworks and stockades, while the main entrenchment was simply a ditch with earth thrown up from it to form a breastwork. The entrance to the outer entrenchment was at about the center of its northern wall. This entrenchment was not finished in April 1815 when the Spanish surveyor and engineer Capt. Vicente Sebastian Pintado saw it, but work likely continued after the date of his visit.

Somewhere "beyond" or "in rear" of the fort was a village area where the families of the Colonial Marines lived. The location of this community remains something of a mystery as "beyond" or "in rear of" depends greatly on the perspective of the person writing the description. Only limited archaeology has taken place at the site as of this writing (2019), and no footprints of original houses known. Pintado, who described the civilian homes as *cabanas*, showed rectangular areas of structures both north and south of the water battery and citadel. It is tempting to believe that these represent organized village areas, but they might also denote the locations of the barracks and storehouses. Archaeologists will have to reveal the answers in the future.[153]

Important councils took place at each end of the river in the month after the Battle of Pensacola. The Grand Council of the Lower Creeks convened at Broken Arrow on November 9, 1814. Col. Hawkins did not attend but was represented by the assistant agent, Christian Limbaugh. He reported that the British intervention was the primary topic and that Little Prince called on his fellow chiefs to declare once and for all which side they would take:

> You have now heard the Talks. All those who are not now willing to protect their own nation will be considered as hostile to the U.S. I have now thrown away the Siminolies. We shall now have to go to war against them. I do now understand what you Cussetaus are about, or what you intend to do. You must now say quickly what you mean to do. There is no time to be considering on it now. If you are for the British, say so.[154]

The chiefs agreed to join the proposed U.S. campaign against Prospect Bluff, and Limbaugh sent Nimrod Doyle to call out Maj. William McIntosh and his warriors from Coweta. The process of enrolling men for the campaign began, even as new intelligence came in from low down on the Flint River:

> …The King of Micco Sookee does what he can to restrain his young people. They are impudent and eager for mischief. A man who called himself a British officer and Tom Perriman visited the King and urged him to go to war and to go out with the Warriors offering him 100 dollrs. For every trader, cowbuyer or other American found in their country and the like some for captured negroes. The

---

[153] Vicente Sebastian Pintado, Map of 1815, Pintado Papers, Library of Congress.

[154] Little Prince, Talk given at Coweta on November 9, 1814, quoted in Christian Limbaugh to Col. Benjamin Hawkins, November 10, 1814, enclosed in Hawkins to Gov. Peter Early, November 15, 1814, Georgia Department of Archives and History.

King answered, begin you first the war and you will then
see what the Red people will do. The head quarters of the
encouragers of mischief is Perrimans. Ten negroes arrived
almost perished from Pensacola and 100 expected to join
the British.[155]

Within three days of this report another arrived with information that
the British were beginning to arrive at the confluence of the Chattahoochee
and Flint Rivers:

We have information from a Talasee Indian who has
just returned from Perryman's settlement, that those in
that quarter intend to commence hostility in a short time.
Ten of the British had just arrived in that neighbourhood
with most of the hostile Indians who were at Pensacola
with a View of building a fort near the confluence of the
waters of Chattohochee and Flint Rivers. He also states
there has been spies on us for some time cloaked by
persons who come from there with the pretense of
remaining in their towns. Two or three has lately gone
back to the places from whence they came, and give the
lower towns to understand those forts are [weakly]
garrisoned and can easily be taken. He states that they
were ready to march against us at a short notice.[156]

Col. Hawkins enclosed these dispatches in a report to Gov. Peter Early
on November 15. He used the opportunity to explain how he planned to
move his force down the Chattahoochee River:

I count on having a force of 7 or 800 at least ready to
act as circumstances may make it necessary within a few
days. I hope soon to hear from General Jackson the
information sent him. I rely on his taking such order as

---

[155] "Information of hostile appearances among the Simenolies and Hostile
Creeks," November 11, 1814, enclosed in Hawkins to Early, November 15,
1814, Georgia Department of Archives and History.
[156] Lt. Lewis to Col. Benjamin Hawkins, November 14, 1815, enclosed in
Hawkins to Early, November 15, 1814, Georgia Department of Archives and
History.

the importance of the subject requires. I have not heard from the a.d.q.m. General on my application to him. We ought to have some batteauxs in Chattohochee to float down provisions. They are easily made of two trees with a batten piece of a foot or more in width, easily managed with oars or poles, and indispensably necessary for transporting supplies and eventually to cross our men over rivers and Creeks. Probably you may have authority to take order on this subject, or the General who commands the detachment about to march to aid Genl. Jackson. I some time past communicated to Genl. Pinckney at his request that Flint river was boatable during the Winter and Chattohochee at all seasons.[157]

The simple bateaux described by the agent were commonly used on the Chattahoochee, Flint, and Apalachicola Rivers, as were similar craft hollowed from single large logs. One found near Apalachicola in the 20th century is more than 50-feet long and was designed so that the rudder could shift from one end to the other.[158]

Lt. Col. Nicolls meanwhile called for the chiefs allied with the British to convene for a council at Prospect Bluff. It took time for his runners to go out and for the chiefs to plan and travel to the lower Apalachicola. Food was very short, but work went forward on the new fort and a second smaller one just below the confluence of the Chattahoochee and Flint:

> I have directed the *Childers* to leave here two six pounders, and I have sent one six pound field piece to Lieut. Col. Nichols for the defence of the Bluff. He has already begun to build a Fort which I think will be attended with many advantages. It will be necessary to furnish him with heavy cannon, and as I entend to send the Transport to Providence the moment she is clear, for provisions, we shall request His Excellency Governor Cameron to send down in her as many as he can spare.

---

[157] Hawkins to Early, November 15, 1814, Georgia Department of Archives and History.

[158] This bateaux or "trader's canoe" was on display at the Apalachicola Art Center in 2019.

I beg leave to inform you that the ships of the squadron are on two-thirds allowance of provisions with scarcely enough to last one month.

The Lieut. Colonel had only two hundred and twenty barrels of flour brought down in the *Mars Transport* and Thirty he brought from Pensacola. I have in consequence directed Captain Umfreville of the *Childers* to hire a vessel at Providence and send her down here immediately with provisions under convoy of the *Cockchafer* or any other man of war that may be there. – The *Sophie* and *Carron* have no medicines, nor has the detachment, and our supply is getting very short. I enclose a letter from the Surgeon of this ship stating the medicines the ships and troops are most in want of.[159]

The last week of November found the Americans and British still eyeing each other warily from opposite sides of the Spanish border. The sounds of axes, shovels, and hammers rang out at Prospect Bluff as the walls of the new fortress rose higher day by day. Work also started on a second fort that likely had no name in 1814. It is commonly called Nicolls' Outpost today. The land along the Apalachicola immediately below the Florida border consists of a wide floodplain. This created problems for the British, who hoped to build the new post as close to the confluence of the Chattahoochee and Flint Rivers as possible. The tall bluffs that rose on either side of the floodplain swamps were too far back for mounting cannon that could control the river.

The British solved this difficulty by building their new fort atop a prehistoric Native American mound on the east side of the river about one mile below the confluence. The mound was tall enough to protect the fort itself from floodwaters, although the surrounding ground was liable to be inundated during high water. The new fort was much smaller than the one underway at Prospect Bluff, its dimensions constrained by the size of the flat-topped mound. No diagrams or detailed descriptions are known to exist, but the outpost was an earthwork redoubt surrounded by a ditch with an added log stockade. Its artillery included a Cohorn mortar and a 5½ inch howitzer. Cohorns are often thought of as small, portable weapons,

---

[159] Commodore Sir James A. Gordon to Admiral Sir Alexander Cochrane, November 19, 1814, Cochrane Papers.

the ones used by the British during the War of 1812 were large and fired 24-pound shells. Both pieces could lob explosive shells high enough into the air for them to crash through the decks of any American vessel that might try to enter the confluence. The fort's garrison included 180 Royal and Colonial Marines. Both white and black soldiers were present.

Creek warriors and spies submitted numerous reports to Col. Hawkins, the contents of many of which survive. Virtually no written reports from British spies still exist, but there is clear evidence that Nicolls and Woodbine were equally engaged in spying on their enemies. One such mission by several Seminole warriors led to bloodshed deep in the settlements along the Georgia frontier:

> Three Seminole Indians went a few days ago to Fort Lawrence and delivered themselves up, saying they belonged to one of the parties lately on our frontier, and had been compelled to flee for safety in consequence of an affray with some British soldiers who were along.... [T]he commanding officer determined to send them to Fort Hawkins for further examination, and accordingly started them off with a guard of three men. The Indians were permitted to loiter along the road till night, when at a signal they rose on the guard, wounded one of them severely with a knife, and effected their escape.[160]

U.S. officials reasonably concluded that the Seminoles were spies who used a ruse to scout the strength of Fort Lawrence, a post on the Federal Road between Fort Hawkins and the Chattahoochee River. The site is in modern Taylor County, Georgia. Militia officers blamed Fowltown for this and other raids, accusing Neamathla and his warriors of stealing livestock. Most of the attacks did not result in injury or death on either side, a sign that the warriors still abided by their agreement with Woodbine to follow British rules of war.

---

[160] *Georgia Journal*, November 23, 1814.

Several of Neamathla's warriors crossed the Flint River near Aumuccalee – which the Georgians called "Chehaws" – and Lt. Col. Allen Tooke led 150 militia soldiers down to investigate. Capt. Timpoochee Barnard and some of his Yuchi warriors joined in, while the rest of Barnard's men went to Hartford to restock their supplies. Tooke tried to enlist the Chehaw warriors in his effort to catch the British-allied ones from Fowltown:

> I understood that three Indians supposed to be hostile were seen the day before I reached Chehaw a few miles below that Town aiming for the Ocmulgee and enquiring for Col. Hawkins'. I asked about it and they denied it at first but soon finding that I knew the fact too well for it to be disputed they admitted it. I then insisted on their detaching some of the young men in pursuit of them and pursue them until they overtook them. At first some of the chiefs appeared willing but after some debate they refused. I mentioned our cutting a road through their country on to the Fork of the Rivers. They made no reply.[161]

The Aumuccalee chiefs also declined to send a delegation down the Flint River to negotiate with the leaders of the pro-British towns. Tooke hoped that such talks would stall a major attack on the frontier, but the Chehaws just wanted to stay out of it. The militia officer noted that many of the warriors were "well supplied with British muskets and ammunition which they acknowledged to have drawn from the British down at Perryman's." Still, he expected that most would fight on the side of the United States if the necessity arose.[162]

The existence of spies on both sides of the border was confirmed by Lt. Col. Nicolls, who noted the presence of the Georgia soldiers at Aumucalee in a report to Admiral Cochrane:

> ...The Brother of the Foule Town Chief is just arrived, he says two hundred enemey's cavalry came into the Chief's

---

[161] Lt. Col. Allen Tooke to Gov. Peter Early, November 21, 1814, Hargrett Rare Books and Manuscripts Library, The University of Georgia Libraries, Telamon Cuyler Collection, Box 47, Folder 04, Document 07.
[162] *Ibid.*

town and asked their leave to [attack] and chastise the
Foule Town people for stealing their Horses, but
unfortunately they would not let them. If they had the
Foule Town people would have brought them down to
me. The Chehaws are but lately armed and they are very
faithful.[163]

The colonel may have been confused about the identity of the
individual who arrived at Prospect Bluff to deliver the news. The "brother
of the Foule Town Chief" was most likely Neamatha, the actual Fowltown
chief. The chief of Aumuccalee was a prominent individual called "Old
Howard." He was an uncle of the Coweta war chief William McIntosh. It
is certainly possible that he was a brother of Neamathla, but there is no
documentation or oral history to support such a close relationship. Nicolls
also confirmed that the weapons and ammunition seen by Lt. Col. Tooke
on the Flint River came from the British.[164]

The end of November 1814 found the British solidly entrenched at two
points on the Apalachicola River. The cannons of the British Post at
Prospect Bluff and its sister fort near the confluence controlled the river,
blocking access to both the Americans and the Spanish. Col. Hawkins,
who weeks earlier reported that he would march in a "few days," still had
not gotten his planned campaign off the ground.

The only real threat to materialize against the posts on the
Apalachicola that year came from the west.

---

[163] Lt. Col. Edward Nicolls to Admiral Alexander Cochrane, December 3, 1814,
Cochrane Papers.
[164] *Ibid.*

8

MAJOR BLUE'S CAMPAIGN

THE MOST SIGNIFICANT THREAT TO THE BRITISH POST AT PROSPECT BLUFF was set in motion by Maj. Gen. Andrew Jackson as he withdrew from his successful raid on Pensacola. He ordered Maj. Uriah Blue of the 39th Infantry Regiment to lead a major force deep into the woods and swamps of Northwest Florida. The allied Creek force under Col. Benjamin Hawkins and a Georgia militia command under Brig. Gen. David Blackshear would operate independently but in support of his operations. The objective was to locate and attack Red Stick refugee camps, British-allied Seminole towns, and the British encampments on the Apalachicola River.

Jackson drove the British from Pensacola Bay with his November attack but failed to corner the Prophet Francis, Peter McQueen, and the Red Sticks as he hoped. He fell back from Pensacola, already anticipating a move to New Orleans, which he believed would soon be the target of a major British attack. The movement of the main army, however, would leave Mobile and the territory along the Alabama and Tombigbee Rivers open to attack. The British and Red Sticks were a formidable force, and they had opted to withdraw instead of fighting at Pensacola. They still posed a very real danger to Jackson's left that he needed to neutralize.

The general ordered Maj. Uriah Blue of the 39th Infantry to take command of a large force and drive east as far as the Apalachicola River. His command would consist of mounted Tennessee volunteers and a large allied force of Chickasaw, Choctaw, and Creek warriors. The frontiersman

Davy Crockett was one of the Tennesseans assigned to his command, which numbered well over 2,000 men. They were well-armed but had great difficulty in finding provisions. Maj. Blue reported one-month after Jackson's capture of Pensacola that he was still waiting to take the field:

> I am sorry to inform you that I still remain here, while Genl. Coffee remained here, it was impossible for me to get one ear of corn, he got all the corn that was in the neighbourhood, consequently I had to send a considerable distance up the river for what little corn I could get. The improbability of procuring boats, together with the badness of the weather, rendered it impracticable for necessary supply to be furnished me to move – I shall start in the morning to a certainty – It was obvious to me if I had to wait untill we could be properly furnished with corn that I should never get off. I thought proper to dismount a part of my mounted men making pack horses of their horses, as it is impossible to carry waggons on owing to the rodes being so extreamly bad – by which means I get off altho I am not so well furnished as I would wish. The contractors have disappointed me not having as much beef as I would wish to drive on we will start with 20 days rations of flour by the time that is gone I am in hopes we shall be in a country where we can get beef a plenty.[165]

Blue left Fort Montgomery near Fort Mims at the beginning of the second week of December and marched swiftly for the Perdido River. He crossed into Spanish Florida and struck the Escambia River north of Pensacola. Crockett recalled that part of the U.S. force moved immediately on the refugee camps in the Escambia swamps:

> …[O]ur spies on the left came to us leaping the brush like so many old bucks, and informed us that they had

---

[165] Maj. Uriah Blue to Maj. Gen. Andrew Jackson, December 7, 1814, Jackson Papers, Library of Congress.

discovered a camp of Creek Indians, and that we must kill
them. Here we paused for a few minutes, and the prophets
pow-wowed over their men awhile, and then got out their
paint, and painted them, all according to their custom
when going into battle. They then brought their paint to
old Major Russell, and said to him, that as he was an
officer, he must be painted too. He agreed, and they
painted him just as they had done themselves.[166]

The scouts led the soldiers to an island in the swamp where Red Stick
men, women, and children were beating Coontie root for food. Deep water
prevented Blue's men from approaching, and as they were discussing how
best to reach the island, the sounds of gunfire suddenly erupted:

...With that we all broke, like quarter horses, for the
firing; and when we got there we found it was our two
front spies, who related to us the following story:—As
they were moving on, they had met with two Creeks who
were out hunting their horses; as they approached each
other, there was a large cluster of green bay bushes
exactly between them, so that they were within a few feet
of meeting before either was discovered. Our spies
walked up to them, and speaking in the Shawnee tongue,
informed them that General Jackson was at Pensacola,
and they were making their escape, and wanted to know
where they could get something to eat. The Creeks told
them that nine miles up the Conaker, the river they were
then on, there was a large camp of Creeks, and they had
cattle and plenty to eat; a further, that their own camp was
on an island about a mile off.[167]

The Choctaw warriors talked, smoked, and shook hands with the two
Red Sticks before shooting one and clubbing the other to death. The two
slain Creek warriors were then decapitated:

---

[166] David Crockett, *A Narrative of the Life of David Crockett of the State of Tennessee*, Philadelphia, 1834: 107-108.
[167] *Ibid.*: 108-109.

> When we reached them, they had cut off the heads of both the Indians; and each of those Indians with us would walk up to one of the heads, and taking his war club would strike on it. This was done by every one of them; and when they had got done, I took one of their clubs, and walked up as they had done, and struck it on the head also. At this they all gathered round me, and patting me on the shoulder, would call me "Warrior—warrior."[168]

After beating the two heads, the Choctaws scalped them, and the detachment continued forward. They soon found a trail leading through the swamp to the Conecuh River. The soldiers followed it and soon came to a spot where "a Spaniard had been killed and scalped, together with a woman, who we supposed to be his wife, and also four children." Crockett recalled that he felt "mighty ticklish" at that moment, but continued with the other soldiers and the Choctaw warriors until they hit the river opposite the Red Stick camp:

> It was now late in the evening, and they were in a thick cane brake. We had some few friendly Creeks with us, who said they would decoy them. So we all hid behind trees and logs, while the attempt was made. The Indians would not agree that we should fire, but pick'd out some of their best gunners, and placed them near the river. Our Creeks went down to the river's side, and hailed the camp in the Creek language. We heard an answer, and an Indian man started down towards the river, but didn't come in sight. He went back and again commenced beating his roots, and sent a squaw. She came down, and talked with our Creeks until dark came on. They told her they wanted her to bring them a canoe. To which she replied, that their canoe was on our side; that two for their men had gone out to hunt their horses and hadn't yet returned. The canoe was found, and forty of our picked Indian warriors were crossed over to take the camp. There was at last only one

---

[168] *Ibid.*: 109-110.

man in it, and he escaped; and they took two squaws, and ten children, but killed none of them, of course.[169]

The troops did not attack the large Red Stick village reported to be up the Conecuh, but Maj. Blue sent a detachment down the peninsula opposite Pensacola. This force attacked Red Sticks found there, killing some and capturing others. The prisoners were sent back to Fort Montgomery with a guard of allied Native Americans. Crockett reported hearing that "after they left us, the Indians killed and scalped all the prisoners.[170]

The skirmish mentioned by Crockett took place near Garcon Point in what is now Santa Rosa County, Florida. The detachment sent down the east side of the Escambia cornered the Red Sticks, but after a brief skirmish, the warriors started to retreat across the bay to Pensacola. A second force led by Capt. William Boyles, who until recently had lived in Spanish Florida, cut them off. Maj. Blue reported that Boyles and his men "received them with a warm fire—but did not much execution, it was thought they killed a few."[171]

Boyles pursued some of the Red Sticks into Pensacola, surprising the Spanish and briefly occupying the city. To his surprise, his men brought in one of the most sought-after Maroons in the Spanish borderlands:

> The prisoners taken amount in the whole to eighty one, among them are four negroes – one named Joe taken in Pensacola by Capt. Boyles when he pursued the enemy, Joe had been wounded by Maj. Chiles's party, while he was making his escape in a canoe. He was the fellow who led the Red Sticks in the attack of Ft. Mimms, there is likewise another negroe fellow who was at the fall of that place – among the prisoners are 15 warriors – all the prisoners I send this day for Fort Montgomery.[172]

Survivors of Fort Mims claimed that Joe met the Red Sticks on their way to Fort Mims and gave them vital intelligence on the strengths and weaknesses of the stockade. He was seen fighting alongside them during

---

[169] *Ibid.*: 110-111.

[170] *Ibid.*: 112-113.

[171] Maj. Uriah Blue to Maj. Gen. Andrew Jackson, December 18, 1814, Jackson Papers, Library of Congress.

[172] *Ibid.*

the battle and was the key leader of a group of Maroons who joined in the war against the United States. Despite the wounds he received while crossing the bay from Garcon Point to Pensacola, he escaped U.S. custody yet again and disappeared into the Northwest Florida wilderness.

While Maj. Blue was operating against the Red Sticks along the Escambia and in Pensacola, dramatic events took place at Pensacola Bay. A massive British fleet appeared in the Gulf of Mexico and its flagship, HMS *Tonnant*, soon anchored in the deep water off St. George Island. Aboard was Admiral Sir Alexander Cochrane, the commander of British forces in North America. The fleet was on its way to attack New Orleans and so confident was Cochrane that he brought a printing press along. He planned to use it for printing notices to communicate directly with the citizens of Louisiana and other states, but gave it a trial run at Apalachicola Bay:

> Hear! O ye brave Chiefs of the Creek and other Indian Nations.
>
> The great King George, our beloved father, has long wished to assuage the sorrows of his warlike Indian children, and to assist them in gaining their rights and possessions from their base and perfidious oppressors.
>
> The trouble our father has had in conquering his enemies beyond the great waters, he has brought to a glorious conclusion; and peace is again restored amongst all the nations of Europe.
>
> The desire, therefore, which he has long felt, of assisting you, and the assurance which he has given you of his powerful protection, he has now chosen as is chiefs by sea and land to carry into effectual execution.
>
> Know then, O Chiefs and Warriors, that in obedience to the Great Spirit which directs the soul of our Mighty Father, we come with a power which it were vain for all the people of the United States to oppose. Behold the great waters covered with our ships, from which will go forth an army of warriors, as numerous as the whole Indian nations; inured to the toils and hardships of war – accustomed to triumph over all opposition – the constant favourites of victory.

The same principle of justice which led our father to wage a war of 20 years in favour of the oppressed nations of Europe, animates him now in support of his Indian children; and by the efforts of his warriors, he hopes to obtain for them the restoration of those lands of which the people of the bad spirit have lately robbed them.

We promised you by our talk of last June, that great fleets and armies were coming to attack our foes : and you will have heard of our having triumphantly taken their capital city of Washington, as well as many other places – beaten their armies in battle, and spread terror over the heart of their country.

Come forth then, ye brave chiefs and warriors, as one family, and join the British standard – the signal of union between the powerful and oppressed – the symbol of justice, led on by victory.

If you want covering to protect yourselves, your wives and your children, against the winter's cold, - come to us, and we will cloth you. If you want arms and ammunition to defend yourselves against your oppressors, - come to us, and we will provide you. Call around you the whole of your Indian brethren – and we will show them the same tokens of our brotherly love.

And what think you we ask in return for this bounty of our Great Father, which we his chosen warriors have so much pleasure in offering to you? Nothing more than that you should assist us manfully in regaining your lost lands – the lands of your forefathers – from the common enemy, the people of the United States; and that you should hand down these lands to your children hereafter, as we hope we shall now be able to deliver them up to you, we have forced our enemies to ask for a peace, our good Father will on no account forget the welfare of his much-lov'd Indian children.

Again then, brave Chiefs, and warriors of the Indian nation, at the mandate of the Great Spirit, we call upon you to come forth arrayed in battle to fight the great fight of justice, and recover your long-lost freedom. Animate your hearts in this sacred cause – unite with us as the sons of one common father, - and a great and glorious victory will shortly crown our exertions.

Given under our hands and seals on board his Brittanic Majesty's ship Tonnant, off Appalachicolo.

ALEX. COCHRANE.

JOHN KEANE.

Dec. 5, 1814.[173]

The Prophet Francis and Peter McQueen were at Prospect Bluff when the proclamation arrived, so it was translated for them. They asked the interpreter—probably Lt. Hambly—to respond in kind:

Great and illustrious Warrior,

We have received the letter you sent to us by Colonel Nicolls. You say well, great Chief, that our breasts are filled with the glorious love of liberty, and, protected by our great and good father, we will live or die free, of which we have given hard proof, by choosing to abandon our country rather than live in it as slaves. We thank you for the supplies you have sent and promised to send; we receive them with unbounded gratitude: but for them we should all have perished. Be pleased to send our love and duty to our good and great father, King George. He has shown that he has not forgot his once happy children, and we bless the Great Spirit for freeing him from his enemies in Europe. Our long absence from him we liken to the longings of a father for a lost son; our happiness, like a father who has found one. Your sons whom you have sent to our aid we hail as brothers on the shores of the sea, but we hope soon to embrace them in the land of our forefathers. Our distress has been beyond the power of our tongues to tell you; we were driven from our homes, and our clothes and household utensils taken from us. From that time until we took your sons by the hand, famine, nakedness, and their accompanying miseries have been our lot. Our fathers were true men to your fathers; they

---

[173] Adm. Sir Alexander Cochrane and Maj. Gen. John Keane to the Great and Illustrious Chiefs of the Creek and Other Indian Nations, December 5, 1814, Mercer University.

told us to be so always. They are dead, but their truth remains with us, and we implore our good father to continue his paternal assistance, for we have fought and bled in his cause. Pray of him, great chief, to keep a port on this coast, for the Spaniards are weak, frail friends. In our time of distress they turned us into the woods like dogs, but since your sons came here we walk like men in their streets. The chief you have sent to us we receive as we ought; we will obey him in all things. We have made him our kind warrior and Commander in Chief. We will get all the black men we can to join your warriors. We thank you also for your promise of protecting our rights on a general peace taking place. We will do our best to unite all our red brethren, and form a strong arm, that will be ready to crush the wicked and rebellious Americans when they shale dare to insult our father and his children. We hope you will always keep a chief here with us, for as long as he stays among us, our ways will be shown to us, and we will walk in them. We pray to the great spirit for, and give our blessings to your father, and to you, and tell him we will fight bravely under his colours.

In the name of our brothers,
JOHN X FRANCIS, Warrior of Tuskeege.
PETER X MC QUIN, Warrior of Talase.[174]

Adm. Cochrane invited Francis, McQueen, Thomas Perryman, Cappachimico, and other chiefs to join him aboard the *Tonnant* for dinner. Not all his officers were enamored of their dinner guests:

> ...I find I have not yet, however, mentioned to you the arrival of our magnanimous allies Kings Capichi and Hopsy (or Perriman), with their upper and second warriors, the Prophet Francis, Helis Hadjo, the ambassador from the Big Warrior, &c., &c. We had the honour of these Majestic Beasts dining with us two days in the 'Tonnant,' and we are to be disgusted with a similar

---

[174] John [Josiah] Francis and Peter McQuin [McQueen] to Hon. Sir Alexander Cochrane, December 1814, *The Times of London*, August 15, 1818.

honour here to-day. All the body clothes they get they put on one over the other, except trowsers, which they consider as encumbrances it should seem in our way of using them, and they therefore tie them round their waists for the present, in order to convert them into leggings hereafter. Some of them appeared in their own picturesque dresses at first, with the skin of a handsome plumed bird on the head and arms; the bird's beak pointing down the forehead, the wings over the ears, and the tail down the poll. But they are now all in hats (some cocked, gold-laced ones), and in jackets such as are worn by sergeants in the Guards, and they have now the appearance of dressed-up apes.[175]

The chiefs accepted Cochrane's invitation to join the expedition as observers. The British officers were then full of hope for the outcome of their New Orleans Campaign and expected to easily brush the American army out of the way and take the Crescent City.

On the same day that Sir Edward Codrington, Adm. Cochrane's fleet captain and executive officer, described the Red Stick leaders as "dressed-up apes," Maj. Gen. John McIntosh ordered Brig. Gen. David Blackshear's brigade to move in support of the white and Native American troops under Maj. Blue and Col. Hawkins:

> Brig. Gen. Blackshear will march, with Col. Wimberly's regiment of infantry, direct from this encampment to Hartford, on the Ocmulgee River, and proceed from thence by opening a road in the most direct way to the Flint River, bearing in mind that he must apprize me, from time to time, of the strength and movements of any hostile Indians that he may acquire a knowledge of on his march, - taking special care that the information sent to me may be the best his means may afford or admit of, keeping in view the object of his march, - to wit, to deter any hostile or marauding party of

---

[175] Sir Edward Codrington to his daughter, December 14, 1814, included in *Memoir of the Life of Admiral Sir Edward Codrington*, (Abridged edition): 239.

Indians from committing acts of violence or making predatory excursions upon the frontiers of the State of Georgia most exposed to their savage fury, making every effort at the same time to arrive at the Flint River as speedily as possible, giving me the earliest information of that event.

Upon Gen. Blackshear's arrival at the Flint River, he will proceed to select a proper situation as a place of deposit for provisions, and throw up a small breastwork, with pickets around it, and two blockhouses at right angles of the same, about sixteen or eighteen feet square, which will be sufficient to secure the work from assault on every side. A subaltern's command will be sufficient for this station, who will remain and occupy it until otherwise ordered or relieved. His Excellency the Governor will detachment two hundred horsemen to join the general at this point, as soon as, in his opinion, a sufficient time has been allowed to this detachment to reach Flint River.[176]

Gen. McIntosh informed Blackshear that Maj. Blue was operating in Spanish Florida with 1,600 mounted troops and a large auxiliary force of Choctaw, Chickasaw, and allied Creek warriors. Col. Hawkins was being ordered down the Chattahoochee River from Fort Mitchell with another large Native American force. If the situation required, McIntosh was prepared to join the operation with his full command. The general knew that a major British fleet had arrived on the Gulf Coast and that Jackson was in New Orleans and calling for troops to move in that direction. He did not realize that any hope of cooperating with Blue's movement against the Fort at Prospect Bluff was about to slip away.[177]

Maj. Blue left his camps along the Escambia River on December 19, 1814. Short on supplies, he planned to live off the land and by raiding Red Stick camps for corn and other provisions. Things do not always go as planned, as the major reported to Gen. Jackson on December 27:

---

[176] Maj. Gen. John McIntosh to Brig. Gen. David Blackshear, December 14, 1814, Telamon Cuyler Collection, Hargrett Rare Book and Manuscript Library, The University of Georgia Libraries.
[177] *Ibid.*

On the 26th I arrived at Holmes' village on the Choctawhatchee. The enemy had deserted some time before my arrival – we destroyed their houses.

In the vicinity of the village my Indians took one scalp and three prisoners.

On my way here near the Yellow Water Creek – ten prisoners were taken – by my Indians.

My command at this time are without provisions of any kind. The horses are unable to go any farther. I am on my return march to Fort Montgomery – I will endeavour to scout what Indians may be on the Yellow Water.

If I had been able to procure provisions at Holmes as I had calculated on – I would have routed all the Indians in this quarter, but owing to the want of provisions I am compelled to return.[178]

Davy Crockett wrote in his autobiography that the soldiers of Blue's command left Fort Montgomery with 20 days' rations of flour and eight days' rations of beef, on which they lived 34 days before reaching Holms' town on the Choctawhatchee River:

...We were, therefore, in extreme suffering for want of something to eat, and exhausted with our exposure and the fatigues of our journey. I remember well, that I had not myself tasted bread but twice in nineteen days. I had bought a pretty good supply of coffee from the boat that had reached us from Pensacola, on the Scamby, and on that we chiefly subsisted.[179]

The hoped to take the supplies of the Red Sticks and continue the march, but Holms anticipated them and removed the food—and people— from his town:

...We traveled all night, expecting to get something to eat when we got there. We arrived about sunrise, and near the

---

[178] Maj. Uriah Blue to Maj. Gen. Andrew Jackson, December 27, 1814, Jackson Papers, Library of Congress.
[179] David Crockett, *The Autobiography of David Crockett...*: 115.

place prepared for battle. We were all so furious, that event the certainty of a pretty hard fight could not have restrained us. We made a furious charge on the town, but to our great mortification and surprise, there wasn't a human being in it. The Indians had all run off and left it. We burned the town, however; but, melancholy to tell, we found no provision whatever. We then turned about, and went back to the camp we had left the night before, as nearly starved as any set of poor fellows ever were in the world.[180]

Holms' successful retreat from the west side of the Choctawhatchee River ahead of the attack doomed Uriah Blue's campaign against the Fort on the Apalachicola. The provisions of his army were completely exhausted. He detached 500 of the Tennesseans and ordered them to head across country to Fort Jackson at the confluence of the Coosa and Tallapoosa Rivers. The starving main body then retraced its trail back to the Escambia in a desperate search for food.[181]

Crockett gave a vivid description of the suffering experienced by the men in both columns:

...We passed two camps, at which our men, that had gone on before us, had killed Indians. At one they had killed nine, and at the other three. About daylight we came to a small river, which I thought was the Scamby; but we continued on for three days, killing little or nothing to eat; till, at last, we all began to get nearly ready to give up the ghost, and lie down and die; for we had no prospect of provision, and we knew we couldn't go much further without it.[182]

At this last desperate moment, the soldiers with Crockett reached the margin of a large prairie. They turned their horses loose to graze and found a large game trail. They pursued it and shot two turkeys. As they were cooking these over an open fire, a party that had been sent forward in search of supplies arrived with a small quantity of flour. The discovery of

---

[180] *Ibid.*: 115-116.
[181] Blue to Jackson, December 26, 1814.
[182] Crockett, *The Life of David Crockett*: 118.

a bee tree followed, and the soldiers felt themselves return to the ranks of the living.[183]

The large force from Fort Montgomery was out of Florida and on its way to the forts on the Alabama and Tallapoosa River before either Blackshear's or Hawkins' columns were ready to march. The first U.S. campaign against Prospect Bluff had failed, but the officers and men on the Chattahoochee and Flint Rivers were still willing to try.

The Red Stick chief Holms and his followers crossed over to the east side of the Choctawhatchee River. They settled in the reach stretch of country known as the Holmes Valley—possibly in chief's honor—and built a new town. They were living there four years later when U.S. troops once more came searching for them.

The British, meanwhile, were on the move. Nicolls and his Royal Marines were taken aboard the ships of Cochrane's fleet, while the Colonial Marines and his Native American allies remained behind to guard the forts on the Apalachicola. Adm. Cochrane and Maj. Gen. John Keane were determined to have New Orleans. Maj. Gen. Andrew Jackson was equally determined to defend it. Heavy fighting broke out south of the city near Chalmette on December 24, 1814, when Jackson led a night attack on the British army. Neither side knew it, but the War of 1812 was officially over. Commissioners from the United States and Great Britain signed the Treaty of Ghent earlier that same day.

---

[183] *Ibid.*: 118-119.

9

THE HAWKINS CAMPAIGN

NEWS OF MAJ. URIAH BLUE'S FAILURE to reach the Apalachicola took time to reach Fort Mitchell on the Chattahoochee River. Col. Benjamin Hawkins and his Native American force camped around the fort, waiting for supplies and more recruits to arrive. Brig. Gen. David Blackshear's Georgia brigade was still struggling to reach its jumping-off point on the Flint River, but there was no reason to believe that it would not be there and ready for action soon.

The arrival of Admiral Cochrane's fleet off Apalachicola Bay confused American authorities as to the strength and location of the British invasion force. The slow communications of the time added to the confusion when news of ships at Apalachicola reached American authorities at the same time as the first reports that a British fleet was off the Belize or mouth of the Mississippi River. Fears grew that the enemy planned simultaneous attacks on New Orleans, Mobile, and the Georgia frontier. These fears assumed a new level when another invasion force reached the waters of Cumberland Island on the Georgia coast.

Maj. Gen. John McIntosh was at Fort Mitchell, readying his force of Georgia militia for a march through the Creek Nation to Mobile. He knew that with so many new and massive warships on the coast, the Royal Navy could blast past Fort Bowyer even if it failed to reduce the little fort. If the British attacked Mobile in force, he would need extra troops. The only ones readily available were in Brig. Gen. David Blackshear's brigade, then camped on the west side of the Ocmulgee River near Hartford, Georgia.

Blackshear on December 30 that he would march for the Flint on the next morning:

> I have the honor of communicating to you that I arrived at Hartford on Thursday evening after my departure from Camp Hope, where I found my flat not finished; but, by the time I had my tools helved and ground, it was ready for our transportation aross the river. On Tuesday, the 26th, we began to cross the river. Owing to some obstructions, did not get the army over until yesterday evening. As soon as I got a sufficient number of my troops over, I detached two companies to clear a road and make a bridge across the first creek, - which is the most important in my route, and which is now complete.[184]

Blackshear started west on New Year's Eve, pushing through a trackless wilderness. His pioneers cleared a path ahead of the main body as it advanced. Their supplies were very short. They seldom had more than one day of forage on hand for the horses. "We have no contractor," he wrote, "no soap, none of the parts of a ration except flour, hogs, and salt." Despite such difficulties, his command was moving, and he promised to keep it marching.[185]

Maj. Gen. McIntosh wrote to Gov. Early on the same day, expressing confusion over whether he should order Blackshear to follow him west to Mobile or allow the downriver campaign to continue. He asked that the governor make the final decision:

> I wish to God I had been a month in advance! I did not think, under existing circumstances, that I would order Gen. Blackshear to retrace his steps with all expedition and follow me with zealous industry. There is no other mode by which he can ever join me, as the idea of cutting a road across the country to be timely to render aid in the present urgent case is chimerical, in my opinion, and

---

[184] Brig. Gen. David Blackshear to Stephen F. Miller, *Memoir of Gen. David Blackshear*, Philadelphia: J.B. Lippincott & Co., 1858, Appendix: Papers Referred to in Memoir, pp. 403-468.
[185] *Ibid.*

would defeat every object of his usefulness. If you think with me, you can give that order positive; otherwise, if you conceive the frontiers of the State of Georgia may be benefited from his services, let him be retained for that service.[186]

McIntosh convinced himself that Mobile was the point in greatest danger and that the British force opposing Blackshear and McIntosh was smaller than reported. "I believe no other enemy is in his route but a few Seminole Indians, not exceeding three hundred," he wrote to Early, "which might have been subdued by one or two companies of foot and a troop of horse."[187]

Reports from Prospect Bluff, however, indicate that the American general underestimated the danger. Even after the withdrawal of Nicolls and the Royal Marines for the New Orleans attack, there were 3,551 warriors and soldiers in the two forts on the Apalachicola. These included 170 Maroon recruits for the Colonial Marines, 760 Miccosukee and Seminole warriors, 400 "Chihaw" warriors (probably including the men from Fowltown and Okitiyakani), 800 Red Stick Creeks and 1,421 Lower Creeks. The number of Red Stick warriors did not include Holms' band on the Choctawhatchee or the group on the Conecuh. Col. Hawkins reported that warriors from Florida continued to strike deep into Georgia:

> The chief warrior of Mic,co,soo,kee led a party of his warriors towards the frontiers of Georgia, ten in number, and killed five white people, and carried the scalps to the British below the confluence of the Flint and Chattahoochie. There are a few white troops at Forbes's store (18 miles up the Apalachicola on the East side). The store was surrounded with a ditch. 32 warriors of Choctaws from Fort Jackson (a part of those who had surrendered there) and a great many red clubs were there. The runaway and stolen negroes were close by the store; Provision short, bisquit only. So great the scarcity of meat

---

[186] Maj. Gen. John McIntosh to Gov. Peter Early of Georgia, January 1, 1815, Stephen F. Miller, *Memoir of Gen. David Blackshear*, Philadelphia: J.B. Lippincott & Co., 1858, Appendix: Papers Referred to in Memoir, pp. 403-468.
[187] *Ibid.*

that the Choctaws subsisted partly on old stinking cow hides.

The supplies of Indian goods, arms and ammunition very abundant. Two houses of dry goods and four of saddles, brass kettles, arms and ammunition. There were some vessels back of the Islands opposite the mouth of the river, with troops on board, and some of the troops were landed and could be seen from the mouth of the river.[188]

Hawkins, like many white Americans of the 19th and 20th centuries, did not recognize the black men on the Apalachicola as real soldiers. Yet some of the Maroons had been training as Colonial Marines for six months. They were well-equipped and well-armed, proficient with muskets and artillery. Food shortages were chronic at the British posts but enough trickled in to keep them and their families alive. The Maroon and Native American settlements built around the two posts were massive, and the British did their best to feed not only the soldiers and warriors but thousands of women and children too.

Maj. Gen. McIntosh was still at Fort Mitchell when Hawkins penned his report. He informed Gov. Early on the same day that he was preparing to march for Mobile. He told the governor that he had decided against withdrawing Blackshear's column from the campaign against the forts at the confluence and Prospect Bluff:

> …Weighing all the circumstances, and the distance I am placed from Genl. Blackshear, and the improbability of his being timely to render services in the present urgent call at Mobile, I have determined to direct him to pursue the object of subduing any hostile tribes of Indians over (or) British in that quarter–which, when effected, to follow me to Mobile. Colo. will cooperate heartily with him in the defeat of the Indians or British in that quarter and will leave this for the fork of the Chattahoochee and

---

[188] Col. Benjamin Hawkins to Maj. Gen. John McIntosh, January 4, 1815, Hargrett Rare Book and Manuscript Library, The University of Georgia Libraries, Telamon Cuyler Collection, Box 76, Folder 25, Document 18.

Flint rivers about the 9th inst. with seven hundred Indians, fine fellows, heartily engaged in our cause.[189]

The "Colo." Mentioned by the general was Benjamin Hawkins. Enough boats were nearing completion at Fort Mitchell for the agent's Native American force to start its move down the Chattahoochee River. The rest of the warriors planned to march by land, scouting the lands between the Chattahoochee and Flint as they moved. The lead Creek chief with the expedition was Maj. William McIntosh, who has sometimes been confused with Gen. McIntosh.

Gen. McIntosh reported that part of Maj. Uriah Blue's column had emerged from the wilderness at Fort Decatur on the Tallapoosa River. This news was serious because it meant Blue would not be cooperating with the forces under Hawkins and Blackshear. Meanwhile, rumors grew of a British invasion of St. Marys and Cumberland Island. Enemy boats appeared at Sapelo Island, and British ships suddenly showed up at Amelia Island on the Florida side of the international border. The civilian population along Georgia's Atlantic seaboard was nervous, and it did not take long for protests to arise over Blackshear and his men being sent away from the coast for a campaign down the Flint River:

> I am requested by a large portion of the Inhabitants of this [i.e., McIntosh] County, as their Representative to pray your Excellency, to countermand, the order for the marching of the Detachment to the Indian frontier, it is the opinion of the whole County, that, we have nothing to fear from Indian invasion, as they have sufficient employment at home, whilst our whole Sea Coast has much to apprehend from British spoliation. Those men now under orders to march; are drafted from the Sea Coast, leaving their families and property completely exposed.[190]

The fear voiced by the state representative from McIntosh County was justified. British troops descended on Cumberland Island just three days later on January 13, 1815:

---

[189] Maj. Gen. John McIntosh to Gov. Peter Early, January 4, 1815.

[190] Rep. Francis Hopkins to Gov. Peter Early, January 10, 1815, Hargrett Rare Book and Manuscript Library, The University of Georgia Libraries, Telamon Cuyler Collection, Box 77, Folder 30, Document 13.

We have at length certain accounts of the enemy having landed at Cumberland Island. An express passed through this place to-day, at 2 o'clock, P.M. for Camp Covington, addressed to Gen. Floyd, from Capt. Massias, the commanding officer at Point Petre. By the express we have learnt the following particulars – that the enemy landed on Tuesday and Wednesday last in two divisions, one at Plum Orchard and the other at Dungeness, in thirty barges, containing about two thousand men, blacks and whites. A great part of the fleet (8 or 10 vessels) were off St. Andrew's bar, and many of their barges were within that bar on Thursday last. Two or three of the British barges attempted to pass the fort at Point Petre, but were fired on and compelled to retreat. It is not yet known how many troops they have actually with them, or what their intentions are – we think that it is the van of a force destined against the southern coast, which in all probability will desolate the sea islands between this and St. Mary's, and then make an attack on Savannah: To-Morrow we shall be able to give a further and more particular account.[191]

It did not take the British long to move against St. Marys and the American battery at Point Peter (also spelled Point Petre). Both sides suffered casualties, but Capt. A.A. Massias and his small command from the U.S. Rifle Regiment stood no chance against the powerful British force sent against them by Admiral George Cockburn. The town was looted, and its citizens fled for safety. U.S. troops started gathering on the north bank of the Altamaha River to make a stand, but without reinforcements stood little chance of stopping the British.[192]

Brig. Gen. Blackshear, meanwhile, was slowly working his way west. The new road opened by his army struck the Flint River just north of Cedar Creek in what is now Crisp County, Georgia. Work began on a new supply depot—often called a "breastworks"—on high ground overlooking the river swamps. Blackshear's works are often confused with Fort Early,

---

[191] *Savannah Republican*, January 15, 1815, 8 p.m.

[192] Letters from St. Mary's, January 18, 1815, published in the *American Telegraph*, February 15, 1815.

which U.S. troops built nearby a few years later. His original fort, however, was a short distance north of the later one. As the work of building the new depot was underway, Gov. Peter Early penned stunning new orders for the general:

> I feel a deep conviction that you ought to pursue the original destination of the army. The destruction of the Red Sticks by Major Blue is a circumstance which also has its weight. It has diminished very much the causes which gave rise to your being detached from the main army. The Seminoles will, it is to be presumed, be deterred from committing hostility; and should they continue to manifest an unfriendly temper, I must send against them another force.
>
> You will therefore consider yourself ordered to join Gen. McIntosh with the least possible delay. The route to be taken must be left to your own discretion.
>
> Should you have reached Flint River, and boats should have met you from above, possibly you may deem it advisable to ascend the river to the Agency. I presume, however, that you will consider it most advisable to retrace your steps, and, if boats should have come down, to order them to return, sending in them some of your heaviest baggage. [193]

Early advised Blackshear to march through the woods to Coweta on the Chattahoochee via Timothy Barnard's place further up the Flint. The route was reported to be high and sandy and would make the movement easier for the soldiers than retracing their route back to Hartford and then marching around via Fort Hawkins.[194]

Communications were not instantaneous in 1815, and it took days for the new orders to reach the Flint River. On the Chattahoochee, meanwhile, a spy returned from a mission down to the Apalachicola with new information on the British presence there:

---

[193] Gov. Peter Early to Brig. Gen. David Blackshear, January 6, 1815, Stephen F. Miller, Memoir of Gen. David Blackshear, Philadelphia: J.B. Lippincott & Co., 1858, Appendix: Papers Referred to in Memoir, pp. 403-468.
[194] *Ibid.*

He saw twenty white and forty black soldiers below the forks of the river, about two miles east of the little old fields, where the Commissioners of Limits encamped: one officer commanded, in British uniform. They had not fort or ditch. They had one house built and were about to build another. They came up by land, and one boat came up with their provisions and other stores. He saw about thirty white and sixty black soldiers at Forbes's Store, - In all, ninety, which he counted. Five are officers, - the whites dressed in red, the blacks in blue. They have four cannon, and seven mortars about seven-inch, two feet long, fixed on carriages with two low wheels, and the stores surrounded with a ditch and about two hundred hostile Indians. He saw a number of black women and children at the stores. The men were all soldiers.

He went by land down the west side of the Chattahoochee to Jack Mealing's [*i.e.* Mealy's], twenty five miles or thereabouts below the forks, cross the Appalachicola and went down the eastern side to Forbes's store. The way pretty good for horse and foot. From the forks there are two creeks to Is-te-foo-mul-gee [Estiffanulga], a bluff twenty miles below Mealing's [Mealy's]; small streams thence to the stores. It is thirty miles from Is-te foo-mul-gee to the Store, in all, about seventy-five miles. He-te-he-hee had settled at Cho-co-mith-lo, a bluff about five miles below the forks, but are to move up to the settlement at the commissioners' old camp. The Mic-co-soo-kee people brought three scalps the day before he got to the Store, which they got near the St. Illa [Satilla]. They were men's scalps, and were killed on horseback. He saw a large supply of goods and ammunition of good quality for the Indians.[195]

Unaware that Gov. Early had already ordered Blackshear to march to his support with his entire brigade, Maj. Gen. McIntosh concluded his dispatch with orders that he send one battalion to reinforce him:

---

[195] Maj Gen. John McIntosh to Brig. Gen. David Blackshear, January 9, 1815, Stephen F. Miller, *Memoir of Gen. David Blackshear*, Philadelphia: J.B. Lippincott & Co., 1858, Appendix: Papers Referred to in Memoir, pp. 403-468.

Under these circumstances, I am compelled to call for a battalion from your detachment, as you will then have a sufficient number with Col. Hawkins's reinforcement, (which will consist of at least one thousand warriors,) who will march to-morrow or next day down the Chattahoochee, and co-operate with you in all matters for the eventual subjugation of all hostile appearances in that quarter; and, as this detachment was particularly intended for the defence of Mobile and New Orleans, five hundred detached for the Georgia frontier defence is all I can sanction with the information I am now possessed of. If additional aid is required, the Executive of Georgia, or General Pinckney, whose district you are in, will furnish it.[196]

Gen. McIntosh learned two days later that Early had ordered Blackshear's entire force to withdraw from the campaign and move in support of the main militia force then making its way through the Creek Nation. He rescinded his order to send one battalion and told Blackshear to come with all his men.[197]

Neither McIntosh nor Early seems to have considered that their successive and contradictory orders would confuse Gen. Blackshear. The governor made things even worse on January 9 when he read McIntosh's communique instructing Blackshear to send just one battalion west. Deciding he could provide enough men from elsewhere, he now ordered the general to turn around, go back to the Flint, and continue his campaign with his entire force![198]

There were now five sets of orders on the road to Blackshear's brigade, each of them instructing it to do something different. The first of these reached the unfinished fort on the Flint River on January 8, 1815.

---

[196] *Ibid.*

[197] Maj. Gen. John McIntosh to Brig. Gen. David Blackshear, January 11, 1815, Stephen F. Miller, *Memoir of Gen. David Blackshear*, Philadelphia: J.B. Lippincott & Co., 1858, Appendix: Papers Referred to in Memoir, pp. 403-468.

[198] Gov. Peter Early to Brig. Gen. David Blackshear, January 10, 1815, Stephen F. Miller, *Memoir of Gen. David Blackshear*, Philadelphia: J.B. Lippincott & Co., 1858, Appendix: Papers Referred to in Memoir, pp. 403-468.

Gen. Blackshear had just sent his wagons back to Hartford for more supplies:

> These operations, however, were suspended by the reception of despatches from his Excellency on the evening of the 8th, embracing copies of your letter to him, and from General Winchester to yourself, as well as orders requiring me to retrace my route and pursue you with the least possible delay. I accordingly sent immediately on in pursuit of my wagons a man authorized to order them to return without delay to this place. Should my wagons arrive this evening, (of which I have no doubt,) I shall take up the line of march early to-morrow morning, and cautiously exercise every expedient to pursue you with the utmost expedition.[199]

The situation rapidly devolved into a comedy of errors for Blackshear. Turning his men around, he started back to Hartford from where he would begin his march to reinforce Blackshear. After only two days on the road, however, he received the orders that he would not be needed after all. Accordingly, he turned west again and marched back to the Flint to begin his operations against the forts on the Apalachicola. No sooner did he reach a point about 12 miles from his new fort, though, than the third set of orders arrived, once again directing him to reinforce McIntosh! He dutifully turned his column around again and started for Hartford.

Blackshear was much more concerned over contradictory intelligence flowing in from Col. Hawkins than he was with the marching and countermarching. The agent first reported that as many as 10,000 British troops were landing at the mouth of the Apalachicola, but then had forwarded the intelligence that only 150 redcoats were at the forts at the river. The general could not help but wonder if Hawkins were not trying to mislead the army for sinister purposes:

> Duty to my country impels me to apprise your Excellency that while such reports can transform a British army of fourteen thousand from one number to another

---

[199] Brig. Gen. David Blackshear to Maj. Gen. John McIntosh, January 11, 1815, Stephen F. Miller, *Memoir of Gen. David Blackshear*, Philadelphia: J.B. Lippincott & Co., 1858, Appendix: Papers Referred to in Memoir, pp. 403-468.

until it is reduced to fifty whites and a few blacks, the citizens of Georgia may be scalped with impunity. I beg leave to remark that the colonel has arranged every thing to his mind. He has furnished the Indians with arms, ammunition, rations, - for all sorts and denominations; has as many under pay as soldiers as he may choose to break sticks for, (a muster-roll being out of the question.) In doing this, it was necessary to make reports of various kinds, and as variable in their features, until Gen. McIntosh has gone on to Mobile and left an imperious general order for me to pursue him. And then he can make just as many British or hostile Indians as are necessary to keep himself and Indians under pay and rations; and in one night he can receive reports from confidential runners and civilize all the rest, and nothing to do but break another bundle of sticks, and take his new civilians into pay and rations, and stay at their homes quietly, while we are beating through the wilderness, making roads to transport provisions and funds to such of his most happy and favored people as he may choose to point out.[200]

Blackshear apologized to Early if his sentiments were too forceful but pointed out that two more of his men had died of sickness the previous night. He was worried about his home state but would follow all the orders that he received. He compared the dedication of his men to the warriors under Hawkins, a force that he did not like:

When the militia are called into service, they must be mustered by an officer of high responsibility; every man must be present and inspected, and if not able to perform drudgery, he is sent home and is glad to return without pay or rations. If he is able-bodied, he must do duty, be frequently inspected, reported every day, and punished if he fails to do his duty, (which is right.) But contrast this with the situation of the colonel and his scalping myrmidons. By this your Excellency will perceive that all

---

[200] Brig. Gen. David Blackshear to Gov. Peter Early, January 14, 1815, Stephen F. Miller, *Memoir of Gen. David Blackshear*, Philadelphia: J.B. Lippincott & Co., 1858, Appendix: Papers Referred to in Memoir, pp. 403-468.

your indefatigable exertions and arrangements for the defence of our beloved State are broken in upon by the artifice of that one old man, who does nothing but write and talk, and talk and write.[201]

The general turned for Hartford and began his final march to reinforce McIntosh. Gov. Early promised to send 500 mounted men to carry out the expedition down the Flint River. Before he could do so, however, a flood of reports about the British landing on Cumberland Island and sacking of St. Marys reached the state capitol in Milledgeville. Early now took control of the situation and ordered Gen. Blackshear to get ready for a fight:

> ...A great crisis in our State has occurred, which has determined me to assume a responsibility in relation to yourself and the regiment under your command which no other condition of things would justify.
>
> Our State is actually invaded by the enemy, in large force. It is invaded in its most vulnerable point. I have official intelligence that two ships-of-the-line, seven frigates, and a number of smaller vessels have entered St. Andrews' Sound, made a landing on Cumberland Island, and are there establishing themselves. I have further intelligence that their barges occupy all the sounds and inlets between St. Mary's and Brunswick, inclusive.
>
> The defence of our own land is the first and most imperious duty. Were the regiment under your command without the State, on its route to Mobile, I should not interfere with it; but, under existing circumstances, I should think it criminal inattention to my own greatest duty to suffer the force to pursue its destination. You are already in the field, prepared at all points, and at the very spot most favorable for marching to the relief of the sea-coast. Before other troops could be collected, organized, and marched there, insurrection on one side, and Indian massacre on the other, may have produced their full measure of ruin. The enemy have black troops with them.

---

[201] *Ibid.*

Under all these circumstances, I take on myself the responsibility of ordering you with the force under your command to shape your course, without delay, to the point invaded.[202]

Early's specific mention that Cockburn's force included "black soldiers" shows the psychological effect alone of Cochrane's plan to turn the slaves of the Americans against them. Blackshear was just 5 miles from Hartford when he received the governor's orders, and he immediately turned for the coast, ordering supplies to Fort Barrington on the Altamaha, by which point he planned to march. His involvement in the campaign to the Apalachicola was over.

Col. Hawkins started down the Chattahoochee River much later than expected but finally reached the borderlands on around February 10, 1815. He learned while on the march that Blackshear's column was turning for the coast, but still believed that Gov. Early would send a militia force to cooperate with him:

I only know incidentally that a British force is come against your seacoast, that General Blackshear was ordered there, And it may be General Clark also. On this supposition I have to state to you the President has accepted my resignation of the agency for Indian affairs, and Mr. Limbaugh is to take charge of them till a successor is appointed. Of course if General Clark does not come, with the cooperating force, a man of skill and abilities should be selected. I shall continue in the present crisis of our affairs until such a man arrives, or in the possible event of my receiving a commission to command the enrolled Indians.[203]

---

[202] Gov. Peter Early to Brig. Gen. David Blackshear, January 19, 1815, Stephen F. Miller, *Memoir of Gen. David Blackshear*, Philadelphia: J.B. Lippincott & Co., 1858, Appendix: Papers Referred to in Memoir, pp. 403-468.
[203] Col. Benjamin Hawkins to Gov. Peter Early, February 12, 1815, Hargrett Rare Book and Manuscript Library, The University of Georgia Libraries, Telamon Cuyler Collection, Box 76, Folder 25, Document 20.

No men were coming down the Flint to assist the agent. The British invasion forced the governor to rush every available man in this state to meet the threat. Savannah was threatened and with it all of Georgia.

Hawkins reached Tocktoethla, the town of Col. Thomas Perryman, with a force of fewer than 1,000 warriors. The assistant agents and a few other white men accompanied the expedition, but Lower Creek and Yuchi fighters provided the bulk of its strength. It was a very small force with which to oppose the 3,551 men that the British had on the Apalachicola. Hawkins did not realize it, but he was in a very dangerous situation.

The boats from Fort Mitchell navigated the Chattahoochee River without difficulty, and the agent reported that the river was "fine for boating." No obstructions interfered with the trip down, which Hawkins estimated to be 112 miles. He and his men halted at Perryman's place in what is now Seminole County, Georgia, to establish camp. The scouts he sent forward to the head of the Apalachicola soon returned to warn him that the British were strongly fortified just below the forks of the rivers:

> The Hostile force below the forks of the Rivers on the East of apalatchecola are about 300 who have entrenched themselves have a breast work abt. 4 feet high and One Howitzer and one Cohorn. They have 100 whites, 80 blacks and the remainder Indians. They are endeavouring by all the means in their power to increase their force with Simenolies & There is a Spanish officer among them whos rank I know not from Pensacola, Hugh McGill with some colored people. He ordered a Half breed my informant, who knew him well, out of their fort as being opposed to him and the British.[204]

Hugh McGill, mentioned in Hawkins' report of February 12, 1815, was a former sergeant in the U.S. Army's 2nd Infantry Regiment. He deserted and fled with his family to Pensacola, where he joined with the Colonial Marines upon their arrival in the Spanish city. He may have been one of the spies who provided intelligence to the British before their deployment to the Gulf Coast.

The artillery pieces at the upper fort were more powerful than might be suspected. The howitzer was a light 5 ½ inch gun weighing roughly

---

[204] *Ibid.*

1,700 pounds (carriage included). It fired a 5 ½ inch explosive shell with impressive accuracy at ranges of up to 800 yards. It was less accurate past that point, but the shells exploded into as many as 20-30 jagged pieces when they exploded. Each could maim at up to 250 feet from the point of explosion. The howitzer also fired case shot – called canister by American gunners – to drive back attacking infantry at close range. These loads consisted of small balls backed into tin cans that burst open upon firing. The balls spread out like shot from a shotgun. The coehorn (or cohorn) was larger than the small, portable mortars of the same name that are familiar to many reenactors of today. The one at the British fort fired 24-pound explosive shells but could be moved and fired by a small gun crew. Designed for lobbing shells high into the air and then down through the decks of boats or into the ranks of advancing soldiers, it was a lethal anti-personnel weapon. It was most effective when fired at close range.

Hawkins did not realize it at the time of his February 12 report, but the British forces withdrawn from the Apalachicola for the attack on New Orleans were back. Andrew Jackson's army achieved a stunning victory over the British at Chalmette on January 8, 1815. Lt. Col. Nicolls returned to Prospect Bluff with his Royal Marines and additional reinforcements from the Second West India Regiment. Made up largely of black men from Jamaica and other Caribbean islands, the regiment was badly shot up at the Battle of New Orleans. When he heard of the American agent's presence with a large armed force just north of the border, Nicolls rushed additional troops to the upper fort (commonly called Nicolls' Outpost):

> …Colo. Nicolls with 200 troops white and black and an assemblage of 500 Warriors is just below the forks. They have an intrenched post picketed, with one Howitzer and one cohorn. The Indians are mostly from the Simenolies of East Florida, and Oketyocanne, Fowl town, and Cheauhau within our limits. They are well supplied with cloths and munitions of War. McQueen and Francis are in Uniform. Every party as they arrive give the War whoop, fire their guns and paint for war. The Indians chastised by Jackson are very humble. The Colo. is gone down today as he says "for his supplies to march towards Charleston, where he soon expects to hear of the arrival of Lord Hill, with a powerful force. He is to set free Negros, compel the Americans to restore back the lands to the Indians, and

make every thing submit to him as he marches along. He will bring his cannon up the river with him." He is a great boaster promises any thing and every thing to attach the Indians to his party.[205]

The Royal Navy sent a shore party to assist in the anticipated fight against Hawkins. "Eight men in the yawl with a Carronade" from HMS *Borer* went up to the forks. (Note: A carronade was a short naval cannon that could fire a heavy projectile). William Rawlins, the commander of the *Borer,* reported that the American force threating the upper fort was composed of 50 white cavalry and around 900 Creek warriors.[206]

Hawkins called his position above the forks "112 Mile Camp" or "Camp 112 Mile." It was at a point later called Fairchild Landing. Thomas Perryman and his people evacuated the town at some point before the colonel's arrival, but did not have time to remove all of the arms and ammunition that the British had stockpiled there for them:

> I find that Woodbine and his followers are returned to their head quarters below the confluence of the rivers and most probably [all] who were preparing for acts of hostility against your frontiers. We hear only of one or two straggling parties being out. Since the disaster of the British forces at New Orleans the general opinion among them is they will have peace this spring. If a movement should be attempted from where the enemy are we shall have some fighting but I believe the Indians below are under serious apprehensions for their safety. The women and children in the utmost distress for food. All have fled from between the forks. We have found in their houses 50 muskets and 650 musket flints and have heard of more.[207]

---

[205] Col. Benjamin Hawkins to Gov. Peter Early, February 20, 1815, Hargrett Rare Book and Manuscript Library, The University of Georgia Libraries, Telamon Cuyler Collection, Box 75, Folder 25, Document 21.

[206] Lt. William Rawlins to Rear Admiral Percy Malcolm, February 26, 1815, Cochrane Papers.

[207] Col. Benjamin Hawkins to Gov. Peter Early, February 24, 1815, Hargrett Rare Book and Manuscript Library, the University of Georgia Libraries, Telamon Cuyler Collection, Box 76, Folder 25, Document 22.

Recognizing that he faced a much stronger and better-armed force than his own, Hawkins was now on the defensive and gave up on the idea of attacking either of the British forts. Georgia's failure to send white troops greatly concerned his Native American soldiers, who were especially alarmed that militia troops were garrisoning the forts where their women and children were waiting. They convened a council on the night of February 20 and presented their statement to the agent on the next morning:

> We were enrolled in public service by order of General Jackson, promised soldiers pay and rations, and ordered to take care of this frontier. We had selected some of our best men to garrison the posts, we were promised by Colo. Hawkins and General McIntosh a force of white troops to act with us, and while we were out on duty we hear 300 men have taken possession of the posts, our women and children are there and we well know these men are rude and ungovernable. We find we are to have no meat. If white soldiers were with us and would live without it we could and would do it. We hear not of the white force promised us, and why is it these people did not come to help us, and not stop where they have nothing to do?[208]

The situation was deteriorating. Provisions were running short, and the foraging parties sent out by Col. Hawkins were unable to find many cows that they could confiscate for beef. With his Creek soldiers now disgruntled over the failure of more white troops to support them, the agent did his best to hold the command together in the face of an enemy that was growing stronger by the day. He was very lucky when the situation expectedly resolved itself on February 25, 1815:

> Yesterday about one o'clock I received express from Capt. Limbaugh a copy of the despatch from the postmaster genl of 14th announcing the arrival of a treaty of peace. I immediately sent off two runners with the

---

[208] Statement of Chiefs, February 21, 1815, enclosed in Hawkins to Early, February 20, 1815.

information to the British commandant below. They met a flag of truce bringing information to me from their admiral of the same import, Two officers Lieuts. One of the navy and the other of the army bore the flag. They brought the 9th art. of the treaty only, it being all they had recd. The officers remained with me last evening and returned today. This event yesterday was communicated to ever command who fired a feu de joie, and this morning they paraded in one line as the British officers received with us the line and one other feu de joie was fired.[209]

The firing of a *feu de joie* was a special and rare event. The salute—which is also called the "rippling fire"—was reserved for momentous occasions such as the inauguration of a President. It consists of all the soldiers forming a line and firing in rapid succession one after another. The explosion of fire from the muzzles of the black powder muskets of that day created the appearance of a rippling line of fire. With nearly 1,000 men at his command, two ordered by Col. Hawkins and carried out by his men must have been remarkable to see.

The American agent began sending his men home in detachments, ordering them to spread the word of the truce to everyone they encountered. He instructed William Hardridge to travel down to Prospect Bluff with orders to confer with Lt. Col. Nicolls and then started for home.

The last major campaign of the War of 1812 was over.

---

[209] Col. Benjamin Hawkins to Gov. Peter Early, February 26, 1815, Telamon Cuyler Collection, Hargrett Rare Book and Manuscript Library, The University of Georgia Libraries, Box 76, Folder 25, Document 23.

10

THE BRITISH POST

THE AMERICAN CAMPAIGNS UNDER MAJ. BLUE AND COL. HAWKINS operated with very little intelligence about Nicolls' forts on the Apalachicola River. The commanders knew virtually nothing about the British Post at Prospect Bluff, which developed into a fortress of considerable size and strength over the winter of 1814-1815. The arrival of Nicolls, Woodbine, the Marines, and their Red Stick allies in the weeks after the Battle of Pensacola brought about a dramatic surge in the population at the bluff and an immediate need both for stronger defenses and a reliable supply line.

The task of designing the new fort fell to Lt. Christie of the Royal Marines Artillery. None of his reports are known to exist, and it is unclear whether he incorporated Woodbine's magazine and other existing structures into his plan. Lt. Col. Nicolls, who arrived to inspect the lieutenant's work after a visit to British ships off Apalachicola Bay, was not pleased with what he saw:

> ...Enclosed also is the plan Lieut. Christie of the Royal Artillery drew of this fort during my absence, but I found it so defective that I ordered Captain Henry to execute it differently as you will see by his plan. We have the ditch dug all round 12 feet wide, and six deep. We would get on much faster if we had a larger proportion of entrenching tools; if you can spare any Pray Sir send me

some; also canvas for boats sail. The pull up against the [current] is very severe with loaded boats and those very clumsy. Our Medicines are all expended, and we want a couple of surgeon assistants.[210]

The ditch mentioned by Nicolls in his report to Admiral Cochrane was the moat that surrounded the central citadel. This octagonal fortification was built of earth and wood and stood back from the crest of the bluff at what would become the center of the post. The moat or ditch is still visible today, especially during times of heavy rains when it fills with water. The principal magazine was inside this work, but it was not just a magazine. Neither was it covered with earth nor was it mound-shaped or 30-feet high as some writers have suggested.

The British built the citadel on the designs of Sébastien Le Prestre de Vauban, Marquis de Vauban, a prominent French military engineer who lived more than 100-years earlier. It is reminiscent of the fortress that Vauban designed at Neuf-Brisach in the French region of Alsace but on a much smaller scale. It was the last of the fortresses designed by the famed engineer to Louis XIV and is considered part of this "Third System." Neuf-Brisach consisted of an octagonal citadel surrounded by moats and outer defenses. While the British Post at Prospect Bluff was not of the size and scope of Neuf-Brisach, which enclosed an entire town, it bore remarkable similarities to the World Heritage Site.

There is no readily accessible stone at Prospect Bluff, so Capt. Robert Henry of the Royal Marine Artillery used the longleaf pines that grew in profusion there to form the outlines of the citadel. Some of these were cut into 50-foot lengths to form the outer wall and an equal number at 30-feet to form the interior. The ends were notched "log cabin" style to form morticed joints. The 30-foot logs were then stacked horizontally to form the shape of an octagon. Each of the eight walls was of equal length, and each angle was of equal degree. Inside the wall was an open area that served as a *place d'armes* or parade ground for the fort.

Eighteen feet out from this inner wall, the British built a second almost identical wall using the 50-foot logs. It surrounded the inner one. Work

---

[210] Lt. Col. Edward Nicolls to Adm. Sir Alexander Cochrane, December 3, 1814, Cochrane Papers.

also started on a ditch or moat surrounding the twin walls. Earth removed from the ditch was packed between the two log walls to create a solid rampart. The moat was deepened and widened as the outer wall grew in height, creating extra earth for the filling of the rampart. The larger circumference of the moat allowed for the removal of enough dirt to pack between the two walls until the rampart was 18-feet thick and 12-feet high. The top was planked over to form a gun deck for artillery, and castle-like crenellations completed the exterior height of 15-feet.[211]

The result was a very strong fortification that could be defended by a small garrison against an overwhelming force. The grand magazine—one of three eventually built at the fort—was buried deep inside the earthen wall. A sally port or gate pierced the rampart on the western side of the citadel, where warships firing from the river could not hit it. A drawbridge spanned the ditch on the same side as the sally port.

As the citadel was under construction, the British also built a redan or triangle-shaped battery immediately at the point where the bluff projected slightly near its southern end. The base of the triangle was left open, but the sides were built in the same design as described above. Nicolls placed his heaviest artillery behind these walls where it could fire up and down the river at approaching vessels. The battery controlled a visible stretch of the Apalachicola that was more than 3 miles long.

The building of the fort was a labor-intensive process. Not only did the Royal and Colonial Marines work on the defenses, but help also poured in from the Native American towns in the British alliance. "Their brave and faithful old Chief Cappachimico who has adhered to England through all difficulties, is here with me and 70 of his men helping me to build the Fort," Nicolls wrote of the Miccosukees on December 3, 1814. He also made use of the Cuban militia that he forcibly embarked from the Barrancas while evacuating Pensacola. These soldiers were initially put ashore in deplorable conditions on St. Vincent Island, but the colonel soon moved them up to the bluff to help with the manual labor.[212]

Lt. Col. Nicolls also reported on December 3 that 50 Miccosukees were on their way to raid the Georgia frontier. The rest of the Red Sticks

---

[211] See Pintado, 1815, and Poe, 1963.

[212] Lt. Col. Edward Nicolls to Adm. Sir Alexander Cochrane, December 3, 1814.

from Pensacola were coming and would arrive within a few days. He believed that they would make good soldiers, but they feared the Creeks allied with the United States would move in behind them when they advanced to engage American troops. The Red Sticks learned this lesson at the Battle of Horseshoe Bend. The colonel, however, planned to deal with this by bribing the Big Warrior and his followers:

> I am waiting the arrival of the other Chiefs, for I now find that before I advance it is absolutely necessary to have the Upper Town Creeks in our alliance. Those people justly dread the idea of their allowing them in the rear when they are engaged with the Americans as was lately the case. I am therefore taking every possible step to gain them over and as I have before told you, I must give them money as well as presents across the line as lately the Americans have failed paying them from inability. If you can send me a small sum, say (pound symbol) 500, Wm. Hambley thinks it would buy them all…by the presents and that some or as much of it as you can in Gold it being more portable, and in their opinion a more valuable present. They have also been led to believe that a force of Troops was coming to aid them. If you possibly can spare a battalion of Marines or black troops, I am sure it would be of the greatest benefit to the service, and red clothing is much wanted.[213]

Admiral Cochrane arrived off Apalachicola Bay in the days that followed, and Nicolls went down to meet him, taking with him Cappachimico, Thomas Perryman, William Perryman, the Prophet Francis, Peter McQueen, and others. Capt. Robert Henry remained behind to command at Prospect Bluff. So many Native American allies poured in on him, however, that he soon pleaded for help from Capt. William Rawlins (or Rawlings) of HMS *Borer*, a 14-gun warship then off St. George Island:

---

[213] *Ibid.*

In consequence of the vast number of Indians pouring in upon us daily, I feel it absolutely necessary to request you will be pleased to demand supplies of provisions from the Commander in Chief for us.

We now victual two thousand and two hundred men, women and children, and by letters from Lieut. Smith who is in advance, I find there are five hundred Indians within two days march of us: I must therefore beg leave to urge the necessity of your loosing no time in procuring supplies as the service we are upon may suffer seriously by reducing the Indians to short allowance and much more by turning them back altogether for want of provisions.

We may hourly expect Lieut. Col. Nicolls, but to await one week for him, might reduce us to extreme necessity. If you think proper to dispatch any of our vessels, you will see the necessity of putting her in charge of some of your own hands, as the Marines on board are not capable of taking them to sea. I shall be glad to have the honor of hearing from you.[214]

Rawlins immediately loaded provisions into a small schooner belonging to the Royal Marine detachment and sent it up the river to Capt. Henry. He urged the land commander to stretch them as far as possible and to be as economical as he could. The captain considered taking his ship over the bar into Apalachicola Bay, but soundings convinced him that it was not worth the risk. His report to Admiral Cochrane provides a good understanding of the difficulty that the British faced in getting supply ships into the bay:

I should have felt myself justified in proceeding in His Majesty's Sloop under my command with the above information, but a considerable delay would have taken place, as we were obliged to take out our provisions guns and stores &c., and to start nearly the whole of the water

---

[214] Capt. Robert Henry to Capt. William Rawlins, December 18, 1814, Cochrane Papers.

before we could get over the Bar, and event hen we hung for a few seconds on the break of it, from frequent Soundings I am convinced there is not more than ten feet water upon it: and at present we have not a sufficiency of small vessels down the river to put our guns provisions &c. into to enable us to cross the Bar and reembark them without considerable delay, and then only with a fair wind and settled weather from the very indifferent way the small vessels are found.[215]

Rawlings had previously warned the admiral that the sails of the small sloops and schooners used to move supplies back and forth from the ships offshore and storehouse on St. Vincent Island up to Prospect Bluff were in dismal condition. He now reported the same of the island storehouse where arms and other supplies were stored while awaiting transport:

I beg to acquaint you that the Store House, containing the arms &c. on the island of St. Vincent, is only a temporary hut, consisting of stakes and the leaf of the Palmetto trees and by no means secured, against the effects of the weather so little so that the arms which have been stacked out of the cases, are very materially injured by the rain. I shall therefore clean and put them in the best state I can; and afterwards embark them on board the Transport Brig *Mars*, for their preservation as well as security. Major Nicolls had withdrawn the Spanish Guard to Head Quarters previous to my arrival here. – I have reason to suppose the present Store House is within the reach of the surf during the hurricane months. If therefore a Store House is to be established on that island, I beg to suggest that a more elevated site will be necessary for it.[216]

---

[215] Capt. William Rawlins to Adm. Sir Alexander Cochrane, December 21, 1814, Cochrane Papers.
[216] Capt. William Rawlins to Adm. Sir Alexander Cochrane, December 21, 1814, (Second letter of same date), Cochrane Papers.

The "Spanish Guard" mentioned in the captain's report was the detachment of 200 Cuban militia taken from the Barrancas. The shipment of provisions sent up to the bluff did little to relieve the desperate conditions there. Five hundred Eufaula warriors arrived at the fort, bringing the total number of Native Americans there to more than 1,600 men, 450 women, and 55 children. These were in addition to the 200 Spanish soldiers and the 150-180 Colonial Marines with their families. Capt. Henry wrote directly to Admiral Cochrane to explain the situation and urge him to send provisions as soon as possible:

> In the absence of Lt. Col. Nicolls I beg leave to acquaint you, that from the number of Indians daily arriving here, a speedy supply of provisions will be absolutely necessary to prevent our sending them back, a circumstance that might seriously effect the service we are upon, as there are several wavering towns lately joined us from the Americans Lines; And to send those back without assistance and without the presents promised them, would be placing them in the hands of the Enemy.[217]

Other Creek and Seminole groups were reportedly on their way to the bluff, where the mass of humanity was already on half-rations of beef. Henry reported that eleven days of bread and flour remained in stock at the post, and he had only a few calves on the hoof left. Warriors went out to drive in free-range cattle from as far away as the Georgia frontier, but the rivers and creeks had started their annual mid-December rise, and it was difficult to get stock to the fort by land.[218]

The situation got much worse on December 23 when 1,000 more Lower Creek warriors arrived at Prospect Bluff to join the British. Their unexpected appearance threw the post into a complete crisis. Capt. Henry distributed almost everything in his storehouses to them, but the requirement that he feed well over 3,000 Creeks and Seminoles, plus

---

[217] Capt. Robert Henry to Adm. Sir Alexander Cochrane, December 22, 1814, Cochrane Papers.
[218] *Ibid.*

another 1,000 British and Spanish soldiers and Maroon women and children, depleted his provisions. He sent the warriors out into the woods with their muskets to hunt game and fend for themselves. Capt. Rawlins reported from HMS *Borer* that the men were hunting throughout the Apalachicola River estuary, desperately searching for food.[219]

Rawlins notified Admiral Cochrane that the Marine detachment at the bluff was in "the greatest distress for want of provisions." The necessity of Capt. Henry sending the warriors and their families out to fend for themselves caused a serious disruption in the fort's supply line:

> The evil has attended their dispersion, instead of bringing in the cattle at Head Quarters, they have shot, and applied them to their own use; which has reduced the detachment at Prospect Bluff to very great distress, so much so that they have upon two or three occasions been altogether destitute of meat. As it is probable the Indians will return again shortly, a supply of provisions, will be absolutely necessary for their use, (as well as the detachment) if it is intended, to retain them here.[220]

The pleas for help from Rawlins and Henry took time to reach Admiral Cochrane. First, the two officers had to wait for a ship bound for the fleet to stop off Apalachicola Bay. It took even longer for that vessel to sail west to the coast of Louisiana, where Cochrane's fleet anchored during the operations against New Orleans. The December dispatches, of course, arrived to find the admiral and other senior officers distracted by the fighting against the American army under Maj. Gen. Andrew Jackson. Nicolls was present in the camps below Jackson's lines at Chalmette with the chiefs who had gone to observe the expected American victory. His delegation included Col. Thomas Perryman and Capt. William Perryman from the Seminole towns on the lower Chattahoochee and Apalachicola Rivers; Cappachimico of Miccosukee; the "Old Factor," a Yuchi chief;

---

[219] Capt. William Rawlins to Adm. Sir Alexander Cochrane, January 16, 1815, Cochrane Papers.
[220] *Ibid.*

Peter McQueen, leader of the Talisi (Tallassee) Red Sticks, and the Prophet Josiah Francis. Some of their families accompanied them.[221]

The presence of Nicolls and the chiefs at the Battle of New Orleans allowed them to meet many observers, some of whom left fascinating descriptions of their appearance and conduct. Among these was Benson Earle Hill, an artillery officer assigned to Cochrane's flagship HMS *Tonnant*:

> ...On its quarter-deck I saw, for the first time, the Indian chiefs, who, we were led to believe, would prove valuable allies to us in our present undertaking. A British officer, Colonel Nicholls of the Marines, had, for some time past, been domesticated with them; from his account of their prowess, and attachment to our cause, most favourable results were anticipated. These savages belonged to the Creek and Choctaw tribes; their deputation was formed of some five or six men. They were fantastically attired; two of the principals had on large ill-made coats of scarlet serge, with a profusion of marine buttons, tinsel epaulettes, and small stars on their breasts. This attempt at European costume scarcely covered their filthy check-shirts and deer-skin leggings.[222]

The observations of Hill and others are racist by modern standards but reflect the thoughts and reactions of British officers on their first encounters with Native American leaders. His description of the Muscogee practice of ear mutilation is particularly fascinating:

> ...One of these was pointed out to me as [Thomas] Perimond, King of the Muscogies. He was of an advanced

---

[221] Certificate of Lt. Col. Edward Nicolls for January 16-25, 1815, enclosed in Capt. D.E. Bartholomew to Adm. Sir Alexander Cochrane, February 6, 1815, Cochrane Papers.

[222] Benson Earle Hill, *Recollections of an Artillery Officer: Including Scenes and Adventures in Ireland, America, Flanders, and France*, Volume I, London: Richard Bentley, New Burlington Street, 1836: 298-300.

age, and remarkably fair complexion for a red skin. This was accounted for by one of his companions, who stated that his lady-mother had played false with an English deserter – proving that the court of Muscogy was no more exempt from scandal than that of Muscovy. A large hoop of gold hung from his majesty's nose, and his unsymmetrical ears were adorned with silver rings. The rest were badly clad, after their own fashion; but all of them exhibited the peculiarity of having the external cartilage of the ear cut, and hanging down on the shoulder in unseemly flesh, resembling the cadaverous appendage to the neck of a turkey-cock. As a mark, I presume, of distinction, one of the warriors wore a band of silver round his head, with numerous small bells attached to hit; above these was stuck some wild bird, whose putrescent state proved that it must have been killed many days.[223]

Hill's commented that the attire and appearance of the chiefs were "as unlike the fanciful arrangement of feathers, seen in pictures or on the stage, in Mexican or Indian costume, as possible." The role of the entertainment industry in the public's perception of Native American culture was as evident in 1815 as it is today.[224]

The artillery officer was on the deck of the *Tonnant* when the British attacked the schooner USS *Seahorse*, sloops-of-war USS *Tickler* and USS *Alligator*, and Gunboats Nos. 5, 23, 156, 162, and 163 at the Battle of Lake Borgne on December 14, 1814. The chiefs joined him there to watch the distant battle, giving him a particular opportunity to observe the Prophet Francis:

...The chiefs were attended by a prophet, on whose predictions they relied implicitly...Amongst the spectators collected to witness the attack on the schooner, were the Indian chiefs, who appeared deeply interested in the proceedings; and no sooner was the destruction

---

[223] *Ibid.*
[224] *Ibid.*

effected, than the prophet, in a fit of inspiration, commenced a palaver with his countrymen, foretelling the complete success of our Pale Faces on the following day; this was soon made known to us by Colonel Nicholls, who endeavoured to impress upon us that we might depend on the predictions of this gifted seer.[225]

Another officer who met the chiefs and their families was George Laval Chesterton, who was introduced to the military service in 1812 by Lt. Col. Nicolls. Both men were friends of Viscountess Perceval, who later became Countess Egmont. She requested that Nicolls watch over Chesterton, assuring him that that the young man was one of those who thought "gunpowder most excellent snuff."[226]

Chesterton encountered Nicolls again at New Orleans and found the famed Royal Marine suffering from the grievous wounds he received at the first Battle of Fort Bowyer:

> His appearance was not at all improved by additional age and by active and disastrous service, for his enterprises had been unsuccessful.
>
> He had lost an eye; and whether it resulted from his association with his wild Indians, or an affected singularity, or, as some averred, a slight aberration arising from numerous wounds, he certainly had contracted a fantastical deportment, and looked so strangely care-worn, that few could regard him without surprise and comment.[227]

Nicolls offered the young officer a post with his land forces in Florida, but Chesterton had a deep fear of being scalped. He referred his old mentor to his commanding officer, who told the lieutenant colonel that he could

---

[225] *Ibid.*: 300, 328.
[226] George Laval Chesterton, *Peace, War, and Adventure: An Autobiographical Memoir of George Laval Chesterton*, Volume I, London: Longman, Brown, Green and Longmans, 1853: 9-10.
[227] *Ibid.*: 213.

not spare the young officer. Chesterton did enjoy his opportunity to meet the Red Stick, Seminole, and Miccosukee chiefs:

> The Indian chiefs had been arrayed in uniforms sent from England, as presents to them from the Prince Regent. Upon what principal of selection these habiliments were chosen it is hard to contemplate, for anything more ridiculous and ill-suited can scarcely be imagined. They resembled the full-dress jackets of serjeants of the Guards, to which huge cocked hats were added; and the exotic chiefs, some with rings suspended from their noses, chins, and ears, and many with feathers drooping from the hair, exhibited figures much better suited to a pantomime than to a camp. These singular personages strutted about us, equally the objects of merriment and surprise.[228]

Unlike many of the British officers and soldiers, however, Chesterton took the time to talk with the Native Americans of Nicolls' party. They suddenly became very human to him:

> Their followers were numerous, and realised all our previous notions of this remarkable race. Many of them spoke tolerable English (from their casual intercourse with the Americans); and their tattooed bodies, wild deportment, but gentle manner, elicited our curiosity and sympathy. I remember an occasion on which their frail huts took fire, and the consternation that prevailed amongst them; and the frank dependence which they all (females especially) reposed in our willing aid, won our utmost good will. Upon that occasion I assisted a matron, of medium age, in the removal of her portable effects, and got upon terms with the whole family that apprised me there was but a step well understood, between the savage and the civilized.[229]

---

[228] *Ibid.*: 214-215.
[229] *Ibid.*: 215.

The woman mentioned by Chesterton was the wife and mother of one of the Native American families. Unfortunately, he did not mention her name, as his description of her is one of the best written by a European visitor of a Creek or Seminole woman of the War of 1812 era:

> The mother was a fine woman, with a handsome countenance. She was so dexterously tattooed throughout every observable portion of the frame, that not a flaw was discernible in the lines and curvatures intended, doubtless, for embellishent. Her daughter, at least seventeen years of age, was of graceful form, and equally with her mother was thus artistically decorated. There were several other children, and all bore marks indicative of their wild origin. They reposed childish confidence in me, and took my hand and answered to my caresses with all the eager playfulness of any other class of children. The mother spoke very good English, and reasoned upon the war we were waging, with more astuteness than could have been expected from a savage. The fire drove them from our immediate vicinity, and I afterwards sought to renew my acquaintance with them in vain. I saw them no more.[230]

Chesterton also had a brief interaction with the Maroons entering the British lines below New Orleans. Many of these men joined Nicolls' Colonial Marines and the young officer saw some of them again in the military camps of the land forces at Mobile Point during the second attack on Fort Bowyer (February 7-12, 1815):

> The runaway negroes, who hoped by our patronage to disenthrall themselves from the rigours of slavery, were numerous and of all ages and marketable promise. Amongst them, again, I observed the everlasting buoyancy of animal spirits. They were good tempered,

---

[230] *Ibid.*: 215-216.

The Fort at Prospect Bluff

and unceasingly mirthful; and their intercourse with us betokened unlimited confidence. They were all removed with the army, and we afterwards saw in our future camp many who first became known to us before New Orleans.[231]

The Battle of New Orleans, of course, was a disaster for the British. Their grand attack on Jackson's lines was hurled back with devastating losses in a battle that lasted just 25 minutes. Maj. Gen. Sir Edward Pakenham, the brother-in-law of the Duke of Wellington, was killed, as was Maj. Gen. Samuel Gibbs. Maj. Gen. John Keane suffered two wounds. Total British casualties were 285 killed, 1,265 wounded, and 484 prisoners or missing in action, a total loss of 2,084 men. Jackson, meanwhile, reported losses of only 13 killed, 30 wounded, and 19 captured or missing in action. Command of the army fell to Maj. Gen. John Lambert, who, after consultation with Admiral Cochrane, decided to withdraw to the fleet. The chiefs were devastated. Benson Earle Hill wrote that Thomas Perryman went from tent to tent seeking alcohol with which to drown his sorrows.

Nicolls and the chiefs went aboard the bomb sloop HMS *Erebus* eight days after the battle of January 8, 1815. They reached Apalachicola Bay on January 22:

> I beg leave to inform you, that the *Erebus* and Convoy left the Anchorage at the Chandelieur Island at noon on the 21st instant and arrived off St. George's Island on the evening of the 22nd. On the 23 the *Florida* was taken close to the Bar, but all the boats belonging to the *Borer & Mars Transport* being up the River, the means for delivering the Cargo was confined to the boats of this Sloop until the evening of the 25th when the boats mentioned came down & one large & two small schooners with them. I directed the whole of the Stores & provisions to be put onboard the *Mars*, and sent the company of the

---

[231] *Ibid.*

West India Regt. To assist in hoisting in, & sending daily at dawn of day a working part of them to the *Florida*. Two days from the weather and extraordinary Strong ebbs in the River our progress was much impeded, but on the morning of the 28th, I sent up the two largest schooners loaded with provisions & the troops on their decks, keeping the boats of the *Erebus*, *Borer*, *Mars* and *Hercules* constantly carrying to the *Mars* what Stores were left, & bringing off sand with them for Ballast & the brig having received Sixty five Tons of sand last night, I weighed at day light this morning with the Convoy.[232]

Capt. D.E. Bartholomew assured Cochrane that he showed proper respect to the Creek and Seminole chiefs aboard his vessel. The supplies sent up from the convoy helped ease the cloud of starvation that hovered over Prospect Bluff, but Nicolls returned to news that Hawkins was approaching the upriver fort with a force of nearly 1,000 warriors:

Brevet Major Nicolls, having by letter bearing date 28th instant represented to me, that he was in great want of ordnance and that he expected to be soon attacked by the Americans, who had built several boats roofed over musket proof. I supplied him from the *Florida* with two long six pounder guns and carriages, with a proportion of shot as under: - Those guns with the ammunition were supplied to the Brig by Government, the other guns onboard her being 9 Pounders & the owner's property I did not remove. I also supplied him from this ship with several Carpenters tools & stores all which I trust will meet your approbation.[233]

---

[232] Capt. D.E. Bartholomew to Adm. Sir Alexander Cochrane, January 31, 1815, Cochrane Papers.

[233] Capt. D.E. Bartholomew to Adm. Sir Alexander Cochrane, January 31, 1815 (second letter of this date), Cochrane Papers.

Capt. Bartholomew sent 100 round shot, ten loads of grape, and 25 rounds of canister for the 6-pounders that he provided to Nicolls. The British rushed troops and warriors up to the outpost, while the Royal Navy sent a yawl armed with a carronade and manned by eight sailors. As Col. Hawkins reported, the force at the upper fort grew to some 800 soldiers, warriors, and sailors. Counting the carronade in the yawl, they had three pieces of artillery—compared to none for the U.S.-allied Creeks—plus a solid fort built atop one of the "tumuli" or prehistoric mounds at what is now River Landing Park in Chattahoochee, Florida. The anticipated battle, however, never took place. News of the signing of the Treaty of Ghent arrived before major fighting could begin.

The end of the War of 1812 marked the beginning of a new phase in the history of the British Post. Hawkins and other U.S. officials expected an immediate withdrawal of Nicolls and his men from the Apalachicola, but Lt. Col. Nicolls had other plans.

11

THE LAST THREE MONTHS

BRITISH FORCES REMAINED ON THE APALACHICOLA RIVER
from February-May 1815, even though the War of 1812 was over. This
extended presence became increasingly threatening to U.S. officials in
Georgia and the Southeast, especially as Lt. Col. Edward Nicolls engaged
in a noteworthy exchange of letters with Col. Benjamin Hawkins.

The final phase of British operations on the Gulf Coast began when
the army landed on Dauphin Island and east of Fort Bowyer on the Mobile
Point peninsula. Maj. Gen. John Lambert moved against the fort with a
determination to take it and open the way into Mobile Bay. His troops were
in position and ready to begin constructing siege lines by February 8:

> ...We broke ground on the night of the 8th, and advanced
> a firing party to within one hundred yards of the fort
> during the night. The position of the batteries being
> decided upon the next day, they were ready to receive
> their guns on the night of the 10th, and on the morning of
> the 11th the fire of a battery of four eighteen pounders, on
> the left, and two eight-inch howitzers on the right, each at
> about one hundred yards distance, two six-pounders at
> about three hundred yards, and eight small cohorns
> advantageously placed on the right, with intervals
> between one hundred and two hundred yards, all
> furnished to keep up an incessant fire for two days, were

prepared to open. Preparatory to commencing, I summoned the fort, allowing the commanding officer half an hour for his decision upon such terms as were proposed. Finding he was inclined to consider them, I prolonged the period at his request, and at 3 o'clock the fort was given up to a British guard and the British colours hoisted, the forms being signed by Major Smith, military secretary, and captain Ricketts, R.N, and finally approved of by the Vice-Admiral and myself, which I have the honour to enclose. I am happy to say, our loss has not been very great; and we are indebted for this, in a great measure, to the efficient means attached to this force. Had we been obliged to resort to any other mode of attack, the fall could not have been looked for under such favourable circumstances.[234]

The fall of Fort Bowyer netted 366 prisoners for the British, Lt. Col. William Lawrence of the Second Infantry among them. Andrew Jackson was stunned by Lawrence's surrender, especially after that officer's tenacious defense of his post in September 1814. Lambert's army and artillery, however, were prepared to demolish the fort's weak land face, and the American officer saw no alternative that would not lead to the slaughter of his men. The capture of the fort opened Mobile Bay to the Royal Navy. Gen. John Coffee wrote to his wife from New Orleans that rumors of peace had reached that place but that he was unsure what the British would do:

> The enemy the last accounts were laying off Mobile, and it was uncertain if they would attack the town of Mobile or not. I believe it is certain that Admiral Cochrane, the principal naval commander, has left the fleet, and has gone to the Chesapeake, for either reinforcements or to be ready to meet any dispatch vessels that may be sent on the subject of a treaty – perhaps next mail will bring us intelligence of something that may alter

---

[234] Maj. Gen. Sir John Lambert to Earl Bathurst, February 14, 1815, *The Times of London*, April 19, 1815.

our destination, but without it, I don't expect to leave here untill the complete fulfillment of our term of service which will be on the 28th of this month, so that we have no certainty of leaving this untill that time, and it will take us from thirty to forty days to reach home.[235]

The feared attack never came. News of the Treaty of Ghent slowly spread through the fleet, and the British stood down their plans for offensive operations. A copy of the treaty reached Apalachicola Bay with the arrival of HMS *Thames*. Lt. Col. Nicolls was at the fort near the confluence, preparing for battle when he first learned of the new developments. He went down to the bay to learn more:

> I have the honor to acquaint you that I have received from Captain Irby of the Thames, Letters from the Commander in Chief acquainting me of a Treaty of Peace being signed by the Commissioners of the United States and those of England which has been ratified by the Prince Regent that when it receives the ratification of the President of the United States is to be considered final, and all hostilities to cease, also directing me to act on the defensive only until such ratification takes place and t recommend the same to the Indians; all of which I have complied with.[236]

The distance between the two British forts is around 80 miles, but the channel of the Apalachicola was even more twisting and turning in that day than it is now. It took one full week for Nicolls to reach Prospect Bluff and the bay and then for his dispatch to make it up to the outpost. Mere chance and the extra cautious attitude on the part of Col. Hawkins are all that prevented an outbreak of fighting. The American commander knew he was outgunned, so he focused instead on blocking the departure of

---

[235] Gen. John Coffee to Mary Donelson Coffee, March 3, 1815, "Letters of General John Coffee to his Wife, 1813-1815," *Tennessee Historical Magazine*, Volume II, Number 4, December 1916: 294.

[236] Lt. Col. Edward Nicolls to Rear Admiral Percy Malcolm, February-March 1815, Cochrane Papers.

raiding parties from the outpost. He pushed his camp forward about one mile from its original position at Tocktoethla to find better cane for the horses. He noticed that most of the British-allied warriors were withdrawing back below the Florida line, although several small parties were still out. He informed Gov. Peter Early that he intended to stay on the defensive and did not expect to fight unless they British advanced. If they did so, he would resist them.[237]

Hawkins underestimated the strength of the parties of warriors that Nicolls had sent against the Georgia frontier. "I fear that sad mischief will be done by the parties I have detached," the latter officer wrote." He had no way of communicating news of peace to them.[238]

As Nicolls sent couriers to find and bring in the war parties, Col. Hawkins debated a raid on Miccosukee to find beef for his men. He told Gov. Early that unless he received new information by February 27, he would act on "my own views as will best secure your frontiers during the sojourn of the enemy on your seacoast." He reported hearing rumors that Gov. Mateo Gonzales Manrique of Pensacola had sent an armed vessel to retrieve "McGill and the Spanish negroes," a reference to American deserter and current Colonial Marine Hugh McGill and the Cuban militia force that the British forcibly embarked from the Barrancas. Although he had not met Lt. Col. Nicolls, he told Gov. Early that the Irish officer was "quite the blustering braggadocio."[239]

The news of peace reached both forces at the forks on February 25, 1815, and bitter enemies instantly became friends. British officers visited the American camp for what has jokingly been called the "Battle of the Barbecue" and the firing of the *feu de joie* salutes described in the previous chapter. The British carried only the 9th article of the Treaty of Ghent when they arrived at 115 Mile Camp, but it was one of vital importance to their Red Stick allies:

> The United States of America engage to put an end
> immediately after the Ratification of the present Treaty to
> hostilities with all the Tribes or Nations of Indians with

---

[237] Col. Benjamin Hawkins to Gov. Peter Early, February 24, 1815.
[238] Lt. Col. Edward Nicolls to Rear Admiral Percy Malcom, February-March 1815.
[239] Col. Benjamin Hawkins to Gov. Peter Early, February 24, 1815.

whom they may be at war at the time of such Ratification, and forthwith to restore such Tribes or Nations respectively all the possessions, rights, and privileges which they may have enjoyed or been entitled to in one thousand eight hundred and eleven previous to such hostilities.[240]

The article further required each side to prevent their American Indian allies from making further attacks. Its requirement that all seized "property" be returned to the Indians was one of enormous implications. Maj. Gen. Jackson had imposed the Treaty of Fort Jackson on the Creek Nation on August 9, 1814, stripping the Native Americans of more than 23 million acres of land as compensation for U.S. losses in the Creek War. The British believed that Americans should restore this territory to the Creeks. The United States, however, did not agree. U.S. authorities maintained that the Creek War of 1813-1814 was not part of the War of 1812 and that the Fort Jackson treaty which ended it had nothing to do with the British or the Treaty of Ghent. This stance was at odds with earlier U.S. claims that the Red Stick war was instigated by the British.

Hawkins and his men started evacuating 115 Mile Camp on February 26, 1815. The colonel divided his command into several columns and ordered them home by different routes to spread the word of the signing of the peace treaty and afford them better chances of finding food. Nicolls also set about concluding the business of war on the Apalachicola, but his methods were different:

> …The Indians who first engaged in the War are in a most wretched state, and I hope Provisions will be sent to me for them soon, with the last supply I got we have no only three weeks for our own people and we are obliged to victual several Indians who are necessary to our movements; in ten days from this I am to have a general meeting of the Chiefs at our Fort on the Forks of the Chatahouche and Flint Rivers, to the collectively I shall communicate the terms of Peace, but for the individuals

---

[240] Treaty of Ghent, Article the Ninth, December 24, 1814.

to whom I have already communicated it they have replied that unless they have free communication with us and a British officer kept with them they are sure of destruction.[241]

Nicolls scheduled the general meeting or council for March 10 at the upper fort and announced plans to evacuate the outpost soon after that date. "As soon as I hear from the American Colonel commanding opposite to me that the Treaty is accepted," he wrote, "I shall cause my advance to retire to this post [*i.e.*, Prospect Bluff]." He informed his Red Stick and Seminole allies that Admiral Cochrane had ordered him to leave them "plenty of arms, ammunition &c., and even cannon, with which they are well pleased." The chiefs requested that he or a different officer of his command remain with them as an agent, telling Nicolls that the "presence of a British officer is indispensable."[242]

The lieutenant colonel knew that the request of the Seminoles and Creeks for a British officer to be placed in control of their affairs in Florida was an insult by Spain. The dying empire still held legal possession of the colony, but Nicolls warned Rear Admiral Percy Malcolm that the Indians would attack the Spanish if they tried to block their request:

I have told them that if it is the will of my Government, I will remain and see justice done to them with pleasure, they are very much exasperated against the Spaniards, and it is as much as I can do to prevent them from driving the Garrison of St. Marks, and indeed all the other Garrisons out of the Province. They positively declare that if Spain does not suffer them a free communication through the Appalachicola river between them and the British they will declare war without quarter against her Subjects. I think it would be good policy in our Government to demand from Spain such terms, for

[241] Lt. Col. Edward Nicolls to Rear Admiral Percy Malcolm, February-March 1815.
[242] *Ibid.*

> unless that is the case we can never get to the Indians to
> supply them with powder, arms & c....[243]

Nicolls anticipated future fighting when he wrote of his allies that "we may always calculate on their assisting us either against Spain or America." He could not have imagined that Great Britain and the United States were embarking on 200 years of friendship and peace.

The American force left 115 Mile Camp before the end of February 1815, but the British continued to garrison both of their forts on the Apalachicola. Nicolls and other officers did what they could to restrain their allies from further attacks against the United States. Rear Admiral George Cockburn, who learned of the ratification of the Treaty of Ghent on March 15, sent out a call to "the Chief of any Indian tribe on or near the border of Georgia" to refrain from further action. His letter reached Col. Nicolls through American officers as well as an enclosure in a dispatch from Rear Admiral Malcolm.[244]

The leaders of the Red Stick Creek, Lower Creek, Seminole, Miccosukee, and other groups allied with the British convened at the upper post on March 10, 1815. It was ten months to the day since HMS *Orpheus* arrived off Apalachicola Bay. The Muscogee people had been dealing with the British in one way or another since 1674. The council at Nicolls' Outpost, however, was the last time the two nations ever signed a proposed treaty. The document they produced was the last agreement ever concluded between British officers and American Indians in what is now the United States east of the Mississippi River.

The important Native American leaders present included Cappachimico, Thomas Perryman, the Prophet Francis, Peter McQueen, Homathlemico, and three men named Eneah Emathla (Neamathla). One of these was the Fowltown chief who achieved note for his defiance of U.S. expansionism in the years 1817-1836. When U.S. troops raided his home in 1817, they found a British uniform coat with epaulets and a letter

---

[243] *Ibid.*

[244] Rear Admiral George Cockburn to the Chief of any Indian tribe on or near the Border of Georgia, March 10, 1815, Hargrett Rare Book and Manuscript Library, The University of Georgia Libraries, Telamon Cuyler Collection, Box 82, Folder 18, Document 01 (signed aboard the HMS *Albion* off Cumberland Island).

signed by an officer affirming that Neamathla was a true friend of the British.

The agreement requested continued support—military and otherwise—from Great Britain but did not end there. The chiefs were angry with John Forbes and Company for the firm's alleged support of the United States in the War of 1812. Anger also still simmered among the Miccosukee and others over the Forbes Purchase, which took more than one million acres from the Lower Creeks, Miccosukees, and Seminoles in place of payment in cash for debts owed to the trading company by the entire Creek Nation. The Nicolls' Outpost council allowed the chiefs to rescind the Forbes Purchase, and they did so. Col. Nicolls considered this action to be one of great importance:

> …They have by a public act in full assembly confiscated the lands given to and all the property of the house of Forbes & Co. for breach of contract with them and for endeavouring to prevent them from joining us – Indeed I know this to be true for I have intercepted letters from [John] Forbes at St. Augustine and from [James] Innerarity the Mayor of Mobille which if they are to be considered as British will shew them to be guilty of Treason, and I personally know the partner of the house at Pensacola [i.e., John Innerarity] to be the greatest rascal on earth, one who has abused the British in the grossest terms, and praised the Americans in the strongest manner, of which I have seen written proofs by his own hand.[245]

Other discussions took place at the council, but the topics remain unknown. Nicolls, Capt. Henry Ross of the British Rifle Corps, and Capt. Joseph Roche of the 1st West India Regiment represented the British at the talks. Lt. William Hambly served as interpreter. The document produced at the talks still survives. It was addressed to King George III and signed by 30 chiefs. They expressed their desire to live independently and requested that Great Britain maintain open ports for them at the mouths of the Apalachicola, Alabama, and St. Marys Rivers:

---

[245] Lt. Col. Edward Nicolls to Rear Admiral Percy Malcolm, February-March 1815.

...[F]or if our communication is once more cut off from his children, we shall be totally ruined; we have fought and bled for him against the Americans, by which we have made them our more bitter enemies, and as he has stood the friend of oppressed nation beyond the great waters, he will surely not forget the sufferings of his once happy children here. We therefore rely on his future protection and his fatherly kindness: we will truly keep the talks which his chief has given us, if he is graciously pleased to continue his protection.[246]

The chiefs went on to explain that the formerly prosperous Seminoles were now in a desperate condition, despite assistance from the British for which they were thankful:

...[F]amine is now devouring up ourselves and our children, by reason of our Upper Town brethren being driven down upon us in the time the corn was green, and now their miseries and necessities cause them to root up the seed of our future crop, so that we sow in the day we are obliged to watch at night. Was it not for the powder we get from your chief, the whole of the nation would be in dust: the Red Sticks have shot and eat up almost the whole of our cattle, for they have seen their children digging in the woods for want, and who can blame them, when they are pressed by such cruel necessity? Thus are we situated, and are only looking to the departure or the stay of your children, as the signal of our destruction or prosperity.[247]

Among the starving children referenced were the son and daughters of the Prophet Francis himself. He had tried to preserve lands of the

---

[246] Address of the Indians to the King of England, on the Conclusion of the Treaty of Peace, March 10, 1815, *The London Times*, August 13, 1818.
[247] *Ibid.*

Muscogee and stop the "Manifest Destiny" of the United States, but now was a refugee far from home. One of his daughters, Milly, soon became one of the most remarkable women in North American history. She saved the life of a Georgia militiaman named Duncan McCrimmon three years later. Often called the "New" or "Creek" Pocahontas, she sparked a national debate about the humanity of Native Americans when she explained that she intervened in the planned execution of McCrimmon out of mercy and humanity. Many whites of her day did not believe that American Indians possessed such qualities. Since it was common for chiefs and warriors to bring their families to important councils, Milly likely was present at Nicolls' Outpost when the treaty was signed.[248]

The chiefs also explained that John Forbes and Company had not kept its promises to settle lands granted it with "British men" and to maintain affordable supplies of merchandise for Native American use:

> ...[I]nstead of their doing this, they have attempted to settle our lands with Americans, and have refused to supply us with powder, when we were attacked by our enemies, and have urges us to declare for the Americans against the British, and have offered rewards to us for that purpose; and they have actually written to their agents who reside among us, desiring them to obstruct the British officers all in their power from assisting us, and to represent to them, alas, how impossible it would be for them to succeed against the Americans.[249]

The agents referenced in the document were Edmund Doyle and William Hambly, both of whom served with the British on the Apalachicola. Creek and Seminole warriors had intercepted letters to them from company officials. "We further annul and declare void our grant or grants of land accordingly," the document continued, "warning them [*i.e.,*

---

[248] For more on her life, please see *Milly Francis: The Life & Times of the Creek Pocahontas* by this author.
[249] *Ibid.*

190

company owners] and all belonging to them to never appear again in the nation."[250]

The chiefs also explained the harm done to the Creek Nation by the running of the Federal Road through its territory. They had sent William McIntosh, who they called a "young chief" and who was now their enemy, to protest against the road, but he had betrayed them. They alleged that he was "tricked by the enemy" and unlawfully sold their lands on the Oconee and Ocmulgee Rivers. They asked King George to assist them in ending American use of the road and in having their old lands restored:

> ...The above-mentioned McIntosh holds a commission as Major in the American army, and the Creek Regiment: he has caused much blood to be spilt, for which we denounce him to the whole nation, and will give the usual reward of the brave who may kill him, he having on a recent occasion killed and scalped a brother who was on an errand of peace to our Cherokee brethren, for no other reason alleged against him than his having British arms about him, and in this we are told he has been encouraged by Colonel Hawkins, although long after a peace was declared, and all hostility ordered to cease.[251]

The chiefs concluded with a request that Colonel Nicolls "return our grateful thanks to our good Father and his chiefs." They thanked the colonel and his officers for "their brotherly conduct to us" and declared that they would consider as an enemy anyone who would try to sell any of their lands:

> ...[W]e do further declare, that whosoever shall endeavour directly or indirectly to separate us from him [i.e., King George], or his children, to be the enemy of us and our children, and that we will not trade or barter with any other than the British nation, if the above requests be complied with and we do promise to give grants of land

[250] *Ibid.*
[251] *Ibid.*

> to all such British men as our good Gather shall give
> permission to stay among us, and that we will do our best
> to protect and defend them in their laws and property: and
> we send as our representative, our brave brother Hidlis
> Hadgo (Francis) to our good Father, who is authorized to
> ratify this treaty.[252]

The 30 chiefs then made their marks on the document, while Nicolls, Ross, Roche, and Hambly signed it. The signers included Red Sticks, Lower Creeks, Seminoles, Miccosukees, Alachuas, and Yuchis. It marked the formalization of an alliance among the Native American groups that soon assimilated to become the Seminole and Miccosukee people. It is not a stretch to suggest that the Treaty of Nicolls' Outpost marked the formation of the Seminole Tribe of Florida and the Seminole Nation of Oklahoma as they are known today.

Lt. Col. Nicolls thought that he might remain behind as the British agent to the Creeks and Seminoles. While he was willing to accept the duty if ordered, he also recognized that the Apalachicola would be a lonely and dangerous place for him after the British troops withdrew:

> ...If I am left here after the forces are withdrawn, I hope
> you will be so good as to let me have one or two officers
> of my choice and some non commissioned officers & a
> few Privates, as it is a wild Country to travel through even
> in Peace – and I also request you will e so good as to let
> Captain Rawlins of the Borer remain with me if a vessel
> of war is to be left, - We also want two small Schooners
> that belonged to this place and are now with you [i.e.,
> Rear Admiral Percy Malcolm], and if you can spare us
> any other that does not draw more than 6 feet she will be
> of great service to us.

Nicolls and the other British officers had the future of their Native American allies in mind in late February and March 1815, but the Americans and Spanish were thinking of just one thing—slaves.

---

[252] *Ibid.*

William Hardridge, an emissary sent by Col. Hawkins to meet with Lt. Col. Nicolls at Prospect Bluff, reached the British Post on February 26, 1815. He was received courteously by Captain Ross of the Rifle Corps but told that Nicolls had gone to the Gulf of Mexico for meetings with the admirals. Hardridge's primary mission was to seek the return of slaves who had fled the Georgia frontier and joined the British military. Col. Hawkins had a personal interest in the mission, as some of the people that he kept in bondage were among the Maroons at the bluff. Ross informed Hardridge that Nicolls left no instructions about the Maroons and that no action was possible until he returned. Curiously, Col. Hawkins noted that some of the black recruits that Hardridge saw at the fort had "run away from the negroes and white people." The American reported that provisions were short at the bluff. He saw Creek and Seminole families living on alligators and heard that one woman had eaten her child. Capt. Ross asked him if the United States had withdrawn its troops from the Creek Nation. When Hardridge told him that soldiers remained at posts in the Creek country, Ross explained that the British alone were to protect the Creeks in the future.

The American representative remained at Prospect Bluff for three days, during which time he examined the fort there and saw around 500 Creeks and Seminoles inside the defenses. Whether this number included women and children is not known.

In Pensacola, Gov. Mateo Gonzales Manrique was being pressured by John Innerarity and others their lost slaves back from the Apalachicola River. The British had returned 70 of the Cuban troops, but scores of now liberated slaves from Pensacola remained on the river along with the rest of the Spanish soldiers. The residents of Pensacola didn't care much about the soldiers, but they wanted their slaves:

> ...[I]t is public and notorious that all our slaves were seduced with deceptions and carried off by force in such a way as may be supposed on account of the benefit that would result to Nicolls by the formation of his Colonial

Regiment, by which he would obtain the confirmation of his Colonelcy, and it is known that even the Indians have suffered equal oppressions from Captn. Woodbine and his other Agents, who despoiled them of their slaves, whom they keep in the Fort they have built on the River Appalachicola.

Similar sentiments raged in St. Augustine. Capt. Woodbine had gone there to secure additional recruits and communicate with Admiral Cockburn in the last days of 1814. He encouraged slaves to leave farms and plantations surrounding the old city and obtain their freedom by enlisting in the Colonial Marines. Many did so. Gov. Sebastian Kindelan of East Florida ordered Woodbine out of the province, but the captain caused significant losses in human flesh to the citizens there. Gov. Kindelan appealed to his counterpart in Pensacola for help and Manrique forwarded his dispatch to Capt. R.C. Spencer of the Royal Navy:

> ...[U]pon his return he took away a number of Slaves & horses belonging to different inhabitants and planters of this Province, entrusted to my care, and consider it my duty to claim them for their account and also of the Chua [i.e., Alachua] Indians protected by this Government which the said English Officer had also taken away and encorporated with his detachment. I conceive it incumbent on me to use every exertion in furthering their views and supposing you to have more immediate intercourse with the British Commanders I request you to represent to them in the name of the Spanish Government to that effect.

Manrique also appealed to the British commanders in the Gulf, explaining the case of Spain's government and citizens and seeking help in securing the return of the former slaves from Prospect Bluff. Most of the Maroon men, however, were now members of the British military and had been promised their freedom. Only free men could serve in the armed forces of Great Britain and Col. Nicolls had no intention of returning them to slavery

Human property was the main reason that Spain's surveyor general for West Florida was sent to Havana from Pensacola at the end of February. Capt. Vicente Sebastian Pintado met with Admiral Cochrane there on February 28, 1815, explaining that he had come to "witness the delivery of the salves and effects belonging to the citizens of this Plaza of Pensacola."[253]

Cochrane authorized Pintado to travel to the Apalachicola aboard the British warship HMS *Brazen*, which he boarded the next morning. The ship arrived off Apalachicola Bay on March 6 but did not find Capt. H.C. Spencer, who he was to meet. HMS *Borer* anchored inside the bay, somehow having made it over the bar between St. George and St. Vincent Islands. The *Brazen* continued to Pensacola, where Pintado found Spencer's ship, HMS *Carron*, near the Barrancas. A pilot boat carried the Spanish officer ashore, and he soon arranged a meeting with Capt. Spencer, who agreed to take him to Apalachicola. Dr. Don Eugenio Sierra of Pensacola went along. Pintado noted that the "Majordomo" or chief steward for John Forbes and Company, William McPherson, also came along.[254]

The Spanish captain and his companions finally reached Prospect Bluff after considerable delay:

> ...[O]n April 7 reached that settlement called Loma de Buena Vista or Prospect Bluff on the East of the Apalachicola River in a boat about ten miles from its mouth, where Colonel Nicolls newly arrived from Mobile Point was, and where he had his troops, Indians, and many

---

[253] Capt. Vicente Sebastian Pintado to Sr. Dn. Josef de Soto, April 29, 1815, MSS51045, Vicente Sebastian Pintado Papers, 1781-1842, Manuscript Division, Library of Congress, Washington, D.C.
[254] *Ibid.*

blacks emigrated or brought from the holdings of the Americans, and of the establishments of Indians, and including some of the residents of this Plaza because the greater part had been based on St. Vincent Island by order of Captain Spencer so we had a better chance to act without the presence of the other blacks with the caveat that even though there orders were to make delivery of the slaves (to force refusal) using only persuasion and making him see the horrible and miserable state in which he would stay after the departure of the English troops, declaring solemnly that by no reason should embark on English ships, and offering with our consent the pardon and forgiveness of his past, and manifesting the danger if they were to be caught by the Indians and delivered to their masters in hope of reward on the part of these.[255]

Pintado quickly discovered that the Maroons at Prospect Bluff had no interest whatsoever in returning to slavery in Pensacola. Although Lt. Col. Nicolls advised each one in the officer's presence to "return to their masters," the former slaves already knew that the British would take them "to the English colonies" where they could live as *hombres libre* or free men. The captain told those willing to meet with him that he was following orders to bring them back but would not use force. He warned instead that they would be in destitute condition once the British left:

> ...By these measures I persuaded about 28 to return, but these ones escaped disappearing from the post, and others returned to say that they did not want to come: so of 128 that were taken according to the list that Eugenio Sierra had, only 12 came, some voluntarily, and others by degrees of persuasion. The others are there with orders not to board them. They disarmed and discharged them from

---

[255] *Ibid.*

the service, several of them in my presence, and they were paid their money as soldiers; but having been told that in the licenses that are given to them there is no mention of their color or state slavery, I observed to the Colonel, that each of these licenses was a charter of freedom, because only free men were admitted in the armed service and that they would qualify as such where they went with this document.[256]

Nicolls assured Pintado that either "his government or failing that the philanthropic society would satisfy the worthy masters the price of their slaves who did not want to return to the service of their masters."[257]

Pintado continued his report by observing that hundreds of Maroons remained at Prospect Bluff, many of them armed:

The number of slaves including ours and emigrants or brought from American or Indian settlements that remain there, could reach 250. Of the rest they will embark some fifty or more. The rest, less those of Panzacola, the Colonel told me were armed and those from here seek weapons with much ease, and according to him, have formed a project to go settle in Tampa Bay. This number increased without doubt every day and will be a meeting point of those who left their masters.[258]

A representative from East Florida arrived while Pintado was at the bluff, claiming six of the Maroons there as property and requesting 400 pesos for each. Nicolls indicated that he would support the request for payment. He directed Pintado to Capt. Woodbine regarding others present from St. Augustine and vicinity:

---

[256] *Ibid.*
[257] *Ibid.*
[258] *Ibid.*

...[H]e told me that he had 78 blacks of East Florida, but that these were blacks that were among the Indians for several years and none directly from St. Augustine: He was actually in that plaza escorted by forty and so many of them offered to perform service: that while there several citizens came claiming some of them, and he told them he would not contest them in any way but he could not use force as he had none; also the same Captain Woodbine expected another number of negroes from the border that would join those in Apalachicola and form there a settlement that would consist of as many as 300 families.[259]

Capt. Pintado was a surveyor and military engineer by profession, not a slave catcher. Having done what he could to convince the Spanish Maroons to return to slavery, he ended his efforts and focused his observations instead on the impressive fortifications that the British had built at the bluff:

On my arrival at the Loma de Buena Vista or Prospect Bluff the officers and troops were prepared for the evacuation; and in fifteen days of this date it was totally complete. My first step was to inform myself on the state of the fortifications artillery and other things, and what was intended when they entirely evacuated the post, for which I directed to Colonel Nicolls and asked what he sought to do with the artillery and ammunition that were there and with the works of the fortification that he had made in a territory, although equally owned by the Indians it was undeniably the lawful claim of the sovereignty of H.C.M. as part of West Florida, and by consequence of his domain, and that even the part in which was found the

---

[259] *Ibid.*

works was the particularly property ceded by the Indians with legitimate titles, sanctioned by the Government of this Province, making him aware at the same time the danger that would result if the post was left in the state that it is as it would be a meeting point for all the wicked and a second Barataria which would increase, assisted by the number of blacks there, the unquietness not only of the rest of the province, but also the Gulf of Mexico with raids and piracy.[260]

The officer's fear that the Fort at Prospect Bluff would become a "second Barataria" is interesting. The bluff was the location selected for a pirate base by William Augustus Bowles in 1800. The adventurer had succeeded in building warehouses, barracks, and was constructing a fort when Spanish troops struck and destroyed the complex. Pintado saw—as had Bowles before him—that the Apalachicola River was an ideal base for piratical cruises on the Gulf of Mexico. The twisting channels of its estuary made it possible for small sloops and schooners to elude pursuit, while cannon mounted at Prospect Bluff could control the river for several miles.

Nicolls replied first concerning the redoubt near the confluence of the Flint and Chattahoochee Rivers, telling Pintado that only a few men remained there, and he would have it destroyed if the Spanish officer so desired. He mentioned, however, that he would tell his Native American allies that Spain had requested its demolition.[261]

After considering the matter for a time, though, Nicolls changed his mind and told Pintado that he would leave both forts intact:

> ...[H]e said to me that both this and the other he would leave in the state that they were: that he would leave the artillery that was not of bronze as it had been requested by the Indians, and so had orders and working instructions to give also many weapons, artillery, equipment &c. They

---

[260] *Ibid.*
[261] *Ibid.*

ask for the same equally for the defense and protection of the post that they were charged with until the English Government with our consent decided on the questions that had been made by the natives including free navigation and trade for the river: that in the interim no foreigners would be admitted there, not even to the same Spaniards, and only to the English: they promised however not to commit the least hostility against the Spanish or Americans unless they have express orders of the English Government. This, though very badly satisfied and inclined to enmity with the Spanish Government. I asked him if he would be good enough to answer me by writing and to explain all these points the same way I had asked him: He replied that he could not nor should he account to anyone of the mode of operations in which he was engaged by superior order.[262]

Capt. Pintado noted that despite Nicolls' firmness about his orders, "the said colonel treated me personally with all the attention, urbanity and professionalism that one could wish." Nicolls and Capt. Spencer invited the Spanish officer to observe an impromptu council with some of the British-allied chiefs:

...[Nicolls] told me that the Indians had asked if I was to stay there and if I came with intentions of taking possession of the place to keep when the English evacuated it, in which case he warned me to retire as soon as possible. This is what happened: I did not perceive any hate against me, to the contrary all the war chiefs that I knew or I did not know, by the mere act of carrying the Spanish uniform and rosette, gave me their hand and

---

[262] *Ibid.*

spoke in their languages that I did not understand with gentle faces and demonstrations of friendship.[263]

The chiefs asked the British to provide them with two 12-pounder cannon and the necessary ammunition and implements. Nicolls and Spencer agreed, but instead of two 12-pounders, they had four 24-pounders taken from the frigate HMS *Cydnus* and sent to Prospect Bluff. Pintado witnessed the movement of these guns and further reported that the British supplied them with "400 shot, balls, barrels of gunpowder and shells." It took three boats to move all of the ammunition up to the bluff, and the Spanish officer estimated that the total amount of powder alone came to 800 *arrobas* (7,500 pounds). The cannons also were carried up to the fort in small boats or barges as the *Cydnud* was much too large to cross the bar into Apalachicola Bay. Pintado went on to describe the fortifications he saw at Prospect Bluff:

> In the establishment there were four cannons of six on sea carriages and a number of balls for iron cannons no doubt for the service of the Indians, as claimed the Colonel; but these are mounted on the side of the post facing the open ground outside the fortifications. These consist of a redan of wood and mud on the bank of the river and wharf of the post, with an embrasure on each side situated to be able to fire up and down the river. About sixty yards in there is an octagon of logs of wood packed with solid earth with care, which has exterior sides of about 50 feet; but this was not finished, only the rampart, for the merlons and the esplanade were underway when the news of peace was received. They had a shallow ditch. The Octagon and houses of the establishment, which in the greater part consist of a considerable number of cabins, is encircled by a stockade

---

[263] *Ibid.*

of not much strength, leaving open the part along the river; and thirty or forty yards from the stockade to the part of the camp to the countryside is all surrounded with a shallow ditch and earthen parapet, of little depth the one and the other of little height, in the manner of a field entrenchment.[264]

The only boats that Pintado saw for the use of the fort were a few flatboats and *piraguas*. He noted that "many gifts" were distributed to the Native Americans and the British were leaving "considerable spares for the next year to the charge and care of a man named William Hambly, who is or was an officer among them who remains there I have understood enjoying half his pay."[265]

The Spanish captain was back in Pensacola by the end of April 1815. He reported that the British were starting to evacuate Prospect Bluff and that he saw ships and transports anchored offshore, ready to carry out the effort.

---

[264] *Ibid.*
[265] *Ibid.*

12

THE EVACUATION

THE BRITISH EVACUATION OF PROSPECT BLUFF was long and slow. Just as the process of moving supplies and armament upriver to the fort had been tedious and difficult, so too was the effort to move soldiers and their families downstream to the bay in small boats. St. Vincent Island once again served as a way station. People were brought down in boats, sloops, and barges and put ashore on the island. From there, they moved out to the ships in launches and longboats. It took days to move each boatload, and there was always the risk of a sudden squall or accident. Plus, the weather was growing hot. May is a summer month for all practical purposes in Florida. The warmer the temperatures, the more miserable conditions became for the families waiting for transportation on St. Vincent Island.

The Native Americans, of course, stayed behind in Florida and adjoining areas that, until the imposition of the Treaty of Fort Jackson, were part of the Creek Nation. The Miccosukees and Seminoles slowly returned to their towns, carrying supplies of arms and ammunition with them. Nicolls promised to leave additional powder, lead, muskets, and other material for their use in the magazines of the fort. The future of the Red Sticks was more uncertain. Holms and his people remained near the "Big Spring" of the Choctawhatchee (today's Washington Blue Spring) in Northwest Florida, far-removed from white settlements. The Prophet Francis was going to England with Lt. Col. Nicolls to press the case of the Red Sticks and Seminoles for recognition and assistance. His followers planned to relocate west to the Wakulla River, where they could receive minimal supply and support from the Spanish garrison at San Marcos de Apalache. Peter McQueen planned to relocate near Miccosukee with the Tallassee, Atasi, and others. The large fields would at least provide minimal provisions, and they would also be close to the Spanish post. Neamathla and the Fowltown people resettled on the former site of Perryman's town after Hawkins withdrew his force back up the Chattahoochee. Thomas Perryman moved his town across the river to the proximity of Telmochesses, the village of his son William. Groups of Yuchi and others settled in the same vicinity. The Alabama King and others remained near Pensacola.

Prominent residents of Pensacola realized that they needed to act fast if they hoped to obtain the return of slaves who had left them for service in the British Colonial Marines. A group of these individuals petitioned Gov. Mateo Gonzales Manrique for his assistance in early March:

> The undersigned Inhabitants of this Town with all due respect represent to your Excellency, that since the month of August last, when the English forces that were in Appalachicola under the command of Colonel Edward Nicolls, and Capt. Woodbine, were admitted into the Town, and lodged in the only Fort that protected the place, they began to experience many oppressions and vexations on the part of the said Colonel, and the different parties of Indians whom he recruited here into his Service; he not only arresting by his own authority and causing to be arrested sundry Inhabitants, but also depriving them of their property, and the means of procuring their necessary Subsistence, such as, their Slaves, horses, and small vessels, violating what he had decidedly offered in his Proclamation of the 26th of said month, which he published with a solemnity in this place, at the head of the Troops that he brought under his Command and of the Indians of his Party and in that of the 29th of same month, addressed to the Louisianians, in which he enlarged his

offers: In this the said Colonel offered to the Inhabitants of the United States of America to whom he addressed himself, protection and Security of their property, persons and slaves, if they united with him, or remained neutral in the invasion that he projected against the province of Louisiana, exciting even those of the State of Kentucky, with other matters; but what was our Surprise at seeing on his return from the attack that he unsuccessfully made with his troops and four vessels of war of H.B. Majesty on the American Fort at the Point of Mobille, that the Troops and Indians who came by land, should have plundered in violation of the said proclamation, sundry peaceable inhabitants, stripping them of their property and even of their clothing, destroying their harvests already collected, carrying off their slaves and horses, without their being able to obtain their restitution, although repeatedly reclaimed.[266]

The document marked a dramatic turning point in the history of the Fort at Prospect Bluff. The thousands of Red Stick refugees who fled into Florida after the Battle of Horseshoe Bend were the primary focus of the British, Spanish, and Americans from March 1814 through February 1815. The end of the War of 1812, however, changed the focus to the colony of Maroons or escaped slaves that Nicolls had assembled on the Apalachicola.

Edward Nicolls was one of the first successful abolitionists to set foot in North America. He liberated well over 1,000 men, women, and children from slavery by offering men of color the chance to enlist in the British military. The laws of Great Britain held that the country's soil was free. Its ships and foreign military posts were likewise considered free soil. By simply walking through the gates at Prospect Bluff, the outpost near the confluence, or San Miguel at Pensacola, male Spanish slaves or Maroons from the United States could enlist in the Colonial Marines and become permanently free. Their families became free simply by coming with them.

---

[266] Citizens of Pensacola to Gov. Mateo Gonzales Manrique, March 1815, Cochrane Papers.

Historians often represent the families gathered at Prospect Bluff as being escaped slaves from the United States, but the majority were from Spanish Florida. And their "owners" believed unquestioningly in their right to possess other human beings. In their eyes, Nicolls was an outrageous outlaw for setting free the people that they claimed as their own:

> The said Colonel following up his destroying system and idea of devastation to our prejudice, placing us on a parallel with his Enemies and treating us with yet great acrimony, during his stay in this place, made recruits of our slaves, causing them to be carried off by means of his Crimps or Recruiters to Fort St. Michael which was garrisoned by his Troops, some by deceitful offers that he never fulfilled, others by art and force, clothing them with a kind of uniform and red caps, obliging them to work day and night before our eyes, treating with contempt and outrage our just reclamations, in the most impertinent manner, and with the most insulting expressions, and when he disposed his retreat in the Month of November last, on account of the approach to this place of the Army of the United States of American commanded by Major General Jackson he took advantage of the hurry and confusion caused by this sudden surprise to complete his work, carrying off even to Negro Women and their infant children, as is public & notorious augmenting in such manner our losses & aggravating to the highest degree our ruin by the loss of at least two-thirds of our slaves, and all the small craft that we had for the traffic of the Bay and Rivers that disembogue into it, even the Government Barge, of which notable deeds, the annals of History furnish few parallels.[267]

---

[267] *Ibid.*

The Spanish governor forwarded the petition of his citizens to the commanders of the British fleet in the Gulf, making clear to them that he stood on the side of the slaveholders in his city:

> It is one of the most sacred duties of Spanish Governors to defend, shelter, and protect the lives and properties of the Inhabitants of the Countries confided to their care, and in discharge of this duty, I consider myself so much the more obliged to accede to the Supplications of those who have signed the memorial, as although their respectful petition had not existed, I could not have omitted, or have done otherwise than express myself to your Excellencies, in order to engage you to comply with the demand of the persons injured and to persist in my endeavours until the end was obtained in case my Exclamations should not be attended to on the part of your Excellencies.[268]

Gonzales went on to pen a litany of complaints against Nicolls. The relationship between the two men soured in October and November of the previous year when the governor dithered as Jackson's troops approached the city, leaving the British lieutenant colonel unable to cobble together a suitable defense. The British officer had already voiced his opinions of the Spanish governor in a letter to Admiral Cochrane. Now it was the governor's turn:

> Your Excellencies must equally know that the conduct of the said Colonel in the degree that it was ungrateful for the good reception that he received in the Country was contrary to what he aught to have observed towards the Individuals of a friendly and even allied Nation which had distinguished him in Europe – that is to an enemy it is not permitted to do further injury than what may be necessary for obtaining the end for which War is

---

[268] Gov. Mateo Gonzales Manrique to the British Commanders, March 9, 1815, Cochrane Papers.

undertaken that which is done to a friend through the medium of Craft and perfidy, neither can nor ought to be excused, and in fine, that it being in Spanish Territory, where Colonel Nichols has perpetrated his excesses and injustice and it being to Spanish Territory whither he has carried off, and in which he keeps the property of which he has despoiled these inhabitants, aggravates the insult done to the Spanish Nation, and is an additional motive why the English Commanders without consulting other laws than those of Spoilation the same in all Nations should determine on the entire restoration of the property taken by force and fraud and on the endemnifaction of the losses consequent thereon.[269]

The task of trying to satisfy Spanish claims fell to Capt. Robert C. Spencer of HMS *Carron* and the British victualling agent Robert Gamble. They sailed from the mouth of Mobile Bay for "Pensacola and Appalachicola" on March 6, 1815, accompanied by HMS *Forward* and "a few of the small Schooners hired at Pensacola."[270]

In a compromise with the citizens of Pensacola—and primarily John Forbes and Company, the largest claimant—the British were willing to pay reasonable amounts for losses. They would not, however, return former slaves who did not wish to go. Mr. Gamble faced the double duty of trying to supply the Royal Navy ships for their return voyages to the Bahamas and Jamaica, while also working to settle the claims of the Spanish residents. He found that John Forbes and Company was the only trading firm in Pensacola and despite the company's British roots, it now took full advantage of the situation by charging the agent a 25% premium for accepting British money:

I have purchased here ninety six barrels of flour and one thousand nine hundred & eighteen pounds of Bacon, the Flour and 958 lbs. bacon have been put on board the

---

[269] *Ibid.*
[270] Rear Adm. Percy Malcom to Adm. Sir Alexander Cochrane, March 9, 1815, Cochrane Papers.

Forward for your disposal and which I recommend being first used; The remainder of the Bacon Captain Spencer has directed to be sent to the *Carron* as it is very uncertain if we shall get any [portable soup] to carry to Sea with us – and from the claims that have been put in I fear we shall be detained at Apalachicola much longer than we expected; As Captain Spencer writes you on this subject I shall not enter into it farther than to state that it will be very desirable to spare us all the Cash you can, as Bills on the British Government are at a discount of 25 p. Cent and at the present moment there is only one house in the place that will take them, and consequently set their own price.[271]

The *Carron* left Pensacola with the rented schooners and reached the Apalachicola in mid-March. Capt. Spencer's biographer wrote that Rear Admiral Malcolm had selected him "for the delecate service of settling all their claims and dismissing them from our service." The reference is to the black soldiers at Prospect Bluff. Each was paid for his services and give a certificate documenting the dates of his duty in the Colonial Marines. The Spanish Captain Pintado, who was present for part of this process, objected because these certificates were freedom papers, but the process continued. "This was completely arranged to the entire satisfaction of his Majesty's government," wrote the biographer, "not withstanding the prejudices and wild habits of the Indians, amongst whom Captain Spencer lived encamped at Prospect Bluff, far up the Apalachicola river, for upwards of a month."[272]

The Colonial Marines faced a critical choice as they received their discharges from the service. They could leave with the British, who

---

[271] Robert Gamble, Victualling Agent, to Rear Adm. Percy Malcom, March 11, 1815, Cochrane Papers.

[272] Lt. John Marshall, *Royal Navy Biography; Or, Memoirs of the Services of All the Flag-officers, Superannuated Rear-Admirals, Retired-Captains, Post-Captains, and Commanders, Whose Names appeared on the Admiralty List of Sea-Officers at the commencement of the year 1823, or who have since been promoted*, Supplement:--Part III, London, 1829: 260.

offered to resettle them in a place where they could live in peace and freedom, they could return to slavery in either Spanish Florida or the United States, or they could remain behind at the soon-to-be evacuated fort. Many had t their immediate families with them, but brothers and sisters, parents, and other relatives remained in slavery not far away in or near Pensacola, St. Augustine, or in the United States. The British officers warned them that remaining at the fort would be difficult, and they would have to fend for themselves. The only guarantee of living in peace as citizens of Great Britain meant moving far away from Florida.

It was a difficult choice, and as might be expected, only a handful decided to return to slavery. The majority chose to leave with the British, but a group of around 80-100 men and their families decided to stay behind and live at Prospect Bluff. More than 90 percent were from Spanish Florida and knew that Spencer and Gamble were compensating their former "owners." They believed they had nothing to fear from the Spanish and saw no reason why the United States would take an interest in them. Nicolls did his best to leave them ready to defend themselves. A deserter who slipped away from his Royal Marine forces in early April 1815 gave U.S. Maj. Gen. Edmund P. Gaines an idea of the strength of the fort:

> Samuel Jervais, being duly sworn, states: That he has been a sergeant of marines in the British service for thirteen years past; that about a month ago he left Appalachicola, where he had been stationed for several months; that the English colonel (Nicholls) had promised the hostile Indians at that place a supply of arms and ammunition, a large quantity of which had been delivered to them a few days before his departure, and after the news of a peace between England and the United States being confirmed had reached Appalachicola; that, among the articles delivered, were, of cannon, four 12 pounders, one howitzer, and two cohorns; about three thousand stands of small arms, and near three thousand barrels of powder and ball; that the British left with the Indians between three and four hundred negroes, taken from the United States, principally from Louisiana; that the arms

and ammunition were for the use of the Indians and negroes, for the purposes, as it was understood, of war with the United States; that the Indians were assured by the British commander that, according to the treaty of Ghent, all the lands ceded by the Creeks, in treaty with General Jackson, were to be restored; otherwise, the Indians must fight for those lands, and that the British would in a short time assist them.[273]

The deserter was Samuel Jervais, a sergeant from Nicolls' command. His information was more or less correct, but he left before the British significantly increased the firepower of the fort. Instead of the four 24-pounders mentioned in the deposition, they decided instead to mount four 24-pounders in the water battery. Two aimed upriver and two down. They could reduce any vessel that came within one mile to matchwood. Four additional guns, all 6-pounders, were mounted on the eastern walls of the main citadel. These could control the land approaches to the post. The final armament also included five other pieces, among them the howitzer mentioned by Jervais.

To provide better protection for the houses or *cabanas* where those who were remaining behind lived, the British officers supervised the preparation of an outer entrenchment that surrounded the entire complex. It was still under construction when Pintado saw it in April 1815. Rectangular in design with full bastions on its eastern corners and half bastions on its western or river ends, this work he described as "a shallow ditch and earthen parapet, of little depth the one and the other of little height, in the manner of a field entrenchment." The captain's description might technically be true, but this entrenchment is the best-preserved part of the fort today.[274]

Nicolls planned eventually to retrieve the 300-350 men, women, and children that he was leaving behind. For the time being, however, there was not enough room in the ships for everyone to go.

---

[273] Deposition of Samuel Jervais, May 9, 1815, *American State Papers, Foreign Relations*, Volume 4: 551.

[274] Capt. Vicente Sebastian Pintado to Sr. Don Josef de Soto, April 29, 1815, Pintado Papers, Manuscript Division, Library of Congress.

As the British continued their preparations to leave Florida, they assured the Native Americans that Article Nine of the Treaty of Ghent required the United States to return lands seized during the war. Great Britain believed that this included the 22 million acres taken from the Muscogee (Creek) people by the Treaty of Fort Jackson. The United States disagreed. The article in question is simple:

ARTICLE THE NINTH.
The United States of America engage to put an end immediately after the Ratification of the present Treaty to hostilities with all the Tribes or Nations of Indians with whom they may be at war at the time of such Ratification, and forthwith to restore to such Tribes or Nations respectively all the possessions, rights, and privileges which they may have enjoyed or been entitled to in one thousand eight hundred and eleven previous to such hostilities. Provided always that such Tribes or Nations shall agree to desist from all hostilities against the United States of America, their Citizens, and Subjects upon the Ratification of the present Treaty being notified to such Tribes or Nations, and shall so desist accordingly. And His Britannic Majesty engages on his part to put an end immediately after the Ratification of the present Treaty to hostilities with all the Tribes or Nations of Indians with whom He may be at war at the time of such Ratification, and forthwith to restore to such Tribes or Nations respectively all the possessions, rights, and privileges, which they may have enjoyed or been entitled to in one thousand eight hundred and eleven previous to such hostilities. Provided always that such Tribes or Nations shall agree to desist from all hostilities against His Britannic Majesty and His Subjects upon the Ratification

of the present Treaty being notified to such Tribes or Nations, and shall so desist accordingly.[275]

Great Britain believed, with a degree of logic, that the Red Sticks were still at war with the United States when the signing of the Treaty of Ghent took place on December 24, 1814. The Prophet Francis, Peter McQueen, Homathlemico, the Atasi King, the Alabama King, Holms, and Red Stick leaders were in Florida and still in arms with thousands of warriors behind them. None of these participated in the signing of the Treaty of Fort Jackson, which was attended almost exclusively by chiefs allied with the United States.

The question was whether the Creek War of 1813-1814 ended with the Treaty of Fort Jackson or whether it continued until after the signing ceremony at Ghent, Belgium. The United States maintained that the Fort Jackson treaty ended the war and that the War of 1812 was a separate conflict. U.S. troops, however, continued to pursue and fight Red Stick forces as late as Christmas Day 1814—the day after the Ghent signing— when Maj. Uriah Blue's forces attacked Holms' town on the Choctawhatchee River in Northwest Florida.

The Red Sticks and Seminoles made their position clear in a letter to Admiral Cochrane on April 2, 1815:

> We, the undersigned, chiefs of the Muscogee nation, declared by his Brittanic majesty to be a free and independent people, do in the name of said nation agree to the 9th article of the treaty of peace between his Brittanic majesty and the United States – and we do further declare, that we have given most strict and positive orders to all our people, that they desist from hostilities of every kind against the citizens or subjects of the United States.
>
> Given under our hands at the British fort, on the Appalachicola, this 2nd of April 1815.
>
> HEPOOETH MICCO X

---

[275] Treaty of Peace and Amity between His Britannic Majesty and the United States of America, December 24, 1814, Library of Congress.

CAPPACHI MICCO X
HOPOY MICCO, T.P. [Thomas Perryman][276]

Military officers and civilian authorities in the United States, however, gave no regard to such declarations. Their position that the War of 1812 and Creek War were separate events was firm, and they had no plan of returning 22 million acres to the Muscogee. American settlers were already viewing the new lands with hungry eyes:

> We are informed by an intelligent gentleman who accompanied Col. Hawkins on his late expedition down the Chatahouchie, that the quantity of fertile land included in the cession of territory made by the Creek Indians to the United States, and falling within the ultimate limits of this State, is much greater than had been supposed. He represents the land bordering on the Chatahouchie and on many of the creeks which empty into it, to be of very superior quality, and affording settlements the most desirable he has seen in the southern states. He speaks also in high terms of the beauty of the Chatahoochie river and of its fitness for navigation.[277]

On the same date that the above account appeared in *The Georgia Journal*, the first British troops left Apalachicola Bay. HMS *Herald*, an 18-gun sloop-of-war, weighed anchor off St. George Island and sailed for Jamaica on April 5, 1815. Onboard were Capt. Joseph Roche's company from the 1st West India Regiment as well as a drummer and three lieutenants from the Royal Marines. Roche and his men had been on the Apalachicola River since shortly after the Battle of New Orleans, and he was a witness to the treaty signing at Nicolls' Outpost on March 10, 1815.[278]

---

[276]Hepooeth Micco, Cappachi Micco, and Hopoy Micco to Adm. Sir. Alexander Cochrane, April 2, 1815, published in the *Western Citizen*, July 8, 1815.
[277] *The Georgia Journal*, April 5, 1815.
[278] Ship muster for HMS *Herald*, ADM 37/4660, National Archives of Great Britain.

Another company-sized departure came ten days later on April 15 when HMS *Seahorse* sailed for England. She carried 64 soldiers from the garrison.[279]

The next group to leave was a big one and included not just men, but women and children too. Nicolls ordered two lieutenants, a sergeant, and a private from the Royal Marines to board HMS *Borer* for transport back to England on April 21, 1815. On the same day, he ordered aboard the same ship a large "party of black people for passage to Bermuda." This was the first group of families to leave for freedom in British territory. Upon reaching Bermuda, they were transferred to HMS *Goree* and carried to Halifax, Nova Scotia. Some remained there permanently, adjusting to the rigors of the new climate, but others soon relocated to Trinidad.[280]

Two ships—HMS *Carron* and HMS *Cydnus*—left the next day. *Carron* carried a large group of Maroon refugees supervised by Lt. Robert C. Ambrister. After a brief stop in the Bahamas for Ambrister to disembark, they were put ashore at Bermuda on May 22. *Cydnus*, meanwhile, sailed with 81 of Nicolls' Colonial Marines aboard. The four 24-pounders left at Prospect Bluff came from this vessel. She reached Bermuda on June 13, and the men went ashore to join their families. They remained in service there as a supernumerary battalion until 1816.[281]

In Georgia, meanwhile, William Hardridge's long-awaited report of his visit to the fort finally reached Col. Benjamin Hawkins at Fort Hawkins. This dispatch is included in its entirety here because Hardridge was the only U.S. official to visit the post during its British occupation:

> I arrived at prospect bluff at Forbes's store the 26.
> Feby. and delivered the dispatch to Capt. Ross
> commanding his B.M. troops at that garrison. Capt. Ross
> informed me that Col. Nicolls had left that about six days

---

[279] Ship muster for HMS *Seahorse*, ADM 37/5439, National Archives of Great Britain.

[280] Ship muster for HMS *Borer,* ADM 37/4633, National Archives of Great Britain.

[281] Ship muster for HMS *Carron* and HMS *Cydnus*, National Archives of Great Britain.

before his arrival there and gone to sea to see the admirals and they could not say what time he would return. I waited three days. Capt. Ross said he knew nothing about the negroes run away from the Negros and white people and could not do any thing on it, until the arrival of Col. Nicolls. It is uncertain when they would leave there they had as yet rec. no orders to embark. I left there on the 30th. I was in the British fort and saw all their works and saw many of the runaway negroes. The Indians are all inside the fort and issued rations the same as soldiers both Indians by report 500. As much as I have learned the British are determined to keep the Negros. They have joined them as soldiers and they have given them their freedom. Provisions is very scarce and the Indians in the Country are living altogether on Alligators. I have heard for a certainty an Indian woman eat her own child. Capt. Ross said the Indians who did mischief killed a man and stole horses between Forts Perry and Lawrence was small parties from Fowltown and gone out four days before peace. The British have given positive orders not to trouble any other man or do any more mischief to go home to their fields and go to planting.

Capt. Ross enquired of me positively if the U.S. soldiers had yet left the Creek Nation. I told him no. He then answered they were obliged to leave the nation. The U.S. was not to keep any garrison in the nation. His B.M. was to protect the Indians in the future.[282]

The statement that Capt. Ross knew nothing about the Maroons who had run away from "the Negros and white people" is curious. It appears to imply that some of the escaped slaves who made their way to Prospect Bluff had fled black owners. Ironically, even as he worked to help Lt. Col. Nicolls assure the freedom of slaves in Florida, Capt. George Woodbine

---

[282] William Hardridge to Col. Benjamin Hawkins, included in Hawkins to Gov. Peter Early, April 24, 1815, Telamon Cuyler Collection, Hargrett Rare Book and Manuscript Library, the University of Georgia Libraries.

of the British forces became a wanted man in Great Britain for his role in the slave trade before he joined the war effort:

AFRICAN INSTITUTION – SLAVE TRADE, PERJURY, OUT-LAWRY. ONE HUNDRED GUINEAS REWARD.

Whereas, at the Assizes, and General Session of Oyer and Terminer, holden at the Castle of Exeter, in and for the country of Devon, on Saturday, the 18th July, 1812, a Bill of Indictment for PERJURY, committed in a certain proceeding, instituted in the High Court of Admiralty, touching the employment of a certain ship or vessel, called the GALLICIA, in the Slave Trade, was at the instance of the Directors of the Africa Institution, preferred, and found against George Woodbine, otherwise called JORGE MADRESILVA, who acted as Super Cargo on board the said ship or vessel at the time of her capture, by His Majesty's ship Amelia, off the coast of Africa, in the year 1811; and the said George Woodbine, otherwise Jorge Madresilva, not having appeared to the same Indictment, he hath since been Out-lawed by due course of law. Notice is therefore, hereby given, that whoever shall apprehend the said George Woodbine, otherwise called Jorge Madresilva, and cause him to be lodged in the Castle of Exeter, or any other of His Majesty's Gaols in England, shall receive a REWARD of ONE HUNDRED GUINEAS from the Directors of the said Institution.[283]

Woodbine never faced justice in London. He was not a career officer like Nicolls, nor was he an abolitionist. A Jamaican merchant and trader, he later attempted to wrest control of Florida from Spain, but his plans fell apart.

---

[283] *London Times*, April 25, 1815.

HMS *Aetna*, a 386-ton bomb vessel, was the next British vessel to leave the waters off Apalachicola Bay. The term "bomb vessel" refers to the fact that the *Aetna* carried two large mortars in addition to more standard armament. These lobbed explosive shells or "bombs" high into the air over enemy targets. She was one of the Royal Navy ships that bombarded Fort McHenry on September 13-14, 1814. Her shells were among the "bombs bursting in air" that inspired Francis Scott Key to write America's National Anthem. She weighed anchor off St. Vincent Island on April 25 and set sail with a large party of refugees aboard.[284]

Most of the British soldiers had left Prospect Bluff, but Nicolls continued to linger with a small force to oversee the landing of additional supplies and arms for the former Colonial Marines who were staying behind. The British Native American allies would also benefit from this arsenal. Writing from the fort on April 28, he addressed Col. Hawkins in response to a letter from the American agent left behind by William Hardridge the previous month. As was becoming an obsession for U.S. officials, Hawkins had been most concerned about seeing the black British troops return to slavery. Nicolls made clear that would not happen:

> ...On the subject of the negroes lately owned by citizens of the United States or Indians in hostility to the British forces, I have to acquaint you, that according to orders, I have sent them to the British colonies, where they are received as free settlers, and lands given to them. The newspaper you sent me is, I rather think, incorrect; at all events an American newspaper cannot be authority for a British officer. I herewith enclose you a copy of a part of the 9th article of the treaty of peace relative to the Indians in alliance with us, they have signed and accepted it as an independent people, solemnly protesting to suspend all hostilities against the inhabitants of the United States.[285]

---

[284] Master's Log for HMS *Aetna*, ADM 52/4404, National Archives of Great Britain.
[285] Lt. Col. Edward Nicolls to Col. Benjamin Hawkins, April 28, 1815, *Western Citizen*, July 8, 1815.

The British officer complained of a recent attack by a "party of American horse" on Boleck's (or Bowleg's) town on the Suwannee. These men, he reported, had killed one of the Seminoles and wounded another. They stole cattle plundered a party of Seminoles that was on its way back from a peaceful visit to St. Augustine. Nicolls asked Hawkins to investigate and promised to do the same if any of the Creeks should cause trouble in the American settlements. He then got down to the business of the British interpretation of the Ninth Article of the Treaty of Ghent:

> The chiefs here have requested me further to declare to you (that in order to prevent any disagreeable circumstance from happening in the future) they have come to a determination not to permit the least intercourse between their people and those of the United States. They have in consequence ordered them to cease all communication directly or indirectly with the territory or citizens of the United States – and they do take this public mode of warning the citizens of the United States, from entering their territory or communicating directly or indirectly with the Creek people. They also request that you will understand their territories to be as they stood in the year 1811.[286]

The year 1811 was important because the Ninth Article specified that white and Native American land ownership be restored to its status as of that year. Nicolls was telling Hawkins not only that Americans should desist from all communications with the Muscogee, but that they should do so on all lands owned by the Creeks in 1811—including those taken by the United States at Fort Jackson.

The Royal Marine followed with another letter on May 12, demonstrating to Hawkins the seriousness of the British-allied chiefs in keeping their promise to punish any chiefs or warriors who committed acts of violence against American settlers:

---

[286] *Ibid.*

In my letter to you on the 28th ult. I requested you would be so good as to make enquiry into the murder and robberies committed on the Seminoles belonging to the Chief called Bow-Legs, at the same time declaring to you my determination of punishing with utmost rigor of the law any one of our side who broke it. Of this a melancholy proof has been given in the execution of an Indian of the Atophalga town [*i.e.,* Attapulgus] by Hothly Poya Tustunnuggee, Chief of the Ocmulgees, who found him driving off a gang of cattle belonging to your citizens, and for which act of justice I have given him double presents and a Chief's gun, in the open square before the whole of the Chiefs, and highly extolled him. These, sir, are the steps I am daily taking to keep the peace with sincerity.[287]

Nicolls accused the American agent of failing to act with similar sincerity. Another group of men from the United States had attacked Boleck and murdered two more of his people. When he inquired as to what proof they had of U.S. settlers being responsible for the outrage, the Seminoles told him the bloody clothing of the slain men was found in the camp of the perpetrators. Nicolls told Hawkins that he had convinced the Seminoles to remain on the defensive but to put to death anyone else who attacked them. He also emphasized that the situation on the frontier had changed and a much more formidable adversary now faced the Americans:

…They have given their consent to await your answer before they take revenge; but sir, they are impatient for it, & well armed as the whole nation now is, and stored with ammunition and provisions, having a strong hold to retire upon in case of a superior force appearing. Picture to yourself sir, the miseries that may be suffered by good and innocent citizens on your frontiers, and I am sure you will

---

[287] Lt. Col. Edward Nicolls to Col. Benjamin Hawkins, May 12, 1815, *The Georgia Journal*, June 7, 1815.

lend me your best aid in keeping the bad spirits in subjection.[288]

Nicolls' letter indicates that he held a final a large council of chiefs at Prospect Bluff on May 11, 1815. The meeting was likely the last such conference between the British and the Native Americans of the Southeast. More than 200 years of diplomatic history was finally at an end.

Hawkins said as much when he replied to Nicolls on May 28:

> The treaties you have made for the Creek Nation, with the authority created by yourself for the purpose, must be a novelty. It would surprise me much to see your Sovereign ratify such as you have described them to be, with a people such as I know those to be, in the territories of his Catholic Majesty – I shall communicate what has passed on the subject between us to the officers of Spain in my neighborhood, that they may be apprised of what you are doing.[289]

The agent's letter was long and involved but ultimately useless. Unless he happened to see it later in an English newspaper, Lt. Col. Nicolls never read it. HMS *Forward* sent her boats up the river to Prospect Bluff with a final shipment of supplies on May 14. By the next day, Nicolls, the last of his men, the Prophet Josiah Francis, and his retinue were aboard. The little 12-gun brig "made signal to sail away," raised anchor, and left the waters off Apalachicola Bay on May 16, 1815.

The British campaign on the Gulf Coast was over.

---

[288] *Ibid.*

[289] Col. Benjamin Hawkins to Lt. Col. Edward Nicolls, May 28, 1814, *Georgia Journal*, June 7, 1815.

13

THE NEGRO FORT

THE BRITISH WITHDRAWAL FROM THE APALACHICOLA created a situation unlike any that had ever happened before in North America. An organized colony of free blacks lived independently under its governance a mere sixty miles from the southern border of the United States. Not even the inhabitants of the earlier and noteworthy Fort Mose on the outskirts of St. Augustine could have made such a claim. They lived a prosperous and free existence but were subject to the governance of Spain. The Maroons at Prospect Bluff, however, lived under their leadership and by their own devices. Many of them were well-educated, and all possessed valuable skills that prepared them to thrive in the isolated wilderness.

The United States Army was aware of British plans to leave the Fort at Prospect Bluff in the hands of a part of their former Colonial Marines almost from the point that Nicolls left the post. Maj. Gen. Edmund P. Gaines, a hero of the War of 1812, was at Fort Stoddert north of Mobile when he interviewed the British deserter Sergeant Jervais:

> I am unable to say how far the statement of Jervais is entitled to credit; but I have examined him attentively, and am under a strong impression that he has stated the truth, and that the supplies mentioned in his deposition are not mistaken for those delivered last fall, but have really been delivered since the ratification of the treaty had been officially announced to the British troops at

Appalachicola. These supplies were, however, brought to Appalachicola previous to the ratification of the treaty.[290]

Gaines also recognized—contrary to the position of Maj. Gen. Andrew Jackson and others—that the Red Stick Creeks were not defeated. He informed the acting-Secretary of War Alexander J. Dallas that he planned to travel from Fort Stoddert to Forts Montgomery and Claiborne as quickly as possible to learn more about the plans of the Native Americans. If they were determined to continue the fight, he would "assemble a force to meet them." U.S. forces were downsizing due to the end of the War of 1812, but the general thought he could assemble around 1,000 men from what remained of the 2nd, 9th, 24th, and 39th Regiments:

> With this force I shall be able to keep the Indians in check; and with another thousand, to consist of Choctaws and volunteers, I should feel sufficiently strong to make a decisive stroke upon the depots at Appalachicola, which, I persuade myself, the Government may be at liberty to sanction; for, until these depots (if they really exist) are destroyed, our frontier cannot but continue to be extremely insecure.[291]

Gaines ordered the commanding officers at the various posts still occupied along the frontier to keep their men ready for active service and placed requisitions to equip a small train of field artillery with fixed ammunition, tools, and camp equipage. Like other American officers, he blamed Spain for allowing the enemies of the United States to establish depots and operate from within the limits of Florida. That nation was bound by treaty, he noted, "to restrain, by force, all hostilities on the part of the Indian nations living within her boundary."[292]

---

[290] Maj. Gen. Edmund P. Gaines to Acting-Secretary of War A.J. Dallas, May 14, 1815, *American State Papers, Foreign Relations*, Volume 4: 551.
[291] *Ibid.*
[292] *Ibid.*

"If she does not restrain them," he continued, "we may conclude that she has endeavored to do so, but is unable. Can she blame us, then, for restraining them, ourselves?"[293]

Part of the problem as a difference in how the United States and Spain viewed the territorial rights of the Native Americans. The Americans, for example, technically believed that the Muscogee were independent but, in practice, felt that they lived within the limits of the United States and Spain. The Red Sticks and Seminoles in Florida, accordingly, were subject to the authority of the King of Spain. In the eyes of Spain, however, the Muscogee comprised an independent nation with territorial rights to their lands. Spain claimed only the coastal areas as far inland as the tidal influence and other specific lands obtained by the treaty. The rest belonged to the Native Americans. They could not dispose of it without the approval of the King, but otherwise, Spain pretended no authority over their territorial integrity.

For this reason, Spanish authorities did not consider the British forts on the Apalachicola to be violations of either their territory or neutrality. The presence of the redcoats there was between Great Britain and the Creeks. The United States held a different view.

A "gentleman of respectability" in Bermuda reinforced the opinions of U.S. authorities on May 21, 1815. He was a subject of King George III but opposed his country's policy of liberating and arming slaves. He learned from Capt. Rawlings of HMS *Borer* that Nicolls had raised a force of nearly 300 Maroons at Prospect Bluff and that Spencer and Pintado had failed in their efforts to convince them to return to slavery. Rawlings further told him that the British were giving them artillery, ammunition, and the intact fort:

> I have since learned that the Carron, which must have sailed from Appalachicola previous to the Borer, is arrived at Nassau, on her way to Bermuda, with 176 slaves of all ages. As she is daily expected, and as Captain Spencer is now on his way here, it might be as well to wait their arrival before you make any official communication

---

[293] *Ibid.*

to your Government on the subject. It is, however, obvious that, were you in possession of the whole facts, no time ought to be lost in recommending the adoption of speedy, energetic measures, for the destruction of a thing held so likely to become dangerous to the State of Georgia. The Spaniards are not in a situation to do it, but I dare say would co-operate. I have learned that the whole of the slaves brought from the United States have been sent to Nova Scotia, with the exception of a few that were lately shipped to the island of Trinidad, in His Majesty's ship the Levant, and such as have enlisted in the colonial marines were in these islands. A few stragglers have contrived to get on shore in the Bermudas, and, by the connivance of their colonized friends, to remain, very contrary to the wishes of the inhabitants, who are, in general, desirous of getting rid of them.[294]

In a postscript the writer added that the 176 "slaves" (actually now free people) aboard were "unquestionably" bound for Trinidad. These refugees from the Apalachicola constituted the first wave of more than 800 former British Colonial Marines who settled on the island in the years 1815-1816. The story of the "company villages" established by some of these families is well known. These communities formed according to the companies in which the men had served, but they post-date those founded by the Prospect Bluff Maroons (or "Bluff People"). The refugees aboard the *Carron* settled near Port au Spain on the west coast of Trinidad.[295]

Maj. Gen. Gaines learned more about the situation at Prospect Bluff on May 22 when new intelligence arrived from Mobile. A group of Maroons from Prospect Bluff voluntarily returned to slavery in the city:

---

[294] Memorandum of a gentleman of respectability at Bermuda, May 21, 1815, *American State Papers, Foreign Relations*, Volume 4: 552.
[295] John McNish Weiss, *The Merikens: Free Black American Settlers in Trinidad 1815-1816*, McNish & Weiss, London, 2008.

Some negro men belonging to Don McGill, of Mobile, taken some months ago to Appalachicola by the British, voluntarily returned a few days past. Their statement of the supplies and negroes left by the British corresponds with that contained in the deposition of Jervais, enclosed in the letter which I had the honor to address to you on the 14th instant. The negroes add that there are at Appalachicola nearly 800 Indian warriors, and that the negroes were permitted to remain with the Indians as freemen, or to return to their masters, as they should elect, and that but few had agreed to return.[296]

The general concluded his report to the acting secretary of war with additional intelligence from "a very intelligent negro man belonging to D. Kennedy, at Mobile." This individual reported that Nicolls was still on the Apalachicola with "900 Indians and 450 negroes under arms." The British had left Prospect Bluff one week before Gaines received this news, but with the slow communications of the day, he had no way of knowing.[297]

Nicolls and the Prophet Francis reached Amelia Island on Florida's Atlantic Coast during the first week of June 1815:

A letter from a gentleman in Fernandina to his correspondent in this city, dated June 10, states, "that the English brig of war *Forward*, of 14 guns, and a transport in company, put in there on Wednesday last for water and provisions; last from Matanzas, bound to Bermuda. Lieut. Col. Nichol and Capt. Woodbine, with an Indian Chief, were on board – also, about 50 ***** troops.[298]

The report from the uniquely named *Savannah Museum* newspaper used asterisk symbols "*****" instead of the word "negro," as was its

---

[296] Maj. Gen. Edmund P. Gaines to Acting-Secretary of War Alexander J. Dallas, May 22, 1815, *American State Papers, Foreign Relations*, Volume 4: 552.

[297] *Ibid.*

[298] *Savannah Museum*, June 15, 1815.

custom anytime it referred to black British troops. This prevented literate enslaved men in the city from realizing they could obtain freedom by taking up arms with Great Britain. The "Indian Chief" mentioned in the account, of course, was the Prophet Josiah Francis. Capt. Woodbine was already in the vicinity, and if he went aboard the *Forward*, it was to meet Nicolls there.

East Florida's new governor Juan Jose de Estrada was unaware of Nicolls' presence off Fernandina when he wrote to Gov. Peter Early of Georgia on June 15 reporting that the British officer was still at Prospect Bluff:

> Although my predecessor had given notice some time since to the Captain General I now repeat it, informing him that Col. Nicolls remains in the British Camp on the Appalachicola with the Indians that have been inimical to the United States, exercising over them an assumed superintendancy, as he shows by his letter to Col. Hawkins, Agent of the Creek Indians. – I am sure his excellency will take the most prompt and necessary measures to stop such conduct, and of the result you shall be duly advised.[299]

The Spanish governor was responding to a demand from Early that he act to suppress British acts against the Georgia frontier. The Americans by then, however, were consumed with rumors about Capt. Woodbine. One of the most prominent surfaced on June 17 that he "went through this city [*i.e.,* Savannah] last night in disguise, on his way to Washington" carrying dispatches from Lt. Col. Nicolls to the U.S. Government. There is no known documentary support for this claim.[300]

A report on the next day raised a more serious specter for the planters in Georgia and the Carolinas:

---

[299] Gov. Juan Jose de Estrada to Gov. Peter Early, June 15, 1815, *Georgia Journal*, July 19, 1815.
[300] *Savannah Republican*, June 17, 1815.

...[Woodbine] has left in West Florida three hundred ---- - well organized, with eight pieces of cannon. The source from which I have my information I pledge myself to you to be authentic – I am not warranted to mention names. In the name of our abused and insulted country, I call on you to use all means in your power to cause this scoundrel to be arrested and sent to his own country in irons – in this case I think that "vigor beyond the law" ought to be exercised. Our southern ----- property will not be worth holding, unless most energetic steps are taken to repress the insidious attempts of our inveterate enemies, the British.[301]

The *Savannah Republican* this time resorted to the use of blank spaces instead of the word "negro" to hide the race of the armed men on the Apalachicola and the type of "property" that the writer feared would not be worth holding. The continued existence of the Fort at Prospect Bluff and the decision of the British to leave it fully intact and armed in the hands of their former Colonial Marines was a growing concern across the Southern frontier. Some American officers even began to see a plot to seize the Floridas in the measure combined with Great Britain's slow evacuation of its coastal footholds:

A letter from an officer at Charleston, S.C. dated July 1, says: "There are at Amelia a transport & brig of war with black troops, Indians, and marines under Colonel Nichols from Apalachicola. They say they are only waiting for more men and money to take possession of the Floridas." If this be the case, strong precautionary measures on that frontier will be necessary on the part of the United States.[302]

---

[301] Gentleman on St. Simons Island to a Gentleman in Savannah, June 18, 1815, *Savannah Republican*, June 29, 1815.
[302] *New Jersey Journal*, July 18, 1815.

The main reason for the slow departure of British troops was a shortage of supplies and the time required for transports and other vessels to remove soldiers and families to other places before returning to pick up more. By early July, however, the first wave of Maroon settlers from Prospect Bluff was safely in Trinidad, and Admiral Sir Alexander Cochrane finally replied to Gov. Mateo Gonzales Manrique in Pensacola:

> I have the honor to acknowledge receipt of your Excellency's Letter of the 25 ult. And it is with Extreme regret I learn that the Slaves at Apalachicola have not gone back to their Masters. And I also feel sorry that it has not been in my power to bring back the Spanish Soldiers from that vicinity. The services upon which I have been engaged have not permitted of my detaching any vessel from my fleet to bring back these troops, but in a few days I will dedicate a sloop of war solely to that purpose. It is necessary in relation to the Negroes that I should be clearly understood by your Excy. as having no sort of control over any of those not actually taken by the British Marines, for such as thought proper to join the Indians, your Excellency must make application to their Chiefs. Situated as I am with so few white Troops at Appalachicola it would be attended with much hazard the making use of forcible measures which accordingly I must decline.[303]

The admiral's letter was written well before July 10, the date which appears on it, but it likely was withheld until all British troops were safely away from the Apalachicola and the Maroon families opting to evacuate were at Trinidad, Halifax, Bermuda, and elsewhere. The British by then had settled with all willing Pensacola residents for their economic losses.

---

[303] Adm. Sir. Alexander Cochrane to Gov. Mateo Gonzales Manrique, July 10, 1815, "Documents Relating to Colonel Edward Nicholls [sic.] and Captain George Woodbine in Pensacola, 1814 [sic.]," *Florida Historical Quarterly*, Volume 10, Number 1, July 1931: 52

John Forbes and Company, however, continued to fight for reimbursement for decades to come.

Lt. Col. Nicolls, now once again Brevet Maj. Edward Nicolls, enjoyed a rare return to his home in mid-August, bringing with him several surprise guests:

> PORTSMOUTH, August 14. – ...The *Forward*, Lieutenant Banks, arrived here on Saturday from Pensacola, last from Bermuda, in 42 days: left lying there the *Maidstone*, Captain Skipsey; *Araxes*, Captain Bligh; and *Rinaldo*, Captain Carter, from Jamaica, bound to Halifax. The *Forward* had two transports under her convoy, with part of the marine artillery on board, from Pensacola, which she was obliged to leave at Bermuda to be hove down; in consequence of their being so leaky. Major Nicholls, who had the command of the marine battalion serving in Florida, is come home in the *Forward* with an Indian Chief, who has greatly distinguished himself by assisting the British against the Americans in that country.[304]

The "Captain Bligh" mentioned in this report was not the well-known Lt William Bligh, who achieved one of the greatest navigational feats in seafaring history by piloting an open boat 4,000 miles with little food or water following the 1789 mutiny on the *Bounty*. This officer was Capt. George Miller Bligh, a distinguished officer who was aboard HMS *Victory* at the Battle of Trafalgar and was present when Vice-Admiral Horatio Nelson died from wounds received in that landmark fight against the French.

The intelligence of the British departure from Prospect Bluff reached St. Stephens in that part of the Mississippi Territory that is now within Alabama by July 15, 1815. Eastern newspapers copied reports from the

---

[304] "Ship News," *The Morning Post* (London), August 16, 1815.

community in August, and the Spanish governor at St. Augustine confirmed the news in a letter to Gov. Early on September 11.[305]

Concern over Nicolls' activities on the Apalachicola traveled from Washington, D.C., to U.S. Ambassador John Quincy Adams in London by September 1815. He further learned of the presence of the Prophet Francis in England and raised concerns on behalf of the United States to Lord Bathurst:

> I said that the American Government had been peculiarly concerned at the proceedings of Colonel Nicholls, because they appeared to be marked with unequivocal and extraordinary marks of hostility. "Why," said Lord Bathurst," to tell you the truth, Colonel Nicholls is, I believe, a man of activity and spirit, but a very wild fellow. He did make and send over to me a treaty, offensive and defensive, with some Indians; and he is now come over here, and has brought over some of those Indians. I sent for answer that he had no authority whatever to make a treaty, offensive or defensive, with Indians, and that this Government would make no such treaty. I have sent him word that I could not see him upon any such project. The Indians are here in great distress, indeed; but we shall only furnish them with the means of returning home, and advise them to make their terms with the United States as well as they can." Perceiving that I had particularly noticed his declaration that he had declined seeing Colonel Nicholls, he said that he should perhaps see him upon the general subject of his transactions, but that he had declined seeing him in regard to his treaty with the Indians.[306]

---

[305] Report from St. Stephens dated July 15, 1815, reprinted in the Charleston *City Gazette*, August 31, 1815; Governor of Florida to Gov. Peter Early of Georgia, September 11, 1815, East Florida Papers, University of Florida.

[306] John Quincy Adams, "Extracts of a letter from Mr. Adams to the Secretary of State, stating the substance of a conversation with Earl Bathurst," dated: London, September 19, 1815, *American State Papers, Foreign Relations*, Volume 4: 554.

The wily New Englander recognized an attempt by Bathurst to couch the true intentions of the British government regarding Nicolls. Bathurst had been "good-humored and conciliatory," but Adams saw through his subterfuge and realized that while the British would not sanction the treaty signed at Nicolls' Outpost, that was as far as they would go regarding their war hero.[307]

Even so, the American ambassador put the words of Lord Bathurst in writing on September 25, 1815:

> It was with the highest satisfaction that I understood your lordship, in the name of the British Government, to disavow the proceedings of all those officers, of which it had been my duty to complain; and that I received from you the assurance that orders had long since been given for the restoration of the post of Michilimackinac to the United States; that instructions had been given to promote, by all suitable means, the restoration of peace between the Indians and the United States; and, particularly, that Colonel Nicholls, in pretending to conclude a treaty, offensive and defensive, with certain Indians belonging within the jurisdiction of the United States, had not only acted without authority, but incurred the disapprobation of His Majesty's Government.[308]

Great Britain did not approve Nicolls' treaty with the Red Sticks, Miccosukees, and Seminoles, but as Adams predicted in his letter to Secretary of State James Monroe, took no disciplinary action against Maj. Nicolls, who was following the orders of Admiral Cochrane.

The Prophet Francis learned of the disavowal of the treaty while in England that fall, but the Native Americans and Maroons in Florida did not hear that Great Britain rejected their alliance for another year.

---

[307] *Ibid.*

[308] Amb. John Quincy Adams to Earl Bathurst, September 25, 1815, *American State Papers, Foreign Relations*, Volume 4: 554.

The colony at Prospect Bluff showed promise in the fall of 1815. The return of peace to the frontier allowed the men, women, and children there to focus on building new lives. They worked now only for themselves and each other, enjoying the prospects that freedom offered. American officers who saw the results of their efforts the next year reported that their fields extended up and down the river nearly 50 miles from the fort. In these, they grew corn, melons, squash, beans, sweet potatoes, and other crops. They raised stocks of fowl, swine, and cattle for both beef and milk. One of their farms—or "plantations" as the Americans called them—was on the present site of Apalachicola. Others were located in hammocks and spots of good ground along the margins of the estuary and river swamps and up its tributary creeks.

The British left a small schooner and a couple of sloops at Prospect Bluff. Several of the Maroons were experienced shipbuilders and supplemented these with new vessels that residents used to fish in the river, estuary, and Apalachicola Bay. These waters teemed with oysters, shrimp, and a variety of both salt and freshwater fish. The surrounding forests provided whitetail deer, squirrel, rabbits, and opossum as well as a variety of nuts and edible plants and roots. Coontie, which looks like a palm but is more closely related to the pine, produced starchy tubers or "arrowroots." It grew in profusion along the Apalachicola and was used to make flour.

Trade with the Seminoles, Miccosukees, and Red Sticks also helped supply the needs of the community. Bahamian smugglers and probably a few Spanish ones also continued to do business with the Maroons. The colony that Nicolls, a white British officer, planted, was now thriving under black management.

The British had left the storehouses at Prospect Bluff well stocked with provisions, but the summer of 1815 proved to be a good one for growing food. No one at the bluff knew it yet, but they were very fortunate. The climate of the world was undergoing dramatic change due to the largest volcanic explosion in the recorded history of the world. The volcano Tambora on the Indonesian island of Sumbawa erupted on April 10, with a blast that was 100 times more powerful than the 1980 explosion of Mount St. Helens in Washington. The eruption killed 12,000 people in an instant and spewed ten cubic miles of ash and other debris into the atmosphere. This ejecta spread across the northern hemisphere, changing the climate so dramatically that 1816 is remembered to this day as the "Year without a Summer." Crop failures led to starvation and disease that killed untold thousands of people around the world. The impact would reach the Southeast in the following year.

Defense, meanwhile, remained a priority for the community. The men—and possibly the women—continued to drill, and the British colors were raised over the fort each day. Nicolls later recalled that a woman named Mary Ashley helped to fire the morning and evening gun. Military discipline was maintained at the fort, with Sergeant Major Garcon as the commander. A sergeant's guard watched over the wharf to and sally port to prevent access by unauthorized persons. Gunners maintained the cannons in useable condition, while others kept the wooden parts of the fort in good repair. Based on Pintado's account of the incomplete state of the defenses, there is strong archaeological evidence that Garcon and his men continued working on perfecting them after the departure of the British troops and other refugees. The outer entrenchment, for example, is much deeper and stronger than described by Capt. Pintado, especially in its bastions, which were solidly built field works. The moat and connected defenses of the octagonal citadel were also more strongly built than indicated in the Spanish officer's report. It seems unlikely that so much physical labor took place in the three weeks between Pintado's visit and the date of Nicolls' departure.

The United States made no immediate move against the post. Maj. Gen. Gaines, who showed the highest immediate interest, was sidelined by "a severe attack of bilious fever in leaving the Creek Nation" just as he was on his way to visit Maj. Gen. Andrew Jackson after analyzing the strength of his troops. He wound up in a sickbed for weeks and was unable to confer with Jackson until late July. A lack of intelligence and the heat of the summer season prevented the American officers from moving.[309]

It was during the summer and fall of 1815 that U.S. officials and newspaper editors began calling Prospect Bluff the name by which many

---

[309] Maj. Gen. Edmund P. Gaines to Brig. Gen. Daniel Parker, Adjutant and Inspector General, July 29, 1815, Office of the Adjutant General, Letters Received, National Archives.

remember it today: "Negro Fort." Several visits were made to the post that year by individuals who relayed information to military authorities in both the United States and Spanish Florida. Among these was William McGirt, a Creek warrior and the nephew of Sandy Durant:

> ...[M]y Uncle resides 40 miles this side of the British fort. After I had been with my Uncle for several days, I told him of my intention to go and see the British fort, "he says he did not think it was safe for me to go there, when Colo. Nicolls left the fort he left positive orders with Lt. Hambly commanding officer of His Britannic Majesty's forces, on Appalatchicola, to take all prisoners that came from the United States." I told him that I was a native of the Creek Land, and came to get presents, he then & myself went together to the British fort, and made myself known to Lt. Hambly and what my business was and what I came for.[310]

McGirt wrote of his visit in a July 20 letter to Christian Limbaugh, the Assistant Agent under Benjamin Hawkins. He reported that Hambly warned that he was under orders to confine any white man that came down from the United States. McGirt explained that he was not white but Creek and had come to ask for presents. The lieutenant allowed him to stay overnight, but would not let him into the citadel of the fort:

> ...I saw the British fort which is build on the east side of Apalatchicola. I was not permitted to go inside the fort, saw only the outworks, is build very strong & large & supposing it covers about two acres of ground they are still at a working at the fort daily. There are no British troops there at present, none but negros I did not count them. I suppose there is 100 of them, under arms, and a good many of them are gone about and off from the fort to make little crops of corn. They keep sentrys & the

---

[310] William McGirt to Christian Limbaugh, July 20, 1815, James Fletcher Doster, *The Creek Indians and their Florida lands, 1740*-1823, Volume II, Creek Indians, Indian Claims Commission docket no 280, 148-149.

negros are saucy and insolent, and say they are all free. They have a vast deal of goods there for the Indians. Several houses filled with and a great deal of ammunition, everything plenty, corn and rice aside; no scarcity. The fort might easily be taken at this time as the negros are generally out in the day. I saw but five cannons, them was very large.It is very probable there are a great many inside the fort, which I could not see—[311]

Hambly asked whether the United States had evacuated its military posts in the Creek Nation and McGirt told him no. The lieutenant replied that this was a violation of Article 9 of the Treat of Ghent. He also asked about the status of plans to survey the lines of the Treaty of Fort Jackson cession. McGirt told him that he understood the surveyors would start to work that summer. When Hambly heard this, he ominously warned that his orders were to attack the surveying party if it attempted to divide the Creek lands.[312]

Perhaps the most detailed account to reach American hands that summer came from Ned, "a free man of colour," who abandoned the fort and went to Mobile. He arrived there at about the same time as William McGirt's visit to the Apalachicola:

> Fort appalachacola is situated on the east side of the river Appalachacola about sixty miles below the junction of the Chattahoochee and Flint rivers.
>
> The walls of the fort are made of timber filled in with dirt and are about thirteen foot through—The space within the walls is about twenty yards square—There is none large pieces of cannon mounted on the walls.
>
> There is Three Hundred and Eighty casks of Powder and Five Hundred casks of cartridges in the Fort.

---

[311] *Ibid.*
[312] *Ibid.*

> There is Two Hundred and fifty negros armed with
> muskets commanded by a French negro called Garscon—
> They are drilled and perform regular Guard Duty.[313]

Other correspondents gave similar reports. Kendal Lewis and William Hardridge, for example, went down the Apalachicola. Sandy Durant warned them of the danger to their lives, but they made it as far as William Hambly's home at Spanish Bluff. He confidentially told them that he wished the fort destroyed but begged them not to repeat his comments as he would lose his life if the word got out.[314]

The Spanish commandant at San Marcos de Apalache, meanwhile, sent a detail to the Apalachicola in search of provisions for his command. The Maroons stopped them from entering the fort and warned them away, but not before they saw two vessels armed with cannon. The report from San Marcos contributed to John Innerarity's belief that the fort was turning into a base for piracy.[315]

These different reports made clear to both the Americans and the Spanish that the fort was turning into a permanent settlement. The United States was unwilling to allow the existence of a large community populated by free blacks near its borders. As 1815 turned into 1816, the flurry of letters being exchanged by various officials grew. Lost in the discussion, however, was a report from Timpoochee Barnard that most escaped American slaves were going not to Prospect Bluff but to the Suwannee River instead (punctuation enhanced for clarity):

> When we got to Miccosookee we found they were
> gone off to the mouth of Suwanne since the information
> he got from the Chif of Miccosookee is as follows—they
> informed him that run away blacks were constantly
> coming from St. Marys and from other parts of Georgia

---

[313] "Statement of Ned, a free man of colour," enclosed in Maj. Gen. Edmund Gaines to William H. Crawford, Secretary of War, February 20, 1816, Secretary of War, Letters Received, National Archives.

[314] Kendal Lewis and William Hardridge, Report, August 6, 1815, Secretary of War, Letters Received, National Archives.

[315] Francisco Casa y Luengo to Jose de Soto, July 5, 1815, Papales de Cuba, University of Florida.

to that place near the mouth of the Suwanne river many of those that were at the fort at the mouth of the rivers are gone on there. The information he got from the Chiefs at Miccosookee and blacks also say that there are four hundred collected there fit to bear arms exclusive of the women and children and that they are well furnished with arms and ammunition which they have received by water carriage from the mouth of the rivers the red people say that those blacks have a red pole set up in their town and are dancing the red stick dance.[316]

The younger Barnard was on a mission to recover his family's lost slaves, but the chiefs of Miccosukee urged him not to go. Cappachimico had just returned from such an effort:

A few days before he got to Miccosookee seven of Caupitcha Micco's blacks had made their escape to the mouth of Suawanee and he was afraid to go in their town after them, one of young Durant's that lives low down on these river snot long ago made his escape to the Sauwannee he sent seven red men after him they went to where he was and aught him and tied hi the blacks rushed on them and turned them loose the Aulautcheewau Chief, Old Paine brother, went up to try and stop the blacks from the assault the blacks pushed him down on his back and ordered him off.[317]

Cappachimico told Barnard that the Maroons on the Suwannee originated from both the United State s and Spain, as well as from Creek and Seminole country. The chief also asked the young war chief to carry a message to Col. Benjamin Hawkins, begging him to do something about white cattle thieves that were roaming along the border. Hawkins

---

[316] Timpoochee Barnard, quoted in Timothy Barnard to Benjamin Hawkins, March 1816, James Fletcher Doster, *The Creek Indians and their Florida lands, 1740-1823*, Page 162.
[317] *Ibid.*

confirmed that the cattle rustling was done by whites but died before he had time to do anything about it.

Photographs
Section Two

Brig. Gen. Sir Edward Nicolls, GCB,, painted later in life, commanded the British Marines at Prospect Bluff. He fought in more than 100 battles. Royal Marine Barracks

Admiral Sir Alexander Cochrane, GCB, sent the Royal Marines to the Gulf Coast ahead of his New Orleans campaign. National Portrait Gallery, London

Abraham received his military training as a Colonial Marine at Prospect Bluff. He fought in the Seminole Wars and survived the Trail of Tears.

Neamathla (Eneah Emathla) was one of the Native American chiefs who joined the British on the Apalachicola. He lived to fight the United States again in the Seminole and Creek Wars. Library of Congress

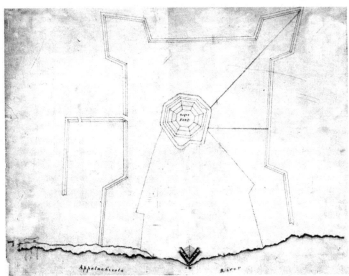

James Gadsden mapped the British Post or Negro Fort at Prospect Bluff in 1818. This representation of the fort has the the later Fort Gadsden structure removed to show only the British works. The octagonal citadel is the site of the explosion. National Archives

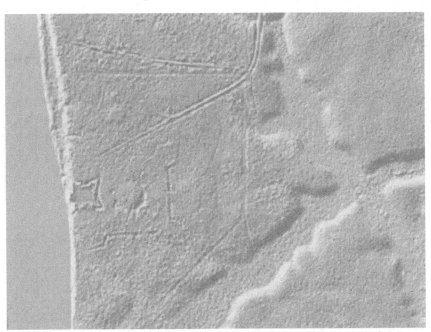

The outline of the fort is clearly visible in the left side of this lidar image. The deep areas at right are creeks and swamps. Northwest Florida Water Management District

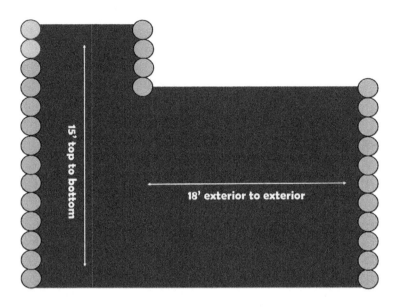

A cross section of the walls that surrounded the octagonal citadel of the British post. The round circles are logs. The black areas show the thickness of the earth fill

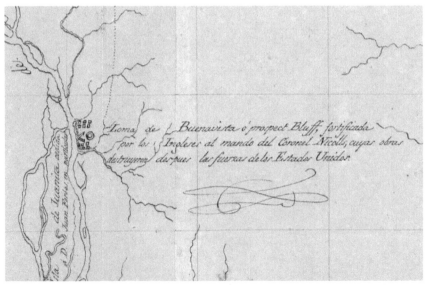

3This 1815 map by Capt. Vicente Sebastian Pintado shows the octagonal citadel and water battery of the Fort at Prospect Bluff. Library of Congress

4Brig. Gen. Duncan Lamont Clinch as he appeared later in life. He was a young lieutenant colonel during the 1816 attack. National Archives

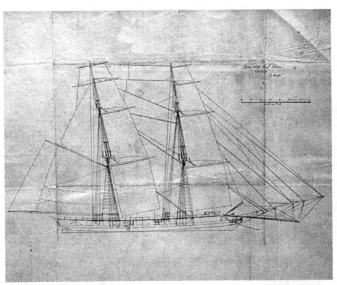

5Gunboat No. 149 and Gunboat No. 154 were built using a similar design to this representation of a "Jeffersonian Gunboat." They were twin masted vessels with a single large gun in the bow.

The noted Civil War photographer Matthew Brady took this image of Maj. Gen. Edmund P. Gaines late in the general's life. The bullet wound he received in the Seminole Wars is clearly visible in his cheek. National Archives

A reconstructed blockhouse stands on the site of Fort Gaines, the U.S. post from which the army began its move on the Negro Fort.

Brig. Gen. William McIntosh, the war chief of Coweta, held the rank of major during the 1816 campaign. He served under Andrew Jackson in the Creek War of 1813-1814.

Fort Scott is overgrown and isolated today. It was the command post for Clinch's campaign in 1816. The site is protected by federal law.

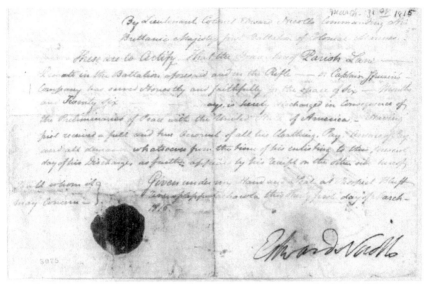

The discharge or "freedom papers" of Parish Lane, a private in the Colonial Marines, hold the signature and seal of Lt. Col. Edward Nicolls. Library of Congress

Julee's cottage in Pensacola was the home of Julee Panton, a free woman of color. It is a rare surviving example of a cabana or cabin in use at the time of the Negro Fort expedition and is now part of Historic Pensacola Village.

This soldier served in the West India Regiments, one company from which was at Prospect Bluff. At least one of the prisoners taken after the explosion was from Jamaica, the origin point of the regiment.

Water still fills the moat that surrounded the octagonal citadel during times of heavy rain. The walls were on the ground visible at left.

The water battery of Fort Gadsden is largely intact today. The earthworks at this spot are more substantial than the rest of the fort and they probably survive from the original British Post. The river is visible in the background.

The ditch of the outer entrenchment of the British Post or Negro Fort is visible in the center of this photograph. The fallen trees were toppled by Hurricane Michael.

Another view of the outer entrenchment of the British Post shows the ditch. The higher ground at left is part of the breastwork of the outer defenses.

The citadel of the Negro Fort stood at the center of this photograph. It was octagonal shaped and had walls of log and earth that were 18-feet thick and 15-feet tall. The explosion took place here on July 27, 1816.

Susie Goodhope and her trained dog Shiraz search for the location of the mass grave where the victims of the 1816 explosion are buried.

An examination of potential graves underway at the so-called "Renegade Cemetery." These graves likely hold U.S. soldiers, not the Maroons killed in the 1816 explosion.

14

THE CAMPAIGN BEGINS

THE LAST DAYS OF THE NEGRO FORT began with the arrival of the Little Prince at Fort Gaines on May 8, 1815. Former Lt. William Hambly and a cadre of chiefs from the Lower Creek territory were with them, their last-ditch effort to convince warriors living near and below the Florida line to attack and take the fort was a failure:

> …[T]he Prince told me that he had done every thing that lay in his power to induce the lower Indians to go against the Negro Fort, and to let the white people alone, but that they were crazy and would not listen to him. That they had deceived him for some time, but that at last he had discovered that they were determined on their own destruction, and that I might do as I pleased with them.[318]

Hambly told Lt. Col. Duncan L. Clinch that the members of the party ran for their lives from the Seminole and Red Stick country with warriors from Fowltown in hot pursuit. He and the Little Prince barely escaped with their lives:

---

[318] Lt. Col. Duncan L. Clinch to Maj. Gen. Edmund P. Gaines, May 9, 1816, Andrew Jackson Papers, Library of Congress.

...[A] party of Tuttelosees pursued them with the intention (if taken) to keep the Prince a prisoner and to burn himself [i.e., Hambly], he further states it, as his opinion that they cannot raise more than 500 men that will go to War. Tuttelosees & Micesookees are the principal investigators, but he thinks most of the Towns on the Flint below Barnett's [i.e., Barnard's], and several Towns on the east bank of the Chattahochee will join them.[319]

Clinch informed Maj. Gen. Gaines on the next day that a string of chiefs from towns near Fort Gaines was coming into the post to solicit advice about what they should do. He told them to stay at home and make their crops of corn, which were already in the ground. When his troops approached, however, the chiefs and warriors should come out and meet him without arms. He further told them of plans to make a census of the towns and that any warriors who left to join the opposing forces could never return. If any of the towns welcomed such men back, then the entire village would face destruction. The Little Prince responded by ordering all chiefs wishing to remain friendly to the United States to see the lieutenant colonel.[320]

The U.S. troops were preparing to move. Clinch informed Gen. Gaines that he was "extremely anxious to move down on those fellows"—a reference to the Seminoles and Red Sticks—and planned to do so as soon as he had a sufficient supply of provisions and ammunition. He also ordered two companies of the 4th Regiment of Infantry then on the march from Charleston to leave their heavy baggage at the Creek Agency on the Flint River and join him at Fort Gaines as soon as possible:

> I then propose leaving all my heavy baggage and a sufficient number of men to man the boats at this post, and move the balance of my command down the River by rapid Marches, and destroy every hostile town between

---

[319] *Ibid.*
[320] *Ibid.*

this and the confluence of the two rivers—after which my boats can drop down with ease and safety in two days—I will then select a strong position on the Flint, fortify my camp, move up the [Flint] River, and destroy all the towns to Burges' old place, and order the command left at the Agency to decend the Flint with our supplies.[321]

The lieutenant colonel would then invade Spanish Florida and "strike a blow in another quarter." What he meant by "another quarter" would soon become clear.

Even as Lt. Col. Clinch was outlining his plans to destroy the Native American towns around the confluence of the Flint and Chattahoochee River, runners were on their way to Fort Gaines with new orders from Maj. Gen. Gaines. These specified that Clinch was to cautiously descend the Chattahoochee to the confluence and build a new post directly on the Spanish border:

Until you are perfectly satisfied as to the strength and healthiness of the position which you may select for a permanent post, you may limit yourself to a temporary work, as I have before suggested, to be thrown up at a convenient point for the present security of your command, until you have it in your power to select a proper site for the intended fort. You will probably find a handsome and suitable bluff on the left or East side of the junction of the rivers. Examine and report to me the situation of the Country at, and for eight or ten miles above the junction, noting the different sites which appear to you most eligible—the distance of each from the river, & from the junction of the two.[322]

---

[321] *Ibid.*

[322] Maj. Gen. Edmund P. Gaines to Lt. Col. Duncan L. Clinch, April 28, 1816, Andrew Jackson Papers, Library of Congress.

At the same time, the general approved the provisioning of a force of Lower Creeks that Col. Benjamin Hawkins was raising for an attack on the Negro Fort. The warriors would receive 300 barrels of government corn but would not be enrolled in the service of the United States or paid for their services. Should this experiment fail, Gaines informed Maj. Gen. Andrew Jackson on May 15, the U.S. Army would destroy the fort:

> ...Should they fail, I shall then avail myself of the discretionary power which you have been pleased to confide to me and shall adopt such measures as may appear best Calculated to Counteract Indian hostility and at the same time to break up the Negro establishment, which I have reason to believe is acquiring strength and additional numbers.[323]

The borderlands were a hive of activity as Gaines wrote his letter to Jackson. Maj. David E. Twiggs of the 7th Infantry was on the march to the Conecuh River, where he was to build another new fort. At the same time, Capt. Alex Cummings was en route from Charleston, South Carolina, to Fort Hawkins with the last battalion of the 4th Infantry. The latter movement placed all three battalions of the regiment on the frontier.

Gaines remained at Camp or Fort Montgomery as these movements began. One week later on May 22, he outlined his plans for the campaign to Commodore Daniel Patterson, commandant of the U.S. Navy station at New Orleans:

> I have determined upon an experiment by water, and for this purpose have to request your co-operation; should you feel authorized to detach a small gun-vessel or two as a convoy to the boats charged with our supplies up the Appalachicola, I am persuaded that, in doing so, you will

---

[323] Maj. Gen. Edmund P. Gaines to Maj. Gen. Andrew Jackson, May 14, 1816, Andrew Jackson Papers, Library of Congress.

contribute much to the benefit of the service, and the accommodation of my immediate command in this quarter. The transports will be under the direction of the officer of the gun-vessel, and the whole should be provided against an attack by small arms from shore. To guard against accidents, I will direct Lieutenant Colonel Clinch to have in readiness a boat sufficient to carry fifty men, to meet the vessels on the river and assist them up.[324]

The general told Patterson about the murders of Johnson and McGaskey and the capture of the two soldiers at Fort Gaines. He also gave details about the construction and armament of the Negro Fort and promised that "it shall be destroyed" if the ships met with any opposition to their passage.[325]

One day later, on May 23, Maj. Gen. Gaines penned order for Lt. Col. Clinch to begin his move down the Chattahoochee River. "If your supplies of provisions and ammunition have reached you," he wrote from his headquarters at Fort Montgomery, "let your detachment move." The soldiers were to carry 25 days rations, and an additional supply of food was to move by water from Fort Gaines. Disapproving of Clinch's earlier plan to march down the river burning Native American towns, however, Gaines urged him to move by boat and with caution:

> ...The force of the whole nation cannot arrest your movement down the river on board the boats, if secured up the sides with two-inch plank, and covered over with clapboards; not could all the nation prevent your landing and constructing a stockade work, sufficient to secure you, unless they should previously know the spot at which you intended to land, and had actually assembled at that place previous to or within four hours of your landing; but

---

[324] Maj. Gen. Edmund P. Gaines to Commodore Daniel T. Patterson, May 22, 1816
[325] *Ibid.*

your force is not sufficient to warrant your march to the different villages, as suggested, by land. The whole of your force (except about forty men, or one company, for the defence of Fort Gaines) should be kept near your boats and supplies until the new post shall be established. You may then strike at any hostile party near you, with all your disposable force; but even then you should not go more than one or two days' march from your fort.[326]

The general also urged Clinch to be wary of William Hambly. Gaines was suspicious of the former British lieutenant and could not divine his motives in suddenly appearing to be a friend of the United States. He went on to explain the movement of the supply transports from Pass Christian, Louisiana, to Apalachicola Bay. Heavy guns and other ordnance supplies would be aboard them to assist in reducing the Negro Fort:

...Should the boats meet with opposition at what is called the Negro fort, arrangements will immediately be made for its destruction; and for that purpose you will be supplied with two eighteen-pounders and one howitzer, with fixed ammunition and implements complete, to be sent in a vessel to accompany the provisions. I have, likewise, ordered fifty thousand musket cartridges, some rifles, swords, &c. Should you be compelled to go against the negro fort, you will land at a convenient point above it, and force a communication with the commanding officer of the vessels below, and arrange with him your plan of attack. Upon this subject you shall hear from me again, as soon as I am notified of the time at which the vessels will sail from New Orleans.[327]

---

[326] Maj. Gen. Edmund P. Gaines to Lt. Col. Duncan L. Clinch, May 23, 1816, *ASPFA*, Volume IV, Page 559.
[327] *Ibid.*

The new fort at the confluence of the Chattahoochee and Flint Rivers, Gaines continued, "must be established speedily...Even if we have to fight our way through the ranks of the whole nation."[328]

There was no direct road from Camp or Fort Montgomery at Tensaw in present-day Alabama to Fort Gaines on the Chattahoochee River, so dispatches were slow to arrive. Couriers had to follow a round-about way between the two posts, and it took one week for the general's orders to reach Lt. Col. Clinch. The letter was still en route when Capt. Amelung finally reached Pensacola and delivered Maj. Gen. Jackson's communique to Gov. Mauricio de Zuniga. The governor wrote back on May 26, giving Jackson basic information on the location and history of the Prospect Bluff fort, while also explaining that some Spanish citizens also disapproved of its existence. He explained that Nicolls and Woodbine and enlisted slaves belonging to Spanish subjects and pronounced himself willing to move against the fort if properly supplied and reinforced. The governor told Jackson that he was seeking authority for a campaign from the Captain General of Cuba, a campaign that "exactly corresponds with ours as to the dislodging of the negroes from the fort, the occupying it with Spanish troops, or destroying it, and delivering the negroes who may be collected to their lawful owners."[329]

Despite the claims of many historians that Jackson directly ordered or even led the expedition to destroy the Negro Fort, he was at his home in Nashville and distant from the scene of action. There is no documentation to suggest that he did more than authorize Gen. Gaines to use his discretion in the matter. Events were already outpacing both Jackson and the Spanish governor by the time Amelung reached Pensacola, and Zuniga penned his reply.

Lt. Col. Clinch received his orders and prepared for an immediate movement down the Chattahoochee River to the confluence. At the same

---

[328] *Ibid.*
[329] Gov. Mauricio de Zuniga to Maj. Gen. Andrew Jackson, May 26, 1816, *ASPFA*, Volume 4, pp. 499-500.

time, a party of Upper Creek warriors located the alleged killers of Johnson and McGaskey and turned them over to the garrison at Fort Jackson. The two soldiers captured with the herd of beef cattle near Fort Gaines, in turn, were given up by the Fowltown warriors in a clear peace offering to the army. Most of the cattle were returned.[330]

The prospects of a war with the Red Sticks and Seminoles appearing to diminish, Gaines rescinded a request that Georgia call out its militia. He made no changes, however, to the gathering campaign against the fort at Prospect Bluff. Lt. Col. Clinch put the operation in motion on June 7, 1816, when he began his long-awaited trip down the Chattahoochee. Five days later he reported from Camp Crawford, the new post he set up on the Flint River in what is now Decatur County, Georgia:

> I was very desirous to have found a suitable site for a fortification nearer the Confluence of the two rivers, than the one I have selected, but the situation of the country would not admit of it. The land near the Confluence is very low and subject to inundation for several miles up, on the west side of the Flint, on the east side, there is a range of hills that runs between a half and a quarter of a mile from the river, but the intervening space is of a low, swampy cast and also subject to inundation. I had learnt before leaving Fort Gaines that there was a considerable pine bluff about seven miles up on the east side of the river. On reaching it I was disappointed in the site, but determined at once on landing my command, and on reconnoitering the country on both sides the river as the labour and fatigue in ascending in our heavy boats was very great.[331]

---

[330] Maj. Gen. Edmund P. Gaines to Maj. Gen. Andrew Jackson, June 3, 1816, Andrew Jackson Papers, Library of Congress.
[331] Lt. Col. Duncan L. Clinch to Maj. Gen. Edmund P. Gaines, June 12, 1816, Andrew Jackson Papers, Library of Congress..

The number of potential sites for a fort in the confluence vicinity was extremely limited. The territory, both south and west of the forks, belonged to Spain. This removed the high bluffs at present-day Chattahoochee from consideration. Lt. Col. Nicolls built a fort atop one of the prehistoric mounds at today's River Landing Park during the War of 1812, but like the towering bluffs that overlooked the site, this location was also in Spanish territory. As Clinch observed, the actual point of land formed by the joining of the Chattahoochee and Flint Rivers was also unsuitable. The peninsula was low and swampy and in places only "three or four feet wide." Spain built the mission of La Encarnacion a la Santa Cruz de Sabacola on the high ground overlooking the peninsula in 1675, but the site was not suitable for the U.S. military's purposes due to the expanse of swamp that surrounded it and separated it from the rivers.[332]

Clinch instead continued to look up the Flint River, first leading his men through the swamps to the foot of a high range of hills on the south or east side of the Flint. The site proved unsatisfactory:

> ...[T]he distance from the river, the difficulty of ascending it, and the want of water, induced me to take a small party of men in a Canoe and explore the river until I could find a more eligible site, and to my great satisfaction I had not proceeded more than a mile before I discovered a high pine bluff on the west side of the river and on examining determined at once on occupying it. The bluff is not more than half as high as the one at Fort Gaines, but the site is rather a more military one in as much as it commands the country round it.[333]

The bluff described by the lieutenant colonel rises only seven feet above the normal level of Lake Seminole today, but before the completion of the Jim Woodruff Dam in 1958, it rose an impressive 35-40 feet above the Flint River. The surface formed a broad plateau of more than 12-acres

---

[332] *Ibid.*
[333] *Ibid.*

and was ideal for the construction of a military post. Its location on a sharp bend of the river allowed for the placement of cannon to control not only the channel but the low-lying swamps on the opposite shore. Good water was also present:

> ...On examining for water we have discovered two of the most extraordinary springs (if they may be so called) that I have ever seen, within less than half a mile of the site. They are at least 90 feet in circumference, and twenty or thirty deep, the water cool, well tastes, and I have no doubt will prove healthy which is the most important consideration (in my opinion) in selecting a military site.[334]

Lake Seminole now covers these springs. Archaeological research shows that they attracted human settlement for thousands of years, as did the actual bluff selected by Clinch for his new fort. Evidence shows Native Americans lived on the site during the Woodland (400-900 A.D.), Mississippian (900-1450 A.D.), and Creek (1450-1816 A.D.) eras. Archaeologists found no evidence of burial or ceremonial mounds on the bluff, but believe it long served as a habitation or village site.

Clinch followed his orders and built a temporary log fort on the bluff, letting Maj. know Gen. Gaines that he was in place and waiting to hear from the gunboats and transport ships:

> I have thrown up a pretty strong temporary work, erected a store house and have my command under shelter and comfortable in a few days, and feel confident we can repel the whole Creek Nation were they to attack us. I shall send a confidential Indian down the river to the bay with a letter to the Commanding officer of the Gun Boats, in the course of two days, with instructions to remain in

---

[334] Nancy Marie White *et. al.*, "Archeology at Lake Seminole," unpublished report, Cleveland Museum of Natural History, 1981.

sight of the bay...If the vessels do not arrive with some supplies very soon we shall be entirely destitute of provisions before we can get them up the river.[335]

Lt. Col. Clinch named the new outpost Camp Crawford to honor Secretary of War William Crawford of Georgia. It is better known today by its later name of Fort Scott. As the troops worked to complete their stockade and huts, the marine phase of the campaign took shape. Commodore Daniel Patterson agreed to the request from Maj. Gen. Gaines for naval cooperation, ordering Lt. Commander Charles E. Crawley to take command of the ships sailing for Apalachicola Bay. On July 19 he sent Crawley a copy of the letter from Gen. Gaines to acquaint him with the situation into which he would be sailing:

> ...[W]ith that letter for your guide, convoy the transports with ordnance, provisions, &c. up the River Apalachicola and Chattahoochie to such point or points as may be required if practicable, should you meet with opposition from the Negroe Fort, situated as stated in the letter on the lower river, the Military Commanding Officer will have orders to destroy it, in which you will cooperate, the plan of attack to be concerted between yourself and him, the Transports will be under your direction entirely. In the event of Hostilities between the Indians and the U.S. you will if practicable afford any aid with your vessels in your power to the Army. Remain in that River & cooperate with them untill it shall be necessary to return here for provisions but if you cannot aid them in their operations you will then return immediately bringing with you the transports.[336]

---

[335] Lt. Col. Duncan L. Clinch to Maj. Gen. Edmund P. Gaines, June 12, 1816.
[336] Commodore Daniel T. Patterson to Lt. Commander Charles E. Crawley, June 19, 1816, Letters Received by the Secretary of the Navy from Captains,

Patterson authorized Crawley to take U.S. Gunboat No. 149 under his command to go with his vessel, a cutter stationed at Pass Christian. The two transport ships secured to carry the army's supplies were the fast schooner *General Pike*, laden with provisions, and the smaller vessel *Semelante*, which carried the cannon and other ordnance supplies that Gaines had promised Clinch.[337]

The commodore knew that Lt. Commander Crawley was at sea but expected him to return to Pass Christian in time to lead the flotilla. Just in case, however, he sent the orders undercover to Sailing Master Jairus Loomis, who commanded Gunboat No. 149:

> The enclosed dispatch for Lieut. Commdr. Crawley is transmitted under cover to you least he might not arrive at the Pass Christian by the time the Transports laden with Ordnance, Provisions &c., mentioned to you verbally when here, shall arrive and be ready to proceed to their place of destination in which case you will consider them as addressed to you and act accordingly, in that event you will take under you Command Gun Boat No. 154 together with the transports and proceed in execution of those instructions—In the performance of the duties therein pointed out, it will be necessary to act with vigor & judgement and you will refrain from any act of hostility against a Spanish Force, or violation of their rights and laws. You will make no delay in your departure from the Pass Christian after the arrival there of No. 154 & the Transports.[338]

---

compiled 1805-1885, M125, Roll 50, National Archives (hereafter Letters Received from Captains).

[337] *Ibid.*

[338] Commodore Daniel T. Patterson to Sailing Master Jairus Loomis, June 19, 1816, Letters Received from Captains.

The request from General Gaines that the Navy supply gunboats to escort his supply ships filled a need beyond a probable attack on the Negro Fort. Pirates were a very real threat on the Gulf of Mexico in 1816. Many of the former Baratarian "privateers" were ignoring the pardon they received after the Battle of New Orleans and were again seizing ships and cargos. Other pirates from other places also prowled the coast. The *General Pike* especially was known to carry rich cargoes along the Atlantic seaboard and Gulf Coast, so she and the *Semelante* undoubtedly mounted small cannons and other weaponry for their defense. The two naval vessels assigned to escort them were standard "Jeffersonian Gunboats" of the War of 1812 era. Named for President Thomas Jefferson, who was a fierce supporter of their deployment, the gunboats were purely defensive. Designed to patrol and defend America's coasts and rivers, they were not large enough for extended sea voyages. Congress authorized the building of nearly 300 Jeffersonian Gunboats, but fewer than 200 launched. When the United States declared war on Great Britain in 1812, the U.S. Navy consisted of a mere seven frigates, four schooners, four ketches, and 170 gunboats. Frigates like the USS *Constitution* ("Old Ironsides") quickly proved their worth against the Royal Navy, but the gunboats were all but worthless in combat. At the Battle of Lake Borgne, Louisiana, for example, the British captured all five Jeffersonian Gunboats committed to action in short order, along with two of three remaining American vessels, without committing a single warship to action.

Gunboats No. 149 and No. 154 were typical vessels of their class. They each had two masts and carried a crew of around 20-30 men. They were about the size of a small modern shrimp boat, and each carried a single long 9-pounder cannon in the bow. Other than a swivel gun or two, muskets, swords, and pistols were the only other arms aboard. The gunboats were no match for the British, but they were more than capable of dealing with most pirate vessels in the Gulf. Their representations in movies aside, most real pirate ships were small sloops or schooners, and they rarely carried more than one or two small cannons. Most had no artillery at all.

The transports and Gunboat No. 154 sailed from New Orleans, and by June 24 were at Pass Christian. Lt. Commander Crawley was not back from the sea, so on that date, Commodore Patterson ordered Sailing Master Loomis to assume command of the flotilla and sail for the Apalachicola. With Gunboat No. 149 as his flagship, Loomis led the four vessels to sea and began the journey east along the coasts of Mississippi, Alabama, and Northwest Florida. Sailing Master James Bassett commanded Gunboat No. 154 and a third officer, Midshipman Alexander W. Luffborough, "though much indisposed & having sent in his resignation to the Department very handsomely volunteered his services." The little flotilla passed the Spanish capital of Pensacola without incident and reached Apalachicola Bay on July 10, 1816.[339]

The sailors soon spotted a Creek chief on the shore. He proved to be John Blunt, a former resident of Upper Creek town of Tuckabatchee, who now lived on the Apalachicola. He supported the British during the War of 1812 but was now an ally of the United States. He proved to be the "confidential Indian" that Lt. Col. Clinch promised Gen. Gaines he would send to the bay as a messenger to the commander of the ships. The sailors took Blunt aboard ship for an interview with Sailing Master Loomis:

> ...At this place I received despatches from Lieutenant Colonel Clinch, commanding the fourth regiment United States infantry, on the Chattahoochee river, borne by an Indian, requesting me to remain off the mouth of the river until he could arrive with a party of men to assist in getting gup the transports; desiring me also to detain all vessels and boats that might attempt to descend the river.[340]

---

[339] Commodore Daniel T. Patterson to Benjamin W. Crowninshield, Secretary of the Navy, August 15, 1816, Letters Received from Captains.

[340] Sailing Master Jairus Loomis to Commodore Daniel T. Patterson, August 13, 1816, Letters Received from Captains.

Loomis agreed to blockade the mouth of the river while waiting for Clinch to come down. He asked Chief Blunt to go back to Camp Crawford with this news and then settled in to wait.

15

THE WATERING PARTY ATTACK

THE TUCKABATCHEE CHIEF JOHN BLUNT MOVED QUIETLY through the wilderness, carrying news of the flotilla's arrival to the new American fort. The distance was more than 120 miles, and the journey took time. Several days also passed before Garcon and the men at Prospect Bluff learned that American ships were in the bay. The intelligence probably came from a Maroon who had cleared a small farm on the site of present-day Apalachicola. The name of this individual is unknown, but references to his "plantation" appear in U.S. military reports of the campaign.

Garcon responded to the news by ordering a detachment of men into one of the small vessels left for their use by the British. They left the Negro Fort and sailed 20-miles down to the mouth of the river, reaching the bay on July 15, 1816:

> On the 15th I discovered a Boat pulling out of the River, & being anxious to ascertain whether we should be permitted peaceably to pass the Fort above us, I dispatched a Boat with an officer to gain the necessary information. On nearing her, she fired a volley of musketry into my Boat, and immediately pulled in for the

River. I immediately opened fire on them from the Gun Vessels but with no effect.[341]

Garcon later told American officers that his final orders from the British were to defend the river and not allow the passage of vessels flying the U.S. or Spanish flags. The volley of musketry from the Maroon boat left no doubt that the men aboard were serious about their mission. The thunder of the cannons from the two gunboats, meanwhile, confirmed that the Americans also were ready to fight. Unsure of what to expect next, Garcon called for reinforcements, and the Choctaw chief led his warriors down from the Negro Fort in response. Sixty fighters from the fort now waited onshore just inside the mouth of the river to see what the ships would do next.

While the Maroons and Choctaws waited at Apalachicola Bay, John Blunt reached Camp Crawford on July 15. Lt. Col. Clinch at once assigned Maj. Enos Cutler to take command during his absence and hand-picked 116 men for the expedition downstream. The soldiers divided into two companies under Brevet Maj. Peter Muhlenberg and Capt. William Taylor and climbed into their boats on July 17. Sixty men remained behind under Maj. Cutler to guard the fort while they were away.[342]

Clinch led his boats down the Flint to its confluence with the Chattahoochee. Turning south into the Apalachicola River, he crossed the international border into Spanish Florida. He planned to storm the Negro Fort should the men there try to stop the transports from passing. He gained unexpected support for the expected attack on the same day that he left Camp Crawford:

...On the same evening I was joined by Major [William] McIntosh with one hundred and fifty Indians, and on the

---

[341] Sailing Master Jairus Loomis to Commodore Daniel T. Patterson, August 15, 1816, Letters Received from Captains.

[342] Lt. Col. Duncan L. Clinch to Col. Robert Butler, Adjutant General of the Department of the South, August 2, 1816, Jackson Papers, Library of Congress.

18th by an old chief called Capt. [Sam] Isaacs and the celebrated chief Kotcha-hajo or Mad Tiger at the head of a large body of Indians, many of whom were without arms. My junction with these Chiefs was accidental their expedition having been long since projected. Their object was to capture the negroes within the Fort and restore them to their proper owners. We held a council…and [an] agreement was entered into.[343]

The agreement described by Clinch specified that if joint force could take the fort, "the Indians are to have all the Powder (Cannon excepted) small arms, clothing &c. & Fifty Dollars for every grown negro taken by them, not the property of the Creek Nation." The army, meanwhile, would take possession of the "cannon, ordnance stores &c. & of all the property the Indians cannot carry from the Fort." Kendal Lewis, a resident of Coweta, served as the interpreter for the council. The lieutenant colonel soon regretted his promise to give the Creeks all the powder and small arms they could carry away. When he signed the agreement on July 18, however, he had no idea of the extent of the arsenal stored in the Negro Fort.[344]

As the soldiers and Native Americans negotiated their alliance, the first blood of the campaign was spilled near the mouth of the Apalachicola River. The ships had been at sea for sixteen days and by July 17 were running low on freshwater:

On the 17th at 5 A.M., I manned & armed a Boat with a swivel & musketry & four men, and gave her in charge of Midshipn. [Alexander] Luffborough for the purpose of

---

[343] *Ibid.*

[344] Articles of Agreement entered into on the 18th July 1816 by Lt. Col. D.L. Clinch, on the part of the U. States & the Chiefs Capt. Isaacs, Kotcha-harga, & Majr. McIntosh on the part of the Creek Nation, enclosed in Clinch to Butler, August 2, 1816, Jackson Papers, Library of Congress.

procuring fresh water, having run short of that Article. At 11 A.M. sailing Master Basset who had been on a similar expedition came along side with the body of John Burgess, O.S. [Ordinary Seaman] who had been sent in the Boat with Midshipn. Luffborough; his body was found near the Mouth of the River, shot through the heart. At 4 P.M. discovered a man at the mouth of the River on a Sand Bar. Sent a Boat and Brought him on Board, he proved to be John Lopaz O.S. the only survivor of the Boat's Crew sent with Midshipn. Luffborough.[345]

Sailing Master Loomis stumbled into a trap by sending a small boat into the mouth of the river. After the exchange of fire on July 15, Garcon and the Choctaw chief hid their fighters along the shore, anticipating that the Americans would come into their river. Seaman Lopaz (or Lopez) described the scene:

He reports that on entering the River, they discovered a Negro on the Beach near a plantation, that Mr. Luffborough ordered the Boat to be pulled directly for him, that on touching shore he spoke to the Negro, and directly received a volley of musketry from two Divisions of Negros & Indians, who lay concealed in the bushes on the Margin of the River. Mr. Luffborough, Robert Maitland, & John Burgess were killed on the spot. Lopaz made his escape by swimming & states that he saw the other Seaman Edward Daniels made prisoner. Lopaz supposed there must have been Forty Negroes and Indians concerned in the Capture of the Boat.[346]

The violence of the attack shocked the sailors aboard the American gunboats. Many of them were veterans of the Battle of New Orleans, but

---

[345] Loomis to Patterson, August 15, 1816.
[346] *Ibid.*

an encounter with Red Stick Choctaws was a new experience for them. The bodies of Luffborough and his men were scalped and otherwise mutilated. Their boat was taken, and the prisoner, Edward Daniels, was carried to the Negro Fort to face an even more gruesome fate.

The exact site of the attack on the watering party is unknown. Many writers speculate that the name of Bloody Bluff, a low rise on the east bank about three miles below Prospect Bluff, originates with the deaths of Luffborough, Maitland, and Burgess. The details in Loomis's report, however, make this identification impossible. Bloody Bluff is seventeen miles up the Apalachicola from the bay, and a row up to that point by five men in a small boat in the time allowed is impossible. Not only would the party have to reach the bluff by pulling against the current, but the body of John Burgess then would need to float seventeen miles back down to the mouth of the river. Since Luffborough left Gunboat No. 149 at 5 a.m. and Sailing Master Bassett came alongside with Burgess' body at 11 a.m., the six-hour absence of the midshipman's party did not allow enough time for a round trip of 34 miles.

Lopaz, the survivor from Luffborough's party, said that the attack took place "on entering the river." The east side of the Apalachicola for miles above its mouth is marsh and wetland, completely unsuited for agricultural purposes. It could not have been the location of the "plantation" near which the sailors spotted a Maroon man. The opposite or west side of the river, however, is habitable, as is demonstrated by the presence there of the city of Apalachicola today. Small springs along the margins of this higher ground provided freshwater, a necessity that allowed people to live on the site for thousands of years. Luffborough was looking for water, not a long trip up the Apalachicola River. The farm he spotted and the man he approached "on entering the river" were undoubtedly along the shore where Apalachicola now stands.

Loomis had no way to communicate news of the disaster to Lt. Col. Clinch, but it did not take long for the army officer to learn of the attack:

I ordered the Chiefs to keep parties in advance and to secure every negro they fell in with and to join me near the Fort. On the 19th they brought in a prisoner taken the evening before. He had a scalp which he said he was carrying to the Seminoles. He further stated that the Black Commandant and the Chactaw Chief had returned to the Fort from the Bay the day before with a party of men, with information that they had killed several Americans, and taken a Boat from them.[347]

The Americans later learned that Edward Daniels, the prisoner taken during the watering party attack, "was tarred & burnt alive." The final death toll from the encounter included:

Alexander W. Luffborough, Midshipman, Killed in Action.
John Burgess, Ordinary Seaman, Killed in Action.
Edward Daniels, Ordinary Seaman, Captured and Executed.
Robert Maitland, Ordinary Seaman, Killed in Action.

The small boat under Sailing Master Bassett brought the body of John Burgess back to Gunboat No. 149. The sailors probably buried him at sea in Apalachicola Bay rather than risk a return to shore. The reports make no mention of the discovery of the body of Edward Daniels at the Negro Fort, and its fate is unknown. The reports likewise are silent on any recovery of the bodies of Midshipman Luffborough and John Burgess.

Higher up the Apalachicola River, now aware of the violent encounter near the bay, Lt. Col. Clinch and his command continued their downstream journey. The Creek warriors under McIntosh, Isaacs, and Mad Tiger swept down the east bank of the river, capturing some of the Maroons as they advanced. Clinch noted, however, that "a number of them had left their

---

[347] Clinch to Butler, August 2, 1816.

fields and gone over to the Seminoles on hearing of our approach." He also reported that "their cornfields extended nearly fifty miles up the river."[348]

Commodore Patterson, who benefited from discussions with Loomis, Bassett, and others, summed up American concerns about the size and success of the Maroon settlement in his report to Secretary of the Navy Benjamin W. Crowninshield:

> ...[T]he Country in its vicinity is of manifest importance to the U. States & particularly those states bordering on the Creek Nation, as it had become the general Rendezvous for Runaway Slaves & disaffected Indians, an asylum where they were assured of being received; a strong hold where they found arms & ammunition to protect themselves against their owners & the Government...add to which that the Force of Negroes were daily increasing & they felt themselves so strong & secure that they had commenced several plantations on the Fertile Banks of the Apalachicola which would have yielded them every Article of sustenance & which would consequently in a short time have rendered their establishment quite formidable & injurious to the neighbouring States.[349]

The army command reached Brickyard Creek at the northern end of Prospect Bluff late into the night of July 19-20, 1816. The beginning of the Battle of Negro Fort was at hand.

---

[348] *Ibid.*

[349] Commodore Daniel T. Patterson to Benjamin W. Crowninshield, Secretary of the Navy, August 15, 1816, Letters Received from Captains.

16

THE BATTLE OF NEGRO FORT

LT. COL. CLINCH COULD NOT SEE THE FORT he came to attack when he arrived within one mile of it on the night of July 19-20, 1816. His boats hove to shore at the north end of Prospect Bluff, but the Negro Fort stood at its very southern edge. Garcon and the occupants of the fort knew that the soldiers were approaching due to the sweeping movement of the Creek warriors down the east bank of the river. Maj. McIntosh, Capt. Isaacs and Mad Tiger moved through scattered fields and small farms for 50 miles before reaching the bluff. They captured some Maroons, but most in their path either fled for the Seminole towns or retreated into the fort. The small size of his force prevented Garcon from opposing the approach of the white and Creek soldiers. He and the other defenders stood by their guns and waited for the morning.

Clinch's boats reached the mouth of Brickyard Creek, which defines the north end of the bluff, at 2 a.m. He brought his men ashore under cover of darkness and formed a junction with the Creek warriors who were already spreading out in the trees along the stream. Chief Blunt met him upriver two days earlier to report that he had been unable to get through to the bay with a message for Sailing Master Loomis that the troops were on their way. Clinch now sent him out for another attempt.[350]

---

[350] Lt. Col. Duncan L. Clinch to Col. Robert Butler, August 2, 1816, Jackson Papers, Library of Congress.

The lieutenant colonel still wanted to storm the fort. He had yet to reconnoiter its defenses for himself, but he prepared nonetheless, but daylight revealed the foolhardiness of his plan:

> …My plan of attack was communicated to the Chiefs, and a party of Indians under Major McIntosh were directed to surround the Fort. Finding it impossible to carry my plans into execution without the assistance of Artillery, I ordered Major McIntosh to keep one third of his men constantly hovering around the Fort and to keep up an irregular fire—this had the desired effect as it induced the enemy to amuse us with an incessant roar of Artillery without any other effect than that of striking terror into the souls of most of our red friends.[351]

Other sources indicate that Clinch downplayed the effect of the cannon fire that Garcon rained down on his men. The four six-pounders in the fort were atop the central citadel from which they could fire in all directions. With their 4-pounder field gun, 5 ½-inch howitzer, and Congreve rockets, the Maroons easily swept an arc from the junction of Brickyard Creek with the river around to Fort Gadsden Creek. For one mile out from the fort, the ground was open, creating an excellent field of fire for the former Colonial Marine gunners. The water battery stood on a point that projected slightly from the river face of the bluff. This projection enabled Garcon to bring two of his four 24-pounders into action as well. Clinch's first headquarters were well within range. Dr. Marcus C. Buck, a surgeon with the 4th Regiment of U.S. Infantry, wrote two weeks later that the fort's fire forced Clinch back from his first position:

> …On the morning of the 20th we arrived within three fourths of a mile of the fort, and about six in the morning the enemy opened a fire of round shot, shell, grape, and

---

[351] *Ibid.*

rockets, which was continued with occasional intermission until the explosion of the [27th], but with little injury on our part. In the evening the Colonel chose a more secure position for our camp, until the gun boats and transport, which contained our ordnance, should arrive, and which were then ascertained to be farther from the Fort than was expected.[352]

Dr. Buck's statement that the cannon fire of the Negro Fort did "but little injury" is different from Clinch's claim that it did "no injury." This difference in wording suggests that the surgeon may have treated minor wounds on the first day of the battle. The Creek warriors under Maj. William McIntosh were the most exposed of the attackers, and it is reasonable that a few were wounded. Clinch likely was referring only to the white soldiers of the 4th Regiment in his report, while Dr. Buck probably treated any wounds in the total force – Native American and white. From the evening of July 20, the lieutenant colonel kept his men out of range of the fort, while assigning Maj. McIntosh and the Creek warriors the task of keeping the garrison penned up.

The Maroons may have made at least one sortie from the fort as the Creek warriors closed in around them. A correspondent of the *Augusta Chronicle* wrote that "the negroes made a sortie on the Indians under M'Intosh on the second morning of their besieging the fort, when a direful conflict ensued—the tomahawk and scalping knife (so close was the engagement) were the only weapons used, the negroes however, were driven into the fort." The writer was a "gentleman immediately from Mobile" who probably gained his information as he passed through the Creek Nation. The accuracy of his statement is unknown. He was not an eyewitness to the battle.[353]

---

[352] Dr. Marcus C. Buck, Surgeon, to His Father, August 4, 1816, published in *The Army and Navy Chronicle*, February 25, 1836, pp. 115-116.
[353] *Augusta Chronicle*, August 16, 1816.

Many modern writers describe the Battle of Negro Fort as a brief encounter between the fort's gunners and the men aboard the American gunboats. It was a fierce encounter that began on the morning of July 20 and continued until the morning of July 27. The Creek warriors hovered around the fort for seven days, sniping at any Maroon who showed his or her face above the defenses. The fighters in the fort, likewise, continued their artillery fire day after day, keeping the U.S. soldiers at bay.

The outbreak of the battle allowed John Blunt to make his way past the fort and reach Apalachicola Bay, where hailed the American ships. The chief went by canoe, probably by passing through the channel on the backside of Forbes Island which forms the west bank of the Apalachicola River opposite the fort:

> On the 20th July I received by a canoe with five Indians despatches from Col. Clinch, advising that he had arrived with a party of Troops & Indians at a position about a mile above the Negroe Fort: requesting that I would ascend the River & join him with the Gun Vessels; he further informed me that he had taken a Negro bearing the Scalp of one of my unfortunate Crew to one of the unfriendly Indian Chiefs.[354]

Sailing Master Loomis was worried that men from the fort might attack his vessels as they made their way upriver and declined to move. The killing of Midshipman Luffborough and the men of the watering party revealed the danger to his crews of fire from the riverbanks. He sent Blunt back upstream with a message for Clinch that he needed help to make the requested ascent.

At the Negro Fort, meanwhile, the fighting continued. Dr. Buck described how the attacking force focused on surrounding the post and destroying the nearby fields. "The troops were employed in scouring, foraging, preventing the escape of the enemy, and destroying their

---

[354] Sailing Master Jairus Loomis to Commodore Daniel T. Patterson, August 15, 1816, Letters Received from Captains.

provisions, which consisted of green corn, melons, &c.," he wrote. As he directed these operations, Lt. Col. Clinch—who remained so far back that he had yet actually to see the fort—became confused with the dates. In his report on the battle, he described events as taking place one day after they occurred.

An example was the decision to send forward a white flag and demand the surrender of Garcon and his followers. Clinch said that this took place on July 23, but other accounts indicate that July 22 was the actual date:

> ...In the evening a deputation of Chiefs went into the Fort and demanded its surrender, but they were abused and treated with the utmost contempt. The Black Chief heaped much abuse on the Americans, and said he had been left in command of the Fort by the British Government, and that he would sink any American vessel that should attempt to pass it: that if he could not defend it he would himself blow up the Fort. The Chiefs also informed me that the negroes had hoisted a red flag and that the English Jack was flying over it.[355]

The red flag was a traditional symbol that the occupants of the fort would give no quarter to any enemy that fell into their hands. Likewise, it symbolized their determination to fight to the death. The Mexican general Antonio Lopez de Santa Anna raised one outside the Alamo in 1836 as a message that he would put all of its defenders to the knife. Clinch's statement that the chiefs "informed" him of the flag reveals that he still was so far away that he could not see the fort.

Dr. Buck was present when the delegation of chiefs went forward to meet Garcon:

> ...During this time the friendly Indian Chiefs sent in a flag to the fort, but the garrison refused the terms offered,

---

[355] Clinch to Butler, August 2, 1816.

unless they should be sanctioned by the Chiefs of Fowl Town, Mickasooka, &c., observing that they wished to fight, and had gone into the Fort for no other purpose. We were pleased with their spirited opposition to the imbecile measures of our Indians, though they were Indians, negroes, and our enemies. Many circumstances convinced us that most of them determined never to be taken alive.[356]

Other accounts show that Garcon responded to the surrender demand with cannon fire. Sailing Master Loomis verified in his report by noting that "on the 22d there was a heavy Cannonade in the direction of the Fort."[357]

Inside the fort, women and children joined the men in contributing to their defense. Mary Ashley was 18-years old when she came to the fort with her husband during the British occupation. An escaped slave from St. Augustine, she survived the battle and her role in defending the Negro Fort became known as she tried to secure her release from bondage years later:

> …Mary Ashley had the courage and sagacity to hoist and pull down the colours morning and evening for four days, firing the morning and evening gun, shotted, into the enemy's camp, in hope that the absent garrison would hear it, and come to their assistance.[358]

The reference to the "absent garrison" clearly refers to the men who either escaped or were captured by the American force as it approached and encircled the fort. Maj. Edward Nicolls, who by 1843 was a full colonel, learned of Ashley's part in defense of the post from an unknown

---

356 Dr. Buck to his Father, August 4, 1816.
357 Loomis to Patterson, August 15, 1816.
358 Col. Edward Nicolls to Sir John Barrow, September 11, 1843, "The Sessional Papers of the House of Lords, 1845," *British and Foreign State Papers, 1844-1845*, Volume XXXIII, London, 1859, Page 11.

correspondent. Later events suggest the informant was either George Woodbine, Alexander Arbuthnot, or Robert Ambrister. In addition to Mary Ashley's role in the battle, Nicolls also described how other women and children helped by "filling cartridges" with powder from the "grand magazine" in the citadel at the center of the fort.[359]

How many people were in the fort is still a disputed question. Nicolls wrote in 1843 that lack of transportation forced him to leave behind 350 men, women, and children. At the time of the battle, his informant told him, there were only 60 men in the fort. This estimate is consistent with Lt. Col. Clinch's statement that "the fort contained about one hundred effective men including twenty five Chactaws, and about two hundred women and children." Dr. Buck wrote his father that there were around "three hundred souls" in the fort. Sailing Master Loomis, who was closely involved in the later search and inventory of the fort, said that the defenders included "three hundred Negroes, men, women & children, and about 20 Indian warriors of the Renegade Choctaws." William Hambly, the former commandant of the fort, added some confusion with a statement that 40 people were killed in the fort—as compared to the number of 250-270 given in other accounts—but he appears to be referring only to Maroons who escaped from the John Forbes and Company. Clinch could have stormed the works with relative ease had there been only a handful more than 40 men, women, and children to defend them.[360]

Clinch and Nicolls were probably accurate in their estimates that 100 men—25 of whom were Red Stick Choctaw warriors—went into the fort as the American force closed in. With them were 200-220 women and children, many of whom took part in the fight or filled cartridges. Mary Ashley, for example, served on a cannon crew, and there is little doubt that other women and older children did the same.

---

[359] *Ibid.*

[360] Nicolls to Barrow, September 11, 1843; Clinch to Butler, August 2, 1816; Dr. Buck to his Father, August 4, 1816; Loomis to Patterson, August 15, 1816; William Hambly to John Forbes, August 1816, Papers of John Forbes and Company, University of West Florida.

With force this size, Garcon could not defend the entire fort. Most defenders went into the central citadel, the octagonal structure with thick ramparts of earth packed between log walls. The 6-pounder cannon on the gundeck could sweep the approaches to the fort on all sides, both inside and outside the outer entrenchment that encircled the entire complex. Garcon may have ordered parties of skirmishers into the outer entrenchment during times of immediate danger, but he did not have enough people to place men to defend the breastworks throughout the battle. Instead, he concentrated on defending the "A" shaped area defined by the citadel and the inner stockade.

With most of the people inside the citadel, Garcon and 20-30 of the men occupied the water battery where they could fire its 24-pounders. There is even a dispute about the weight of these cannons. Lt. Col. Clinch reported the capture of one 32-pounder and three 24-pounders in the fort. The inventory prepared by subordinate officers in cooperation with the navy, however, listed the heavy guns as four 24-pounders. The discrepancy is difficult to explain, but the *General Pike* took four 24-pounders to Louisiana after the battle.

The defenders knew from their reconnaissance at Apalachicola Bay that four American ships were at the mouth of the river. They undoubtedly expected them to come upstream, but day after day, they did not. With cannon and rocket fire, meanwhile, they kept the soldiers and Creek warriors at bay, all the while hoping that reinforcements would soon arrive from the Seminole and Miccosukee villages in the area. Couriers sent out by the Maroons reached Fowltown, Miccosukee, and other communities as the battle was underway. Warriors and chiefs started organizing a relief force to raise the siege. They did not arrive in time.

The fighting continued on July 23, 1816. Sailing Master Loomis reported the arrival at the bay of new couriers from Lt. Col. Clinch:

> ...On the 23d I received a verbal message from Col.
> Clinch by a white man & two Indians who stated that Col.
> Clinch wished me to ascend the River to a certain Bluff &

wait there until I saw him.—Considering that by doing so in a narrow & crooked River from both sides of which my Decks could be commanded & exposed to the Fire of Musquetry, without enabling me to act in my own defence, & also that something like treachery might be on foot, from the nature of the message, I declined acting, retained the White man and one of the Indians as hostages, and dispatched the other with my reason for doing so, to Col. Clinch, that his views & Communications to me in the future must be made in writing & by an officer of the Army.[361]

Clinch responded by sending down Lt. Wilson and a detachment of 13 men from the 4th Regiment. They reached the gunboats on July 24 and informed the naval commander of their orders to assist him in bringing his vessels upriver. Wilson told Loomis that he could now ascend in safety. The ships at once started up the Apalachicola:

On the 25th I arrived with the Convoy at Duelling Bluff, about four miles below the Fort, where I was met by Col. Clinch, he informed me that in attempting to pass within Gun shot of the fortifications, he had been fired upon by the Negroes, & that he had also been fired upon for the last four or five days whenever any of his troops appeared in view; we immediately reconnoitered the Fort and determined on a scite to erect a small Battery of two Eighteen pounders to assist the Gun Vessels to force the navigation of the River, as it was evident from their hostility, we should be obliged to do.[362]

Duelling Bluff was the slight elevation on the east side of the river known today as Bloody Bluff. The original name suggests that the modern

---

[361] Loomis to Patterson, August 15, 1816.
[362] *Ibid.*

name may refer to duels that took place there in the years before the establishment of the Negro Fort. Clinch moved his headquarters to the bluff and ordered Brevet Maj. Peter Muhlenberg and Capt. William Taylor to prepare the site for the battery:

> I went on board of Gun Vessel 149 about 4 miles below the Fort. I had previously determined on a position in the rear of the Fort for erecting a battery, but on examining the two Eighteen pounders, I found them mounted on heavy garrison carriages, which rendered it almost impossible to get them to the spot selected, as they must have been taken through a cypress swamp. After reconnoitering the river below the Fort in company with the Commandant of the Gun Vessels, I determined to erect a battery on the west side, and ordered Brevet Major Muhlenburgh and Capt. Taylor to cross with their companies, leaving Lieut. McGavock and a party of men with the main body of the Indians to secure the rear.[363]

The soldiers crossed the river and cleared away the timber and underbrush from the proposed battery site. It was nearly two miles downstream from the fort, extreme range for the two 18-pounders shipped from New Orleans aboard the *Semelante*. How far the men went in building the battery is not known. Garcon and other leaders could undoubtedly see the work underway on the west bank far down from the water battery. If they had a spyglass, they might have even seen the soldiers cutting trees. The purpose of the work would have been unclear.

The Battle of Negro Fort had been underway six days by the evening of July 26, 1816. Lt. Col. Clinch and his land force failed even to approach, much less damage, the fortifications at Prospect Bluff. He only knew what he could see from afar. The fort was much stronger than expected, and

---

[363] Clinch to Butler, August 2, 1816.

while its artillery fire had been ineffective at ranges over one mile, that would change as soldiers and warriors tried to get closer. The potential of a bloodbath for the lieutenant colonel's men was obvious.

Clinch also started second-guessing his decision to erect a battery for the two 18-pounders:

> On the 26th the Col. began to clear away the Brushwood for the erection of the Battery; he however stated to me that he was not acquainted with Artillery but that he thought the distance was too great to do execution. On this subject we unfortunately differed totally in opinion, as we were within point blank range. He however ordered his men to desist from further operations. I then told him that the Gun Vessels would attempt the passage of the Fort in the morning <u>without his aid</u>.[364]

The lieutenant colonel made no mention of this disagreement in his report to Col. Robert Butler, the adjutant general for Maj. Gen. Andrew Jackson. There was a difference of opinions, though. Other eyewitness accounts confirm that Clinch believed that his artillery was too light and his force too small to take the fort. Had he prevailed in his views; the Battle of Negro Fort might have ended with the withdrawal of the American forces on July 27. Loomis was wrong in his assessment that the battery was in "point blank range" of the fort. Two miles was the extreme range for 18-pounders of the day, especially mounted in a rough battery on a riverbank. The navy officer's determination to continue the fight, however, turned near victory for the Maroon forces into a shocking defeat.

---

[364] Loomis to Patterson, August 15, 1816.

17

"THE EXPLOSION WAS AWFUL"

A RED SKY DAWNED OVER PROSPECT BLUFF on the morning of July 27, 1816. Ash thrown into the atmosphere by Mount Tambora still impacted the climate of North America, giving the daylight sky a strange red tint. The effect was visible as far south as the Gulf of Mexico, but the defenders of the fort were used to it by then and probably thought nothing of it. The same was true for the men in the forces surrounding them.

What the defenders did notice was their state of growing exhaustion. The fighting had gone on for seven days and nights, with those inside the fort never knowing when the Americans might rush forward to storm their walls. There was no shortage of supplies in the fort, and the success of the defensive efforts so far was obvious. Exhaustion, however, was unpreventable. On the other side, across the battlefield, the soldiers and warriors were also tired. They had lived for one week in primitive conditions, wading through cypress swamps and sluggish creeks. Each time a cannon fired, they worried that a shot or shell would end their existence. Congreve rockets skittered across the ground until they exploded or showered incendiary material. One found still intact at the site still contained pine resin. Lt. Col. Clinch's easy victory bogged down into a siege. Provisions were still plentiful. Foraging parties brought in green corn and melons from the Maroon fields, and there were free-range chickens, cattle, and hogs roaming the woods. The fort, though, was not an easy place to approach. Soldiers and warriors alike were often wet and covered with mud.

The final day of the Battle of Negro Fort began shortly before 5 a.m. Lt. Col. Clinch incorrectly wrote in his report that it was July 28, but the actual date was July 27, 1816. The disagreement that started between the army and the navy on the previous day continued, with the commanders of each force taking credit for the outcome. Clinch wrote that he exercised total command that morning:

> ...In the course of the evening, after consulting with the Commanding Officer of the Convoy, I directed him to move up the two Gun Vessels at day light the next morning. About six in the morning they came up in handsome stile and made fast along side of the intended battery. In a few minutes they received a shot from a thirty two pounder, which was returned in a gallant manner.[365]

Sailing Master Loomis presented the details of the attack in similar terms but expressed frustration with Clinch and claimed full credit for the navy. After describing the difference of opinion over the usefulness of the projected land battery, he told the army officer that his gunboats "would attempt the passage of the Fort in the morning without his aid." The vessels left Bloody Bluff well before sunrise:

> ...At 4 A.M. on the morning of the 27th we began warping the Gun Vessels to a proper position. At 5, getting withing Gun Shot the Fort opened upon us which we returned, & after ascertaining our real distance with cold shot, we

---

[365] Lt. Col. Duncan L. Clinch to Col. Robert Butler, August 2, 1816, Jackson Papers, Library of Congress.

commenced with hot shot (having cleared away our Coppers for that purpose).[366]

Another account, which supported the navy's point of view, was written by a "gentleman of the first respectability" in New Orleans to the editor of Niles' *Weekly Register*. Penned in the days after the gunboats returned from the expedition, it takes a particularly harsh view of Lt. Col. Clinch's actions before the last day of fighting:

> ...Our vessels were ordered to co-operate with the army. I am sorry to say they received no support whatever, and that, on the contrary, they were dissuaded from attempting to pass or destroy the fort, as being impracticable from the size of their guns, only [9] pounders and but two of them. – Not disheartened, however, our gallant little band, less than 50 in number, all told, began to warp up, every now and then throwing a shot to ascertain the distance correctly – the negroes firing their large guns, but evidently without skill. As soon as they found their shot reach the village in the rear of the fort, they determined, as they say, to see if they could not make a bonfire, having previously cleared away their coppers to heat the shot, neither of them having a furnace.[367]

The argument between the army commander and the naval officer continued for years to come. For the occupants of the Negro Fort, however, the details of who ordered the attack did not matter. Their fates were determined by what happened next. Dr. Marcus C. Buck watched from the

---

[366] Sailing Master Jairus Loomis to Commodore Daniel T. Patterson, August 15, 1816, Letters Received from Captains.

[367] A Gentleman of First Respectability to the editor of the Weekly Register, n.d., republished in the *Republican Star or Weekly Advertiser*, Septembe4 24, 1816.

riverbank at the planned battery site as the gunboats exchanged fire with the water battery of the fort:

> ...On the morning of the 28th about sun rise, a fire from the fort was commenced on the gun boat, which was promptly returned. The 5th shot, which was the first hot shot thrown, entered the magazine, and sealed the fate of the garrison. You cannot conceive, nor I describe the horrors of the scene.[368]

The shock of seeing the explosion is also clear in the words of Lt. Col. Clinch:

> ...The contest was but momentary, the fifth discharge a hot shot from Gun Vessel 154 commanded by sailing Master Basset entered the magazine and blew up the Fort. The explosion was awful and the scene horrible beyond description. Our first care on arriving at the scene of destruction was to rescue and relieve the unfortunate beings that survived the explosion. The war yells of the Indians, the cries and lamentations of the wounded, compelled the soldier to pause in the midst of victory and to drop a tear for the sufferings of his fellow beings, and to acknowledge that the Great Ruler of the Universe must have used us as his instrument in chastising the blood-thirsty and murderous wretches that defended the Fort.[369]

Sailing Master Loomis was less descriptive, saying only that the first hot shot from his gunboats, "entering their Magazine, blew up and completely destroyed the Fort." The writer in New Orleans gave a more detailed account from the naval perspective after talking with the crew members:

---

[368] Dr. Marcus C. Buck to his Father, August 4, 1816.
[369] Clinch to Butler, August 2, 1816.

...It seems somewhat extraordinary, and almost miraculous, but the very first shot fired by Mr. Basset, a judicious, cool and very promising officer, who commanded gun vessel No. 154, entered their principal magazine and blew up the fort! The concussion was felt at Pensacola, a distance of 60 miles. The fort contained about 300 negroes and 20 disaffected Indian warriors with their families – 270 were killed, and the remainder all mortally wounded; only 8 escaped unhurt.[370]

How the crew of Gunboat No. 154 could have lobbed a 9-pound hotshot for nearly two miles and scored a direct hit on the main magazine of the fort has been a mystery since 1816. Many Seminoles, Miccosukees, and Red Sticks—with some prompting from Bahamian trader Alexander Arbuthnot—believed that William Hambly told the boat crews how to target the magazine. There is no evidence in the military records or Hambly's correspondence that this happened. The archaeological evidence suggests that the magazine door faced away from the direction of the cannon shot. Edward Nicolls, who corresponded with individuals who had firsthand knowledge of the explosion, provided the most likely explanation of what happened in an 1843 letter to Sir John Barrow:

...[O]ne of the vessels firing a gun with a red hot shot, fired it more to get rid of it than from any expected consequence, the shot glanced off a tree, and flew out of its course among some loose powder that some of the women were filling cartridges from at the grand magazine door, and which communicated to 300 five-and-a-half-inch shells, and about 300 barrels of powder, blew the whole of the battery or citadel, which stood in the centre

---

[370] Gentleman to the editor of the Weekly Register, 1816.

of the fort, to atoms, destroying all the men and several of the women and children.[371]

Nicolls's ricochet explanation is consistent with the report of Sailing Master Loomis, who said the gunboats were trying to fire over the fort and set fire to the village beyond. A major controversy over the incident erupted in 1819, following the publication of the naval officer's report. Lt. Col. Clinch—by then the colonel of the 8th Regiment—felt that Loomis criticized him unfairly and responded with his questions about the nature of the explosion:

> I should not at this late period have troubled either you or the public, on this subject, had it not been for the many false statements contained in the official report of Sailing Master J. Loomis, as published in the National Intelligencer of last April. – To notice one of which will be sufficient to convince every unprejudiced mind, of the incorrectness of this flaming report. He states that the position selected by me, & himself, was within P. Blank shot for nine pounders, for although the caliber is not mentioned, it must have been implied, as he had only common nine pounders on board of his boats. – The point selected by me, (more with a view of conducting an experiment, than with the prospect of effecting a breach in the wall of the fort) as measured by Major Fanning (an able and practical artillerist three thousand & ninety yards, with a gradual incline [torn] from the Fort to the position selected, the walls of the fort must have been at least fourteen feet high – under all these circumstances, even admitting that a ball thrown from a nine pounder, would range three thousand & ninety yards, what must

---

[371] Col. Edward Nicolls to Sir John Barrow, September 11, 1843.

have been its elevation, to have entered a magazine of the Fort.[372]

The colonel's reference to Maj. A.C.W. Fanning, a seasoned artillerist, was significant. Fanning commanded the American garrison left at Fort St. Marks (San Marcos de Apalache) by Maj. Gen. Andrew Jackson in the spring of 1818. When Spanish soldiers returned per agreement to reoccupy the post in 1819, Fanning shifted to Prospect Bluff, where Fort Gadsden now stood on a small part of the footprint of the original British Post. Clinch, now a full colonel with the 8th Regiment, asked Fanning to measure the distance of the shot that destroyed the Negro Fort. The major responded on June 11, 1819:

> In compliance with your request I have measured the distance from this point to the place where the gun boats lay at the time of its distruction, and found it to be three thousand & ninety yards.—The calculation of this distance, however, would be subject to some correction since the instrument I used for taking angles was very impractical.[373]

The effective range of a long 9-pounder during the War of 1812 era was 793-902 yards. The maximum range of these guns was 1,695 yards, or a bit more than half the distance of 3,090 yards that Fanning measured from the point where the gunboats fired to the site of the explosion. How Sailing Master Bassett was able to launch a red-hot cannonball for a distance twice the range of his gun is difficult to explain. Survivors of the explosion, however, left no doubt that a cannonball caused the blast. Most likely, Bassett fired with his 9-pounder at maximum elevation to give the

---

[372] Col. Duncan L. Clinch to --- ------, October 29, 1819, Adjutant General, Letters Received.
[373] Maj. A.C.W. Fanning to Col. Duncan L. Clinch, June 11, 1819, Adjutant General, Letters Received.

shot the altitude needed, while using a much larger powder load than normal to achieve the necessary range.

The massive explosion that destroyed the fort was unlike anything the sailors or soldiers had ever seen—with one exception. Brevet Maj. Peter Muhlenberg suffered severe wounds when a powder magazine exploded during the American attack on York, Canada, during the War of 1812. He was the chief of staff for Gen. Zebulon Pike, who died when a flying brick struck him. The odds of Muhlenberg witnessing two such explosions are incredibly small, especially since he survived the one at York while men died all around him. Unfortunately, no account of his observations of the Negro Fort destruction is known to survive.

Dr. Marcus C. Buck, the surgeon attached to Clinch's command, was one of the first soldiers to enter the fort and what he saw was overwhelming:

> …In an instant, hundreds of lifeless bodies were stretched upon the plain, buried in sand and rubbish, or suspended from the tops of the surrounding pines. Here lay an innocent babe, there a helpless mother; on the one side a study warrior, on the other a bleeding squaw. Piles of bodies, large heaps of sand, broken guns, accoutrements, &c. covered the scite of the fort. The brave soldier was disarmed of his resentment, and checked his victorious career to drop a tear on the distressing scene.[374]

Dr. Buck and others confirm that the U.S.-allied Creek warriors stormed the fort in the minutes after the explosion. Lt. Col. Clinch and other officers were hard-pressed to stop the indiscriminate slaughter of wounded survivors. Fires ignited by the blast complicated rescue efforts when they threatened another magazine:

---

[374] Dr. Buck to his Father, August 4, 1816.

...So soon as the flame was extinquished, (which endangered our troops, from its probable communication with another magazine between the picquets and parapet containing one hundred and fifty kegs of powder,) their attention was directed to the restoration of the life of those who were least injured. They succeeded with fifty out of three hundred souls who were in the fort. Amongst these were the Negro and Indian Chiefs; but they enjoyed but a short respite from the Indians. The Indian Chief was scalped alive, and stabbed, the Negro Chief was shot. By the great exertions of our human Col. And his officers, the other sufferers were saved from such a death; but several have since died of their wounds.[375]

The "Negro Chief" shot by the Creek warriors after the battle was Garcon. He was likely at the water battery directing cannon fire against the American gunboats when the devastating hotshot was fired. It was possible to see a cannonball with the human eye as it arced through the air toward its target. Garcon may well have followed its trajectory and been looking at the central citadel when it exploded. An unidentified officer writing from Camp Crawford on August 5 mentioned that the Maroon commander suffered eye damage:

> The fifth...shot passed through their magazine, and a dreadful explosion ensued. Some of the negroes and Choctaws were found at a considerable distance from the fort – all torn to pieces! Nearly every soul, in the den of robbers, perished. The number of men, women and children amounted in all to about 300. The chief of the Choctaws was found alive, but very much bruised and burnt. The chief of the negroes (whom they called

---

[375] *Ibid.*

seargeant-major) was also found alive – but quite blind. These two the Indians scalped and shot.[376]

Lt. Col. Clinch reported that Maj. McIntosh, Capt. Isaacs, and Mad Tiger "passed sentence of death on the outlawed Chactaw Chief and the black commandant Garson for the murder of the four Americans, and the sentence was immediately carried into execution." Sailing Master Loomis provided a bit more detail in his report to Commodore Patterson:

> ...Among the Prisoners were the two chiefs of the Negroes & Indians. On examining the Prisoners they stated that Edward Daniels O.S. who was made Prisoner in the Boat on the 17 July was tarred & burnt alive. In consequence of this savage act, the Chiefs were executed on the spot by the friendly Indians.[377]

Accounts vary as to the number of wounded who survived the explosion. Dr. Buck, who was in the best position to know, said that there were 50, including Garcon and the Choctaw chief. Lt. Col. Clinch confirmed this by estimating that there were 100 men and 200 women and children in the fort, "not more than one sixth part of which were saved." Sailing Master Loomis thought there were 320 men, women, and children in the fort, 270 of whom died instantly in the explosion. "The greater part of the rest," he wrote, were "mortally wounded, but three escaped unhurt." His statement also supports Dr. Buck's estimate that 50 people survived, at least temporarily. The sailing master gave another statement to the *Louisiana Gazette* not long after his return to New Orleans. "The number of persons in the fort previously to the explosion could not be precisely

---

[376] Officer at Camp Crawford to a Gentleman in Charleston, South Carolina, August 5, 1816, published in the *Early American Newspaper*, September 10, 1816.

[377] Loomis to Patterson, August 15, 1816.

ascertained," he reported, "about 200 were buried and a great number could not be extricated from under the ruins."[378]

Of the survivors, only eight had any connection to slaveowners in the United States. Clinch prepared a list on August 4 after his return to Camp Crawford:

Names	"Owners"
Lamb	Col. Benjamin Hawkins
Elijah	W. Lewis of Georgia
Abraham	W.B. Howel of Georgia
Jo	Capt. Bowen of Georgia
Batture	"Frenchman" in Bay St. Louis, Mississippi Territory
Jacob	William Morgan
William	"Dulendo a 'Jew King' Jamaica"
Charles	"Said he belongs to John Sharp, but it is supposed he is owned by some gentleman in Virginia, as he arrived at Pensacola in the English vessel *Sea Horse*"[379]

All of the other survivors came from either Spanish Florida or the Creek Nation. John Innerarity, a partner in John Forbes and Company, reported from Pensacola on August 13 that "six negroes who escaped unhurt in the Fort when it blew up have been brought here among the number Castalis [Castalio] whom I have sent to the Public Works with a chain about his leg in consequence of his having prevented several of our

---

[378] Jairus Loomis, Statement to the *Louisiana Gazette*, published in issue of August 19, 1816.

[379] List of prisoners confined at Camp Crawford, August 4, 1816, enclosed in Clinch to Butler, August 2, 1816.

negroes from returning." He went on to note of the survivors that "about 20 are left there wounded."[380]

Among the wounded left at the fort was Mary Ashley, who served with a cannon crew atop the citadel. "This poor woman was cut and most cruelly used by these lawless miscreants," wrote Col. Nicolls many years later, "her free papers destroyed, and herself, children, and the rest of the survivors sold into slavery."[381]

The sheer volume of munitions, weapons, and military supplies found in the fort shocked the American officers. Clinch and Loomis agreed to a joint inventory and assigned Lt. Henry Wilson of the 4th Regiment and Sailing Master Bassett to complete the task. Their report shows how well Lt. Col. Nicolls supplied his Maroon allies before leaving the Apalachicola:

> 48 Shovels, 26 Spades, 55 Pick Axes, 1 Broad Axe, 3 Crow Bars, 1 Cooper's Axe, 1 Crank, 2 Hoes, 550 Muskets (80 complete), 340 Pair of Shoes, 23,500 Flints, 125 Sets Back Accountrements, 20 Sets Buff Cavalry, 514 Old Black & White Belts, 1852 Cartridge Boxes, 1 Box Cartridge Boxes, Lott Cooper Hoops, 1 pn. Tin Scales, 1 Lott Tackle, 7 Cross Cut Saws, 3 Whip Saws, 2 Double Blocks, 1 Lott Bayonets, 1 Lott Sundries, ½ Cask Spikes, 1 Box Cooper Hoops, 1 Cask, 1 Schooner, 1 Cutter boat, 1 Gig boat, 3 flats, 3 – 24 Pd. Cannon & Carriages, 2 – 9 Pounders & Carriages, 2, 6 Pd. & Carriages, 1, 6 Pd. Field Carriage (spiked), 3 Ammunition Carriages, 1 gun Limber, 2 Corn Mills, 1 Lott Tockle Blocks, 1 4 lb. Swivel, 1 2 pd. Swivel (Spiked), 1 Brass Howitzer mounted complete, 460 old belts, 40 New

---

[380] John Innerarity to James Innerarity, August 13, 1816, "Letters of John Innerarity and A.H. Gordon," *Florida Historical Quarterly*, Volume XII, July 1933, Number 1, pp. 37-39.
[381] Col. Edward Nicolls to Sir John Barrow, September 11, 1843.

Carbine Belts, 8 Sword Belts, 1 32 Pd. Cannon & Carriage.[382]

The inventory did not include cannonballs, shells, and other artillery projectiles, which the officers reported they were unable to collect and count. The summary also did not include property destroyed in the explosion, which Lt. Col. Clinch indicated was extensive:

> ...The property taken and destroyed cannot have amounted to less than two hundred thousand dollars. From the best information I could obtain there was in the Fort about three thousand stand of arms, from five to six hundred barrels of powder and a great quantity of fixed ammunition, shot, shell, &c.—One magazine containing 163 barrels of powder was saved, which was a valuable prize to the Indians.[383]

Sailing Master Loomis had additional inventories taken after the ships returned to Pass Christian and New Orleans. They indicate that the on-site tally was inaccurate and incomplete:

> Inventory of Articles Shipped on Board the Schooner General Pike from the Negro Fort to New Orleans today 4 – 24 pdr. Cannon, 4 – 6 pdr. do. do., 1 – 4 pd. Field Piece, 7 Ship Carriages for the first mentioned Guns, 3 Ammunition Waggons, 502 Muskets Good & bad, 1200 Bayonets, 1100 Bayonet Scabbards, 1816 Cartouche Boxes, 290 Bayonet Belts, 220 Cartouche Belts, 150 Gun Slings, 17 Sword Belts, 17 do. Knots, 16 Carbine Belts,

---

[382] "Inventory of Military Stores Captured at The Negro Fort East Florida," prepared by Lt. Henry Wilson and Sailing Master James Bassett, July 1816, Enclosed in Clinch to Butler, August 2, 1816, Jackson Papers, Library of Congress.

[383] Clinch to Butler, August 2, 1816.

33 Buff Straps, 22 Haversacks, 75 set black accoutrements in 3 Boxes, 2 small boxes of Musket Balls, 5500 Gun flints, 5 + Cut Saws, 1 Whip Saw, 170 – 24 pdr. shot, 24 stand 24 pdr. Grape, 20 for 6 pdr. do., 17 Cannister 24 pdr., 70 Shells, 80 Round 5 pdr. Shot, 2 Boxes loose Grape, 14 Water Casks with hoops & heads, one set harness for field, 1 lot Copper Hoops, 1 lot loose Blocks.[384]

In addition to these materials shipped to New Orleans aboard the *General Pike*, another stock of captured weaponry and supplies was taken to Camp Crawford by Lt. Col. Clinch:

1 Brass Howitzer mounted complete, 24 spades, 48 shovels, 54 Pick axes, 1 Broad Axe, 1 Cooper's Axe, 2 Cross bars, 2 Hoes, 120 Pair of Shoes, 1 Pair Tin Scales, 1 Tackle, 2 Cross Cut Saws, 1 Cart, 1 Cutter Boat, 3 Flats, 700 Spikes, 460 Old Belts, 40 new Carbine belts, 8 sword belts, 2 casks Flints, 100 Cartridge Boxes, 1 Box containing 20 Muskets, 1 Corn Mill, 50 Copper Hoops, 4 sets of Harness, 1 set Cart Harness.[385]

The final tally included 12 pieces of artillery, 522 muskets, 1,200 bayonets, and 23,500 gun flints. This haul does not include muskets, pistols, bayonets, flints, and other items claimed by the Creek allies.

The campaign cost the United States Midshipman Alexander Luffborough and three sailors killed. The death toll among the Maroons, however, was horrifying. Dr. Buck and Lt. Col. Clinch agreed that 250

---

[384] Inventory of Articles shipped on the Schooner General Pike, signed by Jairus Loomis at "Prospect Bluff River Appilachacola", July 30, 1816, Letters Received from Captains.

[385] "Articles recd. By Lt. Col. Clinch for the use of his command," signed for by Lt. Col. Duncan L. Clinch, July 1816, enclosed in Clinch to Butler, August 2, 1816.

men, women, and children died in the explosion. Sailing Master Loomis placed the death toll at 270 people. Of the 50 survivors, only six escaped without injury. Garcon and the Choctaw chief, wounded and captured alive, were executed by Creek warriors. The soldiers thought most of the survivors were mortally wounded, but six went to Pensacola and eight to Camp Crawford. The military reports note that about 20 of the others were still alive when the ships sailed from Prospect Bluff. William Hambly's letter of August 28, however, shows that the actual number of wounded left to die at the fort may have been significantly larger.

The final death toll of the explosion was between 250 and 300, making the projectile fired by Sailing Master Bassett the deadliest cannon shot in American history.

18

AFTERMATH AND SURVIVORS

THE STATE OF THE MEN, WOMEN, AND CHILDREN INJURED IN THE EXPLOSION of the Negro Fort was one of great misery. Many were severely burned, their bodies now covered with blisters and charred flesh. Broken bones, head injuries, damage to internal organs, shrapnel wounds, and loss of hearing and vision would be common in the wake of such a traumatic blast. Antibiotics were unknown in 1816, and infections soon raged. First, Dr. Buck and later William Hambly and his family tried to help the injured, but there was little they could do. They had neither the medicines nor the training to deal with such catastrophic injuries.

U.S. soldiers and their Native American allies occupied the fort for days after the explosion. They spent this time guarding against a surprise attack by reinforcements coming to the aid of the Maroon families, gathering and packing supplies for shipment to either New Orleans or Camp Crawford, foraging for food, and destroying the homes and fields of what had been the largest settlement of free blacks in North America. The American officers got their first real look at the fort they had taken:

> ...It stood on the east side of the river about twenty five miles from the Bay, and one hundred and twenty by water from this Post [*i.e.,* Camp Crawford]. Its circumference was about _____ feet. The parapet was about fifteen

high and eighteen thick, and defended by one 32, three
24's, two 9's, two 6 Pounders and an elegant 5 ½
howitzer. It was situated on a beautiful and commanding
bluff, with the river front, a large creek just below, a
swamp in the rear, and a small creek just above which
rendered it difficult to be approached by Artillery. But
under all these disadvantages it was taken without the loss
of a single man on our part.[386]

Lt. Col. Clinch left the estimate of the fort's circumference blank in
his report to Col. Robert Butler. Lt. Vicente Sebastian Pintado's earlier
estimate that each side of the 8-sided citadel measured 50 feet, however,
places the distance at 400 feet. This length was the circumference of the
inner citadel, not of the stockades that connected it to the river or the outer
entrenchment that surrounded the entire complex. Sailing Master Bassett
added that it "was a regularly constructed fortification, built under the
immediate eye & direction of Col. Nichols of the British Army."[387]

The explosion of the "grand magazine"—as Col. Nicolls named it—
destroyed one of three powder magazines in the fort. Modern
archaeologists have yet to locate the remaining two, although one was
somewhere between the "piquets" or stockade and the main citadel. The
third was probably near the water battery. Soldiers and sailors found other
stocks of powder hidden outside the stockade in the houses of the village
area. A participant in the campaign related a harrowing incident at one of
these magazines in an account published many years later:

When the Fort was blown up, Col. CLINCH rushed
into the ruins and ascended the highest point he could
find, in order that the friendly Indians might recognize
him and desist from the work of pillage and slaughter.

---

[386] Lt. Col. Duncan L. Clinch to Col. Robert Butler, August 2, 1816, Jackson
Papers, Library of Congress.
[387] *Ibid.*; Sailing Master Jairus Loomis to Commodore Daniel T. Patterson,
August 15, 1816, Letters Received from Captains.

One of his men discovered that he was standing on a Magazine, towards which the fire was rapidly communicating, and called his attention to the fact just in time for the Colonel's escape and for the safety of the Magazine.[388]

Sailing Master Loomis sounded the river and quickly determined that it was too shallow for the schooner *General Pike* to continue upstream to Camp Crawford. "I found it impassable for vessels drawing more than 4 ½ feet water," he wrote, "consequently Col. Clinch took the provision from the *General Pike* into Flats & lightened the *Semelante* to enable her to ascend the River as high as Fort [*i.e.,* Camp] Crawford." The capture of the cutter, flatboats, and other vessels at the fort made this operation easier. Clinch had the two 18-pounders and ordnance stores removed from the *Semelante* and placed on smaller boats for the journey upstream, ordering Maj. Peter Muhlenberg to lead the flotilla north on July 30, 1816.[389]

The *General Pike* sailed at about the same time, the cargo aboard receipted for, while Gunboats No. 149 and No. 154 lingered at Prospect Bluff for several more days. Lt. Col. Clinch also remained behind with the bulk of the Native American force, and was still there when news arrived that the feared Seminole, Miccosukee, and Red Stick Creek reinforcements were coming down the river:

> ...On the evening of the first inst. I received information that a large body of Seminole Indians were within a day's march of us, and in a few hours the report was confirmed by a letter from Major [Enos] Cutler left in command at Camp Crawford, informing me that a large body of Seminoles were descending the Appalachicola. I immediately ordered Major Muhlenburgh to keep the

---

[388] Unidentified participant, quoted in "Who is Duncan L. Clinch?," *Southern Whig*, September 16, 1847.
[389] Sailing Master Jairus Loomis to Commodore Daniel T. Patterson, August 15, 1816, Letters Received from Captains.

boats together, and to be in readiness to receive them, and directed one hundred Indians to keep with the Boats, and to act in concert if necessary. I advanced with two hundred Cowetas under the gallant Major [William] McIntosh to meet them, but the cowardly wretches dispersed without our being able to get a view of them.[390]

The reinforcements undoubtedly learned the outcome of the battle as they started to descend the river. Lt. Col. Clinch believed that his forces had sealed off the fort tightly enough to prevent the escape of any of the survivors, but William Hambly disputed this in a September statement by noting that "the Negroes that could walk and some Indians have returned." These survivors undoubtedly informed the chiefs leading the relief column that the fort was destroyed and the supplies stockpiled there taken. Stunned by the news, the warriors withdrew until they could learn more.[391]

The flotilla under Muhlenberg continued up the river, paralleled by the two columns of warriors, reaching Camp Crawford by August 4, 1816. A series of letters from Clinch and his officers flowed from the fort on that date, announcing the outcome of the expedition to the world. Dr. Buck's account to his father provided some extra details on the movements of the Seminole relief force:

> While we were carrying on our operations against the fort, the hostile Indians, embodied themselves and had proceeded within thirty miles of us for the purpose of attacking our rear; but the work was accomplished too soon for them, and they made a precipitate retreat on our return. They have since sent word that they wish to make peace. Our friendly chiefs are in consultation as to the measures to be pursued with regard to them. The late affair has created so much terror in their breasts, that I

---

[390] Lt. Col. Clinch to Col. Butler, August 2, 1816.
[391] William Hambly to John Forbes, September 6, 1816, Forbes papers, University of West Florida.

have little doubt but it will secure us from future hostilities with them.[392]

The crews of Gunboats No. 149 and No. 154 remained at Prospect Bluff after the departure of the army, completing the salvage of the captured artillery and supplies. The sailors finished their work by the night of August 2. "On the 3rd August after setting fire to the remaining parts of the Fort & Village," reported Sailing Master Loomis, "I left the River."[393]

In Apalachicola Bay, however, the naval commander faced one final confrontation when the American gunboats emerged from the river to find that two armed Spanish schooners awaited. The vessels had arrived from Pensacola a few days before, and the commanding officer, Don Benigno Garcia Calderon, decided to blockade the river's mouth and wait for the U.S. vessels to return. He now sent one of his officers in a small boat to meet with the American officers. They informed him of their destruction of the Negro Fort and capture of its artillery and other supplies, prompting a demand that Loomis surrender the material to Spain:

> The officer whom I sent on board the vessel under your command, having informed me that on the morning of 27th July last, you had taken and destroyed the fort of Appalachicola, in which were several negroes, runaways from Pensacola, and that the artillery, ammunition, &c. which belonged to said fort, had been embarked by you on board the vessels of this division under your command, I consider it my duty to demand of you in the name of my government, all the artillery and ammunition which you have taken possession of, as belonging to a fortress established in the territory of his catholic majesty, which demand, I do not doubt you will accede to, considering

---

[392] "An officer of the Southern army [i.e. Dr. Marcus C. Buck] to his father, near Winchester, Va.," August 4, 1816, published in the *Nashville Whig* on October 16, 1816.

[393] Loomis to Patterson, August 15, 1816.

the perfect harmony which exists between my government and that of the United States of America: I also request the favour of you to give me a circumstantial account of what occurred in the taking and destruction of said fortress, in order that I may communicate the same to the governor of the province of West Florida. May God preserve you many years.[394]

The Americans were conducting military operations on Spanish soil without the approval of Gov. Mauricio de Zuniga in Pensacola Caught red-handed, they could have provoked a battle between the two nations by refusing Calderon's demand. Loomis, however, placated the Spanish officer:

> Yours of this date I have had the honor of receiving. As respects your demands I shall transmit them to the government of the United States.
>
> The property captured on the 27th of July, 1816, on the Appalachicola river, in East Florida, I consider as belonging to runaway slaves, who had absconded from the United States and elsewhere, to protect themselves against their proper masters. The fort was defended under the English flag accompanied with the bloody flag, therefore I consider it my duty to hold the said property until I receive further instructions from the commanding naval officer of the New Orleans station.[395]

The two commanding officers agreed to deliver an inventory of the cannons and other captured supplies to their respective governments for adjustment. The vessels then sailed back to Pensacola in company. Commodore Patterson later reported from New Orleans that the Spanish seemed complacent about the matter:

---

[394] Don Benigno Garcia Calderon to J. Loomis, August 3, 1816.
[395] J. Loomis to Don Benigno Garcia Calderon, August 5 [*sic.*], 1816.

...Mr. Loomis states to me, that the officer afterwards
informed him, his demand was made without any
authority from the governor of Pensacola, but simply
upon his own, deeming it his duty to do so, expressing at
the same time the pleasure he felt at the destruction of the
fort, and the gratification it would afford to his
government.[396]

Conflict avoided, the *General Pike* and her escorts reached the naval
station at Bayou St. John in New Orleans on August 12, 1816. The cannons
and other supplies were unloaded there and disappeared into the supply
system of the U.S. Navy. The eventual fate of the Negro Fort guns is not
known.

Among those who returned to Pensacola aboard the armed schooner
Maria was Edmund Doyle, the former keeper of the John Forbes and
Company trading post at Prospect Bluff. His existence during the
American campaign, according to William Hambly, had been a precarious
one:

On the 15th of July, I had the opportunity of making
don Edmund Doyle aware of the actions of his country.
His canoe, I learned, had been confiscated and impounded
by [Sandy] Durant. After last Thursday's destruction of
the Negroes that happened on the 28th of July, Doyle
escaped determined to be there on the 31st of July.[397]

Like Lt. Col. Clinch and others, Hambly was confused in his dates.
The fort blew up on July 27, which was not a Thursday but a Saturday. He
made his way to Prospect Bluff, where the military turned the survivors

---

[396] Commodore Daniel T. Patterson to Benjamin W. Crowninshield, Secretary of
the Navy, September 6, 1816.
[397] William Hambly to John Forbes, September 6, 1816.

over to his care. Doyle, meanwhile, reached Apalachicola Bay and went aboard the Spanish schooners. Calderon refused to allow him to go up to the fort and he sailed back to Pensacola aboard the *Maria*. To Hambly, meanwhile, fell the unexpected challenge of caring for the most severely wounded of the surviving Maroons. Fury raged among them and their allies, the Red Stick Creeks, Seminoles, and Miccosukees formerly aligned with the British:

> The Negroes that could walk and some Indians have returned, and they say that the attack has merited the displeasure of the Honorable Governor, Jésus, and of the entire population of Pensacola. Only if both the Honorable Governor and Mayor would have known to come...If only Spain and Great Britain were at war with the United States of America and if only there would be a provocation to expel the Americans as the consequence of their alliances and the removal of the Indians.[398]

Hambly's letter bears dates of September 6 and September 11, 1816, but these are the dates when it left Pensacola and reached John Forbes. That he wrote it in the week after the explosion is clear from the text. The reference to the return of "the Negroes that could walk and some Indians," for example, appears between two mentions that the destruction occurred during the previous week.[399]

The letter raises serious doubts about the traditional interpretation of Hambly's actions at the time of the battle. Rumors grew in 1817—fed in large part by the Bahamian trader Alexander Arbuthnot—that he allied himself with the Americans and even directed the cannon shot that destroyed the magazine. The allegations were questionable at best but received widespread acceptance from historians. Eyewitness accounts of the engagement, however, do not mention his presence on the gunboats or with Clinch's force during the fighting. Lt. Col. Clinch used Kendal Lewis,

---

[398] *Ibid.*
[399] *Ibid.*

not Hambly, as a translator during his negotiations with Maj. McIntosh, Capt. Isaacs and Mad Tiger. John Blunt was his courier to the gunboats. William Hambly does not appear in the lieutenant colonel's reports until after the battle when he assumed care of the Spanish Maroons wounded in the explosion.

The Spanish citizen's own words clearly show his mixed emotions. He gave information to the Americans, but also remained loyal to King and country in 1816. Speaking of the Maroons and Native Americans still living in the area after the explosion, he wrote:

> ...Because of the destruction of Thursday, they should number themselves with him to become a valiant and glorious force to crack America's yoke and liberate my country. If only there was already an English regiment in place every bit ready to help you in case of surprise war. If only the regiment command had already sent two large barges [or transports] loaded with essentials for use of the garrison and the Indians; but if only the bad weather had not already begun.[400]

Hambly lamented the failure of the Spanish governor of West Florida to seek his counsel, blaming Sandy Durant and "Vega Perriman" for giving bad advice. "Perriman" was likely William Perryman who, along with Durant, was among those who asked for British intervention on the Apalachicola in 1813. The regret that authorities suffered delays in sending "two large barges" or transports filled with supplies for the Negro Fort is very intriguing. The implication is that the Spanish armed vessels that arrived in Apalachicola Bay while the Americans were attacking Prospect Bluff might have been there to occupy and supply the fort, not attack it as U.S. officers assumed.

Hambly was part of an effort on behalf of John Forbes and Company to convince Maroons to return to slavery, but he also warned John

---

[400] *Ibid.*

Innerarity and other officials that most were happier on the Apalachicola. Caring for so many survivors, however, put a major strain on his resources:

> Concerning the discussion of a few days ago, I see myself obligated to withdraw myself from that dangerous situation. In the meeting I learned nothing of what would occur to the slaves under my control who live under my roof. That holds true as well for all the others (Tom, Dick Harry) who eat at my table. There is the Negra Doyle and moreover six children. Lieutenant Davy and two Spanish Negroes have escaped. And others will do likewise, seeking treatment for their wounds and unless your detachment arrives soon to search for them. And, more than that, they see me, for the most part, desperate to obtain whatever food…to provide nourishment. Durant has left in panic of what he feared. And the Negroes and Indians have robbed all that remained of eggs set aside for our meals.[401]

His reference to "the discussion of a few days ago" is unclear. The letter is badly faded, and Hambly's script (in Spanish) is difficult to read. It may have referred to a meeting with Edmund Doyle, but also could mean his talks with the American officers. Lieutenant Davy was a Creek chief who lived on the Apalachicola between Ocheesee and Hambly's home at Spanish Bluff. His rank originated from service with Nicolls during the War of 1812.

The lack of provisions was a major issue on the Apalachicola. A combination of the American raid, the Year without a Summer, thousands of Red Sticks who arrived in the area two years before, and the destruction of the fields of the Prospect Bluff settlement led to food shortages. Starvation, according to William Hambly, caused the deaths of wounded survivors:

---

[401] *Ibid.*

The Indians don't know who to trust, and after awhile, the wounded Negroes die of hunger. His Excellency should have sent something to Doyle to reestablish the trading post here...The Indians overload their seeding, planting in waves. They have completed their harvests and promise to sell to the first one who comes to buy; however, if there is too long of a delay, the American troops will purchase the entire harvest. The Indians that returned from that rout also reported that they expected to be invaded but they had not learned who the invading force would be. Colonel Clinch offered to provide me with grain measurers but I have not seen anything of them which impedes the distribution of the grain which needs to be done in case the Southern Americans make them a visit.[402]

Hambly's letter suggests a much larger number of wounded survivors than previously known. In the chaos following the explosion, many who were able to walk, or crawl, must have escaped into the surrounding woods. When the American troops and especially the allied Creek warriors, termed "murderous savages" by Hambly, withdrew, the survivors appeared seeking food and help. Other than what the Spanish citizen and his family offered, there was little of either.

John Innerarity, head of the Forbes and Company operations in Pensacola, believed that Edmund Doyle could have recovered many of the firm's former slaves had Don Benigno Garcia Calderon taken his schooners up to the fort:

> After being informed by the Officers of the Gun
> Vessels of the blowing up of the Fort, Dn. Benigno

---

[402] *Ibid.*

immediately ordered the 2 Schooners under his command to return here which they did in company with the Gun Boats.

Had they gone to the Fort they could have brought away the wounded, and Doyle would have been able to have collected several of our negros, who are scattered among the Seminoles.[403]

Innerarity told his brother, James, in Mobile that "eight of our negroes are either at the Seminoles or Tampa Bay," and that Hambly had "Dolly's family in his possession."[404]

The total number of survivors will never be known but was larger than the American officers thought. William Hambly rescued some, fed others, and knew of still more who were dying in the woods of starvation. Edmund Doyle returned to the river on a mission to reclaim as many as possible for the Forbes Company and other Spanish interests, even though the British military had compensated these individuals at the end of the War of 1812.

---

[403] John Innerarity to James Innerarity, August 13, 1816, "The Pandon-Leslie Papers: Letters of John Innerarity and A.H. Gordon, *FHQ*, Volume XII, July 1933, pp. 37-39.
[404] *Ibid.*

19

AFTERSHOCKS

THE SHOCKWAVE CAUSED BY THE DESTRUCTION OF THE NEGRO FORT shook the ground more than 60 miles away in Pensacola on the morning of July 27, 1816. In some ways, the earth still shakes today. The State of Florida called the Maroons "renegades" and "outlaws" as late as the 1980s when it decided the site was not worth maintaining as a state park. The U.S. Forest Service, which has owned much of Prospect Bluff since the 1930s, assumed management of the fort and keeps it as the only National Historical Landmark in a Southeastern national forest. U.S.F.S. archaeologists Dr. Andrea Repp and Rhonda Kimbrough opened the door to a new understanding of the site, and the Apalachicola National Forest has brought focus to the significance and multicultural nature of its story.

The first controversy over the U.S. campaign erupted just one week after the naval flotilla reached New Orleans. While it is true that most American public officials and newspaper editors supported the attack, there were exceptions. A curious exchange of thoughts began in the Crescent City after the *Louisiana State Gazette* incorrectly reported that American forces had destroyed the Spanish fort of San Marcos de Apalache (Fort St. Marks). A later issue corrected the mistake and prompted a letter from an anonymous resident:

The Appalachicola depot, the outrage committed on the property of Mr. Forbes of Pensacola, and finally the use to which the depot was appropriated at the close of the late war, were subjects of some speculation at the time, but considered of very little importance than as they served to develope the character of the distinguished Major Nicholls. Your two last numbers have revived the subject and given to the Appalachicola depot an importance which few of your readers would have believed it was ever designed to assume. When Nicolls and Woodbine were arranging their plan of attack upon this section of the union, I felt in common with every honest American, very much indebted to our neighbors, the Dons for the dignified manner in which they supported and preserved their neutrality – and but for some foolish notions of their being the allies of John Bull, I am persuaded that Pensacola would never have served the enemy to refit in, the Barancas would not have been delivered over to the safe keeping of our enemy. Pensacola would not have been the rendezvous of the disaffected Indians, the public square of that place would not have been converted into a Champ de Mars for maneuvering & furnishing those savage enemies with arms and munitions of war; Spanish officers would not have served as pilots for the enemy; in a word, the now celebrated Appalachicola depot would not have been known.[405]

The writer's tongue in cheek style, of course, implicated authorities in Pensacola in hostilities against the United States. He went on to suggest that they might be more involved in the Negro Fort story than previously thought:

---

[405] Anonymous Letter to the Editor, *Louisiana State Gazette*, August 21, 1816.

...[W]hat the devil does this Appalachicola fort, and the blowing up hundreds of its noble defenders and carrying off arms and ammunition mean? We understood at the close of the war that a small supply of arms, ammunition and provisions had been left there for the use of a few fugitive slaves and some disaffected Indians – You now speak of three or four thousand stand of arms, of a regular fortification, of twenty four pounders well mounted, an immense quantity of ammunition, clothing, &c. Some three or four hundred thousand dollars at least must have been expended for the temporary convenience of a few deluded slaves, without the knowledge or approbation of our friends the Dons – You cannot be serious – I fear that your first account of the story must be the true one: Col. Clinch and a few brave tars must have mistaken Fort St. Mark for the works designed for the temporary protection of our wretched negroes, and I am the more inclined to believe that such a sad blunder has been committed from having been assured that a formal demand of all the arms and munitions of war taken, has been made, and the refusal to deliver them most solemnly protested against by the officers of the Spanish government. Do think over the subject seriously, Mr. Editor, and let us poor ignorant folks know how far we can trust our neighbors.[406]

The editor of the *Gazette* did consider the issue and concluded that the letter writer might not be far from wrong. The United States coveted Florida, and this desire for territorial expansion often showed itself in allegations that the "Dons" of Pensacola were perfidious and scheming:

---

[406] *Ibid.*

Though the writer of the above communication assumes the dress of a simple farmer, we suspect that he is a knowing one, and that his inuendoes against the character of our neighbors the Spaniards, are those of a man intimately acquainted with the circumstances of our dispute with them, and who has thought deeply upon the subject. There is such plausibility in his suggestion that altho' this negro fort was built and armed by col. Nicholls, to annoy the United States during the late war, yet that during a subsequent period the armament was purchased by the Spaniards in contemplation of a similar object.[407]

The editor's suggestion that Spain bought the arms of the fort was unfounded speculation. Lt. Col. Nicolls expressed thorough disgust with Gov. Mateo Gonzales Manrique's efforts to both defend Pensacola and maintain his country's neutrality, lecturing both the governor and his own military in a series of fiery letters. That Spain considered the U.S. attack to be a violation of its territorial integrity, however, was true. The country's protests fell on deaf ears, and its demands for the cannon and other supplies seized at the fort went ignored.

The newspaper editor saw something sinister in the Spanish protests:

Is it probable that a British officer would have left more than one hundred thousand pounds worth of property in the hands of a miserable banditti, without the smallest possible prospect of advantage to his sovereign? Or is it likely that in the immense fleet which was in the Gulph of Mexico at the conclusion of the war, room could not be found for 3000 stand of arms, 500 sabres, 200 pair of pistols and a quantity of powder? No. In whatever light the subject is viewed, the inference is irresistible that those articles were purchased by the Spaniards. If it were

---

[407] *Louisiana State Gazette*, August 21, 1816.

not the case, what right had a Spanish officer to demand their restitution from Mr. Loomis? True the fort was not garrisoned by Spanish troops, nor was it commanded by a Spaniard, but equally true that under such circumstances there would have been no possibility of injuring the southern frontier of the United States without incurring certain and summary chastisement.[408]

Missing from the editorial was any mention of the fact that the American attack on the Negro Fort was unprovoked. The Maroons were not engaged in hostilities against the United States, and there is no evidence that they intended attacks. U.S. troops invaded a foreign country under the pretext of looking for an excuse to justify the destruction of the fort. The Maroons and Choctaws provided that justification when they attacked the watering party from Gunboat No. 149, although they likely knew by then that an American operation against them was underway.

Another resident of New Orleans did not question the intent of Spain as much as the purpose of Great Britain in leaving a massive armament at the fort:

I wish Nichols and Woodbine had been in the fort when it blew up. The Spaniards now seem to insinuate that it was an interference with their territory, although they officially told general Jackson, they were not accountable for anything the British did, therefore it was an Indian territory. The fort was commanded by a negro who was taken alive, though since dead, he confessed he fought under British colors, they were up in the fort; his orders were, to let no white man approach the fort, or ascend the river, without the private signal of the British.[409]

---

[408] *Ibid.*

[409] Gentleman in New Orleans to a Gentleman in New York, *Early American Newspaper*, November 5, 1816.

Such thoughts and letters proliferated in American newspapers in the fall and winter of 1817-1818. The arrival of the news in Great Britain, however, inspired different reactions. Lt. Col. Nicolls requested permission to return to Florida and lead his former allies. The Prophet Francis, who was still in residence at Nicolls' home, "sweares he will kill every American in the province as soon as he returns."[410]

A British officer who signed himself only as "Old Soldier" wrote to a London newspaper to express alarm at the actions of the Americans:

> My Correspondent in Georgia writes to me, that a Colonel CLINCH, with a party from new Orleans, accompanied by two gun-boats, and transports with provisions and military stores, invaded the Spanish province of East Florida, and reduced the fort of St. Marks, on the Apalachicola river (from an accidental explosion of the powder magazine).
>
> The garrison, consisting of about one hundred negroes, with a few Indians, were made prisoners.
>
> The public will no doubt be curious to know what reason the American Congress will assign, or what apology they can make, to the Spanish Court, for this most wanton, outrageous aggression of the Spanish territories in a time of profound peace.
>
> The longing and anxious desire of the American Congress to obtain "per fus aut nefus" the possession of the province of East Florida, which, from being the key of the Gulph of Florida, which lay the commerce of the Spanish Colonies in time of war entirely at the mercy of the Americans, is well known.[411]

---

[410] Lt. Col. Edward Nicolls, letter of December 19, 1816, Cochrane Papers, University of West Florida.
[411] Old Soldier to the Editor of the Morning Post, *The Morning Post*, November 2, 1816.

The identity of the "Old Soldier" is not known. His incorrect identification of the fort as "St. Marks" shows that he was not Nicolls or George Woodbine, neither of whom would have made such a mistake. He was, however, remarkably familiar with the activities of the American "Patriots" who launched an effort to revolutionize Florida in 1812:

> Our Jamaica Planters and Merchants ought to look to themselves, as they have certainly the most serious cause of alarm at the prospect of East Florida falling into the hands of the Americans, as in time of war they will have a perfect command of the Gulph of Florida.
>
> This favourite object the Americans have always had in view: witness their countenancing and encouraging a band of banditti and marauders from Georgia, who for ten years invade the province of East Florida, and carried on a most destructive plundering species of warfare to the very lines of the capital of St. Augustine.
>
> Although their shameful, audacious aggressions were well known to the Governor of Georgia and the American Congress, yet they never, by Proclamation, or any public act, ordered these banditti to desist from their spoliations and depredations, but encouraged them to persevere in their lawless enterprises; and, however surprising it may appear, the Spanish nation bore with these insolent aggressions, and never attempted to revenge these insults and outrages, of which the Americans took the most cowardly advantage, well knowing that the Spanish armies were fully employed in expelling the French from their territories, consequently incapable of retaliating on the Americans.[412]

---

[412] *Ibid.*

The writer urged the British government to seek possession of Florida from Spain, pointing that it commanded the approaches to Jamaica. He warned that American agitations against Spanish possessions in modern Texas combined with efforts in Florida foreshadowed an effort to seize the entire Gulf of Mexico.

Also, in 19th-century terms, there was great strategic value in gaining possession of Florida's live oak forests:

> As an inducement to the British Government to accede to the proposals of the Spaniards, it is necessary to mention that the Floridas will furnish a regular supply of naval stores, such as pitch, tar, and turpentine, masts, ship-plank, with live oak of the greatest magnitude for ship-building, with which these provinces abound. There is another circumstance which out to have great weight, as the British will have the exclusive possession of live oak, the Americans will be thereby excluded from its use in forming a durable navy, and be obliged to use their own worthless oak, which will not last above six or seven years, at the expiration of which period they must be at the enormous expense of renewing their whole fleet.
>
> Live oak is a wood of that extraordinary durability, that after the trees have been exposed to the changes and inclemency of the seasons for upwards of a century, it acquires a stony hardness, and will resist the edge of the best tempered steel.
>
> The Americans know its value; their first frigates were built of this wood from trees collected in South Carolina and Georgia; they also procured frames for ten or twelve seventy-fours, which were deposited in their arsenal, but were wisely destroyed by Sir ALEXANDER COCHRANE. There are now only a few scattering trees

in Carolina and Georgia, perhaps sufficient to build a frigate.[413]

The United States, meanwhile, wasted no time in trying to capitalize on the demonstration of power provided by the explosion of the fort. Aware that the loss of the massive stockpile of arms contributed greatly to the weakness of the Creek Indians, they invited a delegation of chiefs to the national capital to start negotiations for cessions of Native American land:

> There have lately arrived in Washington city, led by Gen. M'Intosh and by Major Hughes, United States Factor, eight Chiefs and Warriors, deputed by the head men of the Muscogee or Creek nation, on a visit to the President of the United States. Of the object of their visit (says the National Intelligencer) we are uninformed; but they are, we learn, invested with full powers to treat on all points relating to the nation. – This deputation is composed of the principal officers who enrolled early in the Creek war, and who, under M'Intosh, co-operated with Maj. Gen. Jackson during the whole war, and latterly with their leader, marched against the Negro Fort at Apalachicola, which they united with Col. Clinch in the destruction of.[414]

The First Seminole War of 1817-1818 intervened in such discussions, but the defeat of the Red Stick Creek, Miccosukee, Maroon, and Seminole alliance by Maj. Gen. Andrew Jackson in 1818 cleared the way for a massive territorial expansion of the United States. Not only was the U.S. able to force the cession of Florida by Spain, but negotiations soon resumed that led to the surrender by the Creek Nation of its lands in present-day Georgia. The Treaty of Indian Springs, signed in 1825, was

---

[413] *Ibid.*
[414] *The American*, December 25, 1816.

signed by William McIntosh—who commanded Creek forces nine years earlier at Negro Fort—so infuriating other chiefs that an execution squad killed him. A party that included Menawa killed McIntosh and burned his home. The United States, however, still got its way, and the Creeks signed the Treaty of Washington one year later.

Lt. Col. Nicolls dreamed of the fort at Prospect Bluff serving as an armory from which the Creek, Seminole, Miccosukee, and Maroons could draw weapons and ammunition for self-defense and preservation of their lands. If pressed by American forces, they could fall back on the fort, which was large enough and strong enough to protect thousands of people. The dream evaporated in the smoke and fire of July 27, 1816.

Survivors of the attack reassembled at Nero's Town on the Suwannee River. Maroons founded this community after Tennessee volunteers intervened in East Florida's "Patriot War," killed , burned Bowleck's town on Paynes Prairie, and drove them into the wilderness. The town was closely associated with Boleck ("Bowlegs"), the brother of Payne, and stood near Old Town in what is now Dixie County, Florida. The Alachua town and Nero's Town were in proximity. Nero, the principal Maroon chief, was a well-respected leader with service in Nicolls's Colonial Marines.

It did not take long for the community to attract the attention of Lt. Col. Duncan Clinch, who demanded that the Native Americans surrender their black friends and allies:

> I sent two friendly chiefs with a Talk to Kapishimico, Chief of the Mickasukeys, & the oldest chief of the Seminoles, demanding the surrender of all the Negroes belonging to the Citizens of the U.S.—I further informed him that I had sent my last talk to him, & that unless the Negroes were given up immediately, that a sufficient force would be marched into his country, to drive the Seminoles into the Sea.

The two chiefs that I sent with the Talk returned last
evening [Oct. 27, 1816], & informed me that they had
been in council with Kapishimico, & some of his chiefs
for two days, & that they had determined on giving up the
Negroes.—Kapishimico requested them to inform me that
he wished to remain at peace with us—That he could not
take all the Negroes at once, but as soon as the Upper
Indians, took their Negroes from among them, he would
have the American Negroes taken & given up.[415]

Cappachimico's reply shows that he was a wily negotiator. By
offering to round up any escaped slaves from the United States once Upper
Creeks came down and defeated the Maroons first, he put the onus on the
Americans and their Creek allies. Clinch wanted to do exactly that and had
arranged for Maj. William McIntosh to be at Camp Crawford by October
1 with a force 1,000 warriors. The Coweta chief was delayed first by an
important council and then by his trip to Washington, D.C.

The two unidentified chiefs that Clinch sent to Miccosukee tried to
explain Cappachimico's caution:

…The two chiefs that went (& I have much confidence in
the judgement and friendship of one of them) were of the
opinion that they would make exertions to have the
Negroes taken, but that the Negroes would be too strong
for them, unless they received some assistance from the
Indians above the line.—My own impressions are that
they will not give up the Negroes until they are compelled
to do so, as I know them to be our most deadly enemies,
& nothing but force keeps them quiet.[416]

---

[415] Lt. Col. Duncan L. Clinch to Maj. Gen. Andrew Jackson, October 28, 1816,
Jackson Papers, Library of Congress.
[416] *Ibid.*

Clinch's report of October 28 clearly shows that human property was the focus of the U.S. presence on the border. Spain offered no threat, but the greed for slaves was the driving impetus for the military operations. He wanted to go into Florida and bring back as many as possible:

> From the best information I can obtain, they can raise about 400 Indian warriors, & about the same number of Negroes, that is including all east of the Appalachicola, & below the National boundary line.—The Indians on the Appalachicola are very friendly to us. The distance from this post to the Mickasukeys, is about fifty miles, & then about sixty to the principle Negro Settlement on the Suwanna River.—The country is principally open pine barrens, intersected with large ponds, & a few Swamps, with only two rivers, or Creeks to cross between the Flint & Suwanna.—I would not presume to point out to a Genl. of your experience the species of force most proper to send against those Indians (Should they not comply with the demands made of them) but from my small knowledge of the country & of the Indian character, I am of the opinion that seven or eight hundred Indian warriors (about 200 of them mounted) commanded by Major McIntosh, in addition to the troops at this post, would be the cheapest & most efficient force that could be sent against them.[417]

Clinch might have been ready for more action, but his country was not. The invasion of Florida and the attack on the Negro Fort created great tension between the United States and Spain. The crisis deepened on August 27 when three Spanish ships fired on and captured the USS *Firebrand*, a warship on patrol in the Gulf of Mexico. Spain accused the United States of sending the *Firebrand* to escort piratical vessels that preyed on its shipping. Accusations also flew that the schooner was

---

[417] *Ibid.*

helping filibusterers determined on stealing territory in Texas. The incident took place exactly one month after the destruction of the Negro Fort.

The crisis between the two nations escalated quickly until Luis de Onis, Spain's emissary in Washington, assured the American government that his country had no desire for war. The war hawks still clamored, but the situation cooled significantly. As part of this cooling, the Madison Administration decided to suppress Lt. Col. Clinch's report of the attack at Prospect Bluff. The information was already public thanks to letters from the lieutenant colonel and other officers to friends, family, state officials, and the press, but the President saw no need to exacerbate the situation with a sudden release of the official document. The move stunned Clinch, who until that time believed himself due significant recognition for his victory:

> I have been informed by a friend, who was a short time since at W. City, that it was understood there that my official communication of the affair that took place on the Appalachicola, would be suppressed by the W. Department. I am induced to believe from this circumstance, (& I am certain the citizens of the U. States will be under the same impression) that my conduct on that occation has not met the approbation of the Government.—I have been nearly nine years in the service of my Country, during which time I have always considered myself entirely devoted to her interest, & have been wiling at all times to risk my life in her defence, or for the advancement of her glory.—But my character, & reputation (as a soldier) as small as it is, is my own & my all, & I am not disposed to have it sacrificed to answer the political views of my Government.[418]

---

[418] Lt. Col. Duncan L. Clinch to Maj. Gen. Andrew Jackson, November 15, 1816, Jackson Papers, Library of Congress.

Clinch demanded a court of inquiry to decide whether he followed orders by "marching a party of U. States troops into E. Florida, & causing a fort on the Appalachicola to be destroyed." He believed that Maj. Gen. Jackson, to whom he addressed his request, would understand his need to affirm his honor.[419]

Jackson, however, benefitted from direct communications with Secretary of War William Crawford, Secretary of State James Monroe, and others in Washington. He understood the desire of the government to avoid conflict with Spain—at least for the moment—and replied to Clinch in placating terms. The lieutenant colonel did not receive his court of inquiry. The Madison Administration decided to withdraw the 4th Infantry from the border and shut down Camp Crawford. Orders went out to that effect, and the soldiers soon marched north from the camp, which by then Clinch had renamed Fort Scott. The Red Sticks responded by burning the post and carrying away the supplies left behind.

The evacuation of Fort Scott at the end of 1816 temporarily ended American plans for another invasion of Florida. U.S. authorities did not immediately know that a new threat had appeared on the Gulf Coast.

George Woodbine was back.

---

[419] *Ibid.*

20

WOODBINE RETURNS

GEORGE WOODBINE'S WAR OF 1812 SERVICE IN FLORIDA gave him a chance to view the strength of Spain not only in Pensacola but at St. Augustine and Fernandina in East Florida as well. Never a professional soldier like Nicolls, he saw an opportunity in the European country's weakness. His discharge from the military and return to the Caribbean soon led to a new scheme.

Woodbine was always something of an outlaw. His service with the Royal Marines was one of the most legitimate successes of his life. He came to the attention of the British military, however, because of his experience as a smuggler. Woodbine was one of several Bahamians who smuggled goods into Spanish Florida and traded with the Native Americans and Maroons living there. Such acts were highly illegal. John Forbes and Company held exclusive license to trade in Florida, and anyone else engaging in trade there was violating not only the firm's franchise but the laws of Spain. The risk was great, but so too were the rewards. Trading in untaxed goods allowed smugglers like Woodbine to sell cheaper than the Forbes company while making much larger profits. The Bahamian smugglers used small schooners and sloops to slip in and out of undeveloped Florida bays and harbors.

Smuggling was just one small step from piracy, and the line that separated the two crimes was thin. William Augustus Bowles was the best-known individual to enter Florida with dreams of smuggling and trading only to cross that line. What started as an effort by Bowles and his backers to open new trade with the Seminoles, Creeks, and Miccosukees evolved into a piratical scheme to supply goods—and slaves—not only to the Native Americans but to white Americans as well by preying on shipping in the Gulf of Mexico. There is speculation that Woodbine gained his introduction to Florida as a follower of Bowles, but the proof is elusive.

Woodbine was, without a doubt, involved in slave smuggling. The Royal Navy did not know it when it recruited him, but he faced recent accusations of violating Great Britain's law that banned the African slave trade:

> Whereas, at the Assizes, and General Session of Oyer and Terminer, holden at the Castle of Exeter, in and for the country of Devon, on Saturday, the 18th July, 1812, a Bill of Indictment for PERJURY, committed in a certain proceeding, instituted in the High Court of Admiralty, touching the employment of a certain ship or vessel, called the GALLICIA, in the Slave Trade, was at the instance of the Directors of the Africa Institution, preferred, and found against George Woodbine, otherwise called JORGE MADRESILVA, who acted as Super Cargo on board the said ship or vessel at the time of her capture, by His Majesty's ship Amelia, off the coast of Africa, in the year 1811; and the said George Woodbine, otherwise Jorge Madresilva, not having appeared to the same Indictment, he hath since been Out-lawed by due course of law. Notice is therefore, hereby given, that whoever shall apprehend the said George Woodbine, otherwise called Jorge Madresilva, and cause him to be lodged in the Castle of Exeter, or any other of His Majesty's Gaols in England, shall receive a REWARD of

ONE HUNDRED GUINEAS from the Directors of the said Institution.[420]

When the African Institution offered its reward for Woodbine's apprehension, he was in Florida serving as a captain with the local rank of major in Nicolls's battalion. Ironically, he was by then engaged in one of the most ambitious efforts to liberate slaves in Florida history, and his commanding officer was an outspoken abolitionist.

Woodbine left Florida with most of the other British marines in the late spring of 1815. His visits to Pensacola, St. Augustine, Fernandina, and other settled areas, however, gave him unique insight into the tenuous nature of Spain's grasp on the colonies. The Patriot War of 1812 was closer than those of the present generation might think. Had the governor in St. Augustine not convinced the Seminoles and Maroons to enter the fight on the side of Spain, the effort to seize East Florida might have succeeded. Capt. Woodbine saw this when he visited the old city with a bodyguard of Colonial Marines late in 1814. If he could separate the Seminoles and Maroons from Spain and convince them to join white recruits from the Bahamas, it might be possible to seize control of the colony.

The Fort at Prospect Bluff was an important part of this plan. Its stocks included thousands of muskets, carbines, pistols, swords, bayonets, and a small train of field artillery. The magazines held 500-600 kegs of gunpowder for small arms and cannons. There was enough material to supply an army, which is likely what Woodbine had in mind by 1816.

The former captain was organizing his plan in the Bahamas when news arrived that American troops had attacked and destroyed the fort. His response was to sail for the Gulf Coast of Florida. Woodbine owned a schooner, and it sailed it through the Florida Straits and into the Gulf of Mexico, arriving at the mouth of the Apalachicola in November 1816. Edmund Doyle was back at Prospect Bluff by then, working to reestablish

---

[420] *London Times*, April 25, 1815.

the John Forbes and Company trading post near the ruined fort. He reported on December 10 that Woodbine came and met survivors who came out of the woods to see him. His visit to the bluff was brief:

> Woodbine went from this place to Suwannie, sent for Kenhagee [*i.e.*, Cappachimico] who went to see him there, he told the Indians Col. Nicols would be out here in three months, from that time (about two months ago). Woodbine quit the vessel & remained for some days there. From thence he went to Tampa Bay to get a passage to the Havanna, from thence he said he would sail for Providence.[421]

The growing Maroon community at the Suwannee offered a sharp contrast to the charred ruins of the Negro Fort. Nero and his men had carried arms and ammunition from the fort's magazines to their town before the American attack. While the supply cache was small when compared to the massive arsenal destroyed and seized in the battle, it was large enough to guarantee the security of the adjacent settlements of Nero and Boleck. Woodbine found even more good news on his arrival at the Suwannee. The Maroons there continued to maintain military discipline and carry out the drills they learned from the British. He promised them that he would return soon.

The sudden reappearance of the adventurer ignited the fury of the brothers John and James Innerarity. They despised Nicolls and Woodbine. The British presence on the Gulf Coast cost them severely in cattle and goods, but the loss of slaves was what set the traders off:

> ...Of all the Fiends that ever assumed the human form to disgrace it a torment mankind some of the most atrocious & the vilest were vomited on these Coasts by England during the Last Summer or Fall. On this Subject...I dare

---

[421] Edmund Doyle to John Innerarity, December 10, 1816 and January 28, 1817, Papers of John Forbes and Company, University of West Florida.

touch but slightly; for when I think of it my reason leaves me. Sufficient to say that for the unparalleled wrongs we & others have suffered from these bands of Commissioned robbers, these British Algerines, these barbarians cowardly & treacherous, who flee before their enemies & plunder their allies a Memorial claiming reparations has been addressed to Castlereagh. This was a last resource, for sundry representations addressed to the British Commanders Cochran & Malcolm produced nothing but false promises, equivocation & evasions. Neither indeed do I expect any better result from the others. These High & Mighty gentlemen tread us worthless worms beneath their feet, & think us insolent if they by chance to notice that we writhe with Anquish.[422]

For the Innerarity brothers, the War of 1812 was all about one thing—slaves. Their right to hold others in bondage they felt was absolute, and the British move to free and enlist Maroons at Pensacola, and Prospect Bluff interfered with their liberty as they saw it. Writing from Pensacola in May 1815, John Innerarity mocked Nicolls for the major's involvement in abolitionist causes and belittled his promises to seek restitution for "owners" such as the Innerarity brothers, John Forbes, and others:

...But this apostle of liberty & worthy member of the Philanthropic Society held them spell bound. He did not, however, blind Pintado, Sierra, nor McPherson. They had an opportunity of seeing the latent course, the render plot; perpetual freedom, lands in Canada or Trinidado; the assurance that the British Govt. would pay their masters for their value, his return, abundance of provisions to support them & a well constructed fort to defend them in the interim. All this & more was held out to them. When

---

[422] James Innerarity to John Forbes, August 12, 1815, Forbes Papers, University of West Florida.

Spencer's efforts had failed Col. N. desired Pintado to assure the inhabitants of Pens. That his Governt. would pay the full value of their slaves: of this he was confident and expected to be appointed Commissioner with funds for the purpose; but if the Govt. did not he was sure the Philanthropic Society of which he had the honor of being a member, would; so that the owners might console themselves and rest satisfied that all would work together for their good.[423]

The Seminole chief Boleck (or Bowlegs) supported the British during the War of 1812, but later joined John Forbes and Company and others in attempting to secure the return of slaves after the departure of Nicolls and Woodbine:

A Nassau Paper complains, that the desertion of slaves during the late war was not confined to the United States, but was also practised towards the friendly inhabitants of East Florida, and even the Indians, our immediate allies. In confirmation of this assertion, it quotes the following extract of a letter from a settler in Florida, to his friend at Nassau:--"I have now at my house Bow Legs, King of the Seminoles, who has come to request that I would write to my friend in Nassau, to make inquiry about, and try to get back 14 negro slaves, belonging to himself and subjects, carried away by a Capt. Woodbine, under pretence of making them free." The writer adds, that in this application, he as well as others, are interested, who have been treated in a similar manner.[424]

---

[423] John Innerarity to James Innerarity, May 22, 1815, Forbes Papers, University of West Florida.
[424] *Jackson's Oxford Journal*, November 11, 1815.

Of all the former slave holders aggrieved with Nicolls and Woodbine, only the partners of John Forbes and Company had the resources to do something about it. Nicolls was unreachable to them, but George Woodbine was not. John Forbes went after him in the Bahamian courts, using evidence provided by James Innerarity in Mobile, John Innerarity in Pensacola, Edmund Doyle at Prospect Bluff, and others. He secured a decision against the former captain for lying under oath, but Woodbine was no longer in the Bahamas by the time it came down.

Multiple reports—including that of Doyle—place him on Florida's Gulf Coast during the winter of 1816-1817. The details of his plans are shadowy, but they involved not just Woodbine but former Lt. Robert C. Ambrister and the noted adventurer Gregor MacGregor. Woodbine also knew the sometimes privateer, sometimes pirate Luis Aury, who either took part in the scheme or developed a separate plan of his own. The men wanted to drive Spain from Florida and seize it for themselves.

Well-liked by the former members of the Colonial Marines, many of whom he brought into freedom, Woodbine started the projected campaign by sailing for Prospect Bluff in the fall of 1816. He briefly inspected the ruins of the fort in October but quickly moved on to the Suwannee. His presence there was soon known to the editors of American newspapers:

> ...Before I drop the subject of East Florida, it would be well to mention that the Indians, who, taking advantage of the absence of their inhabitants then employed in besieging St. Augustine, came in from the westward and killed and plundered all they met with, and taking off the negroes to a large amount, for which outrage they have never made the smallest satisfaction, but persist in retaining all they took, and granting protection to all runaway slaves from the United States to Florida, whose frontier inhabitants are daily falling a sacrifice to their resentment, which seems indiscriminately directed against all the white inhabitants, with whom they never

visit or have friendly intercourse. Their head quarters, at present, is about the mouth of Sewanee River, called San Juan de Amajura in the old charts, into which vessels are admitted from New Providence, who supply them with arms and ammunition in exchange for skins, &c. A certain captain Woodbine has been with them, and was lately; he is a British officer, and acquired their confidence during the war, by commanding at the British fort of Apalachicola under col. Nichols.[425]

Leaving the Suwannee after several weeks of consultations with Boleck, Nero, and other leaders, Woodbine sailed for Tampa Bay, where he called briefly on the Maroon communities there. He then sailed for Cuba, and from there by August 1817 to the Bahamas. Gregor MacGregor, meanwhile, visited the United States, rounding up volunteers in the Carolinas and Georgia. He sailed from Charleston in June 1817 with fewer than 80 men and stormed ashore at Amelia Island on the 29th after telling his men, "I shall sleep either in hell or Amelia tonight!"

The island's main community was Fernandina, where the largest threat to his plans was Fort San Carlos. The Spanish commandant, however, overestimated the size of MacGregor's force and surrendered without firing a shot. The Scot adventurer raised the "Green Cross of Florida" flag over the fort and declared the establishment of the Republic of Florida. He printed his own money, encouraged fleeing citizens to return, and sent a detachment to conduct reconnaissance around St. Augustine. Things quickly unraveled, however, as Spanish troops killed, wounded, or captured most of the men from his scouting party. His other supporters objected to being paid in paper money that MacGregor issued himself. And, most significantly, authorities in the United States stopped his reinforcements from leaving port.

By late August, it was clear that things were not going well, and the general—a real rank that he held in the armies of Venezuala—called for

---

[425] *Lancaster Journal*, December 3, 1817.

Woodbine's help. The former captain sailed for Florida in his schooner, the *Venus*, picked up MacGregor and his wife, and sailed for Nassau with them on September 8. They arrived there two weeks later, and MacGregor had a commemorative medal struck. It included the words "I came, I saw, I conquered."

George Woodbine, as best can be determined, never returned to Florida after his rescue of Gregor MacGregor. He settled on the Isla de San Andres off the coast of present-day Colombia in 1817 and took part in MacGregor's expedition against Portobello (Panama). Resettling near Cartagena, he developed a plantation and invested heavily in slave labor. It was this phase of life that led to his doom:

> On the night of the 26th July, Col. George W. Woodbine and his family, consisting of his wife and two sons, were inhumanly butchered at Maraparata, their plantation, about 2 leagues from Carthagena, near the shore of the Bay, in the direction of Boca Chica. The horrid act was supposed to be committed by blacks, from adjoining plantations, with the object of robbery. The dwelling was plundered of all the valuable furniture, and every part broken open and searched, where money would likely have been found – but it was believed none was found, as, after the murder, some gold, &c. belonging to the Colonel, was found deposited in another place. It was not known whether the Colonel's own slaves were accessory to the crime or not – they stated that they fled when the robbers attacked the premises, and the next day gave information of the act in Carthagena. Eighteen blacks residing in the neighborhood of the scene, have been arrested on suspicion, and were to have their trial.
>
> Col. Woodbine, it will be recollected, was the officer who commanded in Florida in 1815. He had resided at the

above plantation for several years past, and bore the character of an honorable gentleman.[426]

The murders created near panic in Cartagena, where many of the residents were slave-owners from other countries. The situation was made worse by the French Consul, who made remarks that the community at large took as being supportive of the killings. The investigation concluded that the uprising was carried out by slaves brought to Cartagena by Woodbine from Jamaica and Isla de San Andres. Except for one woman who was spared due to "special reasons" (*i.e.,* pregnancy), the alleged murderers were hanged.[427]

In the end, the former slave smuggler from Jamaica—who freed hundreds of men, women, and children from slavery in Florida—died at the hands of men and women that he held in bondage. His family died with him.

---

[426] *Alexandria Gazette*, September 5, 1833.
[427] Letter dated "Carthagena, Dec. 3, 1833," published in the *National Gazette*, January 2, 1834.

21

ABRAHAM & POLYDORE

THE SURVIVORS OF PROSPECT BLUFF, whether present at the explosion or not, fought on in Florida for many years to come. Their stories are varied and largely unknown, but in two cases, it is possible to tell something of life after Negro Fort. These are the stories of Abraham and Polydore.

Abraham was around 26 years old when American soldiers dragged him from the smoking ruins of Negro Fort. In his shock, he told them that he was from Georgia and was born in slavery to W.B. Howell. This led to his inclusion in the small group of eight survivors that Lt. Col. Clinch took back to Camp Crawford. His name appears on a list of "negroes in confinement at this post" that the lieutenant colonel sent to Andrew Jackson's staff in Nashville on August 4, 1816.[428]

Clinch sent the list to other officials as well, encouraging them to publicize it so that "owners" could claim their slaves at Camp Crawford. While at least one inquired, no one was willing to travel hundreds of miles through Indian country at the peril of his or her life to retrieve one of the eight held at the fort. Orders arrived in December to evacuate the post, and Abraham once again found his freedom. Whether he escaped or was set

---

[428] Lt. Col. Duncan L. Clinch, "List of Negroes in confinement at this post," August 4, 1816, included in Clinch to Butler, August 2, 1816, Jackson Papers, Library of Congress.

free is not clear, but the latter possibility seems likely. Available U.S. Army records do not mention the survivors again after the troops withdrew to Fort Gaines in early January 1817.

Why Abraham told the soldiers that he was from Georgia is something of a mystery. When he enlisted in the Colonial Marines to find his freedom, he was living in Pensacola as a slave to either Dr. Eugenio Sierra or John Forbes and Company. The appeals prepared by residents of Pensacola in 1814-1815 list Abraham as a slave of Forbes and Company. Other sources, however, indicate that Dr. Sierra claimed him. Sierra may have sold him to the Forbes company before his enlistment. If so, he was one of the few Maroons at Prospect Bluff to come face to face with a former master. Dr. Sierra went with the expedition of Lt. Vicente Sebastian Pintado to the bluff in the spring of 1815. The men who met there with Pintado and Sierra informed them that they had no desire to return to slavery and were now "Hombres Libre" ("Free Men").[429]

The training that Abraham received as a private in the British Colonial Marines served him well. After leaving Camp Crawford (by then renamed Fort Scott) in December 1816, he resettled on the Suwannee River at Nero's Town. The Maroons there reorganized as a battalion following the standards they learned at Prospect Bluff. American reports in 1817-1818 show that they were conducting drills and keeping regular discipline. Nero's fighters responded to calls for help from Neamathla after the U.S. attacks at Fowltown on November 21-23, 1817, and took part in the Scott Battle, the Battle of Ocheesee, and the Battle of Fort Hughes. They fought a successful delaying action at the Battle of Old Town and most escaped across the Suwannee River with the neighboring Alachua Seminoles.

Abraham next appeared on the Seminole reserve created by the Treaty of Moultrie Creek in 1823. He was associated with Micanopy, who rose

---

[429] "Relacion a nombre de los esclavos," May 13, 1815, Papeles de Cuba, Legajo 1796, Packet May, Letter No. 513, Archivo General de Indias, University of Florida; "List of the Negroes belonging to the Inhabitants of the Town of Pensacola," Attachment No. 1, Lt. Jose Urcullo to Gov. Mateo Gonzalez Manrique, January 23, 1815, Forbes Papers, University of West Florida; Capt. Vicente Sebastian Pintado to Sr. Dn. Josef de Soto, April 29, 1815, Pintado Papers, Library of Congress.

to become the primary chief of the Seminoles by the 1830s and was a counselor or "sense bearer" to him. His personality was the first thing that most whites noticed about him:

> We have a perfect Talleyrand of the Savage Court in Florida, in the person of a Seminole negro, called Abraham, who is sometimes dignified with the title of "Prophet." He is the prime minister, and privy councillor of Micanopy; and has, through his master, who is somewhat imbecile, ruled all the councils and actions of the Indians in this region.
>
> Abraham is a non-committal man, with a countenance which none can read, a person erect and active, and in stature over six feet...an enemy by no means to be despised.[430]

Other writers reported that he was "cross-eyed," noting that this "gave to his gentle insinuating manner a very sinister effect." He "inclined forward" in what was considered a "French manner." An 1837 report described him as having a countenance that combined "a vast degree of cunning and shrewdness, and he is altogether a remarkable looking negro."[431]

Abraham, by 1826 was living at Pilaklikaha, a Maroon community in today's Sumter County, Florida. He went with Micanopy's delegation to Washington, D.C., in 1825-1826, serving as an interpreter since he understood both the Seminole and English languages. His services proved so valuable that the chief fully emancipated him from any claims that he was a slave of the Alachua band. By this time, Abraham was married to

---

[430] Officer in Camp near Fort Dade to a gentleman in Newark, May 22, 1837, *Army and Navy Chronicle*, Volume IV, Page 378.

[431] For a summary of these descriptions see Kenneth W. Porter, "The Negro Abraham," *The Florida Historical Quarterly*, Volume 25, Number 1, July 1946, pp. 1-43.

Hagar, the widow of Boleck, with whom he had at least two sons and one daughter.[432]

The 1832 Treaty of Paynes Landing between the Seminoles and the United States formalized an agreement that a delegation of Seminole chiefs would travel to present-day Oklahoma, inspect the lands, and report back on its suitability for settlement. The Seminoles would then decide whether they wished to relocate to the West. The interpreters for the negotiations were Abraham and Cudjo, both of whom had served in the Colonial Marines at Prospect Bluff.[433]

The treaty did not end well for the Seminole. Before white authorities allowed the delegation to return home, the members were forced to sign a document at Fort Gibson, declaring that the lands they saw were suitable for settlement. The United States treated this as an agreement by the entire nation that its "removal" on the Trail of Tears was acceptable. Abraham was a member of the delegation and described the circumstances to the chiefs and warriors in Florida on his return. As might be expected, they decided to resist.

During the years 1832-1835, Abraham was considered by many whites to be a "man for hire." They paid him several hundred dollars in cash to quietly convince the Seminoles to emigrate, not realizing that he at once put the money to use buying arms and ammunition. Cuban fisherman and Bahamian wreckers brought the weapons into South Florida, where Seminoles and Maroons bought them. The warriors assembled a considerable supply in this way by the fall of 1835 when the United States announced that the Seminoles must assemble in January and prepare to depart. Abraham, with a large force of Maroon warriors from Pilaklikaha, joined a Seminole army that assembled on the Fort King Road at today's Bushnell, Florida.

Open warfare erupted on December 28, 1835, when the Seminoles struck Brevet Maj. Francis Dade's column as it marched north on the road. Dade and most of his leading officers were killed quickly, with the

---

[432] *Ibid.*

[433] Treaty of Paynes Landing, May 9, 1832, Library of Congress; "List of Negroes belonging to the Inhabitants of the Town of Pensacola."

surviving men throwing up breastworks of log and fighting for their lives. The soldiers, overwhelmed and outgunned, died one by one until only wounded unable to fight back remained. The wounded were also killed, and only three men lived long enough to escape the battlefield. Abraham and the Maroons provided critical firepower during the fighting and shared the victory with their Seminole allies.

The noted black Seminole went on to fight conspicuously in other battles before reaching an agreement with Maj. Gen. Thomas Sidney Jesup in 1837 to end the fighting. The truce did not hold, but so far as is known, Abraham kept his word to Jesup and took up arms no more for either side during the war, although he did serve as an interpreter and envoy to Seminoles bands continuing the fight. He eventually was sent west to modern Oklahoma, arriving at Fort Gibson on April 13, 1839.[434]

Abraham lived the rest of his life in freedom in the west with the ancestors of today's Seminole Nation of Oklahoma. It was a hard life, especially with speculators and members of other tribes anxious to acquire black emigrants as slaves. He prospered well enough to buy his son Washington's freedom from Micanopy for $300 in 1841. He also offered his services as an interpreter, accepting $300 per year from the U.S. Government in 1843-1845. He returned to Florida in 1852 to translate at negotiations with Billy Bowlegs, visiting Washington and New York before returning home. An eyewitness who met Abraham in the latter city described him in vivid terms:

> ...Time and trial, and anxiety, have made a wreck of Abraham. Yet he is straight, and active, and looks more intelligence out of his one eye than many people look out of two. He is in the full costume of the Seminoles. Turban, *a la Turk,* and a hunting shirt, leggings, etc.[435]

---

[434] Porter, *The Negro Abraham*, Page 29.
[435] *Ibid.*, Page 34.

The writer thought that the Maroon might be 70-80 years old, although he most likely was still in his 60s. That he had lived a hard life is without dispute.

Abraham was still alive in 1870 when a letter published in multiple newspapers noted that "the Negro Abraham, is still alive on Little River at an advanced age of one hundred and twenty years. A gentleman saw him the other day." He was 80-90 years old by then but undoubtedly looked ancient to those who met him. He died not long after this final account of him. His son, Washington, later recalled his father as a man who did so well raising cattle that he hid sacks of gold and silver coin beneath the floorboards of his cabin.

Historian Kenneth W. Porter, an authority on Abraham's life, wrote in 1946 that a gravestone with bearing his name was at a cemetery in Brunertown, a small community "west of the Little River settlement, near Hazel." Brunertown no longer exists as a community but was on Salt Creek between Seminole and Konawa, Oklahoma. The cemetery there now called the Seminole Freedman Cemetery and has the graves of many Maroons who were moved west from Florida. The stone marking Abraham's grave is no longer visible there.[436]

Polydore, like Abraham, was a slave in Spanish Florida before the War of 1812. He was living in or near St. Augustine when Capt. Woodbine visited the ancient city in December 1814. The captain arrived with an escort of armed black fighters, causing great alarm among the local slaveholders. They appealed to Gov. Sebastian Kindelan, who promptly ordered Woodbine to remove them from St. Augustine:

> At the time you stated to me verbally, the motives of your coming to this place, I had the honor to represent to you, in like manner, the orders I had received from my government to observe the strictest neutrality; that I could

---

[436] *Ibid.*, pp. 36-37; Old Brunertown Cemetery Census, Seminole Nation, I.T. website, http://www.seminolenation-indianterritory.org/brunertowncem.htm.

not, therefore, permit any communication with the English vessels which might appear off the bar; that I would give you every facility for a passage to Providence; that you would be pleased to discharge the escort of people of color, which under the erroneous idea of this province being invaded, you had obtained from the Seminoles, as a safe-guard on your journey; all of which I repeat to you officially, for your information and government.[437]

Kindelan went on to outline the limits of Spanish East Florida for Woodbine's benefit, warning him not to conduct land troops or conduct offensive operations against the United States from within the colony. Doing so, he warned, would be a rupture of relations between Spain and Great Britain.

Woodbine replied on the same day, promising that he had no intent to liberate slaves from Spanish citizens:

...[P]ermit me to assure you that I have never used any endeavours to induce the coloured people (los Morenos) of the province to desert; on the contrary, my instructions, since I have been in the Indian territory, have been to give every aid (as far as requisite) to the cause of our good and faithful ally, the Spanish nation; I am only authorized, in case any deserters should come in from the United States of America, to protect and recruit them for the service of H.B.M., agreeably to the proclamation of vice admiral Sir Alexander Cochrane, copy of which I enclose for your information. With respect to the few Indian and coloured people (Morenos) who attended me as an escort, as their appearance seems to have produced some sensation among the inhabitants, from an uneasiness about their

---

[437] Gov. Sebastian Kindelan to Capt. George Woodbine, December 30, 1814, *United States Congressional Serial Set*, Volume 18, pp. 35.

slaves, I have given them orders to withdrew immediately to a greater distance from their neighborhood, and if possible, I will leave this place in the evening. I should not have brought this small escort with me, if I had not been informed by the Seminole chief, Bowlegs, that he had certain intelligence that a party of mounted banditti were committing hostilities against the Spanish authorities in this neighborhood.[438]

Woodbine did, however, liberate slaves from Spanish citizens, and Fernando was among them. Kindelan appealed to his counterpart in Pensacola, Gov. Mateo Gonzalez Manrique, for help in obtaining their return from the British:

…[U]pon his return he took away a number of Slaves & horses belonging to different inhabitants and planters of this Province, entrusted to my care, and consider it my duty to claim them for their account and also of the Chua [i.e., Alachua] Indians protected by this Government which the said English Officer had also taken away and encorporated with his detachment. I conceive it incumbent on me to use every exertion in furthering their views and supposing you to have more immediate intercourse with the British Commanders I request you to represent to them in the name of the Spanish Government to that effect.[439]

Manrique delivered the appeal to Rear-Admiral Sir Alexander Cochrane, but like the claims of the Pensacola residents, it fell on deaf

---

[438] Capt. George Woodbine to Gov. Sebastian Kindelan, December 30, 1814, *United States Congressional Serial Set*, Volume 18, pp. 36-37.
[439] Gov. Sebastian Kindelan to Gov. Mateo Gonzales Manrique, quoted in Gov. Mateo Gonzales Manrique to Capt. R.C. Spencer, March 11, 1815, Cochrane Papers.

ears. British law prohibited the involuntary return of the Maroons to their former owners.

Fernando and the others from the St. Augustine vicinity went to the Apalachicola River, where Edmund Doyle and Lt. William Hambly saw them as they came in:

> It is certain when Woodbine arrived at the Bluff he was accompanied by none of the negroes carried from St Augustine or Lachua, but on the evening of the day of his arrival a large body of men arrived. I saw some of them, and asked them where they came from they told me from Lachua, I asked if any came from St. Augustine. I was told not one, those fellows of course received their lesson along the way: Cassel, Harrison, Ambrister & others now in Nassau I know reported at the Bluff that thro the means of Woodbine twenty negroes of both sexes arrived at the Bluff from St. Augustine, St. Johns & Lachua. Shortly after his arrival Mr. Hambly received letters from St. Augustine requesting him to enquire after some negroes that was carried away from thence by Woodbine. Woodbine denied in my presence him carrying any negro from thence, Woodbine came her prepared for villainy and he took care to evade all evidence except what answered his weakest purposes.[440]

A number of the Maroons from East Florida evacuated to Trinidad ahead of the British withdrawal, but Fernando stayed behind, as did Mary Ashley and Susan Christopher with their husbands and families. He made a life for himself at Prospect Bluff, staying there until the American attack in July 1816. Unlike the others, however, Fernando avoided capture and escaped to the Suwannee River where he took refuge in Nero's Town. He

---

[440] Edmund Doyle to John Innerarity, December 10, 1816, Forbes Papers, University of West Florida.

was living there when Maj. Gen. Andrew Jackson's army struck on April 16, 1818.

> I reached it on the evening of the 16th having marched twenty miles, the Negroes and Indians made a joint resistance against my left column who was endeavouring to turn their right, whilst the right was attempting to cut them off from the river, and my center moving quickly to the attack in front, the poor deluded wretched perceived the danger that threatened, precipitated themselves into the river, where they must have suffered from the brisk fire of the Indians, here we obtained a few cattle and about three thousand bushels of corn.[441]

Nine Maroons died in the fighting, and two fell into the hands of Jackson's men as prisoners. One of them turned out to be Fernando, called "Pollydore" by the general:

> To convince you of the trouble I have taken to transmit information to the legal owners of Pollydore, I will briefly give you a history thereof. Pollydore was captured with arms in his hands at the Suwannee, in April, 1818 – had been enlisted by Major Nicholas [i.e., Woodbine] at St. Augustine in 1813; at the close of the war was handed over to the notorious Woodbine, and by him to the notorious Ambrister. Having been taken with arms in his hands, under the character of a British soldier, our two governments being at peace, his life was forfeighted, and he ought to have died; but being informed that Pollydore belonged to one of the daughters of Mr. Ontego, late Auditor of War at St. Augustine, and this information from Mr. Hambly, I was determined to have

---

[441] Maj. Gen. Andrew Jackson to Rachel Jackson, April

him preserved for them, and immediately wrote to St. Augustine, etc.[442]

Jackson's description of Fernando's capture "under the character of a British soldier" is interesting. It may imply that he was wearing his Colonial Marines uniform. Former Lt. Robert C. Ambrister was in uniform when Jackson's troops captured him on the Suwannee one day later. The general's note that William Hambly interceded on Fernando's behalf is likewise interesting. The former lieutenant was with Jackson when the army reached the Suwannee and either recognized the prisoner or learned his identity by conversing in Spanish with him. Hambly owed his life to Nero, who saved him from execution at the Suwannee following a trial ordered by the Bahamian trader Alexander Arbuthnot. Nero arranged for Hambly to be placed in Spanish custody at the fort of San Marcos de Apalache, where U.S. troops found him when they seized the fort in April 1818. Whether it was his plan or not, Hambly saved Fernando's life just as Nero had done for him. The fate of the other Maroon prisoner captured at the Suwannee is not known.

Now calling him Polydore, Jackson carried the prisoner home with him to the Hermitage in Nashville, Tennessee. The general often suffered for lack of someone able to translate documents written in Spanish, a service that Polydore was able to provide. Jackson soon discovered that the former Colonial Marine was quite literate and had bookkeeping skills as well. He put him to work in the plantation office while he began a four-year effort to track down the Spanish family that claimed him. Using slaves in supervisory roles was not uncommon for Andrew Jackson. Hannah, for example, was the head of household staff at the Hermitage, while Squire was the foreman for the field hands. Richard Ivy Easter noted Polydore's presence in and about Nashville on May 9, 1821. "I saw your Servant Polidore yesterday," he wrote, "and made particular Enquiry your Black family were and how they Conducted, and if he can be relied on,

---

[442] Maj. Gen. Andrew Jackson to Satorius, February 1822.

every thing is going well at your farm." Jackson was traveling at the time.[443]

The general finally succeeded in reaching the Satorios family from whom Fernando or Polydore escaped. One of his letters reached Catalina Mir Satorios at Charleston, South Carolina, in the spring of 1822. Jackson explained how Polydore (or Fernando) came to be in his custody and his decision to spare the man's life (see above). Satorios responded on April 16, 1822:

> If my husband did not present himself (at the time) to lay claim to his slave, as you say he should have done, it was from his having been quite unable to undergo the last fatigue, & he consequently took the liberty of writing to you mentioning his indisposition & not meaning any offense. His letters were written by the hand of Judge Mitchell, & the unhappy man did not live to receive an answer, which he so much desired. I did not write to you myself, hoping to have the pleasure of presenting myself personally to you at St. Augustine, where from the publick papers, I was enduced to suppose you would have fixed your seat of Governmt. But I had not that pleasure, as you went to Pensacola. How ever it was a great consolation to me to have received your letters.[444]

In his letter to Mrs. Satorios, the general proposed buying Polydore from her. The man had been in Jackson's possession since his capture on the Suwannee four years before. Satorios agreed to a price of $500 and expressed her appreciation to Jackson for sparing the escaped slave's life on the battlefield. "I am bound to believe that you not having taken away the life of this ungreatfull negro (as he deserved) was the effect of the

---

[443] Richard Ivy Easter to Andrew Jackson, May 10, 1821, *The Papers of Andrew Jackson, 1821-1824*, 1980, Page 39.
[444] Catalina Mir Satorios to Maj. Gen. Andrew Jackson, April 16, 1822, Jackson Papers, Library of Congress.

divine will," she wrote, "that inspired you with mercy toward him, out of compassion to me, that I might not in my misfortunes, be deprived of his value."[445]

After confusion over proper form, Satorios signed a bill of sale, and Jackson paid the widow with a draft on a Charleston bank. The correspondence does not explain the circumstances of her relocation from St. Augustine to Charleston, which took place not long after the cession of Florida from Spain to the United States.

In a curious missive, however, she did take the time to write directly to Polydore, who she still called Fernando. She questioned him for associating with "el diablo" ("the devil") in the form of Capt. Woodbine and complained of the injustice he had visited on her by seeking his freedom. She called herself a "neutral" though and advised him that "with happiness there is happiness." "I do not doubt that you have experienced many troubles and scares and I hope that they have served as a lesson to you," she continued, "and that from this day forward you will seek liberty not in this miserable world but in the next." She also asked God to grant him a long life and urged him to "treat your new master with fidelity and constancy until his death." It is unknown if the former Fernando responded to her letter.[446]

Polydore did remain with Jackson for the rest of the general's life. A list of the names and ages of the slaves at the Hermitage on January 5, 1829, reveals that "Polladore," who was then "about 40," had married a 25-year-old woman named Sally and had four children: Adaline, age 5, Toney, age 3, Phillip, age 2, and Prissy who was about one month old.[447]

The former Colonial Marine, who, in the eyes of the British government, was a free man, remained enslaved on Andrew Jackson's

---

[445] *Ibid.*

[446] Catalina Mir Satorios to Fernando, July 14, 1822, Jackson Papers, Library of Congress..

[447] "The names and ages of the negroes on Andrew Jackson's farm, Hermitage, this 5th of Jary., 1829," *The Papers of Andrew Jackson, 1829*, Volume VII, pp. 8-9.

farm until 1846 when he was sent to Mississippi (the 7th President died the previous year). Polydore remained there until 1861 when he was moved to the new Louisiana home of Samuel Jackson, the general's grandson by Andrew Jackson, Jr. If he was 40 years old in 1829, then the onetime freedom fighter was around 72 when he arrived in the Pelican State.

Whether Polydore outlived his last "master" is not known. Samuel Jackson enlisted in the Confederate army and was elected 1st lieutenant of Company G, 44th Tennessee Infantry on December 10, 1861. His promotion to captain came four months later. He received a bullet wound to the hand at the Battle of Stones River and suffered mortal wounds at Chickamauga on September 19, 1863. Samuel Jackson died from his wounds on either September 29 or October 2, 1863. He is buried at the Hermitage.[448]

Polydore's gravesite is lost to time.[449]

---

[448] Christopher Young, "Old Hickory's Ties to Chickamauga," Army of Tennessee: A Collaborative Investigation of the Civil War's Western Theater (website), http://bullyforbragg.blogspot.com/2008/12/old-hickorys-ties-to-chickamauga.html, December 21, 2008.
[449] Personal communication with descendants, April 12, 2016.

22

MARY ASHLEY'S STORY

A REMARKABLE STORY UNFOLDED IN CUBA AND THE HALLS OF BRITISH POWER many years after the destruction of the Fort at Prospect Bluff. Mary Ashley petitioned the Spanish government for her freedom from slavery, opening the door to a remarkable story of perseverance and survival. The news reached Great Britain in a letter from Joseph T. Crawford, the country's Consul-General in Cuba:

> Some time during the last war with the United States of America, one of our expeditions occupied a place on the coast of Florida, called "Prospect Bluffs."
>
> Our forces employed a number of the population in the construction of forts, as well as having enlisted many of the coloured inhabitants who served as soldiers during the occupation.
>
> At the time we evacuated the Prospect Bluffs, free papers were given to the soldiers and their families who had served in our ranks; which free papers are said to have been signed by the senior officers of our expedition, whose names were, "White, Woodbine, and Nichols." These particulars have been furnished by Mary Ashley, the widow of a soldier of that name enlisted, during the occupation on her own behalf, and on behalf of her

children now grown up, and consisting of a son and several daughters, as well as on behalf of Susan Christopher, who also received her free papers in the manner above described, but which free papers these poor people have lost, as may well be supposed, under the circumstances which I am about to state to your Lordship.[450]

The circumstances to which Crawford referred, of course, resulted from the American attack on Prospect Bluff. Mary Ashley's emergence in Havana, Cuba, in 1843 brought the story of the forgotten War of 1812 fort to the full attention of the British government:

> According to Mary Ashley's statement, the British forces evacuated the Prospect Bluffs, the defences were blown up, and upon the occupation of that post by the Americans, all those who had been in the British service were obliged to remove.
>
> These people went to San Augustin in Florida, from whence they were embarked to this island and sold into slavery, how and by whom they are unable to describe intelligibly; but the fact of their being kept in that miserable situation, is proof that they were so taken away and placed.[451]

The Consul-General assumed there must be records in Great Britain to verify Ashley's story. Writing to the Earl of Aberdeen, he asked for an archival search to locate any evidence of the "freedom papers" issued at

---

[450] Joseph T. Crawford, Consul-General, to the Earl of Aberdeen, *Correspondence on the Slave Trade with Foreign Powers, Parties to Treaties, under which Captured Vessels are to be tried by mixed tribunals, Class B,* Presented to both Houses of Parliament by Command of Her Majesty, 1844, LONDON: Printed by William Clowes and Sons, 14, Charing Cross, For Her Majesty's Stationery Office, 1844, pp. 42-43
[451] *Ibid.*

Prospect Bluff so he could appeal to the authorities in Cuba for the freedom of Ashley, her children, and her friend Susan Christopher. He noted that she remembered the names of "Captains (as she calls them), at any rate they were officers, "Smith and Prince." Smith was probably Lt. Samuel Smith. Prince was also a well-known figure at the British Post. A non-commissioned officer in the Colonial Marines, he was one of the first to enlist there under Capt. Woodbine. Spanish documents show that Dr. Eugenio Sierra, the surgeon to the Spanish garrison, claimed Prince as a slave. Prior to enlisting he was a master carpenter and Woodbine hired him early during the British occupation to find and bring in other recruits.[452]

The story intrigued Aberdeen, and he ordered the search requested by Crawford. It did not take long for the researchers to find—as many historians have since discovered—that most of the records associated with the British efforts on the Apalachicola were missing:

> No trace of any of the officers named by Her Majesty's Consul-General in Cuba can be found in the books of this office, nor is there any record of the occupation of these mud forts. As, however, it is probable that these forts were erected under the superintendence of officers of the Ordnance Department, a copy of your letter and its enclosure has been transmitted to Mr. Byham,[453]

Aberdeen notified Crawford of the problem, and the Consul-General replied by urging that a search be made of the records in the Ordnance Department. He mentioned that Christopher and the entire Ashley family faced horrible conditions as laborers on a railroad construction project:

---

[452] *Ibid.*

[453] L. Sullivan to Viscount Canning, August 10, 1843, "The Sessional Papers of the House of Lords, in the Session 1845," British and Foreign State Papers 1844-1845, Vol. XXXIII, Compiled by the Library and Keeper of the Papers, Foreign Office, London: Printed by Harrison and Sons, St. Martin's Lane, 1859, Page 12.

I beg leave to express a hope that some record may appear in the Ordnance Department, as to the services which these poor people say they then rendered to the British arms, which may entitle an interference here for their liberation from slavery. They appear to be quite superior to the mass of the miserable creatures who are, like them, suffering; and by the kindness of the Marquess de la Canada Thirry, I was able to keep one of them from working on the railroad, to which all who were in the Casa de Beneficiencia had been ordered, and where the labour and treatment are both extremely severe.[454]

As the correspondence between Aberdeen and Crawford was crossing the Atlantic, Sir John Barrow recalled that Edward Nicolls had served in Florida during the War of 1812. He wrote the famous officer, who was now a full colonel, to see if he remembered either Mary Ashley or Susan Christopher. Nicolls replied from his home at "Shooter's Hill" on September 11, 1843:

...[O]n my leaving the post at the Bluff, in June 1815, I had not transports sufficient to take away about 350 men, women, and children, the former of whom had enlisted in the British forces on the faith of the enclosed Proclamation and my instructions, but they agreed to keep together, under the protection of the Indian Chiefs, until we had an opportunity of sending for them. I then left with each soldier or head of a family a written discharge from

---

[454] Joseph T. Crawford, Consul-General, to the Earl of Aberdeen, October 7, 1843, *Correspondence on the Slave Trade with Foreign Powers, Parties to Treaties, under which Captured Vessels are to be tried by mixed tribunals, Class B*, Presented to both Houses of Parliament by Command of Her Majesty, 1844, London: Printed by William Clowes and Sons, 14, Charing Cross, For Her Majesty's Stationery Office, 1844, Page 57.

the service, and a certificate that the bearer and family were, by virtue of the Commander-in-Chief's Proclamation, and their acknowledged faithful services to Great Britain, entitled to all the rights and privileges of true British subjects, which indeed most of them were, having left the United States when they rebelled against the British Crown, and had, from that time to their joining me, lived with Indians well known under the name of King George's men; and on the first sight of our colours they entered my camp with the most enthusiastic zeal, and continued their service with the strictest good faith and conduct, so much so, that out of 1,500 of them I never had occasion to punish one of them.[455]

The reference to "1,500 of them" included men, women, and children. The actual number of men who enlisted in the Colonial Marines at Prospect Bluff and Pensacola was around 300.

The use of the term "King George's men" is consistent with similar phrases used by other Maroons and free blacks who lived among the Southeastern Native Americans after the American Revolution. Escaping from their "masters" in the newly formed United States, they fought alongside the British military in 1775-1783 before forming settlements at Paynes Prairie and on the Chattahoochee/Apalachicola/Flint river system. The black chief Philatouche, who lived on the Flint, was a powerful leader who supported the rise of William Augustus Bowles among the Lower Creeks and Miccosukees in ca. 1780-1804. Many Maroons served under Bowles's "sun flag" of Muskogee, contributing to both his land forces and "navy" (i.e., pirate) crews.

While the colonel's statement that these individuals formed most of his Colonial Marines might be a slight stretch, they did form a substantial portion of his battalion. There were far more men from the Seminole and Creek country in Nicolls' command than escaped slaves from the United

---

[455] Col. Edward Nicolls to Sir John Barrow, September 11, 1843.

States. Based on identifiable names, escapees from Spanish territory around Pensacola and St. Augustine made up the largest part (see Appendices).

Col. Nicolls continued his account with an account of the destruction of the Negro Fort as provided to him by a correspondent with first-hand knowledge of the episode, part of which appears in an earlier chapter:

> After I left the bluffs, before aid could be sent to them, they were treacherously attacked by the lawless slaveholders on the Georgia frontier of Florida, aided by a flotilla of four heavy gun-vessels [i.e. two gunboats and two transports] from the slaveholding State of Louisiana, the whole amounting to 1,200 men, to which our people had only about 60 of their oldest men, and some women, to oppose, the rest and the Indians being absent hunting and fishing, in the security of the generally acknowledged peace; yet notwithstanding their small number, and with the aid of their strong position, they made a most noble defence; the Americans being about to retire after a 14 days' [i.e. 7 days] siege, had broke up their encampment to retreat, being in fear of the return of the absent garrison, all of whom were strong and expert rifle men, when one of the vessels firing a gun with a red hot shot, fired it more to get rid of it than from any expected consequence, the shot glanced off a tree, and flew out of its course among some loose powder that some of the women were filling cartridges from at the grand magazine door, and which communicated to 300 five-and-a-half-inch shells, and about 300 barrels of powder, blew the whole of the battery or citadel, which stood in the centre of the fort, to atoms, destroying all the men and several of the women and children.[456]

---

[456] *Ibid.*

He went on to describe how Mary Ashley served with a cannon crew during the battle:

> ...Mary Ashley, had the courage and sagacity to hoist and pull down the colours morning and evening for four days, firing the morning and evening gun, shotted, into the enemy's camp, in the hope that the absent garrison would hear it, and come to their assistance. This poor woman was cut and most cruelly used by these lawless miscreants, her free papers destroyed, and herself, children and the rest of the survivors sold into slavery.[457]

The colonel supplied a copy of the proclamation issued by Admiral Sir Alexander Cochrane in 1814, calling for slaves to flee their masters and find freedom by enlisting in the British forces. He was unable to find copies of the victualling list from his time in Florida—which included the names of those receiving provisions from the British—but suggested that the original might be in the archives of the Victualling Office. He also offered his disbelief that the destruction of the fort had the official sanction

> I would further beg leave to observe, that a large sum was paid by the British Government to the United States, as a remuneration for all the slaves that joined us in every part of North America. I also deem it right to observe, that I do not think the General Government of the United States authorized the attack on the Bluff, as I was a manifest breach of the treaty of peace, for I am sure they had not then, and I believe have not now, the power to restrain the white population of their southern States, particularly when the subject of slaves is the question.[458]

---

[457] *Ibid.*
[458] *Ibid.*

Great Britain abolished slavery well before 1843, and the discussion of Mary Ashley's status came on the heels of the *Creole* case. That incident received widespread publicity after Bahamian authorities set free more than 100 slaves who overwhelmed the captain and crew of the American slave ship *Creole* in 1841. American authorities railed against the decision, but the British remained firm in their position that all slavery was illegal in their territory. Any Maroon reaching the Bahamas automatically became free. Nicolls wrote in support of this policy, and his ideas were no different in the case of Mary Ashley:

> I do hope, Sir, Her Majesty's Government will use all possible means to obtain the liberty of the persons in question; such praiseworthy exertions will not fail to have a powerful effect among the very intelligent and useful coloured population of Cuba, the southern States of North America, when, if ever the need should come, we can fully depend on their joining us to a man; and better or braver soldiers I would never wish to serve with, which I am able, ready, and willing to do at a moment's warning.[459]

The colonel was 63 years old in 1843, having retired from active duty eight years earlier. His account provided the British government with testimony needed to seek the liberation from slavery of Mary Ashley, her family, and Susan Christopher. Instructions to that effect were sent to H.L. Bulwar by the Earl of Aberdeen on March 25, 1844:

> DURING the last war between Great Britain and the United States of America, the British forces having occupied a post on the coast of Florida, called Prospect Bluffs, a portion of the population of that part of the country were taken into the British service. On the

---

[459] *Ibid.*

evacuation of the place by the British forces, the commanding officer gave papers of freedom to the persons in question, for themselves and for their families; but on the occupation of the place by the Americans, these persons were obliged to remove.

Accordingly it appears that they went to San Augustin, in Florida, and from there were sent to Cuba, and sold into slavery. I send you a copy of a letter which I have received upon this subject from Her Majesty's Consul-General in Cuba [June 19, 1843], and copies of correspondence thereupon with the Secretary of War.

As there can be no reasonable doubt of the truth of the statements and of the identity of the persons, Her Majesty's Government entertain a confident hope, that upon your appeal to the honour and good feeling of the Spanish Government orders will be given for the liberation of these unfortunate and ill-used individuals and their families. I have therefore to instruct you to represent the circumstances, in a note, to the Spanish Government, and to urge them strongly to the performance of that act of justice.[460]

British officials raised the freedom of Ashley, her family, and Christopher with authorities in Havana in 1844. The outcome is unknown.

---

[460] The Earl of Aberdeen to Sir H.L. Bulwer, March 25, 1844, *British and Foreign State Papers 1844-1845*, Vol. XXXIII, Compiled by the Library and Keeper of the Papers, Foreign Office, London: Printed by Harrison and Sons, St. Martin's Lane, 1859, pp. 368-369.

23

ARCHAEOLOGY

THE HISTORICAL SIGNIFICANCE OF THE FORT AT PROSPECT BLUFF until recently has attracted little interest from archaeologists. This failure by the archaeological and anthropological community to show interest in what was the largest free black settlement in North America in 1814-1816 is difficult to explain. The almost complete lack of concern in scientific research at the site has changed dramatically in recent years, thanks in large part to the efforts of Dr. Andrea Repp, archaeologist for the Apalachicola National Forest, and Rhonda Kimbrough, Heritage and Tribal Government Programs Manager for the National Forests in Florida. The duo, with help from interested historians including former Seminole tribal historian Bill Steele, is responsible for a surge in interest and the recent listing of the site on the National Underground Railroad Network to Freedom list maintained by the National Park Service. The fort's National Historical Landmark data has likewise been updated. Repp and Kimbrough also are spearheading the site's recovery from massive damage sustained during Hurricane Michael in October 2018.

Archaeologically, the British Post or Negro Fort is more intact than anyone realized. The advent of lidar (light detection and ranging) technology allowed archaeologists for the first time to see through the dense forest of trees, underbrush, and palmetto that covers much of the site. The results were surprising. Not only was the central citadel and its moat visible in the imagery, but so too were flood control ditches, the outer breastworks, and more—all dating from the British and Maroon occupation.

Ground-penetrating radar (GPR) revealed even more about the site. A GPR survey of part of the citadel area during a National Park Service remote sensing workshop showed structural details that were not previously known. James Gadsden, a topographical engineer attached to Jackson's army in 1818, mapped the site, showing two unusual projections or "rabbit ears" extending from the west side of the citadel. The GPR data, however, revealed that two similar projections once extended from the north side of the citadel. Instead of being curious anomalies, the projections suddenly started to make sense. The central citadel, as Capt. Pintado described and Capt. Gadsden mapped, was octagonal in design, but the moat or ditch that surrounded may have taken the shape of an 8-pointed star. The discovery resulted from a mere two days of GPR work on just part of the citadel but has changed more than 200-years of accepted understanding about the fort.[461]

Repp and Kimbrough also recognized the misidentification of what Florida historians labeled the "Renegade Cemetery" during the site's state park era. This small burial ground is east of the outer works of the fort and consists of a single brick-enclosed gravesite surrounded by indentations in the ground that likely show other graves. The probable graves are orderly and arranged in rows, not at all what one would expect from the mass burial of hundreds of escaped slaves in the heat of summer after a devastating explosion. The burial site looks more like a military cemetery, and more than 80 U.S. soldiers died at Prospect Bluff when Fort Gadsden stood there in 1818-1821. All lost their lives to sickness of one form or another, but primarily from malaria and yellow fever. What was labeled the "Renegade Cemetery" in the 1960s is more likely the place where these unfortunate men were laid to rest. Only one officer of high rank—Maj. George Peters—died at Fort Gadsden during the U.S. occupation, one

---

[461] The author participated in the recent projects and research described here and these paragraphs are based on his personal observations.

explanation for the extra care taken to surround a single grave with a low brick wall.

If the "Renegade Cemetery" is a U.S. Army burial ground, then where is the mass grave from the 1816 explosion? That question is one of the puzzles to which Kimbrough and Repp have applied innovative techniques. Lidar imagery does not show suspicious areas that could be a mass grave, but an area of slight elevation is noticeable on the ground just south of the path leading from the fort site to the known cemetery. Susie Goodhope helps agencies ranging from the Federal Bureau of Investigation (FBI) to the National Park Service (NPS) find human remains through the use of specially trained dogs. These animals successfully located prehistoric human remains more than 1,000 years old in Mississippi and have assisted in dozens of law enforcement and other investigations. Repp and Kimbrough arranged to have Goodhope come to Prospect Bluff.

The effort to use the "cadaver" or "body sniffing" dogs begin in 2016 and continues. Curiously, the dogs detected no scent of human remains on and immediately around the site of the citadel, where the 1816 explosion killed more than 270 people. They did, however, detect strong scents at the low elevation between the fort and the known cemetery. Researchers used two different dogs to verify the possible discovery independently. Each signaled at the same spot. Crews cleared the area of palmettos, and undergrowth and ground-penetrating radar teams checked the site. The results were inconclusive, but research will continue using innovative technologies.

The real question is whether the bodies of the slain men, women, and children of the Negro fort received any burial at all. Dr. Buck and others noted that the explosion left bodies and body parts strewn over a great area on the surface of Prospect Bluff. None of the official accounts mentions burial. Sailing Master Jairus Loomis, however, told the *Louisiana Gazette* that interment did take place. "A about 200 were buried, he noted, "and a great number could not be extricated from under the ruins."[462]

---

[462] Sailing Master Jairus Loomis statement to *Louisiana Gazette*, published on August 19, 1816.

The short statement confirms the existence of at least two "burial" sites at the fort, one where "200 were buried" and the second area were "a great number" could not be pulled from the wreckage caused by the explosion. It is unknown whether the burials were done in multiple spots or in a single mass grave.

Prospect Bluff suffered a heavy hit from Hurricane Michael in October 2018. The Category 5 storm toppled trees throughout the site of the fort, tearing out electrical systems, damaging the small interpretive museum, blocking roads, trails, and parking areas, and damaging intact archaeological sediments throughout the site. The cleanup brought with it an opportunity for the first real "dirt and shovel" archaeology at the site in more than 50 years.

As trees toppled in the high winds, their roots came up filled with earth. These "rootballs" offered a unique chance to learn more about the site. A small amount of funding for research into the lives of the Maroons who lived at the fort became through the Southeast Archaeological Foundation (SEAF) and a one-week project to excavate and screen the earth from selected rootballs began in 2019. The project was carried out by the U.S. Forest Service, the National Park Service, PaleoWest, and volunteers. Solid evidence of human activity was revealed in the form of small pieces of European and Native American ceramic, rusty bits of metal, musket balls, and other artifacts. Analysis of the data recovered is still underway at this time (November 2019). Future reports will detail conclusions reached from the effort.

Florida State University conducted the only significant past archaeology at the site in 1963. Researchers came to several conclusions about the site that have since been altered by historical research and the use of modern technology. The project did reveal, however, that massive timbers from the citadel remain intact beneath the surface of the site. Unfortunately, the field notes from the project cannot be found, and only a short final report survives.[463]

---

[463] Stephen R. Poe, "Archaeological Excavations at Fort Gadsden, Florida," *Notes in Anthropology*, Volume 1, Florida State University. 1963.

What does the archaeology tell us about the Fort at Prospect Bluff? First, the sheer size of the fortress is astounding. Its outer entrenchments could easily protect the 3,500-5,000 people who lived at the site during the height of its military occupation. These outer breastworks with their ditch and reinforced bastions are more substantial that Capt. Vicente Sebastian Pintado described in April 1814. Work must have continued on them after the British departure. Second, the difference in the elevation and design of the earthworks in the battery area of the later Fort Gadsden (1818-1821) structure suggests that the U.S. Army incorporated the original British redan or water battery into its design. Third, the central citadel was massive, and its base remains largely intact. As described by Pintado and others, it was octagonal in design and built by packing a rampart of earth between two walls of horizontal logs. The resulting wall was 18-feet thick and around 15-feet high. The surrounding moat was at least partially star-shaped, with infantry positions built into the projections created by the points of the star. If fully completed, the moat was an 8-pointed star.

The remains of the citadel also suggest thoughts about the nature of the explosion itself. The southern and eastern sides of the structure and its moat are the best preserved. The condition of this side of the citadel shows that the explosion blew away from this area of the fort and against the western and northern walls. The blast erupted through the weakest point of the magazine—its entry—spraying the interior of the compound with shrapnel and debris. With most of the women and children sheltered in that area, the death toll was horrendous. While much more work remains to be done, preliminary observations show that Col. Nicolls' report that the deadly cannon shot did not score a "direct hit" on the "grand magazine" as many have claimed is likely accurate. The hot shot easily would have blown the magazine if it landed among women and children filling powder bags outside its open door, as the colonel reported.

Much remains for the future to reveal.

CONCLUSION

THE BLAST THAT DESTROYED THE FORT AT PROSPECT BLUFF still reverberates today. No record of a more deadly cannon shot is found in all the annals of North American history. The entire site is, as Rhonda Kimbrough of the U.S. Forest Service has said, sacred ground. While the fort is an archaeological and historical treasure, it is also a vast cemetery. Whether or not a burial site holding the remains of the 270 men, women, and children killed there is found, the blood of these determined freedom-seekers saturated the ground. They died here in a desperate battle to save themselves from lives of bondage and slavery. Prospect Bluff Historic Sites is not just a stop on the Underground Railroad. For many—including those who evacuated to Trinidad in 1814 or escaped to the Bahamas in 1818-1819—it was the gateway to freedom. For those who died at the site, it was as Garcon warned, the place where they determined to give their lives rather than return to slavery. Their spirits are still "hombres libre."

THE PEOPLE OF
PROSPECT BLUFF

This list results from a multi-year effort to name as many of the occupants of the British Post or Negro Fort as possible. It uses data from a number of sources including the two claim lists prepared by citizens of Pensacola in 1815, the correspondence of John Forbes and Company employees, military records at the National Archives, the Andrew Jackson Papers at the Library of Congress, the papers of Admiral Cochrane, the correspondence of William Hambly, and documents from Great Britain, the Bahamas, Jamaica, Bermuda, Newfoundland, and Trinidad and Tobago. Special thanks are due to John McNish Weiss, author of *The Merikens*, for his kindness and assistance in identifying many of the Maroons who arrived in Trinidad from Prospect Bluff in 1814-1822. I highly recommend his book, *The Merikens: Free Black Settlers in Trinidad, 1815-1816*, to anyone interested in learning more about the Maroons who evacuated to Trinidad.

The Trinidad Evacuees

HMS Carron, First Arrival

These individuals arrived in Trinidad aboard HMS *Carron* on July 5, 1815. All embarked from Prospect Bluff in April,

Annisey, George, arrived in Trinidad on HMS Carron on July 5, 1815.

Bowden, John, arrived in Trinidad on HMS Carron on July 5, 1815.

Bowlege (Boleck, Bowlegs), Dora, arrived in Trinidad on HMS Carron on July 5, 1815.

Bowlege (Boleck, Bowlegs), Joe, arrived in Trinidad on HMS Carron on July 5, 1815.

Bowlege (Boleck, Bowlegs), Mary, arrived in Trinidad on HMS Carron on July 5, 1815.

Bowlege (Boleck, Bowlegs), Sarah, arrived in Trinidad on HMS Carron on July 5, 1815.

Bruce, Bravo, arrived in Trinidad on HMS Carron, July 5, 1815. Husband of Sally Bruce.

Bruce, Sally, arrived in Trinidad on HMS Carron, July 5, 1815. Wife of Bravo Bruce.

Dane, Becky, arrived in Trinidad on HMS Carron, July 5, 1815.

Dane, Ester, arrived in Trinidad on HMS Carron, July 5, 1815.

Dane, Hope, arrived in Trinidad on HMS Carron, July 5, 1815.

Dane, James, arrived in Trinidad on HMS Carron, July 5, 1815.

Dover, Joe, arrived in Trinidad on HMS Carron, July 5, 1815.

Dover, Rachel, arrived in Trinidad on HMS Carron, July 5, 1815.

Dover, Wisley, arrived in Trinidad on HMS Carron, July 5, 1815.

Edwards, Ryna, arrived in Trinidad on HMS Carron, July 5, 1815.

Gilbert, Charlotte, arrived in Trinidad on HMS Carron, July 5, 1815.

Gilbert, Samuel, arrived in Trinidad on HMS Carron, July 5, 1815.

Harry, Rose, arrived in Trinidad on HMS Carron, July 5, 1815.

Harry, Seniter, arrived in Trinidad on HMS Carron, July 5, 1815.

Hunson (Hinson?), Robert, arrived in Trinidad on HMS Carron, July 5, 1815.

Kane, Betsy, arrived in Trinidad on HMS Carron, July 5, 1815.

Kane, Charlotte, arrived in Trinidad on HMS Carron, July 5, 1815.

Kane, James, arrived in Trinidad on HMS Carron, July 5, 1815.

Kane, John, arrived in Trinidad on HMS Carron, July 5, 1815.

Kane, Mary, arrived in Trinidad on HMS Carron, July 5, 1815.

Kennard, John (surname also given as Edwards), arrived in Trinidad on HMS Carron, July 5, 1815.

Kennard, Polly (surname also given as Edwards), arrived in Trinidad on HMS Carron, July 5, 1815.

Kennard, Richard, was not a member of the Colonial Marines but arrived in Trinidad in 1815. He was probably the child of John and Polly Kennard.

M'Ley, Jacob, arrived in Trinidad on HMS Carron, July 5, 1815.

Marshall, Alender, arrived in Trinidad on HMS Carron, July 5, 1815.

Marshall Ambola, arrived in Trinidad on HMS Carron, July 5, 1815.

Marshall, Billy, arrived in Trinidad on HMS Carron, July 5, 1815.

Marshall, Elsy, arrived in Trinidad on HMS Carron, July 5, 1815.

Marshall, Lizey, arrived in Trinidad on HMS Carron, July 5, 1815. She also spelled her name "Martial."

Marshall, Naifra, arrived in Trinidad on HMS Carron, July 5, 1815.

Marshall, Selby, arrived in Trinidad on HMS Carron, July 5, 1815.

Marshall, Siebre, arrived in Trinidad on HMS Carron, July 5, 1815.

Marshall, Simon, arrived in Trinidad on HMS Carron at age 10, July 5, 1815. Later worked as a Sawyer.

Marshall, Sophia, arrived in Trinidad on HMS Carron, July 5, 1815.

Marshall, Thomas, arrived in Trinidad on HMS Carron, July 5, 1815.

Marshall, Unity, arrived in Trinidad on HMS Carron, July 5, 1815.

Marshall, Veny, arrived in Trinidad on HMS Carron, July 5, 1815.

Marshall, Nance, arrived in Trinidad on HMS Carron, July 5, 1815.

Phillips, John, born on December 1, 1814, and arrived in Trinidad as an infant on HMS Carron, July 5, 1815.

Phillips, John, arrived in Trinidad on HMS Carron, July 5, 1815.

Phillips, Sophie, arrived in Trinidad on HMS Carron, July 5, 1815.

Quarterman, Stephen, arrived in Trinidad on HMS Carron, July 5, 1815.

Truders, John, arrived in Trinidad on HMS Carron, July 5, 1815.

Trump, David, arrived in Trinidad on HMS Carron, July 5, 1815.

Wilkinson, Joe, arrived in Trinidad on HMS Carron, July 5, 1815.

Fifty-one names identified from HMS Carron's arrival of July 5, 1815. The ship arrived on that date with 58 settlers, leaving seven unidentified.

HMS Carron, Second Arrival

These 65 individuals arrived at Trinidad aboard HMS *Carron* on November 27-29, 1815. All are believed to have come from Prospect Bluff.

Adams, Sophia, arrived in Trinidad on HMS Carron on November 27-29, 1815. Gone from the island by 1823.

Amboise (Ambrose?), Mary, arrived in Trinidad on HMS Carron on November 27-29, 1815. Gone from the island by 1823.

Bowline (Bowley?), John, arrived in Trinidad on HMS *Carron*, on November 27-29, 1815. He was from the Chesapeake region of Virginia. He and three children were living on the island by 1823.

Butler, David, was born in 1778 and arrived in Trinidad on HMS *Carron* on November 27-29, 1815.

Butler, Dolly, arrived in Trinidad on HMS *Carron* on November 27-29, 1815. She disappeared from the records by 1823.

Caesar, Francoise, arrived in Trinidad on HMS *Carron* on November 27-29, 1815. He likely was from Spanish West Florida.

Christopher, Amos, arrived in Trinidad on HMS *Carron* on November 27-29, 1815. He disappeared from the record by 1823.

Christopher, Cook, arrived in Trinidad on HMS *Carron* on November 27-29, 1815. By 1823 he was living with his wife, Dora, and three children.

Christopher, James, arrived in Trinidad on HMS *Carron* on November 27, 1815. He was from East Florida and by 1823 was living with his wife, Mary, and one child.

Christopher, Jenny, arrived in Trinidad on HMS Carron on November 27-29, 1815.

Christopher, Mary, arrived in Trinidad on HMS Carron on November 27-29, 1815. She was married to James Christopher and had one child by 1823.

Christopher, Phoebe, arrived in Trinidad on HMS Carron on November 27-29, 1815. She died prior to 1823.

Christopher, Sampson, arrived in Trinidad on HMS Carron on November 27-29, 1815.

Christopher, Sharp, arrived in Trinidad on HMS Carron on November 27-29, 1815.

Christopher, Thomas, arrived in Trinidad on HMS Carron on November 27-29, 1815. He was married to Minto by 1823 and had 2 children.

Clapham, Alexander, arrived in Trinidad on HMS Carron on November 27-29, 1815. He was married to Mary by 1823 and had one child.

Conjuror, Hannah, arrived in Trinidad on HMS Carron on November 27-29, 1815.

Conjuror, Mary, arrived in Trinidad on HMS Carron on November 27-29, 1815.

Craigey, Sally, arrived in Trinidad on HMS Carron on November 27-29, 1815.

Craigey, Walley, arrived in Trinidad on HMS Carron on November 27-29, 1815.

Dundas, Dominick, arrived in Trinidad on HMS Carron on November 27-29, 1815.

Forbes, Richard, was claimed by John Forbes but escaped slavery in East Florida and went to Prospect Bluff. He arrived in Trinidad on HMS Carron on November 27-29, 1815.

Forrester, Henry, arrived in Trinidad on HMS Carron on November 27-29, 1815. By 1823 he was married to Jenny.

Fuchar, James, arrived in Trinidad on HMS Carron on November 27-29, 1815. He was a child of Susan and Joe Fuchar.

Fuchar, Joe, arrived in Trinidad on HMS Carron on November 27-29, 1815. He was the husband of Susan Fuchar.

Fuchar, Sampson, arrived in Trinidad on HMS Carron on November 27-29, 1815. He was a child of Susan and Joe Fuchar.

Fuchar, Susan, arrived in Trinidad on HMS Carron on November 27-29, 1815. She was married to James Fuchar.

Fuentas, Calis or Calistro, arrived in Trinidad on HMS Carron on November 27-29, 1815.

Goodwin, Wright, arrived in Trinidad on HMS Carron on November 27-29, 1815. He was a child of Susan and Joe Fuchar.

Grant, Monday, arrived in Trinidad on HMS Carron on November 27-29, 1815. He was married to Betta by 1823 and had one child.

Hamilton, Mary Ann, escaped slavery at St. Simons Island, Georgia, and went to Prospect Bluff. She arrived in Trinidad on HMS Carron on November 27-29, 1815.

Hectore, Lewis, arrived in Trinidad on HMS Carron on November 27-29, 1815.

Herera, Ramon or Romeo, arrived in Trinidad on HMS Carron on November 27-29, 1815. He married to Mary and had two children but left the island before 1823.

Jackson, Samuel, was born in 1754 and was 60 years old when he left Prospect Bluff. He arrived in Trinidad on HMS Carron on November 27-29, 1815. He was married to Maggy by 1823.

James, Charles, arrived in Trinidad on HMS Carron on November 27-29, 1815. He was married to Venus in 1823.

Johnson, Thomas, arrived in Trinidad on HMS Carron on November 27-29, 1815.

Joseph, Jean, arrived in Trinidad on HMS Carron on November 27-29, 1815.

Kingsley, Anna (also called Priest), arrived in Trinidad on HMS Carron on November 27-29, 1815.

Kingsley, Barbara (also called Priest), arrived in Trinidad on HMS Carron on November 27-29, 1815.

Kingsley, James, arrived in Trinidad on HMS Carron on November 27-29, 1815. He was married to Elsy by 1823 and had one child.

Kingsley, Jenny, arrived in Trinidad on HMS Carron on November 27-29, 1815.

Kingsley, Mary (also called Priest), was born in 1786, and arrived in Trinidad on HMS Carron on November 27-29, 1815. She died on the island on February 2, 1861.

Kingsley, Polly, arrived in Trinidad on HMS Carron on November 27-29, 1815. She was living on the island in 1823 with her husband, Prince Kingsley, and five children.

Kingsley, Prince, arrived in Trinidad on HMS Carron on November 27-29, 1815. He was married to Polly Kingsley by 1823 and had five children.

Kingsley, Sophie (also called Priest), arrived in Trinidad on HMS Carron on November 27-29, 1815.

Lacoste, Hannah, escaped from slavery in New Orleans and went to Prospect Bluff. She arrived in Trinidad on HMS Carron on November 27-29, 1815.

Lacoste (or Lacross), Castor, escaped from slavery in New Orleans and went to Prospect Bluff. He arrived in Trinidad on HMS Carron on November 27-29, 1815.

Lewis, John, born in 1795, he was 20 years old when he arrived in Trinidad on HMS Carron on November 27-29, 1815.

Marshall, Mena or Menta, arrived in Trinidad on HMS Carron on November 27-29, 1815.

McGill, Ann, was a white American and the wife of Sgt. Hugh McGill. She arrived in Trinidad on HMS Carron on November 27-29, 1815.

McGill, Hugh, a white American, he deserted from the 2nd Regiment of U.S. Infantry and escaped to Pensacola. He enlisted there under Woodbine and went to Prospect Bluff with his family, Ann and James. They arrived in Trinidad on HMS Carron on November 27-29, 1815.

McGill, James, a white American, he arrived in Trinidad with his family on the HMS Carron on November 27, 1815.

Marshall, Mary, arrived in Trinidad on HMS Carron on November 27-29, 1815.

Mitchell, Anthony, arrived in Trinidad on HMS Carron on November 27-29, 1815.

Mitchell, John, arrived in Trinidad on HMS Carron on November 27-29, 1815. He went ashore at Port of Spain with his wife, Rose.

Mitchell, Laurence, arrived in Trinidad on HMS Carron on November 27-29, 1815.

Mitchell, Prince, arrived in Trinidad on HMS Carron on November 27-29, 1815.

Mitchell, Rose, arrived in Trinidad on HMS Carron on November 27-29, 1815. She was married to John Mitchell.

Nelson, John, arrived in Trinidad on HMS Carron on November 27-29, 1815. He was married to Rachael and died at Savannah Grande Village on Trinidad from cancer on January 24, 1861.

Piercy, Edward, arrived in Trinidad on HMS Carron on November 27-29, 1815. By 1823 he was married to Winny and had five children.

Richards, James, arrived in Trinidad on HMS Carron on November 27-29, 1815. Escaped from the Lake Borgne area of Louisiana.

Richards, Judy, arrived in Trinidad on HMS Carron on November 27-29, 1815.

Rosser, Richard, arrived in Trinidad on HMS Carron on November 27-29, 1815.

Sidore, Lewis, arrived in Trinidad on HMS Carron on November 27-29, 1815.

Thomas, Thomas, arrived in Trinidad on HMS Carron on November 27-29, 1815.

William, Williams, arrived in Trinidad on HMS Carron on November 27-29, 1815.

Arrived with Sixth Company

These individuals escaped to Prospect Bluff, but the men volunteered later with the Sixth Company. They arrived in Trinidad with the families of that unit.

Brookes, John, a Colonial Marine who enlisted at Prospect Bluff and later served in the Sixth Company, Colonial Marines, he arrived in Trinidad with the men of that unit but disappeared from the records by 1823.

Shaw, George, a Colonial Marine who enlisted at Prospect Bluff and who later served in the Fifth and Sixth Companies, he arrived in Trinidad. He, his wife (Fanny), and their three children were murdered there in 1824 by Sunbury Cooper.

Shaw, Fanny, the wife of George Shaw, she arrived in Trinidad with him and their three children. Sunbury Cooper murdered the entire family in 1824.

Shaw, _____, child of George and Fanny Shaw, murdered in 1824.

Shaw, _____, child of George and Fanny Shaw, murdered in 1824.

Shaw, _____, child of George and Fanny Shaw, murdered in 1824.

Williams, Tony, enlisted in the Colonial Marines at Prospect Bluff and later served in Sixth Company. He arrived at Trinidad but disappears from the records before 1823.

Wood, John, enlisted in the Colonial Marines at Prospect Bluff and later served in Sixth Company. He arrived at Trinidad but disappears from the records before 1823.

Relocated from Halifax, Nova Scotia, in 1821

This individual escaped to Prospect Bluff and settled first at Halifax, Nova Scotia, but relocated to Trinidad.

Rogers, James, enlisted in the Colonial Marines at Prospect Bluff. He arrived in Trinidad from Halifax in 1821 and lived as a farmer.

Others who arrived in Trinidad

These individuals appear on records in Trinidad which confirm they arrived from Prospect Bluff. In most cases, the circumstances of their arrival are not known.

Bridges, Hannah, reported that she arrived in Trinidad from the Apalachicola.

Christopher, Jenny, reported that she arrived in Trinidad from the Apalachicola.

Forbes, Lemon, claimed by John Forbes, escaped to Prospect Bluff and went from there to Bermuda where he lived until 1822. He relocated to Trinidad that year.

Total Known Trinidad Evacuees: 135

Bermuda Evacuees

Eighty-one Colonial Marines left the Apalachicola aboard HMS *Cydnus* on April 21, 1815. They were evacuated with their families to Bermuda where they remained in service as a supernumerary battalion until 1816. They later relocated to Trinidad.

Total Known Bermuda Evacuees: 81 plus families.

Halifax Evacuees

A "number "party of black people" left Prospect Bluff aboard HMS Borer on April 21, 1815. They were carried to Bermuda and there transferred to HMS Goree for transport to Halifax, Nova Scotia. They landed and settled in Nova Scotia. Some later relocated to Trinidad.

Total Known Halifax Evacuees: Unknown

Deserters

Jervais, Samuel, a white sergeant in the Colonial Marines, deserted from his post and fled to the United States. Maj. Gen. Gaines interviewed him in Mobile, obtaining information on the strength of the fort.

Ned, a "free man of colour," deserted from the Colonial Marines and fled to American territory. He provided information on the defenses to U.S. authorities.

Unidentified, a Colonial Marine deserted and went back to his "owners" near Mobile, Alabama.

Total Known Deserters: 3

Discharge Papers

Discharge papers survive at the Library of Congress for the following individual.

Lane, Parish, a private in the Colonial Marines, served in the Rifle Company. Lt. Col. Nicolls discharged him at Prospect Bluff when the British withdrew in 1815.

Total Known Discharge Papers: 1

Pensacola Maroons

These names appear on the lists of escaped slaves from Pensacola and vicinity provided to Lt. Jose Urcullo in December 1814 and Capt. Vicente Sebastian Pintado in March 1815. Abraham, who is listed under U.S. Prisoners, is not included here.

Harry, age 30, escaped from John Forbes and Company and enlisted in the Colonial Marines. He left Prospect Bluff either before the attack or survived the explosion and joined Nero's Town on the Suwannee. From there he made his way into the Peninsula after Jackson's 1818 campaign. He played an important role in leading Maroon forces during the Second Seminole War.

Tom, age 24, escaped from John Forbes and Company and enlisted in the Colonial Marines. He survived the explosion and went to the home of William Hambly on the Apalachicola.

Tom's wife, name unknown, escaped from John Forbes and Company and accompanied him to Prospect Bluff.

Ben, escaped from John Forbes and Company and enlisted in the Colonial Marines.

Ben's wife, name known, escaped from John Forbes and Company and went with him to Prospect Bluff.

Dick, escaped from John Forbes and Company and enlisted in the Colonial Marines.

George, escaped from John Forbes and Company and enlisted in the Colonial Marines.

Ambrosio, escaped from John Forbes and Company and enlisted in the Colonial Marines.

Sofia, age 24, escaped from John Forbes and Company and went to Prospect Bluff.

Estevan, age 30, escaped from John Forbes and Company and enlisted in the Colonial Marines.

Billy, age 34, escaped from John Forbes and Company and enlisted in the Colonial Marines.

Davy, escaped from John Forbes and Company and enlisted in the Colonial Marines.

Congo Tom, from Africa, escaped from John Forbes and Company and enlisted in the Colonial Marines.

Dundas, escaped from John Forbes and Company and enlisted in the Colonial Marines.

Billy, escaped from John Forbes and Company and enlisted in the Colonial Marines.

Carlos Congo, from Africa, escaped from John Forbes and Company and enlisted in the Colonial Marines.

Carlos Mayamba, from Africa, escaped from John Forbes and Company and enlisted in the Colonial Marines.

Dick, second individual of this name, escaped from John Forbes and Company and enlisted in the Colonial Marines.

Elsy, escaped from John Forbes and Company and went to Prospect Bluff.

Elsy's child, escaped from John Forbes and Company and went with her mother to Prospect Bluff.

Elsy's second child, escaped from John Forbes and Company and went to Prospect Bluff.

Marbry, escaped from John Forbes and Company and enlisted in the Colonial Marines.

Marbry's wife, name unknown, escaped from John Forbes and Company and went with him to Prospect Bluff.

Castalio (or Castalis?), escaped from John Forbes and Company and enlisted in the Colonial Marines. He survived the explosion and was carried back to Pensacola and sent to the "public works" with a chain around his leg.

Harrieta, the wife of Castalio, escaped with him and went to Prospect Bluff. She is not mentioned after the explosion.

Child of Castalio and Harrieta, escaped from Pensacola and went to Prospect Bluff with them, but is not mentioned after the explosion.

Child (II) of Castalio and Harrieta, escaped from Pensacola and went to Prospect Bluff with them, but is not mentioned after the explosion.

Philis, esaped from a Pensacola citizen named Blanco and went to Prospect Bluff. She was later claimed by John Forbes and Company.

Philis's child, name unknown, escaped from a Pensacola citizen named Blanco and went to Prospect Bluff with Philis.

Jose, escaped from Martin de Madrid in Pensacola and enlisted in the Colonial Marines. He probably was the individual named Jose Hambroso who received a discharge certificate at Prospect Bluff. Capt. Pintado inspected this certificate during his visit.

William, escaped from Martin de Madrid in Pensacola and enlisted in the Colonial Marines.

Manuel, escaped from Martin de Madrid in Pensacola and enlisted in the Colonial Marines.

Genere, age 17, escaped from Mme. Morel in Pensaocla and went to Prospect Bluff.

Alexandro, age 7, escaped with Genere from Mme. Morel in Pensacola and went to Prospect Bluff.

Dick, age 30, escaped from William Cooper at Pensacola and enlisted in the Colonial Marines.

Jaque or Jack, age 29, escaped from William Cooper at Pensacola and enlisted in the Colonial Marines.

Carlos, age 26, escaped from Mme. Eslava in Pensacola and enlisted in the Colonial Marines.

Carlos (II), escaped from Mme. Eslava in Pensacola and enlisted in the Colonial Marines.

Agustin, escaped from Mme. Eslava in Pensacola and enlisted in the Colonial Marines.

Ambrosio, escaped from Mme. Eslava in Pensacola and enlisted in the Colonial Marines.

Antoin, age 44, escaped from Mme. Eslava in Pensacola and enlisted in the Colonial Marines.

Antonio, escaped from Mme. Eslava in Pensacola and enlisted in the Colonial Marines.

Prince, escaped from Mme. Eslava in Pensacola and enlisted in the Colonial Marines. He was identified as a sergeant after the British evacuation.

Delores, age 16, escaped from Mme. Eslava in Pensacola and went to Prospect Bluff.

Juan, age 24, escaped from a Spanish citizen named Salas at Pensacola and enlisted in the Colonial Marines.

Agustine (II), age 28, escaped from a Spanish citizen at Pensacola and enlisted in the Colonial Marines.

Francisco, age 26, escaped from Pensacola and enlisted in the Colonial Marines.

Juan, age 16, escaped from Pensacola and enlisted in the Colonial Marines.

Saiva, age 26, escaped from Pensacola and went to Prospect Bluff.

Miguel, age 25, captured in the raid on D'Olive's plantation at Mobile Bay, enlisted in the Colonial Marines.

Agustin (III), age 22, escaped from Don Vicente Folch in Pensacola and enlisted in the Colonial Marines.

Tom, escaped from Don Vicente Folch in Pensacola and enlisted in the Colonial Marines.

Francisco (II), age 36, escaped from Don Manuel Gonzalez in Pensacola and enlisted in the Colonial Marines.

Henrique, age 45, escaped from Don Manuel Gonzalez at Pensacola and went to Prospect Bluff.

Pedro, age 32, escaped from Don Manuel Gonzalez at Pensacola and enlisted in the Colonial Marines.

Simon, age 22, escaped from Don Francisco Gomez in Pensacola and enlisted in the Colonial Marines.

Alexis, age 25, escaped from Don Carlos Lavalle at Pensacola and enlisted in the Colonial Marines.

James, age 25, escaped from a Spanish resident of Pensacola and enlisted in the Colonial Marines.

Marian, age 35, escaped from a Spanish resident of Pensacola named Camirosa and went to Prospect Bluff.

Harry (II), age 19, escaped from a Pensacola resident named McFaison or McFason and enlisted in the Colonial Marines.

Frank, age 25, escaped from a Pensacola resident named McFaison or McFason and enlisted in the Colonial Marines.

Francisco (IV), age 31, escaped from a Pensacola resident and enlisted in the Colonial Marines.

Francisco (V), age 20, escaped from a Pensacola resident and enlisted in the Colonial Marines.

Garcon, age 30, escaped from Don Montero and enlisted in the Colonial Marines. A literate carpenter, he rose to the rank of Sergeant Major and assumed command of the fort after Lt. William Hambly returned home. He commanded the fort during the battle and the explosion blinded him. Creek warriors executed him after an interview by U.S. officers.

Carmelita, Garcon's wife, escaped from Don Antonio Montero in Pensacola and went to Prospect Bluff with her husband and child. Creek warriors executed her after the explosion.

Guillermo, age 2, the son of Garcon and Carmelito, escaped from Don Antonio Montero with his parents and went with them to Prospect Bluff. Creek warriors executed him after the explosion.

Valintin, age 44, escaped from Don Pedro Alba in Pensacola and enlisted in the Colonial Marines.

Jack, age 35, escaped from Don Pedro Alba in Pensacola and enlisted in the Colonial Marines.

Hilario, age 25, escaped from Don Jose Noriega in Pensacola and enlisted in the Colonial Marines. His rank was reported as sergeant of the guard after the evacuation of the British.

Edwardo, age 21, escaped from Don Pedro Philibert in Pensacola and enlisted in the Colonial Marines.

Elias, age 28, escaped from a Pensacola resident named Balderos and enlisted in the Colonial Marines.

Sofia, age 35, escaped from Pensacola and went to Prospect Bluff.

Billy, age 26, escaped from Pensacola and enlisted in the Colonial Marines.

Reuidor (?), age 40, escaped from Don Francisco Barrios at Pensacola and enlisted in the Colonial Marines.

Santiago, age 23, escaped from Pensacola and enlisted in the Colonial Marines.

Ramos, age 55, escaped from Pensacola and enlisted in the Colonial Marines.

Ben, age 30, escaped from Pensacola and enlisted in the Colonial Marines.

Ruben, age 35, escaped from Pensacola and enlisted in the Colonial Marines.

Feodoro (Teodoro?), age 15, escaped from Pensacola and enlisted in the Colonial Marines.

Sam, age 20, escaped from Pensacola and enlisted in the Colonial Marines.

Maria, age 30, escaped from Pensacola and went to Prospect Bluff.

Eugenia, age 28, escaped from Pensacola and went to Prospect Bluff.

Betsy, age 12, probably the child of Eugenia, escaped from Pensacola and went to Prospect Bluff.

Delila, age 22, escaped from Don Luis Piernas at Pensacola and went to Prospect Bluff.

Moses, age 32, escaped from Dr. Eugenio Sierra at Pensacola and enlisted in the Colonial Marines.

Lucas, 24, escaped from Dr. Eugenio Sierra at Pensacola and enlisted in the Colonial Marines.

Simon, age 24, escaped from Dr. Eugenio Sierra at Pensacola and enlisted in the Colonial Marines.

Prince (II), age 26, escaped from Dr. Eugenio Sierra at Pensacola and enlisted in the Colonial Marines. He also could have been the

Sergeant Prince referenced as being at Prospect Bluff after the British withdrawal.

Nelle, age 28, escaped from Dr. Eugenio Sierra at Pensacola and went to Prospect Bluff.

Dominque, age 30, escaped from Don Pedro Senac at Pensacola and enlisted in the Colonial Marines.

Miguel, age 35, escaped from Don Pedro Senac at Pensacola and enlisted in the Colonial Marines.

Cato, age 40, escaped from Don Pedro Senac at Pensacola and enlisted in the Colonial Marines.

Dick (II), escaped from Don Pedro Senac at Pensacola and enlisted in the Colonial Marines.

Susana, age 26, escaped from Don Pedro Senac at Pensacola and went to Prospect Bluff.

Agar or Hagar, age 28, escaped from Don Pedro Senac at Pensacola and went to Prospect Bluff.

Felix, age 8, probably a child of Hagar who escaped from Don Pedro Senac at Pensacola and went to Prospect Bluff.

Gordon, age 5, probably a child of Hagar who escaped from Don Pedro Senac at Pensacola and went to Prospect Bluff.

Prince (III), age 4, probably a child of Hagar who escaped from Don Pedro Senac at Pensacola and went to Prospect Bluff.

Mily, age 2, probably a child of Hagar who escaped from Don Pedro Senac at Pensacola and went to Prospect Bluff.

Florida, age 19, escaped from Don Pedro Senac at Pensacola and went to Prospect Bluff.

Betsi, age 16, escaped from Don Pedro Senac at Pensacola and went to Prospect Bluff.

Prince (IV), escaped from Mme. Eslava at Pensacola and enlisted in the Colonial Marines.

Ambrosio (II), escaped from Mme. Eslava at Pensacola and enlisted in the Colonial Marines.

Harry (II), escaped from Dr. Eugenio Sierra at Pensacola and enlisted in the Colonial Marines.

Sally, escaped from John Innerarity at Pensacola and went to Prospect Bluff.

Rosa, escaped from John Innerarity at Pensacola and went to Prospect Bluff.

Cyrus, age 26, escaped from Don Vicente Ordozgoity in Pensacola and enlisted in the Colonial Marines. He later served as one of the three principal commanders of the Negro Fort.

Dolly, escaped from Pensacola and went to Prospect Bluff with her five children. She survived the explosion and went to William Hambly's home on the Apalachicola River.

Child of Dolly (I), escaped from Penscola and went to Prospect Bluff with Dolly. Some or all of her children survived the explosion and went to the home of William Hambly.

Child of Dolly (II), escaped from Penscola and went to Prospect Bluff with Dolly. Some or all of her children survived the explosion and went to the home of William Hambly.

Child of Dolly (III), escaped from Penscola and went to Prospect Bluff with Dolly. Some or all of her children survived the explosion and went to the home of William Hambly.

Child of Dolly (IV), escaped from Penscola and went to Prospect Bluff with Dolly. Some or all of her children survived the explosion and went to the home of William Hambly.

Child of Dolly (V), escaped from Penscola and went to Prospect Bluff with Dolly. Some or all of her children survived the explosion and went to the home of William Hambly.

Cook, Joe, escaped from Pensacola and enlisted in the Colonial Marines. He survived the explosion and resettled in a Native American village near Pensacola, but Don Philibert seized and jailed him as an escaped slave. The constable released him as a free man due to his British service. He was seized by another slavecatcher in the 1820s after Florida was transferred to the United States. This time he was "sold" to Eulalie Garcon, but filed suite seeking his freedom. Testimony before the circuit judge of Escambia County convinced the court that he was free due to his service in the Colonial Marines. He was set free and lived in Pensacola as a free black until at least the time of the Civil War.

Tomas, escaped from John Forbes and Company at Pensacola and enlisted in the Colonial Marines.

Mary, escaped from John Forbes and Company at Pensacola and went to Prospect Bluff.

In addition to the individuals named here, one Maroon escaped from Don Martin de Madrid, but the name is illegible on the claim lists. Five more escaped from Mme. Eslava, one of them a child. (Total six who cannot be identified by name).

A group of 10 Maroons returned to slavery due to Lt. Jose Urcullo's mission to Prospect Bluff, while another group returned with Capt. Vicente Sebastian Pintado. Both groups are likely included in this list of names.

Total Maroons from Pensacola and Mobile Bay: 116

Known Additional Maroons from St. Augustine, East Florida, and the Creek Nation

These individuals appear in records from Great Britain, Cuba, and the U.S. military.

Ashley, Mary, escaped from St. Augustine with her husband and went to Prospect Bluff. She helped fire cannon during the battle and survived the explosion but was captured and returned to St. Augustine. She was taken to Cuba when Spain surrendered Florida to the United States in 1821 and later appealed for her freedom.

Ashley, _____, husband of Mary Ashley, escaped from St. Augustine and enlisted in the Colonial Marines. He was killed in the explosion.

Christopher, Susan, escaped from St. Augustine with her husband and went to Prospect Bluff. She survived the explosion but was captured and taken back to St. Augustine. She was taken to Cuba when Spain surrendered Florida to the United States in 1821 and later appealed for her freedom.

Nero, leading chief of the Maroons associated with Boleck's (Bowlegs') Alachua Seminoles, he enlisted in the Colonial Marines. He left the fort prior to the explosion and returned to the Suwannee.

Polydore (Fernando), escaped from St. Augustine and enlisted in the Colonial Marines. He was injured in the explosion but escaped capture and went to Nero's Town on the Suwannee. He was captured there by Jackson's troops in 1818. Jackson purchased him for $500 and kept him at the Hermitage as the plantation business manager until his (Jackson's) death. He then went to Mississippi and finally Louisiana.

Abram, escaped from St. Augustine, enlisted in the Colonial Marines, left Prospect Bluff but was captured in 1818.

Augustine, escaped from St. Augustine area, enlisted in the Colonial Marines, left Prospect Bluff after the British withdrawal, captured by Creek warriors during the Angola raid.

Betsy, claimed by Jack Mealy of Ocheesee Talofa, fled to Prospect Bluff and later to the Suwannee. She was captured in 1818.

Billy, claimed by Zephaniah Kingsley, enlisted in the Colonial Marines but left Prospect Bluff after the British withdrawal. He was captured in 1818.

Blanco, enlisted in the Colonial Marines, left with the British in 1815.

Bob, claimed by Robert Gilbert of St. Augustine, escaped and enlisted in the Colonial Marines. He left the fort after the British withdrawal and was captured in 1818.

Bob, claimed by Jack Mealy of Ocheesee Talofa, fled to Prospect Bluff and enlisted in the Colonial Marines. He left after the British withdrawal and was captured in 1818.

Cabasa, Dasana, a Spanish deserter, escaped to Prospect Bluff and later fled to South Florida. He was captured during the Angola raid.

Captain Bush, claimed by the Barnards, escaped to Prospect Bluff and enlisted in the Colonial Marines. He left the fort after the British withdrawal but was captured during the Angola raid.

Cato, claimed by John Addison of the St. Augustine area, enlisted in the Colonial Marines but left Prospect Bluff after the British withdrawal. Creek warriors captured him during the Angola Raid.

Caty, claimed by Don Fatio of St. Augustine, escaped to Prospect Bluff but left after the British withdrew. Creek warriors captured her during the Angola raid.

Charles, claimed by Zephaniah Kingsley, escaped to Prospect Bluff and enlisted in the Colonial Marines. He left after the British withdrew, but Creek warriors captured him during the Angola raid.

Charley, claimed by Don Arredondo of St. Augustine, escaped to Prospect Bluff and enlisted in the Colonial Marines. He left the fort after the British withdrew and Creek warriors captured him during the Angola raid.

Charlotte, escaped from St. Augustine to Prospect Bluff, later lived on the Suwannee and was captured in 1818.

Cudjo, claimed by Jack Mealy of Ocheesee Talofa, escaped to Prospect Bluff and enlisted in the Colonial Marines. He was wounded in the explosion of the fort but escaped into the woods. He was captured in 1818 but escaped again and became a noted figure of the Second Seminole War era.

Cyrus, claimed by Boleck (Bowlegs), escaped to Prospect Bluff and enlisted in the Colonial Marines. He left after the British withdrew but Creek warriors captured him during the Angola raid.

Dianna, escaped from St. Augustine with her mother Nancy, went to Prospect Bluff but left after the British withdrew. Creek warriors captured her in the Angola Raid. She was 9 years old when she was captured.

Dolly, age 6, escaped from St. Augustine with her family and went to Prospect Bluff. She was captured in 1818.

Eve, escaped from St. Augustine to Prospect Bluff but left the fort after the British withdrew. She was captured in 1818.

Flora, claimed by John Addison of the St. Augustine area, escaped with her family and went to Prospect Bluff. She left after the British withdrew but Creek warriors captured her during the Angola raid when she was 6 years old.

Frederick, claimed by Robert Gilbert of St. Augustine, escaped and enlisted in the Colonial Marines. He left the fort after the British withdrew and Creek warriors captured him during the Angola raid.

George, age 61, claimed by John Addison of the St. Augustine area, escaped to Prospect Bluff, left the fort after the British withdrew. Creek warriors captured him during the Angola raid.

Greg, age 32, a "waiting man" to John Clark of Georgia, escaped to Prospect Bluff. His fate is unknown.

Green, age 30, a "waiting man to John M. Dooly of Georgia, escaped to Prospect Bluff. His fate is unknown.

Hannah, age 42, claimed by John Addison of the St. Augustine area, escaped to Prospect Bluff but left after the British withdrew. Creek warriors captured her during the Angola raid.

Hannah's child, name unknown, age 2, claimed by John Addison of the St. Augustine area but escaped to Prospect Bluff. She left with her mother after the British withdrew but Creek warriors captured them during the Angola raid.

Hannah (II), age unknown, claimed by John Perpall of St. Augustine, escaped to Prospect Bluff, left after the British withdrawal. Creek warriors captured her during the Angola raid.

Hannah's child (II), age unknown, claimed by John Perpall of St. Augustine, escaped to Prospect Bluff but left after the British withdrew. Creek warriors captured the child during the Angola raid.

Hector (Sr.), age 51, claimed by John Perpall of St. Augustine, escaped to Prospect Bluff and enlisted in the Colonial Marines. He left after the British withdrew and Creek warriors captured him during the Angola raid.

Hector (Jr.), age 12, claimed by John Perpall of St. Augustine, escaped to Prospect Bluff with his father. He left after the British withdrew but Creek warriors captured him during the Angola raid.

Hector (II), age 46, claimed by a resident of St. Augustine, escaped to Prospect Bluff and enlisted in the Colonial Marines. He left after the British withdrew but Creek warriors captured him during the Angola raid.

Israel, claimed by Boleck (Bowlegs), escaped to Prospect Bluff and enlisted in the Colonial Marines. He was captured in 1818.

Jeffrey, age 32, escaped from Robert Gilbert of St. Augustine, escaped to Prospect Bluff and enlisted in the Colonial Marines. Creek warriors captured him during the Angola raid.

Jenny, age 21, escaped from Zephaniah Kingsley and went to Prospect Bluff. She left after the British withdrew but was captured in 1818.

Jim, age 35, escaped from St. Augustine and enlisted in the Colonial Marines. Left Prospect Bluff after the British withdrew, captured during the Angola raid.

Jim, claimed by Boleck (Bowlegs), enlisted in the Colonial Marines. Captured in 1818.

John, claimed by John Perpall of St. Augustine, escaped to Prospect Bluff and enlisted in the Colonial Marines. He left after the British withdrew but was captured by Creek warriors during the Angola raid.

John, age 35, escaped St. Augustine and enlisted in the Colonial Marines at Prospect Bluff. He left for South Florida and Creek warriors captured him during the Angola raid.

John, age 25, escaped St. Augustine and enlisted in the Colonial Marines at Prospect Bluff. He left for South Florida and Creek warriors captured him during the Angola raid.

John, age 21, escaped St. Augustine and enlisted in the Colonial Marines at Prospect Bluff. He left for South Florida and Creek warriors captured him during the Angola raid.

Kitty, claimed by Boleck (Bowlegs), escaped to Prospect Bluff. She was captured in 1818.

Lewis, age 19, claimed by John Addison of the St. Augustine area, left after the British withdrew and was captured during the Angola raid.

Louisa, age 4, escaped from St. Augustine with her family and taken to Prospect Bluff. They left after the British withdrew and she was captured in 1818.

Magg, age 26, escaped to Prospect Bluff from St. Augustine but left after the British withdrew. Creek warriors captured her during the Angola raid.

Manuel, age 32, a Spanish deserter, fled to Prospect Bluff and enlisted in the Colonial Marines. He left after the British withdrew but Creek warriors captured him during the Angola raid. He died in their custody.

Mary, age 2, the daughter of Nancy, she was likely born at Prospect Bluff in 1816. She was captured in 1818.

Mary, age 21, claimed by William Harvey of St. Augustine, she escaped to Prospect Bluff but left after the British withdrew. Creek warriors captured her during the Angola raid.

Mary, age 26, escaped from St. Augustine to Prospect Bluff. Her fate is unknown.

Molly, age 5, a child of Nancy, escaped with her family to Prospect Bluff from St. Augustine. She was captured in 1818.

Nancy, age 19, escaped to Prospect Bluff from St. Augustine. She was captured in 1818.

Nancy age 21, claimed by John Addison of the St. Augustine area, she escaped to Prospect bluff but left after the British withdrew. Creek warriors captured her during the Angola raid.

Nancy, age 24, escaped from Phelema in the Creek Nation and went to Prospect Bluff. She left after the British withdrawal. Creek warriors captured her during the Angola raid.

Nancy's child, escaped with its mother from Phelema in the Creek Nation and went to Prospect Bluff. The family left after the British withdrawal. Creek warriors captured the child during the Angola raid.

Nancy's child, escaped from Phelema in the Creek Nation with its mother and went to Prospect Bluff. The family left after the British withdrawal. Creek warriors captured the child during the Angola raid.

Nancy, age 36, escaped from John Loften in St. Augustine, and went with her children to Prospect Bluff. She was later captured during the Angola raid.

Nancy's child, escaped with its mother and later captured in Angola raid.

Nancy's child, escaped with its mother and later captured in Angola raid.

Nancy's child, escaped with its mother and later captured in Angola raid.

Nancy, claimed by Boleck (Bowlegs), escaped to Prospect Bluff. Captured in 1818.

Nancy's child, claimed by Boleck (Bowlegs), escaped with its mother and was captured in 1818.

Ned, age 46, escaped from the Barnards of Georgia, enlisted in the Colonial Marines at Prospect Bluff. Creek warriors later captured him in the Angola raid.

Newton, Ben, escaped to Prospect Bluff and enlisted in the Colonial Marines. He later escaped to the Bahamas.

Newton, Ben (Jr.), escaped to Prospect Bluff with his father and later escaped to the Bahamas.

Newton, Dick, a free man of color, enlisted in the Colonial Marines. He later escaped to the Bahamas.

Newton, Elizabeth, a free woman of color, escaped to Prospect Bluff and later to the Bahamas.

Newton, _____, Elizabeth's husband and a free man of color, he escaped to Prospect Bluff. He likely died in the explosion.

Newton, _____, Elizabeth's child, escaped to Prospect Bluff with its mother and later to the Bahamas.

Newton, Lucinda, escaped to Prospect Bluff and later to the Bahamas. She is among those who settled on Andros Island.

Offa, a child of Patty, escaped from John Perpall in St. Augustine to Prospect Bluff with its mother. Creek warriors captured Offa during the Angola raid.

Patty, age 36, escaped from John Perpall in St. Augustina to Prospect Bluff. Creek warriors captured her during the Angola raid.

Peggy, age 7-9, a child of Kitty, claimed by Boleck (Bowlegs), she escaped with her mother to Prospect Bluff. Creek warriors captured her during the Angola raid.

Peter, age 17, a Spanish deserter from San Marcos de Apalache, he went to Prospect Bluff and then to South Florida. Creek warriors captured him during the Angola raid but later released him.

Prince, age 31, claimed by Peter McQueen, he enlisted in the Colonial Marines at Prospect Bluff. Creek warriors captured him during the Angola raid but he escaped.

Queen, a child of Patty, escaped with her mother to Prospect Bluff and was later captured during the Angola raid.

Sally, claimed by Boleck (Bowlegs), she escaped to Prospect Bluff but was captured in 1818.

Sam, claimed by Capt. "McDougle" of St. Augustine, he escaped to Prospect Bluff and enlisted in the Colonial Marines. He was captured in 1818.

Sarah (or Cura?), a child of Patty, escaped with her mother to Prospect Bluff. Creek warriors later captured her during the Angola raid.

Sipsey, age 26, claimed by Boleck (Bowlegs), he enlisted in the Colonial Marines at Prospect Bluff, but Creek warriors captured him in the Angola raid.

Smart, age 23, escaped from Zephaniah Kingsley, enlisted in the Colonial Marines at Prospect Bluff. Captured in 1818.

Suky, claimed by Boleck (Bowlegs), went to Prospect Bluff. Captured in 1818.

Thomas, claimed by Boleck (Bowlegs), went to Prospect Bluff and enlisted in the Colonial Marines. He was captured in 1818.

Toba, age 46, a Spanish deserter, he went to Prospect Bluff and survived the explosion. He was released to William Kennard.

Tom, returned to Edmund Doyle in 1815 prior to the attack on the Negro Fort.

Tom, age 25, a drummer from the Georgia militia who was claimed by George W. Welsh, escaped to Prospect Bluff and enlisted in the Colonial Marines. Fate unknown.

Tyrah, age 38, claimed by John Perpall of St. Augustine, she escaped to Prospect Bluff. Creek warriors captured her during the Angola raid.

Tyrah's child, went with its mother to Prospect Bluff. Captured during the Angola raid.

Valetine, age 18, a Spanish deserter who went to Prospect Bluff, he was captured at Angola and released.

William, age 18, a Spanish deserter who went to Prospect Bluff, Creek warriors captured him in the Angola raid. Released.

Total: 93

Other Maroons and Free Blacks

In addition to the individuals held in slavery when the War of 1812 began, a number of Maroons and free blacks lived on the Apalachicola River just below Ocheesee Bluff in 1814. Their numbers and names are not known. Other volunteers also fall into this category.

Vacapachassie, the chief of a combined Native American and Maroon community, enlisted in the Colonial Marines. Chief John Blunt objected years later to Vacapachassie's elevation to primary chief on the Apalachicola because he served with the British against the United States.

Bennett, John, A free black citizen of Spanish Pensacola, he enlisted in the Colonial Marines as a sergeant.

Total: 2

U.S. Prisoners

Lt. Col. Clinch's command carried these eight men to Camp Crawford after the destruction of the Negro Fort on July 27, 1816.

Lamb, claimed by Col. Benjamin Hawkins, was taken prisoner after the explosion and carried to Camp Crawford. His fate from there is not known.

Elijah, who reported that he was claimed by W. Lewis of Georgia, was taken prisoner after the explosion and carried to Camp Crawford. His fate is unknown.

Abraham, reported that he was claimed by "W.B. Howel" of Georgia, but this may have been subterfuge as he enlisted in the Colonial Marines at Pensacola. Carried to Camp Crawford after the explosion and from there he was set free. He returned to Florida and lived first at Nero's Town on the Suwannee and later in the peninsula. He was sent to Oklahoma on the Trail of Tears.

Jo, reported that he was claimed by Capt. Bowen of Georgia, was captured after the explosion and taken to Camp Crawford. His fate is unknown.

Batture, reported that he was claimed by a "Frenchman" at Bay St. Louis in the Mississippi territory. He was captured after the explosion and taken to Camp Crawford. His fate is unknown.

Jacob, reported that he was claimed by William Morgan. He was captured at the Negro Fort and sent to Camp Crawford. His fate is unknown.

William, said that he was claimed by "Dulendo, a 'Jew King' Jamaica," was captured at Negro Fort. He may have been a member of the West India regiment who remained behind when Nicolls left. He was taken to Camp Crawford and his fate is unknown.

Charles, "said he belongs to John Sharp, but it is supposed he is owned by some gentleman in Virginia, as he arrived at Pensacola in the

English vessel Sea Horse." Captured at Negro Fort, he was taken to Camp Crawford. His fate is unknown.

Total U.S. Prisoners: 8

Total known: 439

Missing from this number are those taken to Halifax aboard HMS Goree. These names were unavailable during this research but exist. The same is true of the families of the Colonial Marines taken to Bermuda aboard HMS *Carron*. In addition, it is impossible to identify most of the Maroons who escaped to the Suwannee or the Maroon villages in the Florida Peninsula.

5th West Indian Regiment at Prospect Bluff

Capt. Joseph Roche's company of the 5th West India Regiment, raised primarily in Jamaica, posted to the Fort at Prospect Bluff and Nicolls' Outpost after the Battle of New Orleans. The company suffered heavy casualties at New Orleans. The roster of this unit was not available during this research but likely exists.

Royal Marines at Prospect Bluff

The men on these lists formed Lt. Col. Edward Nicolls' battalion of Royal Marines. They spent at least minimal time at the British Post, St. Vincent Island, and Apalachicola Bay.
Please note that same individuals appear on several of the lists.

Company drawn from HMS Tonnant

Harrison, John, Lieutenant
Greenwood, Joseph, Lieutenant (transfer from 7th West India)
Allen, William, 2nd Lieutenant

McWilliam, John, 2nd Lieutenant
Robins, Joseph, Sergeant
Green, Abraham, Sergeant
Dignan, Francis, Corporal
Wilson, Alex, Corporal
Thomas, George, Drummer
Bruno, John, Drummer
Loughbridge, Thomas
Jones, John
Owens, Hugh
Bunce, Thomas
Bracegirdle, William
Brioffez, Michael
Hall, William
Howell, John
Trip, Richard
Crank, Charles
Barrett, Walter
Brierley, James
Cronican, Patrick
Rees, ____
Haslam, Jonathan
Price, Richard
Hale, William
Wratton, John
Soames, Henry
Hughes, James
Thaw, James
Beer, Richard
Radway, Joseph
Hindman, Matthew
Brown, William
Cannon, Thomas
Keld, Robert
Griffiths, George
Surrey, Samuel
Hall, John
Bentley, James
Light, James

Gordon, John
Morley, Edward
Beckett, Richard
Smith, George
Thoroughgood, James
Brock, William
Williams, Peter
Pitt, William
Hunt, James
Trott, John
Bell, Joseph
Mitchell, Thomas
Whiting, William
Nudd, Charles
Robson, John, Sergeant of Artillery Detachment
Couldry, John, Corporal of Artillery Detachment
Poole, Robert, Gunner of Artillery Detachment
Cork, Thomas, Gunner of Artillery Detachment
Dyson, James, Gunner of Artillery Detachment
Hurst, Edward, Gunner of Artillery Detachment

Company Embarked on HMS Carron

This company embarked from Pensacola on HMS Carron for the First Battle of Fort Bowyer on September 10, 1814. The men formed part of the land force for the battle and withdrew to Pensacola after the American victory. They withdrew to Prospect Bluff temporarily after Jackson's capture of the Spanish capital before going to Louisiana to participate in the New Orleans Campaign.

Sergeant, J., Lieutenant
Green, Abraham, Sergeant
Hensman, Matthew, Corporal
Wheeler, William, Drummer
Haslam, Jonathan
Sweeny, John
Lethbridge, Robert
Lethbridge, William

Jones, John
Bunce, Thomas
Brioffez, Michael
Wainwright, John
Hall, William
Crank, Charles
Howell, John
Barrett, Walter
Pace, Richard
Dingby, David
Payne, Joseph
Bracegirdle, William

Henry's Company

Capt. Robert Henry and his company embarked from Pensacola aboard HMS *Childers* for service in the First Battle of Fort Bowyer. They returned to Pensacola after the British defeat and then went on to Prospect Bluff when Jackson captured the Spanish capital.

Henry, Robert, Captain, commanded the British Post at Prospect Bluff during Nicolls' absence for the New Orleans Campaign.
Woodbine, George, Captain, attached to Henry's company but acting as major in the Colonial Marines battalion.
Cruikshank, _____, Lieutenant
Harrison, John, Lieutenant
Davis, T., Sergeant
Holiday, _____, Sergeant
Bills, James, Corporal
Beckett, Richard
Tan, Michael
Akins, John
Acoles, Charles
Cronican, Patrick
Goodman, William
Pitt, William
Gordon, John
Moyles, John

Williams, Peter
Morley, Edward
Thoroughgood, James
Harding William
Callant, John
Light, James
Brittain, John
Pace, Richard
Barthy, David
Percy, Edward
Carroll, Peter
Cameron, George
Trott, John
Robson, John, Sergeant of the Artillery Detachment
Couldry, John, Corporal of the Artillery Detachment
Milham, John, Bombardier of the Artillery Detachment
Poole, Robert, Gunner in the Artillery Detachment
Woodend, John, Gunner in the Artillery Detachment
Woodend, John, Gunner in the Artillery Detachment
Dyson, James, Gunner in the Artillery Detachment
Cork, Thomas, Gunner in the Artillery Detachment
Annums, Joseph, Gunner in the Artillery Detachment
Hurst, Edward, Gunner in the Artillery Detachment
Hames, George, Gunner in the Artillery Detachment
Proctor, James, Gunner in the Artillery Detachment
Loveday, John, Gunner in the Artillery Detachment

Embarked on HMS Seahorse

These Royal Marines embarked from the Barrancas and Santa Rosa
Island ahead of Jackson's capture of Pensacola. They were carried to
Prospect Bluff on HMS Seahorse.

Woodbine, George, Captain, also acting major of the battalion of Colonial
        Marines.
Ambrister, Robert C., Lieutenant
Cassell, _____, Lieutenant

Greenwood, Joseph, Lieutenant, transfer from the 7th West India
 Regiment.
Cruikshank, _____, Lieutenant
Harrison, John, Lieutenant
Chapman, James, Brevet Lieutenant
Robson, John, Sergeant
Green, Abraham, Sergeant
Robins, Joseph, Sergeant
Bills, James, Corporal
Wilson, Alex, Corporal
Dignan, Francis, Corporal
Couldry, John, Corporal
Bruno, John, Drummer
Thomas, George, Drummer
Wheeler, William, Drummer
Soames, Henry
Hughes, James
Thaw, James
Trott, John
Radway, Joseph
Malone, Jeremiah
Sabo, Johan
Lee, John
Wheeler, Joseph
Carroll, Michael
Nudd, Charles
Keld, Robert
Surrey, Samuel
Hall, John
Lethbridge, William
Williams, Peter
Light, James
Acoles, Charles
Smith, George
Howman, John
Davis, Thomas
Coxall, Richard
Saxon, Thomas
Tennant, George

Sweeney, John
Kelly, John
Lethbridge, Robert
Owens, Hugh
Bunce, Thomas
Bracegirdle, William
Hall, William
Howell, John
Fotheral, James
Crowley, James
Brittain, John
Goodman, William
Coates, Thomas
Wainwright, John
Fry, Richard
Crank, Charles
Barrett, Walter
Brierley, Walter
Cronican, Patrick
Reed, John
Haslam, Jonathan
Price, Richard
Payne, Joseph
Gurney, Samuel
Burford, Thomas
Smith, William
Stephens, Richard
Tarr, John
Harding, William
Callant, John
Smith, William (II)
De'Ath, William
Lock, Edward
Harris, Charles
Duro, Francisco
Baptiste, Juan
Perdo, Leroy
Gordon, John
Gregory, Benjamin

Vero, Adam
Colville, George
Wallis, David
Greenwood, David
Butler, David
Mitchell, J.
Johnson, Abraham
Wood, John
Serdow, Lewis
Hector, Lewis
Rose, James
Henman, John
Hyde, William
Cannon, Thomas
Pitt, William
Bentley, James
Beer, Joseph
Mitchell, John
Griffiths, George
Greenwood, Daniel
Dandriez, Dean
Gould, John
Jones, John
Thomas, Thomas
Kelly, Thomas
Stone, Thomas
Garey, John
Brown, Charles
Raphael, Joseph
Roper, Richard
Weatherhead, Lewis
Jones, Charles
Patton, John
Butler, John
Prince, John
Carroll, Peter
Delaney, August
Fletchler, Charles
Indian, James

Williams, William
Garey, Martin
McQueen, William
Lock, Edward
Wratton, John
Poole, Robert, Gunner in the Artillery Detachment
Annums, Joseph, Gunner in the Artillery Detachment
Cork, Thomas, Gunner in the Artillery Detachment

Other Royal Marines at Prospect Bluff

Smith, Samuel, Sergeant and Brevet Lieutenant, landed from HMS Orpheus with Woodbine in May 1814. He coordinated training at St. Vincent Island and Prospect Bluff but also explored inland as far as Eufaula Talofa.

Denney, James, Corporal and Brevet Lieutenant, worked with Smith to train Native Americans and Maroons at St. Vincent Island, Prospect Bluff, and elsewhere.

REFERENCES

Newspapers

Alexandria Herald, 1814.

American Telegraph, 1815.

Augusta Chronicle, 1816.

City Gazette, 1815.

Connecticut Spectator, 1814.

Daily National Intelligencer, 1813, 1814.

Early American Newspaper, 1816.

Jackson's Oxford Journal, 1815.

Lancaster Journal, 1815.

Louisiana Gazette, 1816.

Nashville Whig, 1816.

National Gazette, 1834.

New Jersey Journal, 1814, 1815.

New York Gazette, 1814.

Republican Star or Weekly Advertiser, 1816.

Richmond Enquirer, 1814.

Savannah Museum, 1815.

Savannah Republican, 1815.

Southern Whig, 1847.

The American, 1816.

The Farmers Cabinet, 1814.

The Illustrated London News, 1865.

The Morning Post, 1815, 1816.

The Pennsylvania Gazette, December 18, 1811.

The Georgia Journal, 1811, 1812, 1813, 1814.

The Times of London, 1814, 1815, 1818.
The Universal Gazette, 1813.
True American, 1814.
Western Citizen, 1815.
Western Monitor, 1814.

Primary Sources

American State Papers, Volume IV Foreign Relations (1815-1822), Washington: Gales and Seaton, 1834.

American State Papers, Volume I: Indian Affairs (1789-1815), Washington: Gales and Seaton, 1832.

American State Papers, Volume I, Military Affairs (1789-1819), Gales and Seaton, 1832.

Archivo General de Indios, Papeles procedentes de la Isla de Cuba, P.K. Yonge Library of Florida History, University of Florida, Gainesville.

Benjamin Hawkins Letters (various), Georgia Department of Archives and History, Morrow.

Blackshear, David, and Stephen Franks Miller, *Memoir of Gen. David Blackshear*, J.B. Lippincott & Co., Philadelphia, 1858.

British and Foreign State Papers, 1844-1845, Volume XXXIII, London, 1859.

Chesterton, George Laval, *Peace, War, and Adventure: An Autobiographical Memoir of George Laval Chesterton*, Volume I, London: Longman, Brown, Green and Longmans, 1853.

Claiborne, Ferdinand Leigh, Papers, Alabama Department of Archives and History, Montgomery.

Claiborne, John Francis Hamtramck, *Mississippi, as a Province, Territory, and State*, (Volume I), Power & Barksdale, Jackson, 1880.

Cochrane, Admiral Alexander Forrester Inglis, Papers, MS 2328, National Library of Scotland, Edinburgh (University of West Florida microfilm).

Codrington, Admiral Edward, edited by his daughter, *Memoir of the Life of Admiral Sir Edward Codrington*, Volumes I and II, Longmans, Green & Co., London, 1873.

Coffee, Gen. John, "Letters of General John Coffee to his Wife, 1813-1815," *Tennessee Historical Magazine*, Volume II, Number 4, December 1916.

Colonial Office Records, 1570-1990, National Archives of Great Britain.

Correspondence on the Slave Trade with Foreign Powers, Parties to Treaties, under which Captured Vessels are to be tried by mixed tribunals, Class B, Presented to both Houses of Parliament by Command of Her Majesty, 1844, LONDON: Printed by William Clowes and Sons, 14, Charing Cross, For Her Majesty's Stationery Office, 1844

Creek War Documents (various), Alabama Department of Archives and History, Montgomery.

Crockett, David, *The Autobiography of David Crockett of Tennessee*, Philadelphia, 1834.

Cuyler, Telamon, Collection, Hargrett Rare Book and Manuscript Library, The University of Georgia Libraries, Athens.

Doster, James Fletcher, *The Creek Indians and their Florida lands, 1740-1823*, Volume II, Creek Indians, Indian Claims Commission docket no. 280.

East Florida Papers, 1784-1821, P.K. Yonge Library of Florida History, University of Florida, Gainesville.

Foreign Office Records, 1782-1890, National Archives of Great Britain.

Index*Leslie, & Co.*, edited by William S. Coker (microfilm edition), Woodbridge, 1986, West Florida History Center and University Archives, University of West Florida, Pensacola.

Pintado, Vicente Sebastian, Papers, Manuscript Division, Library of Congress.

Poe, Stephen R. "Archaeological Excavations at Fort Gadsden, Florida," *Notes in Anthropology*, Volume 1, Florida State University. 1963.

Porter, Kenneth W., "The Negro Abraham," *The Florida Historical Quarterly*, Volume XXV, Number 1, July 1946.

Records of the Office of the Adjutant General, Letters Received, RG 94, National Archives, Washington.

Records of the Secretary of the Navy, Letters Received from Captains, RG 260, compiled 1805-1885, National Archives, Washington.

Records of the Office of the Secretary of War, Letters Received, RG 107, National Archives.

The Army and Navy Chronicle, 1836, 1837, B. Homans, Washington.

"The Sessional Papers of the House of Lords, in the Session 1845," *British and Foreign State Papers 1844-1845*, Vol. XXXIII, Compiled by the Library and Keeper of the Papers, Foreign Office, London: Printed by Harrison and Sons, St. Martin's Lane, 1859.

United States Congressional Serial Set, Volume 18, Library of Congress, Washington.

Weiss, John McNish, *The Merikens: Free Black American Settlers in Trinidad 1815-1816*, McNish & Weiss, London, 2008.

White, Nancy Marie, *et. al.*, "Archeology at Lake Seminole," unpublished report, Cleveland Museum of Natural History, 1981.

Secondary Sources

Braund, Kathryn, *Deerskins and Duffels: The Creek Indian Trade with Anglo-America, 1685-1815*, University of Nebraska Press, Lincoln, 1993.

Brooks, Richard, *The Royal Marines: A History*, U.S. Naval Institute Press, Annapolis, 2002.

Coe, Charles, *Red Patriots: The Story of the Seminoles*, Editor Publishing Company, Cincinnati, 1898.

Cox, Dale, *Milly Francis: The Life & Times of the Creek Pocahontas*, Old Kitchen Books, Bascom, 2013.

Landers, Jane, *Black Society in Spanish Florida*, University of Illinois Press, Urbana and Chicago, 1999.

Millett, Nathaniel, *The Maroons of Prospect Bluff and their quest for freedom in the Atlantic World*, University Presses of Florida, Gainesville, 2013.

Owsley, Frank, *Struggle for the Gulf Borderlands: The Creek War and the Battle of New Orleans, 1812-1815*, University Presses of Florida, Gainesville, 1981.

Reid, John, and John H. Eaton, *The Life of Andrew Jackson: The Original 1817 Edition*, edited with an introduction by Frank L. Owlsey, Jr., University of Alabama Press, Tuscaloosa, 1974.

Remini, Robert V., *Andrew Jackson and the Course of American Empire, 1767-1821*, Harper & Row, New York, 1977.

Saunt, Claudio, *A New Order of Things: Property, Power, and the Transformation of the Creek Indians, 1733-1816*, Cambridge University Press, Cambridge, 1999.

Waselkov, Gregory A. *A Conquering Spirit: Fort Mims and the Redstick War of 1813-1814*, The University of Alabama Press, Tuscaloosa, 2006.

Waselkov, Gregory A., Bonnie L. Gums and James W. Parker, *Archaeology at Fort Mims: Excavation Contexts and Artifact Catalog*, University of South Alabama Archaeological Monography 12, Mobile, 2006.

Williams, John Lee, *The Territory of Florida, or Sketches of the Topography, Civil and Natural History of the Country, the Climate, and the Indian Tribes from the First Discovery to the Present Time*, University of Florida Press, Gainesville, 1962.

Wright, Amos J., *The McGillivray and McIntosh Traders on the Old Southwest Frontier, 1716-1815*, New South Books, Montgomery, 2001.

Index